THE FIGHTIN' TEXAS AGGIES

10

THE FIGHTIN' TEXAS AGGIES

100 YEARS OF A&M FOOTBALL

GENE SCHOOR

Foreword by John David Crow

Introduction by R. C. Slocum

Taylor Publishing Company
Dallas, Texas

To the Aggies' Greatest Fan . . .

Fran

Photos courtesy of Texas A&M University

Designed by Hespenheide Design

Published by Taylor Publishing Company
1550 West Mockingbird Lane
Dallas, Texas 75235

Library of Congress Cataloging-in-Publication Data
Schoor Gene.
The Fightin' Texas Aggies: 100 years of A&M football / by Gene Schoor.
p. cm.
Includes index.
ISBN 0-87833-860-8
1. Texas A&M University—Football—History. 2. Texas A&M Aggies (Football team)—History. I. Title.
GV958.T44S36 1994
796.332'63'764242—dc20 94-21571
CIP

Printed in the United States of America
10 9 8 7 6 5 4 3 2 1

ACKNOWLEDGMENTS

It would be impossible in this short space to list those Texas Aggie players and coaches, sports editors, writers. and sportscasters across the Southwest and throughout the nation who have contributed their efforts to this book. But herewith is a list of just a few who have helped me.

First and foremost a big note of thanks to those terrific Aggie folk: Head Coach R. C. Slocum, John David Crow, Dave South, Alan Cannon, and Debbie Darrah. Plus thanks to all the outstanding editors and writers who cover the Aggies: Denne Freeman '59, Dave Smith, David McNabb, Mike Rabin, Mike Lutz, Jim Maloney, Rich Luna, Tracey Dodds, Kirk Bohis, Mark Rosner, Doug Hensley, Ray Glas, Barry Robinson, Cliff Broyles, Dan Cook, David Campbell, Kim Corum, Mickey Humphrey, Michelle Brenckman, Pete Greaves, Leanne Smith, Jerry Wizig '55. Additional thanks to Yale Lary, Dave Elmendorf, Cotton Price, Charlie Milstead, John Kimbrough, Harris Mack Browder, and Mike Bynum for their marvelous stories and to all those Aggie players who responded with stories and photographs.

Last but not least, a great tribute to the entire staff of the Aggies Library who helped me unearth those early photos and stories.

Special thanks from the publisher to Richard Bak, Jim W. McGuire '49, Jerry Cooper '63, and Harry Ledbetter.

TEXAS A&M
25
TEXAS
56

CONTENTS

Acknowledgments v

Foreword ix

Introduction xi

Prologue: The Birth of Twin Traditions 1

1 REVEILLE IN BRAZOS VALLEY 5

2 THE GAME CHANGES—AND SO DO THE FORTUNES OF THE AGGIES 13

3 UNCLE CHARLEY MORAN'S SCORING MACHINE 17

4 BIBLE THUMPING 33

5 POST BIBLE 51

6 DEPRESSION NO MORE: 1939 63

7 FROM A BEAR MARKET TO THE BEAR 79

8 BEAR ESSENTIALS 99

9 LOST CUBS 113

10 "MAKE SOMETHING HAPPEN" 121

11 THE WISHBONE COMES TO COLLEGE STATION 135

12 JACKIE SHERRILL SPELLS SUCCESS 153

13 RENEWAL OF FAITH WITH R.C. SLOCUM 169

Appendix: Statistics 191

TEXAS A&M
86
95

FOREWORD

Two of the greatest things about college athletics are the traditions and pageantry. Here at Texas A&M University, we have one of the richest and proudest football heritages in the country. Many of the nation's top coaches, players, and personalities have crossed this glorious campus and gridiron. Gene Schoor does an excellent job of bringing out the stories and the personalities behind the rich history of Texas A&M football.

Deciding which university to attend is one of the biggest decisions in any person's life. I chose to attend Texas A&M University in 1954 to pursue an education and play for Coach Paul "Bear" Bryant. Other than my decision to marry my wife, Carolyn, the decision to attend Texas A&M is the best decision I have ever made. Not only did I receive a quality education, and play for Coach Bryant, but I became an Aggie. Not just for four years, but for a lifetime.

Freshman football players were ineligible to play in 1954. Even though I've had numerous people through the years say how proud they were of me for sticking out the demanding "Junction" workouts, I was not at Junction for Coach Bryant's training. If I had been, I may not be where I am today.

Coach Bryant was a demanding coach, but he helped mold successful men in all areas of life. Just when you think you can't go any further in practice, you reach deep inside yourself and come back with a little extra to push through that drill. The same can be said of life in general. There will be tough times, but those people who push through with something extra will achieve success.

Gene Schoor has brought back some of the stories I am familiar with, and others that I'm not so familiar with. He is a nationally known writer who has done tremendous work on several great schools and their football programs. I believe when you read this book, you will agree he has done an outstanding job.

Even though there are those who believe I have been a part of all of the ninety-nine previous Aggie football seasons, I am truly thankful to be a part of the 100th season of Texas A&M football. I was fortunate to play for this great university and to serve as its athletic director for a period of time. I look forward with anticipation to the future success of our football program. I am very thankful to be an Aggie. Little did I know in the fall of 1954 that "Once an Aggie, always an Aggie!"

Gig 'Em!

John David Crow

22

INTRODUCTION

As the head football coach at Texas A&M University, it is with great pride and honor that I write this introduction to a book which chronicles the proud history of Aggie football.

I have been very fortunate to be a part of Aggie football longer than any football coach in the school's history. The support of the Twelfth Man, the Fightin' Texas Aggie Band, and the former students makes Texas A&M a very special place.

Entering the 100th season of Aggie football, some of the most exciting times are on the horizon. But before we take a look ahead, it's fun to take a look back at where we've been. Gene Schoor is a nationally known writer who takes a look back at our past. He brings out the stories behind the facts and figures.

As a youngster growing up in Texas, I kept up with Texas Aggie football. Little did I know at that time I would have the opportunity to coach at this outstanding university. I believe few people understand how special it is to be an Aggie.

As I tell the current players today, these are some of the best times of your life. Make the most of each situation. The friends and acquaintances you make while at Texas A&M will serve you a lifetime. The education you receive is second to none, and hopefully, you'll enjoy success on the playing field. The lessons in the game of football will help prepare you for life.

Aggies demand excellence, effort, character, class, and loyalty. In accepting the opportunity to attend Texas A&M, one takes on a responsibility to do his or her very best and to succeed.

There truly is a "spirit" which surrounds this outstanding institution. It's hard to tell people exactly how special being an Aggie is, but once you experience it, you'll never forget it.

Hopefully, this book will give some insight into that special "Spirit of Aggieland."

Gig 'Em!

R. C. Slocum

1
2
3
4

THE FIGHTIN' TEXAS AGGIES

PROLOGUE: THE BIRTH OF TWIN TRADITIONS

In 1921, tiny Centre College, from Danville, Kentucky, defeated Harvard 6–0. The loss for Harvard—to the smallest college team it had ever played—was its first defeat since a 6–3 loss to Yale in 1916, and its first intersectional defeat in forty years. Coming as it did at a time when football was the single most outstanding spectator sport in the nation—a subject of enormous interest for some, almost a religion for others—the game had such a tremendous impact on the sporting world that in 1960 the Associated Press named it the upset of the half century. And for one glorious moment Centre College occupied the center of the football universe.

It was a combination of good fortune, hard work, talented players, and the inspired coaching of "Uncle" Charley Moran, former Texas A&M coach from 1909 to 1914, that produced this team of giant killers.

Centre finished the rest of the season undefeated, beating Tulane and Arizona State convincingly. Then, offers for a playoff game started pouring into the offices of Coach Moran. The great Knute Rockne came to the Busy Bee Cafe in Danville to ask Moran to play Notre Dame at Soldier Field in Chicago. But Moran had to turn him down, as he did Yale, Princeton, and even the Rose Bowl. The reason: Moran had already scheduled a post-season battle against the Texas A&M Aggies in Dallas on January 2, 1922.

The 1922 battle in the Dixie Classic between Centre College and the Aggies gave birth to Texas A&M's Twelfth Man tradition, and the dramatic contest had a lasting effect on A&M football. Moreover, it proved that the football played in the Southwest was equal to that offered anywhere in the nation. The Aggies, playing the smartest, most aggressive game in their twenty-six-year history of collegiate football participation, defeated Centre College 22–14. The game, played in Dallas before a jammed crowd of more than 12,000 frenzied spectators, was also considered an upset, because the Aggies were heavy underdogs.

"Just before the opening kickoff," said Sammy Sanders, A&M's outstanding halfback, "the Centre players were putting on a great show. They had these colorful jackets that made the players look even bigger than they were and they began to pass the ball forty and even fifty yards. Their kickers were booting the ball high and far and they looked like a professional team. This added to the pressure on us, and to the fans we looked like a bunch of high schoolers."

As the teams lined up for the kickoff, Centre's great end, Red Roberts, positioned the ball for a

Captain W. C. Weir (fourth from left) and some of the other Aggies who contributed to A&M's historic 22–14 upset of Centre College in 1921. It was a game of firsts: first Dixie Classic (the forerunner of the Cotton Bowl); first A&M bowl game; first game of major national significance for those farmers from the Brazos Valley.

kick down the middle of the field, but Captain Bo McMillin walked over to Red and said: "Kick it toward that little guy in the corner," Sanders recalled. Red obliged, kicking the pigskin right to Sanders. "I was so nervous that I dropped the ball," Sanders remembered, "but

Centre College captain and star halfback Bo McMillin married just a week before his team met A&M in the Dixie Classic. Here he is with his wife moments before kickoff.

once I got under way, the goalposts seemed to be racing toward me." Buck Buckner, another Aggies halfback, said, "You could trace Sammy's run up the field by the number of Centre players who had been blocked out on the runback."

Sanders returned that opening kickoff forty-five yards as the partisan fans roared their approval. Then, after one first down, team captain Heinie Weir took the ball and crashed through his left guard—where he was met by several tacklers and was knocked to the turf, grimacing in pain. He was carried to the sidelines, where it was discovered he had a broken leg.

After Weir's injury, A&M failed to gain any ground, so Tom Miller punted to Tom Bartlett, who caught the ball behind his own goal line. Attempting to run the ball out, Bartlett was tackled by A&M's Fred Wilson for a safety, giving the Aggies a 2–0 lead—the first time Centre had trailed in a game all year.

Centre's heavier line eventually started wearing down the smaller A&M line, causing injury after injury. Sanders and then A. B. Morris were carried off the field, but the Aggies, now playing with a quartet of substitute defenders, fought off the aggressive attack of the Centre offense.

With the first half only seconds from expiring, however, Centre battered its way to A&M's two-yard line. Red Roberts and Bob Covington of Centre took turns attempting to crash through for a score. But the A&M line stood as tall as Davey Crockett at the Alamo and refused to budge. On fourth down, Roberts was stopped at the A&M six-inch mark.

The fans rose and cheered themselves hoarse as referee Ernie Quigley gave the ball to A&M on the two-inch line. It was one of the greatest goal-line stands in Southwest football history. The half ended with A&M in front, 2–0.

At halftime, A&M Coach Dana Bible, realizing that he had half a dozen injured players, remembered E. King Gill, who was in the stands spotting players for sports editor Jinx Taylor. Gill was in civilian clothes when he received Bible's urgent message to report to the team.

Years later, Gill picks up the story:

"I had played on the football team, but was now on the basketball team [he was later named to the 1923 and 1924 all-Southwest Conference basketball teams] and I was spotting the players

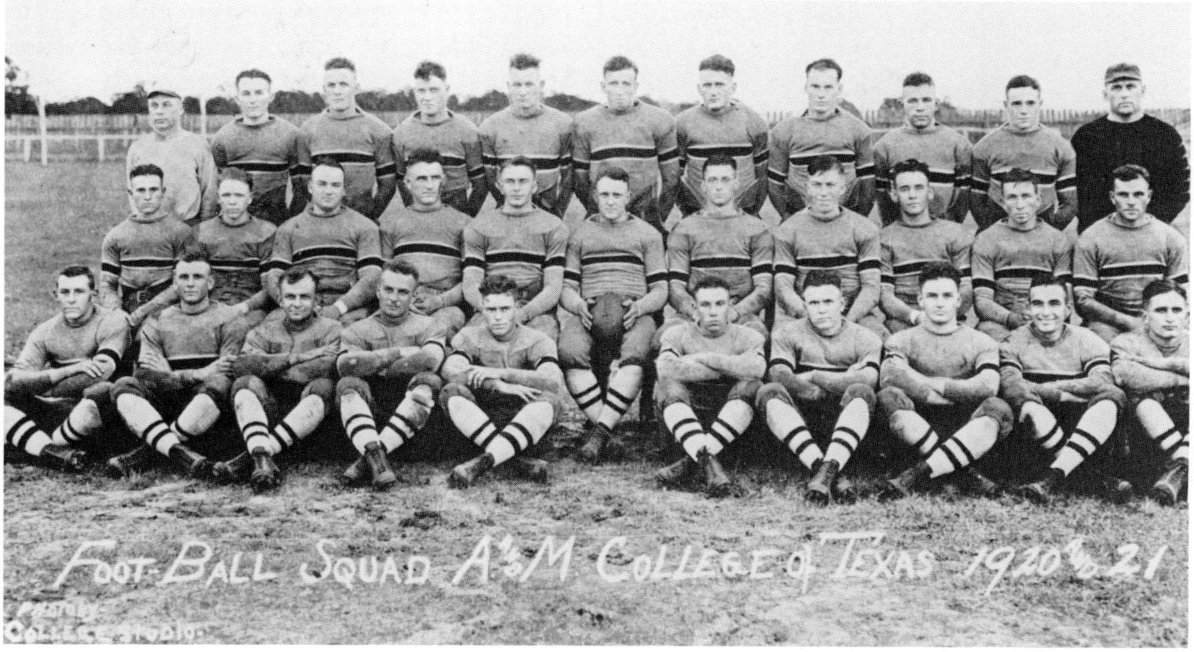

The entire 1920 and '21 Texas A&M team. They elevated A&M football to a position of national prominence—where it has stayed ever since.

for the sports editor of the *Waco News-Tribune* in the press box. I was called down to the A&M bench, and Coach Bible told me to put on a football suit in case I was needed to play in the game.

"There were no dressing rooms at the stadium in those days. The team dressed at the hotel and traveled to the stadium in taxicabs. Anyway, I put on a uniform of one of the injured players. We got under the stands, and the player put on my clothes and I put on his uniform. There were no extra uniforms in those days. Now, I was dressed and ready to play for A&M. But I sat on the bench and was never sent into the game.

These days when Aggie students stand during the entire game, they are reminding the coach, team, and the student body in general that they are ready to do their part. It is this spirit and loyalty that Aggie fans are remembering. (But this by no means was the end of the Twelfth Man story. A new, remarkable chapter would be added by Coach Jackie Sherrill during the 1983 season.)

As the third period began, Centre was unable to pierce the Aggies' line and was forced to punt. The Aggies took over, but on the first play from scrimmage, fumbled the ball. It was recovered by Centre on the Aggie three-yard line. On first down, fullback Jack Snoddy hit a hole over left tackle and went in for a touchdown. The extra point (which was not as automatic then as it is today) gave Centre a 7–2 lead.

Its lead, however, was shortlived. In a show of great respect for his defense, Bible elected to kick off after Centre's touchdown. His faith was rewarded. Centre received the kick and fumbled the ball on the play, as three A&M tacklers drilled the return man. Cap Murrah recovered for A&M at the Centre thirty-three-yard line.

An end-around play, added to A&M's bag of tricks for this game, clicked as Puny Wilson passed the ball to Jake Evans for the Aggies touchdown. McMillan kicked the extra point as A&M regained the lead by a 9–7 margin.

Centre fumbled the ball on its next possession as well, and the Aggies recovered it on Centre's twenty-four-yard line.

Miller raced off tackle for a first down on the fourteen-yard line and Billy McMillan cracked through his own guard for five more. Then Puny Wilson was brought into the backfield

Grabbing a pass from T. F. "Puny" Wilson, end Jake Evans scored the Aggies' first touchdown in the game. It rattled Centre College and the set the stage for the upset.

from his end position and blasted through the Centre line for a touchdown to give the Aggies a 16–7 lead.

The Aggies built their lead to 22–7 on the next series when A&M defensive tackle Ted Winn intercepted a tipped ball and sprinted forty-five yards for another Aggie touchdown. A meaningless Centre touchdown closed out the scoring, and the game ended 22–14.

The upset victory over Centre College, the team that vanquished Harvard, West Virginia, and other Eastern powers, was the biggest victory in the history of Texas A&M football and brought unprecedented national publicity to the Aggies and every member of the team. Sports pages throughout the nation trumpeted the play of Ted Winn, Puny Wilson, Sam Sanders, Cap Murrah, and Heinie Weir and praised the magnificent coaching of Dana Bible.

Commenting on the success of the Aggies, Commissioner Joe Utay, who represented the Fair Organization sponsoring the game, said, "The success of the Aggies-Centre College game assures the post-season tilt as an annual fixture. Our idea in putting on this game was essentially to put the Southwest where it belongs on the football map of the nation. And Texas A&M did that more effectively than we had dreamed possible. The game was a huge success in every way and will be permanent. We are now planning to have the leading Southwest football team play a leading team from another section of the country in what could be a championship game every year."

And so the Cotton Bowl was born—as was one of college football's greatest traditions. The Twelfth Man is Texas A&M's most cherished football tradition, a tradition that has persevered through thirteen head coaches, fourteen Southwest Conference titles, one national championship, and more than 100,000 students. The spirit of the Twelfth Man touches all those who touch A&M—and it sets Aggies apart from their peers.

1

REVEILLE IN BRAZOS VALLEY

As birthday bashes go, the United States' centennial celebration of 1876 was a humdinger. Citizens engaged in a year-long orgy of good old fashioned flag waving, chest thumping and whiskey snortin', with an inordinate share of the excess taking place in Philadelphia, home to the International Exhibition. Here the finest examples of what Mark Twain liked to call the Gilded Age were on display for all to ooh and ahh over: new-fangled inventions like the typewriter, the telephone, and the Westinghouse air brake.

All the star-spangled hoopla obscured some serious problems for the young nation, however. For one thing, there was a depression, severe enough to cause many of the immigrants then flooding the country to change their mind and retrace their trip across the Atlantic. There also was scandal galore, with U. S. Grant's cronies robbing the treasury blind while the old war hero tended to his cigars and horses instead of the presidency. The biggest shock of the year occurred on the eve of Independence Day, when news reached Philadelphia's partygoers of how General George A. Custer had momentarily lost his common sense, and thus his entire command, at the Little Big Horn River in Montana.

For all the bad news concerning the country's economy and its national heroes, Americans clung stubbornly to their dreams, as folks who really don't have any other choice have always done. At College Station in east Texas, a hard-scrabble community located about halfway between Dallas and Houston, some visionaries could still squint into the distance and plot a future as bright as the orange-yellow sun melting like a ball of butter into the horizon.

On October 2, 1976, Texas A&M officially opened its doors as a land grant college and the state's first public institution of higher learning. Every student was a member of the Corps of Cadets, whose structure imitated that of the military. Historically, Texas A&M has commissioned more men (and, since 1963, women) as officers in the U.S. military than any other university in the country, with the exception of the service academies. This military bearing has helped the student body stand tall through some tough times—not the least of which was the rather fitful beginnings of the school's football program.

In 1876 football was just starting its climb to becoming the most popular sport on American campuses. On November 23, just a few weeks after the first squeaks of chalk sounded inside A&M's classrooms, representatives from several eastern universities met in Springfield, Massachusetts, in an attempt to iron out the conflicting rules of play. The American Intercollegiate Football Association grew out of this meeting.

Readers accustomed to the modern game of endzone-to-endzone excitement should understand that the game as played in the nineteenth century was, well, a *snooze*, albeit a violent snooze. The rugby-style game featured long stretches of two groups of players heaving, slapping, kicking and butting against each other as they attempted to move the large, oval-shaped ball using only their feet. Occasionally the ball would squirt out or someone would give it a good boot, at which point the mayhem moved en masse to another spot on the field.

This was brutal, smash-mouth football, a war waged without the benefit of helmets, face masks, mouthguards, shoulder pads or any other meaningful kind of protective equipment. Uniforms consisted of stockings, knee pants, jerseys and caps. Some participants occasionally wore leather nose guards or ear flaps, but these were useless in warding off the inevitable taunts of "Sissy!" from deep inside the "scrum," or pile.

Thanks to pioneers like Walter Camp, by the 1890s the game had become Americanized. There was a greater emphasis on running, and such innovations as blocking, yardlines and a series of downs were in place. The once-common fifteen-man squads had been whittled down to eleven and a scoring system established.

As football gained in popularity, some A&M students thought it only right that their school field a team. In 1894, eighteen-year-old Milt Sims talked a couple of friends, Art Watts and Charley Herndon, into organizing a squad.

"I'd never played the game before," Sims admitted in his old age, "but Herndon, a fine athlete, and Watts had both played some in Dallas." In short order a team of nearly twenty students, most of them novices to the sport, was assembled. Dudley Perkins, still considered one of the best all-around athletes A&M ever produced, trained, managed and coached the team. School colors were selected: red and white.

The equipment was primitive: canvas jackets that laced up the front, some homemade shin guards, and a nose guard to protect Sims' battered proboscis. There was only one football.

As for strategy, there was none. "I don't remember any set plays that we had," said Sims, who was nominated captain and played fullback. "We just got the ball, bucked the line, and anything went. Fists, elbows, knees, anything."

The names of A&M's first team have been blurred by time, but their contribution is in a sense recognized every time the big block T is formed at Kyle Field. For the record, here is the roster of the 1894 squad, the first in a long line of College Station gridders to "Gig 'em!"

Quarterback	Bill Mossenburg
Halfbacks	Hugh F. McDonald, A. Lane
Fullback	Milt Sims
Tackles	Russ Burleson, J. C. McNeil
Guards	John Burney, Jack McGonagill
Center	Bill Krug
Ends	Dudley Perkins, H. T. Chiles
Substitutes	Andy Love, Hiram Coulter, J. Childress, Ed Burgess, Harry Martin, C. Carson, Art Watts, Charley Herndon

Texas A&M's first football game was against Ball High School, which took the train from Galveston to College Station. A&M prevailed, 14–6.

The victory got Sims and his boys feeling a little cocky. "We beat them so easy we got to thinking that we'd like to go over to Austin and play Texas," he recalled. "So we put in a petition and finally got permission."

The A&M eleven arrived in Austin for the big game. From a distance it appeared that the University of Texas, which had opened in 1881, was fielding not a football team, but rather an army of super frontiersmen who shaved with sheet lightning and ate pickled thunderbolts for breakfast. It was an awe-inspiring sight to the out-of-towners.

"Well," explained Sims, "Texas had a professional coach and they wore those big turtleneck sweaters, and when we got there and saw the size of those Texas players, I said to Mossenburg, 'Mossey, if those SOB's are as big as they look from across the field, God help us.' Our team weighed an average of 160 pounds, and those Texas guys looked as if they weighed at least 200 pounds."

On the first play from scrimmage, Mossenburg fumbled the ball. A giant Texas player scooped up the loose leather and lum-

The 1894 Texas A&M team, the school's first. It tested the waters of college football slowly, defeating Galveston High and losing to Texas in its only two games of the year. The loss to in-state rival UT particularly hurt, even in that first season.

bered in for a touchdown. "That kind of took the heart out of us," said Sims, "and they kept on scoring and beat us by 38–0."

The lopsided loss launched what has grown into one of college football's oldest rivalries. Through 1994, A&M and Texas have squared off 101 times. Only Minnesota vs. Wisconsin and Missouri vs. Kansas have dueled each other more often.

Over the years the season-ending game has determined the conference title several times. It has always determined bragging rights for the winner, leaving the loser to mumble "Wait 'til next year" into his drowning-sorrow beverage. "In this part of the country," says current A&M coach R. C. Slocum, "this is the biggest game of the year. There's a lot of families in this state tied to one or both of these universities. That makes for a great rivalry."

Milt Sims, whose self-discipline apparently didn't extend beyond the gridiron, was kicked out of school the following year. The reason can be surmised from his comments in an interview given not long before his death. "Three hundred men and no women at all," he mused. "It wasn't much fun." Presumably Sims took the ball with him when he left, because A&M didn't field a team again until 1896.

The 1896 Farmers (as they were nicknamed in reference to the school's land-grant status) were aided by two volunteer coaches, A. M. Soule and Harry South. Both men were full-time professors at A&M and had played some football. Realizing that the squad, which was made up of students who had responded to a notice calling for players, had little understanding of the game, the two coaches spent much of their time teaching the fundamentals, putting in

Bill Murray was selected as A&M's football coach in 1899, the school's fifth coach in five seasons. Despite winning records in two of the four previous years the Aggies had been shut out by a combined score of 86–0 by Texas. Murray's job was to continue building a solid program—and beat the Longhorns! His first team almost did, losing in a bruising battle 6–0.

a regimen of conditioning, and developing a sense of teamwork.

In the first game of the year, A&M fought Ball High School to a 0–0 tie. Because of A&M's football infancy, high schools, which had fielded teams for years and thus were better organized, could compete evenly with the Farmers and many other college teams.

The following week A&M, displaying marked improvement over its first game, defeated a spirited Austin College squad 22–4. Because there were no formal channels for scheduling, and budgets prevented traveling long distances for games, an up-and-coming program like A&M's had to scramble to find games. In 1896 (and in 1897) the Farmers could schedule only three contests. So their third game of '96 was their last one—a 28–0 pasting of Houston High School.

An experienced football player at several schools, Chuck Taylor took over as A&M's head coach for the 1897 season. The Farmers opened their three-game season with a 10–0 loss to Houston High School. Two weeks later, Add Ran of Waco (the precursor to TCU) pounded out a 30–6 victory over A&M. In its final game A&M claimed its lone victory by defeating Austin College 4–0.

In 1898 A&M hired another new football coach to direct the team: Harry Williams. Williams promptly organized a rugged schedule, including games with Texas, TCU, Austin, and Fort Worth University and then patiently rounded his team into condition for the onset of the season.

There were a number of rules changes in football during the 1898–99 seasons. A touchdown was now worth five points, a field goal was worth five points, the safety two, and the point after touchdown one point. It was left to the discretion of a team captain to substitute a player at any time. Previously, the permission of the referee had been necessary. Football uniforms consisted of moleskin pants and a canvas jacket, joined by a canvas belt. Helmets were worn for the first time; however, many of the players devised other ways to protect their head. A great many allowed their hair to grow, thinking that a bushy head of hair would provide more protection. The first game against Houston High School provided a "good practice session," as A&M romped to a ten-touchdown, 51–0 victory.

The 1898 team won four games, the most in the school's brief history, but failed to knock off Texas.

Their joy, however, was shortlived. The next week, the Aggies traveled to Austin to renew their rivalry with Texas, which they had met only once, in 1894. Texas flattened the Aggies, running through their line at will to register an eleven-touchdown 48–0 victory. It stands as the most lopsided loss in Texas A&M history. In two games with Texas, A&M had been outscored 86–0, a grim statistic that boiled the blood of Aggie players and fans. But revenge would have to wait. Still reeling from the Texas loss, A&M hosted Houston High again the following week and lost, 6–0.

A&M reversed its losing ways, however, in the season's fourth game, pounding out a resounding win at Waco over TCU, 16–0. Wins against Austin College, 22–6, and Fort Worth University, 28–0, closed out the year. The victory over Fort Worth gave the Aggies their most successful season with four wins and two losses.

Despite the record four wins, the coaching merry-go-round continued in 1899. Bill Murray, an experienced coach with a solid reputation, was selected as the fifth A&M coach in five seasons. He set to work immediately to upgrade the Aggies schedule. Regional powers Sewanee, Tulane, LSU, Baylor, and Texas made up the most difficult schedule in A&M's five-year history.

A&M's first game in 1899 was against Houston High School, and the Farmers, playing like a championship eleven, chalked up an impressive 43–0 victory. Sewanee was next. It was in the midst of one of the most incredible records in college football history. On a jaunt of some 3,000 miles by special train, through Texas, Louisiana, and Mississippi, Sewanee defeated six of the top teams in that area in a six-day period, including Texas, A&M (10–0), Tulane (23–0), LSU, Mississippi, and Cumberland. Sewanee carried its own drinking water, had a chef cook its food, and ran up twelve consecutive victories for the season—an unprecedented feat. Most important, Sewanee's iron men helped prove the success of intersectional contests, a popular and important feature of the maturing game.

Following the Sewanee game, A&M rang up three shutout victories: 22–0 over Tulane, 52–0 over LSU, and 33–0 over Baylor. Texas loomed next. In the first half of the biggest game of the year, the Longhorns punched across a touchdown after they blocked an A&M punt on the two-yard line. A bitter argument followed the score, and after twenty minutes of jawing with the officials Captain Hal Moseley and Coach Murray led their Aggies off the field with more than twenty minutes left to play. The game ended in a 6–0 Texas triumph.

The campus newspaper, *The Battalion*, front-paged this wry poem:

"Our players proved they have grit
and played an honest game
The referee robbed us, 6–0
We held the Varsity just the same."

The line against Texas was now: three games, three losses, no points. But the gap was closing and A&M fans eagerly looked forward to the new century—and renewed hope.

By 1900 college football was well on its way to becoming a major national sport, trailing only baseball in popularity. The game, however, was still a crude, rough, and dangerous sport, completely devoid of craft and strategy. There were quick, mass bursts through an opponent's line, creating endless battles at the line of scrimmage. Brute force was the only offensive weapon. Players piled on the ball carrier, roughed up the kicker, and engaged in fierce wedge plays that led to serious injuries in almost every game.

After five seasons, A&M was proving it could play whatever style was necessary to compete at the college level. The next two seasons were disappointing, however, as the Aggies dropped four games to Texas and posted 2–2–1 and 1–4 records in 1900 and 1901, respectively. In the four losses to Texas, A&M was outscored 65–0. Murray's futility against Texas stretched the patience of Aggie fans, so the coach was relieved of his duties for the 1902 season. Texas' dominance of A&M was also probably behind the school's next decision.

The president of A&M and the board of directors agreed that an Athletic Council should be responsible for the selection of coaches, selling

---

THE FIGHTIN' TEXAS AGGIE BAND
100th Anniversary 1994
They've Never Lost a Halftime

The Texas Aggie Band was organized in 1894 by Joseph Holick, maker of the famed Senior boots. From the original 14 members, the band has grown to more than 300—all volunteer, nonmusic scholarship members. In 1924 Lt. Col. Harold Dunn, a professional bandmaster, took over and served until 1945.

Col. Dunn wrote the music for "The Spirit of Aggieland," the official school song. Marvin Mimms provided the words. This and "The Aggie War Hymn" are played at every football game, bringing chills to all. The fight song was written by J. V. "Pinky" Wilson following World War I. Many people believe the band's rendition of the "The Star Spangled Banner" to be the best in America.

Lt. Col. E. V. Adams became band director in 1945 and served for 27 years. Col. Adams perfected the military marching style and invented many precision drills performed on national television to the delight of millions of fans. He was succeeded in 1973 by Lt. Col. Joe T. Haney, composer of "Noble Men of Kyle" and in 1988 by Lt. Col. Ray Toler. Each developed new maneuvers and songs that have kept the Aggie Band unique among college bands.

of tickets for sports events, and the general business direction of all sports activities.

Thus, in 1902 the Athletic Council outbid Ohio State to secure James E. Platt of Lafayette College. Platt had just ended an outstanding three-year career at the school. In 1899 Lafayette won eleven of twelve games, losing only to Princeton. Platt emerged that year as one of the East's top halfbacks.

He was delighted with the turnout at his first practice session. Returning from the 1901 team was Captain Tom Blake, Bill Beilharz, and E. E. Worthing. One pleasant surprise was the appearance of the captain of the 1897 Aggies who had dropped out of school for three years due to injuries.

Platt instituted a number of reforms during the first two weeks of practice. Every player had to run at top speed from his dormitory to the field, then after practice, run back to his dorm. He also added a series of calisthenics and then a rugged scrimmage each day. This regimen of preseason training prepared the Aggies well for their rugged schedule of nine games.

For the first game of the season, Coach Platt's starting lineup included Captain Tom Black, right halfback; Jim Davis, left halfback; and Bill Beilharz at quarterback. The line consisted of E. E. Worthing, center; Joe Benjamin, right guard; Jud Neff, left guard; George Hope, left tackle; Jack Simpson, right tackle; and Josh Sterns, right end.

The revamped Aggies won their first four games, two of them against Baylor, sending them into San Antonio, the site of that year's first game against Texas, on a roll. But the Longhorns played A&M to a scoreless tie, forcing the Aggies to start a new winning streak. The Aggies did so, beating Tulane 17–5 and then blanking TCU and Trinity by a combined 56–0.

November 27, 1902, was a historic date in A&M football. For the first time in their history, the Aggies scored first against Texas en route to an 11–0 triumph. The cadets and alumni painted Austin red and celebrated throughout the night and into the morning.

The unbelievable upset by the Aggies gave them the championship of the South and ended their most successful season at 7–0–2.

The A&M Athletic Council signed Platt to another two-year contract and declared, "Coach Platt is the best football coach A&M has ever had and is a wonderful contribution to our athletic department."

Spalding's Official Football Guide, the college football bible in 1903, discussed the Texas Aggies football program in these glowing terms: "The A&M College of Texas deserves special mention this past season and earned the claim to be numbered among the big four of the Southwest by the ardent athletic support given the team. A&M has not been as well favored as regards financial support, as some of the other Southwest teams, but determination, hard work and superior coaching placed it among the leading teams of the Southwest."

But in 1903, with just three members of the championship team of 1902 returning—Captain Rheinhardt Boettcher, Jim Pirie, and Big Simpson—Platt was forced to start a group of promising freshmen. It was almost an insurmountable job, but Platt was equal to the task. He whipped the team into shape, in preparation for some of the strongest teams in the Southwest, including TCU (twice), Arkansas and Oklahoma for the first time, then Baylor (twice), and Texas, in the annual Thanksgiving showdown. The Aggies faced the toughest schedule of their nine-year football history, yet Platt produced another remarkable season, guiding A&M to a 7–3–1 mark.

"With a bit of luck," said Platt, "we could have won two games this year, games we lost by single touchdowns. Those two games would have given us another championship year. But we'll be better next year."

Little did Platt realize that next year would be his last.

The Aggies went 4–2 in 1904, but the Athletic Council dumped Platt in favor of Bill Bachman for the 1905 season.

Coach Bill Bachman, surveying the twenty-five players who reported for the first practice session in 1905, was pleased with the showing of about fifteen, who had played for Coach Jim Platt, the previous season. They looked bigger, tougher, and more aggressive, and he was optimistic about the kind of season he would have.

For his opening lineup Bachman selected Vic Kelley as the quarterback. He liked the way Vic handled himself and the way his teammates looked up to him as a solid leader. Jim Loving and Chuck Richenstein would be the two halfbacks and Captain Guy Haltom, a rugged, fast-moving youngster, would be the fullback. The linemen included Bob Blake, Bill Boyce, Al Cornell, Jesse Dale, Jim Dean, chunky Felix Puckett, and Bobby Kendrick.

Richenstein and Vic Kelley had played very well for Bryan High School in Dallas, and both players pleaded with Bachman to give Joe Utay a chance in the backfield.

Ordinarily, in those early days of football, a coach would hardly pay any attention to a five-foot, seven-inch back, but Utay was stocky, rugged, and looked tough as nails. Bachman kept his eye on Utay, and after a couple of practice sessions the coach posted him at fullback and alternated him with Haltom. It was a wise move, for Utay developed into one of the most impressive players on the team.

In the opening game of the season, the Aggies blanked favored Houston 29–0. They followed up with shutouts of TCU, Baylor, and Trinity, and after four weeks, had outscored their opponents 115–0. Victories over Austin College and TCU boosted A&M to 6–0 and set the stage for a matchup with tiny Transylvania, a small Kentucky college with an enrollment of 250 and a knack for upsets. True to form, Transylvania knocked off A&M 29–6.

But the Aggies rebounded from defeat, beating Baylor 17–5. It was their seventh win in eight games—just the right tonic as they prepped for the big Thanksgiving Day game against their bitter rivals from Texas.

A&M, with the best record in the South, was heavily favored to defeat a Texas varsity that had lost to Haskell, Vanderbilt, and Transylvania.

But as usual in these traditional rivalries, comparative scores are meaningless, and on this occasion—the twelfth game of the series between these two teams—A&M fell for the eleventh time, 27–0.

The sons of ranchers, farmers, miners, and trappers, A&M students had been brought up to survive tornadoes, snakes, grasshoppers and grass fires, but these continuing losses to archrival Texas had become almost too much to bear. Following the 1905 season, Coach Bachman said, "We won seven of nine games, and in any other school that would be a marvelous record. But I realize that no matter how many games we win, if we don't beat Texas, no one at College Station is happy. We'll get 'em next year."

"Change Those Rules and Reform Football,
or I'll Abolish the Damn Game."

President Theodore Roosevelt in 1900

2

THE GAME CHANGES— AND SO DO THE FORTUNES OF THE AGGIES

The 1905 season ended in a storm of protest against the brutality of the game. Coach Alonzo Stagg of the University of Chicago, writing in the *Chicago Tribune*, said: "Something has to be done immediately about this game, or we shall have to abandon the sport. This past season showed that in 1905 there were 18 deaths and more than 159 serious injuries—injuries so serious that many of the players may never recover their full health."

President Theodore Roosevelt summoned representatives of Yale, Harvard, and Princeton to the White House and told them it was up to them to save the sport by removing every objectionable feature. "Brutality and foul play, inefficient officials, good, sound equipment would certainly help," Roosevelt said. "And if you people, leaders of the sport, don't clean up this game, I will do something drastic, maybe even banish the sport."

At a meeting on December 28, 1905, sixty-two university officials participated in a meeting set up to change and reform football, and a group called the Intercollegiate Athletic Association adopted a program to change the rules to save the game.

At a second meeting on January 12, 1906, a number of rules changes were immediately adopted:

1. Reduce the length of the game from seventy to sixty minutes.
2. Establish a neutral zone separating the teams by the length of the ball.
3. Increase the distance to be gained in three downs from five to ten yards.
4. Prohibit hurdling over players.
5. Guards, centers, and tackles are not permitted behind the line of scrimmage on offense, unless they fall back five yards.
6. When a punt strikes the ground, all members of the kicking team are on side, except the kicker.
7. The field must be marked by lengthwise stripes at five-yard intervals.
8. Legalize the forward pass.

The legalization of the forward pass would revolutionize the game of football. Gone would be the days of heavy-handed mass attacks of brute force and labored progress. The forward pass would enable quick strikes on offense and make the game more exciting and attractive to both player and spectator. This open, streamlined game, however, was not achieved overnight. Mass plays did not die easily, and the revolutionary pass was not universally embraced. Few teams used this new play. And it was not until after the remarkable demonstration by Notre

Dame's Gus Dorais and Knute Rockne against West Point in 1913 that there was a general awakening to the tremendous possibilities of the forward pass.

Bill Bachman concentrated on beating Texas from the very first day his 1906 players reported for practice. The schedule was one of A&M's most difficult, yet exciting, for in addition to two games with TCU, there were games with the colorful Haskell Institute Indians and a two-game road trip against Tulane at New Orleans and against LSU at Baton Rouge. Scheduled for Thanksgiving Day, of course, was the biggest game of the year, against Texas.

In the opening game, with Vic Kelley at quarterback directing the A&M offense, hard-running halfbacks Joe Utay and Lou Hamilton and fullback Jim Ross helped pound TCU for seven touchdowns in a 42–0 rout. The Aggies rolled over their next five foes and felt confident about their annual grudge match with Texas. But the Longhorns used a passing attack to beat A&M 24–0.

Despite coaching the Aggies to a 13–3 record in two seasons, Bachman's inability to win the big one earned him the pink slip, and he was replaced in 1907 by L. L. Larson.

Larson scrapped the Aggies' old-fashioned mass attack, which depended on brute strength, and developed an offense built around speed. He believed in an open style of play and began to experiment with a wide-open, deceptive passing attack. And he had the kind of players, veterans, who responded quickly to this new style of play.

Earl Schultz lettered from 1900–1903. During his four years, A&M posted two winning seasons, including a record seven wins in both '02 and '03. The highlight of his career was A&M's 11–0 road shutout of Texas in 1902, the Aggies' first taste of victory over the Longhorns. It triggered a hearty celebration back home.

In a fast-moving, open attack that featured several fine passes from Kelley to Joe Utay, the Aggies trounced Fort Worth 34–0 in the opener. They were then driven to five days of intense practice in preparation for an early-season game against Texas at Dallas.

This time the Aggies avoided defeat, but they didn't gain victory either, as the two played to a scoreless tie. But A&M won its next five games and stood 6–0–1 on Thanksgiving Day as 6,000 fans watched the visiting Aggies take on Texas for a second time.

In the second period of a scoreless game, A&M fumbled the ball after a Texas punt, and UT recovered it and scored the first touchdown. The conversion was missed and Texas had a 6–0 lead. Toward the end of the second half, the Aggies recovered a Texas fumble on the eight-yard line as Charlie DeWare fell on the ball for A&M. Then Lou Hamilton, behind brilliant blocking, cracked through the Texas line. Hamilton made the extra point, and A&M had a 7–6 lead at the end of the half.

Both teams played conservative football in the third period, neither team gaining much ground. Then in the fourth quarter, A&M, eager and determined for another score, tried a complicated double pass that backfired. Texas' Fred Ramsdell leaped high into the air and took the ball right out of Joe Utay's hands, then shot off on a fifty-yard sprint and scored what proved to be the winning touchdown. It was a brilliantly fought game, but once again A&M was on the short end, this time 11–6.

Although A&M ended the season with a 6–1–1 record against some of the leading teams in the South, they failed to beat Texas in the two games played, so a new coach was on the scene for A&M for 1908.

The Aggies had compiled a 37–9–4 record over a six-season period under three coaches—Jim Platt, Bill Bachman, and L. L. Larson. Their record would prove comparable to the best records of Charley Moran, who took over in 1909, and Dana Bible, who took over in 1917. The trend changed sharply in 1908, when N. A. Merriam took over the head coaching post and led the Aggies to a disheartening 3–5–0 record. It was A&M's first losing season since 1901's 1–4–0.

One other factor in common with the disastrous 1901 season was the double defeat by Texas, in the fifth game of the 1908 season in Houston and the eighth game at Austin. A&M lost 24–8 in Houston and 28–12 in Austin. The loss at Austin was particularly painful as the Aggies blew a 12–0 halftime lead.

Coach Merriam started the 1909 season with an easy win over Austin College, 17–0. But a scoreless tie with TCU prompted mutiny. According to Dutch Hohn, a four-year stalwart at three different positions, "Immediately after the poor showing against TCU, a clamor by the student body went up. By the next night, the student body had raised enough money to pay off Merriam's contract, and he left. His assistant, C. B. Moran, was named to replace him."

End Walter Hyde was one of the few bright spots on the 1900–1901 teams, neither of which finished above .500.

Coach Murray's 1900 edition played to an even 2–2–1 record. Both losses were to Texas, inciting unrest among the Aggie faithful.

When Moran, a pro player-coach with the Massillon Tigers, took over the A&M squad, a member of the A&M faculty asked him if he was teaching his players to be "good losers." Moran countered: "Hell, I didn't come here to lose."

True to his word, Moran led the Aggies to two victories leading up to a November 8 showdown with Texas.

In a driving rainstorm, the Aggies trounced Texas 23–0 for their first victory over the Longhorns since 1902. The spirited win over their bitter foe spurred the Aggies on to overcome every other rival on the schedule. They defeated Trinity and a strong Oklahoma eleven and then, to the utter amazement of all the so-called experts, defeated Texas a second time in a brilliant exhibition, 5–0.

During that second Texas game in 1909, there was a sign displayed by Texas students at the game: "Only once in seven years." After the game, the sign was changed by A&M followers to read: "Twice in three weeks."

It was a year that Aggie alums and cadets talked about for years: 7–0–1 and two lickings of archenemy Texas.

Charley Moran, A&M's new coach, had lived all of sports' great moments. He was a football player; a major league pitcher, catcher, and manager; a college coach; and later, an umpire in the National League. His philosophy was that there was no middle ground—everything was right or wrong, fair or foul, fight or quit. A story told often by Happy Chandler, former baseball commissioner and U.S. Senator among other things, illustrates best Moran's black-or-white view. The two were riding back together from a major league game in which Moran had to make the call on a ball that was fair by inches. "Mr. Moran," said Chandler, "that play was close, wasn't it?" "Son, there ain't none of them close," Moran answered. "They're either fair or foul, out or safe, but above all, they ain't *nothing* until I call 'em."

Charley Moran attended the University of Nashville and the University of Tennessee, each for a year. He coached a fellow named Bob Neyland, who later became head coach at Tennessee and nationally famous as one of football's greatest coaches.

When Moran went to Bethel College as a coach, he was just nineteen years old and played

The 1901 Aggies stumbled to a 1–4 mark and dropped another pair to Texas by a combined score of 49–0. In five games against UT, Murray's teams had failed to score even a point—an unendurable statistic that cost Murray his job. Hired to replace him was J. E Platt, who the next year ended the school's seven-year wait to upend Texas.

on the football and baseball teams—a practice not unusual in college in those early days.

Moran's next stop was Texas A&M. After he left A&M, he coached at Carlisle, Vanderbilt, Centre College, Bucknell, and Tennessee. He also played professional football at Massillon and Grand Rapids, then played professional baseball in the Texas League, and with St. Louis in the American League. He probably was the only baseball player in history to be in the major leagues first as a pitcher, then on his next trip up as a catcher, a switch forced by a sore arm. Then he took a job as a major league umpire for fifteen years.

Moran left Bethel College in 1909 to take an assistant coaching post at Texas A&M, and then when Coach Merriam was fired, Moran succeeded him.

As September 1910 drew near, A&M supporters were asking each other that old and vital question: "Will we beat Texas this year?" Those in position to know what the prospects were did not seem very optimistic. Some important questions would have to be answered on the football field.

Some of the questions had an *if,* before they could be answered: If Roger Hooker, the giant tackle; Arland Ward, the brilliant end; Michael

Following three years of unprecedented success, including 17 victories and the school's first undefeated season in 1902, J. E. Platt stepped down. His successor, Bill Bachman, continued making strides with the program. The 1905 team, shown here, posted a 7–2 mark and scored 180 points for the season, an A&M record that stood until 1910. Bachman departed after the 1906 season, but in two years his teams won 13 games and lost only three.

Joe Utay, a stocky but slightly undersized halfback from 1905–1907, was the Aggies' ablest ball carrier of the early 1900s—and the school's first real star. During his three-year football career, the Aggies posted an impressive 19–4–1 record. After earning his degree, Utay never strayed far from A&M, becoming its athletic director in 1912, helping to organize the first Dixie Classic in 1921, and serving on the board of directors from 1934–1941. He even had a hand in the Aggies' national championship. As chairman of the Athletic Council in 1934, he recommended the school hire Homer Norton, the man who eventually led A&M to the top of college football.

Balenti, the great fullback; and Roc Rugel, another fullback, would return, there would be a winning team. Without these players, only Dutch Hohn, George Barnes, and J. C. Cretcher would be left as a nucleus for the 1910 team.

But Balenti did not return; he was playing professional baseball in the South Atlantic League. Rugel took a job in a Dallas bank, and Lou Hamilton, the greatest athlete ever produced at A&M, had played his four years. There was not a single prospect for the backfield, and the line looked just ordinary.

But Coach Moran just shook his head and muttered to his assistant, "We'll have to work like hell this year." Moran proceeded to select some forty men, including all the 1909 veterans and the most promising of the freshmen, for a pre-practice week at Seabrook as guests of the Seabrook Hunting and Fishing Club. They stayed an additional ten days.

Coach Moran began work with his squad at 6:00 each morning, before breakfast. The players first ran six laps around the half-mile track, then followed with calisthenics, a half hour of passing drills, dummy tackling, and wind sprints. There was no body contact until the players had been at camp for at least a solid week. The workouts were very light until the squad had been toughened; then the heavy work followed, with blocking, tackling, and finally, a fast scrimmage that lasted for a half hour to forty-five minutes. Moran ended the marathon workout with a period of chalk talks. By the end of September, the team was gradually rounding into shape, and Moran was pleased with the results.

The squad returned to the campus, ready for the first game of the season against Marshall School on October 10, and Moran selected his lineup: Captain George Barnes, the biggest man on the squad at six-three and 210 pounds; all-Southern tackle J. C. Cretcher; Dutch Hohn; H. G. Lambert; and ends H. Roy Grissom and George Altgelt. In the backfield, Moran had James Whyte at fullback, Bob Kern at quarterback, and Tyree Bell and Wyatte Beasley.

The Marshall team arrived at College Station four hours late, and the game was postponed for two days to give the visitors a chance to rest after a grueling journey. But when the game started on October 3, the Aggies simply ran over and through their rivals with an avalanche of touchdowns and a 48–0 win. Austin College, A&M's next opponent, witnessed the Marshall-A&M game and wasn't "too impressed with A&M's win."

Austin did get the jump on the Aggies, scoring a touchdown that resulted from an A&M fumbled punt. But the Aggies eventually rang up a 27–5 victory. On October 15, TCU rolled into town and then rolled over, 35–0.

Because of a scheduling mixup in which a preseason invitation to University of Kentucky was mistakenly mailed to Transylvania, Kentucky never made it to College Station. The mistake was not discovered until Transylvania rolled into town. Both teams and officials were embarrassed, but the game was played, and A&M played every man on the squad in wrapping up an easy "practice game" 33–0.

Next, the Aggies met an Arkansas team that employed an unusual tricky offense, with all kinds of lateral passes and other variations, and they lost 5–0.

Returning home after the trip to Arkansas, A&M again defeated TCU, 23–6, in a lackluster effort.

On November 14, the Aggies were ready for the biggest game of the year, at Houston against the Longhorns, who had won five games in a row.

In the third period of the game, with A&M leading 9–8, both teams played cautiously; like two boxers, they sparred with each other, with neither team doing very much, just playing it safe.

But in the fourth quarter, Dutch Hohn and Beasley dove into the Texas line, like Trojan horses, smashing for five, then six yards a carry. Then another seven yards, and then ten, and then Beasley smashed into the line and over the Texas goal line for a touchdown to give A&M a 14–8 advantage as the big crowd literally went wild.

Texas took the kickoff and attempted to pass on every down, but A&M intercepted the ball, and as time ran out, the wild-eyed cadets and fans rushed onto the gridiron to carry their victorious heroes on their shoulders and into the dressing room.

And all over town, the A&M fans painted Houston red as they continued the celebration throughout the night.

KYLE FIELD
Home of the Fightin' Texas A&M Football Team
Home of the Twelfth Man

Kyle Field is named for E. J. Kyle '99, one-time Dean of the School of Agriculture and Ambassador to Guatemala.

The first football games at Texas A&M were played at the drill field (as were baseball games and track meets). The site could accommodate few spectators and the field was in horrendous condition. Dean Kyle, then an instructor in Horticulture, served as President of the General Athletics Association which supervised all A&M-sponsored sporting activities. Committed in general to intercollegiate athletics and in particular to the improvement of A&M's teams, Kyle realized that for athletics to advance at A&M an athletic field was needed. Previously, fans stood or watched from buggies and made contributions when "the hat was passed." These contributions were not enough to buy equipment, hire coaches or pay for trips to away games.

In 1905 Dean Kyle, using part of a field allotted to him for raising crops, installed a fence and bleachers seating 500. He absorbed the entire cost personally. The baseball team used the field in 1905, and the first football game was played in 1906. In appreciation of Dean Kyle's efforts on behalf of A&M athletics, the students named the new stadium Kyle Field.

The first improvement was a covered grandstand in 1907. In 1927 concrete stands were built on the west side and in 1929 on the east and north sides, bringing capacity to 35,000. In 1954, an upper deck was added, enlarging the stadium to 41,500. The next expansion in 1967 raised capacity to 49,000. The first installation of astroturf was made in 1970. In 1979 the stadium was expanded to 72,000 seats, at a cost of $26,126,000.

In honor of the Twelfth Man tradition, a statue of King Gill, the original Twelfth Man, is installed at the north end of Kyle Field—a gift of the Class of '80. The Class of '83 donated the "Spirit of Flame," which is also installed at the north end. The two 100-foot flagpoles at the south end of the field were given in memory of Lt. William B. Blocker '45, who was killed in Italy in WWII.

The original Reveille and subsequent Reveilles are buried near the entrance to Kyle Field.

Four days later, the Aggies took the field against a rugged Southwestern University team. On a rain-slicked field, they eked out a 6–0 victory.

In the final game of the season, the Aggies defeated Tulane 17–0 in a lackluster contest.

A&M closed out the season being named "Champions of the South," and at a victory celebration and banquet given by the Athletic Association, the players were awarded silver footballs. It had been one of the most successful seasons in the sixteen-year history of Texas A&M football.

Dutch Hohn, in a series of recent articles for the A&M yearbook, wrote about those days under Moran:

> Football as we played it at A&M in 1909 to 1911 bore little resemblance to today's game. It was still in a primitive stage. We thought we were smart and tough, and some of us were. But I was forced to agree with Dough Rollins, who helped coach some of the great A&M teams before World War II, when he said, 'Dutch, we should be glad we played when we did. We'd never be able to make these teams.'
>
> The inferior equipment we had to protect us was one example of the primitive football of those days. Another was the matter of the uniforms. We were issued our game uniforms at the very first practice of the season, and if they were ever laundered, I don't remember it. A&M teams in those days could be counted on to get stronger as the season progressed, and before it ended, we usually got pretty high. And talk about overpowering the opposition: this we could be sure of doing, no matter what the score proved to be.
>
> In 1909, when I made the team, not more than fifteen players were ever taken on a trip, and sometimes all of them got to play. Substitutions were infrequent. After I made the first string, I played every minute of every game, except for a five-minute rest period during the TCU game in 1910. I would not admit then or now that I was incapacitated for play, but Moran's story was that for the first four or five minutes, I

Bill Carlin lettered on the 1909 team, first-year coach Charley Moran's undefeated eleven who not only ended a six-year drought against Texas but beat the Longhorns twice that year, the only A&M team to accomplish that before or since. Moran's 1910 Aggies extended the school's winning streak over Texas to three with a 14–8 victory.

was knocked out and unable even to stand on my feet. It was lean pickings for substitutes in those days; they were seldom played in a game.

Recruiting as it is handled now wasn't known then. Coach Moran did do some turn-of-the-century talent scouting, but usually he never knew what players he'd have on his team until practice began in September. Since freshmen were allowed to play then, he looked over the incoming class very carefully each year. I can remember seeing the coach post himself just outside the mess hall one mealtime to scan all the cadets as we marched in. Whenever he saw a likely looking physical specimen, he'd pull him out of line and ask him to report for football.

But football then and now did bear a striking resemblance. The T-formation was commonly used then, in much the same way as today—except the three back men weren't so wide apart.

At A&M, Coach Moran liked to run from the punt formation, and he also used the tandem—with one man back and another man split. One reason he favored the punt formation was that he liked his team to kick often—and on first down.

One other big difference in play then was the use of the dropkick. Today it's unheard of, but it was a potent weapon then, at least in the hands of our fullback, Hamilton.

Frequently, when we were anywhere within forty or fifty yards of the other goal, he'd drop-kick instead of punt, in the hope of getting the ball through the goal posts.

But if some of our techniques were antiquated, we were progressive in one respect. Before the 1910 and 1911 seasons, we went to training camps on the Gulf Coast. In 1910 the camp was at Seabrook, and in 1911 the squad went to LaPorte for two weeks. We slept on cots on the beach and kept our ice, food, clothing, and equipment under a big canvas tent. During the morning we'd dive for oysters, swim, and then, after a light lunch, we'd practice football in a nearby cow pasture.

It was in 1909 that Coach Moran was an assistant to Coach Merriam, and Moran imported four new players of questionable eligibility. They were top players, but I never saw them in class. As I remember, in those days the only requirement for eligibility to play football was that a student must be attending classes for one day prior to the game in which he played. And all the Texas colleges had this rule. It was later on tightened largely because of the generous use Moran made of its liberal possibilities.

With the help of these four 'imports,' we ran up impressive seasons in 1909, 1910, and 1911. In 1911 we went into the Texas game with wins over a good Southwestern team 22–0, Austin 33–0, Auburn 16–0, and Mississippi 17–0. But in the big Thanksgiving game, we dropped a stunner to Texas 6–0.

I think we were just too cocky for the Texas game and we had an off day.

During the second week of football practice in 1911, Texas Coach Bill Wasmund, brought over from Michigan, fell to the ground from the second floor of his house while sleepwalking and died from his injuries. Dave Allerdice was named to replace Wasmund and took over a strong Longhorn team with a 4–1 record on the eve of the A&M game. Texas won a hard-fought battle when Arnie Kirkpatrick recovered a fumble in the end zone.

The very next day, the Texas Athletic Association (on behalf of UT) sent a wire to A&M officials with this terse memo:

"The Texas University Athletic Council greatly deplores the charges in the press regarding the conduct and atmosphere during and after the football games with Texas A&M . . . the action we have now taken is that in view of the controversial heated state of opinion among students and alumni of both institutions, it is in the best interest of Texas that we do not pursue football relations for 1912."

Texas University officials had one primary reason for canceling the football rivalry with Texas A&M: Moran's general football philosophy and attitude, including the use of "ringers" against Texas, and they would not resume their sports activities with A&M until Coach Moran was replaced.

A&M's football program was badly hurt by Texas' actions, for the A&M-Longhorn games provided enough revenue to run the entire A&M sports program.

In 1912 there were additional changes in football rules. The value of a touchdown was increased to six points and a team had to gain ten yards in four downs instead of three.

3

UNCLE CHARLEY MORAN'S SCORING MACHINE

A&M produced a football scoring machine in 1912 like no other Aggie team in history.

Under the marvelous coaching of Charley Moran and the leadership of Captain Ty Bell and such outstanding players as quarterback W. E. Spake, H. G. Lambert, Roark Montgomery, R. A. Kern, and John Lyles, the Aggies opened the season with a runaway 50–0 victory over Daniel Baker. They then routed Trinity 59–0, Arkansas 27–0, and Austin College 57–0.

Oklahoma, which had defeated Texas a week previously, was beaten decisively 28–6 in a game that decided the championship of the Southwest. It was a game that brought out the best in the A&M players, with Kern, Bell, and Ed Vesmirovsky—whose booming punts averaged more than fifty yards—keeping Oklahoma in its own territory most of the game.

The next three games, against the strongest teams in the area—Mississippi, Tulane, and Kansas—were to test the Moran machine to its ultimate.

In the first game, Mississippi State opened the scoring to take a 7–0 lead. But then the Aggies shifted into high gear and ran up a 41–7 win. Next, Tulane fell 41–0. Kansas State, however, slowed the Aggie express, derailing A&M 13–10. This was the first and only defeat for the Aggies, who then ran over Baylor 53–0 to post their eighth victory in nine games.

The 1912 season was the highlight of Coach Moran's tenure at A&M as his Aggies rolled up a record 366 points in winning eight games, while their rivals were only able to penetrate the Aggie defense for twenty-six points.

There was, however, one downer from the season: natural rival Texas was not one of the Aggies' victims because the teams did not play. They wouldn't play the next two years either. Not until 1915 would they meet.

The 1913 Aggies began the season with great expectations but little experience and they were surprised and delighted when they defeated Trinity 7–0, Austin 6–0, and Poly Tech 19–6, but now their eyes were on bigger wins and bigger games.

But their hopes were dashed when the great Dutch Hohn was declared ineligible for playing pro baseball. Dutch had captained the 1911 team, and at various times played at the tackle post and as a guard and was a great pass catcher when he was an end. He was one of the Aggies' great all-around stars, and when he was removed, the bottom fell out and the team practically came apart.

Crestfallen, the Aggies dropped consecutive

games to Mississippi State, 6–0; Kansas State, 12–0; Oklahoma, 3–0; and Haskell, 28–0. Moran did his best to boost the morale of the inexperienced A&M players, and in their next game they responded with a 14–14 tie of Baylor—a moral victory of sorts.

In the final game of the season, at Houston, in a field best described as a "sea of mud," and outweighed by fifteen to twenty pounds per man, the Aggies outfought and outplayed the bigger, more experienced LSU Tigers for three periods. Then with five minutes to play, A&M quarterback H. Bonner completed a flurry of passes to his end, Johnny Garrity. After two more passes to Garrity and Thomas, Bonner went over the LSU goal line. He kicked the extra point to tie the game 7–7 and that's how it stood. Another moral victory.

The inexperienced freshmen of the 1913 squad, which had produced the poorest season since the 1908 team (3–4–2), were now a year older in 1914. They were bigger and had a year of solid varsity experience behind them and they were determined to give the cadets and the alumni the kind of winning season they could crow about.

Led by one of their great stars, two-year captain and fullback Tyree Bell, and aided by such stalwarts as quarterback Verne Scott; halfback Wiley Coleman; ends Garrity and Bill Collins; tackles Benny Faber and Raleigh DeLong; guards Marvin Butler, N. M. Braumiller, and Byron Dickie; and center Frank Cawthon, the Aggies were ready to put their "new" football model on display in the opening game of the season against Austin College.

Following a pep talk by Coach Moran, the Aggies ran onto the field and proceeded to chew up Austin, scoring five touchdowns in running up a 32–0 victory. But there was a distinct letdown a week later against Trinity, and the game ended in a 0–0 tie.

After a week of savage practice, Moran had his players primed as they flattened TCU by a six-touchdown margin, 40–0. But in the next game the Haskell Indians, speedier and more experienced, eked out a 10–0 win.

The following week, the Tigers of LSU rolled into town, but the Aggies were once more in top form as they smashed through and over the LSU defense in an unmerciful display of sheer power, registering eight touchdowns to pound out a stunning 63–9 win.

Charley Moran coached his last game at A&M in 1914. The reason for his untimely departure stemmed from an incident back in 1911, when Texas, accusing Moran of using ringers (illegal players) in that year's Longhorn-Aggie contest, unilaterally canceled the series starting in 1912. When talks began in 1915 about forming a conference including the biggest colleges in the Southwest, Texas, whose membership was considered paramount, stubbornly refused to join if A&M, another school considered a must-have, was admitted with Moran as head coach. Under mounting pressure to release Moran for the good of college football in the Southwest, A&M, with great resignation, fired its most successful coach during the winter of 1915. It paved the way for the formation of the Southwest Conference—and deepened the roots of hostility between Texas's two most prominent college football teams. (Moran went on to a long career as a major league umpire.)

Once again on a roll, and under the driving force of Moran, the Aggies pounded out successive wins over Rice, in a tougher contest than the score indicated, 32–7; Oklahoma A&M 24–0; and Mississippi, 14–7, in a squeaker.

Even though the Aggies finished at 6–1–1, once again there was a general letdown, no climax to a great season, for Thanksgiving Day was devoid of a battle against the rival Longhorns.

The spiritual loss was felt by the players, the cadets and the alumni; without the final Texas game, football seemed rather empty that year.

Late in the season, Texas athletic director Theo Belmont contacted all the major Southwest colleges to set up a conference that would provide strict eligibility rules for not only football but all of the athletic programs. Most of the colleges agreed, and at a meeting on December 4, 1914, the Southwest conference was formally organized. Charter members were Texas, Texas A&M, Baylor, Southwestern, Arkansas, Oklahoma, and Oklahoma State.

Once the agreement was signed, officials of Texas and A&M agreed to resume their football rivalry, and a home-and-home schedule was agreed upon to commence in 1915.

There was, however, a most disturbing note, and it was a major obstacle to the resumption of the big game between the two rivals. While Texas officials stated publicly that the severance of relations between the schools was caused by bad feelings between the two student bodies, they really wanted Moran removed. Aggie backers said it was because Texas had trouble beating Moran's teams. Even that 1911 game that Texas won 6–0 was one that saw the Aggies completely outplay Texas, before the Longhorns recovered a fumble to set up the lone score of the game.

And so Coach Charley, "Uncle Charley," in the interest of bringing Texas and A&M together again, resigned. It was a bitter day in Aggieland when he said his goodbyes, for he was the most popular and the winningest coach A&M had ever had. He was the idol of all the Aggies. In a speech at Dallas, Cy Perkins, a former Aggie, said Moran was the only man he ever saw leave a college for winning too many football games.

In 1915, under new coach E. H. "Jigger" Harlan, a former Princeton all-American, the Aggies upset Texas 13–0 in a game that players dedicated to Moran. During the game, when an Aggie player made a vicious tackle, he would say, "That's for the way you treated Uncle Charley."

Years later, the Moran legacy remained strong. There was a special "Charley Moran Day" in 1938. And in 1948 he was elected an honorary member of the Aggie class of 1913. When Moran died in 1949, twenty-five of his players were invited back to the campus as special guests for the Texas-A&M game. Uncle Charley's granddaughter, Anne Moran, was there to represent Charley.

After Moran left A&M, he became an assistant coach at Carlisle and helped develop the great Jim Thorpe. Then he went on to coach at Centre College from 1917 to 1923, winning big games against Harvard and Princeton and coaching Centre to an undefeated (10–0) season in 1920.

Captain John Rollins of the 1915 team said of the 13–0 victory over Texas that it had inspired a tradition that would prevail in twelve of the next thirteen meetings between A&M and Texas.

"It is certain," said Rollins, that 13–0 was to be a rallying force for the Aggies for years to come, and 13–0 was inscribed wherever it might haunt the followers of the Longhorns, on buses, trolley cars, wagons, automobiles, and public buildings. It mattered little that A&M closed the 1915 season with a 7–0 loss to Mississippi. What really mattered was that a magnificent, treasured rivalry had been restored and in an atmosphere pleasing to both sides."

In his second year at A&M, Coach Jigger Harlan fielded a team that went 6–2 before facing Texas in the annual Turkey Day Festival. That year, the 'Horns, coached by Gene Van Ghent, had a power-laden offense and had run up a 74–0 win over SMU, beaten Rice and Oklahoma in successive games, and were favored to win the SWC title.

Austin's Clark Field was packed with more than 15,000 frenetic fans cheering their favorite team, as the 'Horns and the Aggies clashed.

Nearing the end of the first half with Texas leading 7–0, the Aggies received the ball, and Rollins and Coleman took turns driving the ball, penetrating the Texas defense for five, eight, and ten yards at a time. A&M scored as halfback Frank Litterst tossed a pass to Johnson. The PAT made it 7–7.

In the third period, halfback Rip Long of Texas took the ball from his quarterback, Bill Trabue, reversed his field and sped forty yards through the A&M defense for a touchdown and a 14–7 lead. In the fourth quarter, with A&M battling furiously to score, Bill Trabue of Texas took an Aggie punt, avoided two tacklers, headed for the sideline, and outran three Aggie tack-

lers for a sixty-five-yard TD scamper that wrapped up a 21–7 Texas victory.

The outcome scrambled the SWC race to the extent that no team had a just claim to the conference title. Four teams had lost only a single conference game, and there was no precedent for awarding championships on the basis of winning percentages.

Amid the confusion over who should be considered league champ (an issue never resolved), the A&M Athletic Council decided to replace Jigger Harlan as head coach. Dana X. Bible was named to replace him.

Dana Bible, who was born in Jefferson City, Tennessee, in 1891, played quarterback for Carson-Newman in 1906. There was no coach

The 1914 squad was another of Moran's offensive juggernauts, rolling up 205 points and a 6–1–1 record. In six seasons, the no-nonsense Moran posted a 38–8–4 record, good enough to turn a few heads not only in the South but nationally. His 1912 team, led by lineman Caesar "Dutch" Hohn and fullback Tyree Bell, was a particularly fearsome bunch, one that overpowered its opponents with 366 points (against only 26) en route to 8–1 record. The offensive blitz stood as an A&M record for 73 years.

available, so fifteen-year-old Dana took over. The players furnished their own equipment, handled their own training and other expenses. Dana was a great improviser, even at that early age, and once scored a touchdown on a play he had borrowed from a book on the Rover Boys.

After graduation, Bible took a job at Brandon Prep School in Tennessee. In those early days

Two of Head Coach E. H. Harlan's 1916 Aggies, A. L. Johnson (left) and three-year letterman standout Darrace Burns. Harlan replaced the popular Charley Moran and in two seasons (1915–1916) went a combined 12–5. His first team dumped Texas 13–0 in the first meeting between these bitter rivals since 1911. Because of previous scheduling commitments, the Aggies only played two conference games in the inaugural year of the Southwest Conference. The win against Texas, then, was especially sweet because it represented the Aggies' lone conference victory.

coaches often permitted each other to play. In one game against Chattanooga, Bible was at halfback. Bald at twenty years of age, he had to listen to the jeers of "Grandpa" from the rival student section.

Bible was only twenty-one when he was introduced to the Mississippi College president, and he applied for the football coaching post. But the president, Dr. Provine, suggested he conduct the chapel exercises before he was considered. Bible took up the challenge, conducted the chapel exercises, and got the job.

In 1915, his third year at Mississippi, Bible scheduled a game with big Tulane and, utilizing the same backfield shift as the Tulane team,

defeated the Green Wave 20–8 in one of the big upsets of the season.

While Bible was beating all opponents, the Texas A&M Athletic Council decided it needed a freshman coach to help head coach Jigger Harlan, and offered Bible the post. Bible took the job and was so successful with the A&M freshmen that they played the A&M varsity to a standstill in practice sessions. In 1917 Bible was named head coach.

4

BIBLE THUMPING

Coach Bible remembered the outstanding freshman team he had developed at A&M in 1916, which included such players as Captain Ox Ford, Jack Mahan, Rosey Higginbotham, Tim Griesenbeck, Scott Alexander, Kyle Elam, Cap Murrah, C. R. Drake, G. Martin, and Rip Collins. They were now sophomores, and in early practice sessions were even more impressive than the year before. Day by day they improved and gave every indication they would be outstanding in 1917.

In the opener against Austin, Bible alternated running backs Higginbotham, Mahan, and McKnight. Elam played most downs at quarterback. The linemen were Ford and McMurrey at the tackles, McKnight and Wilson at the guards, Gouger and Alexander at the end posts, and Anderson at center.

A&M scored on its first possession and continued to score two and three times in each period. Bible attempted to keep the score down by putting in every man on the squad, but the reserves were so eager to show how well they could play, they gave their very best, and the result was a smashing 66–0 romp.

The following week, Dallas University, which had provided stiff opposition a year earlier and was even stronger this season came to town intent on beating the Aggies. But A&M, still riding the crest of its smashing win over Austin, played like champions and scored a touchdown on every possession. The Aggies piled up fifteen touchdowns and held Dallas to one first down en route to an incredible 98–0 triumph.

Suddenly, sportswriters were calling the 1917 A&M team the greatest scoring machine in Southwest football history. And no wonder. The Aggies had racked up 164 points to none for their rivals in two games played.

A week later, Southwestern, a team that had always given A&M trouble, found the Aggies on an off day, but A&M still prevailed, further evidence that this was a special team.

At San Antonio the next week, it was A&M versus LSU, and this time it was the marvelous kicking of Rip Collins—whose two field goals and long, high, driving punts that sent LSU back into its own territory for most of the game—that helped the Aggie defense force turnovers and produce a 27–0 win.

Next up was Tulane, coached by an old rival of Bible's, Clark Shaughnessy. The two coaches based their offenses on the famed Minnesota shift. But Bible devised a formidable defense that held the Green Wave scoreless. In the first period, as Tulane failed to gain any ground, A&M racked up three quick touchdowns. In the third period, Tulane finally reached the A&M two-yard line,

Following the 1916 season, Heach Coach E. H. Harlan was replaced by one of his assistants: Dana X. Bible (right, shown with H. B Weir in 1917). A&M officials had been impressed by Bible's coaching success at LSU and hoped he could add a spark. He did more than that. With results that were swift and stunning Bible took A&M to completely unrealized heights. His initial team went undefeated and untied, the first Aggie bunch to accomplish that, and subsequent teams won just about as regularly. In 11 years, Bible posted a near seamless 72–19 record. (He also coached the baseball and basketball teams to SWC championships.)

but the Aggies stuffed 'em, thus thwarting the Green Wave's best scoring opportunity.

A&M managed two more scores, with Mahan, Elam, and McClintock running wild, and defeated Tulane 35–0 for its fifth straight shutout victory.

The Baylor Bears, winners of five straight, including a 103–0 romp over Simmons College, were confident they would take revenge against A&M for their 3–0 loss in 1916. But early in the first period, Rip Collins intercepted a Baylor forward pass, broke through two tacklers, and raced thirty-five yards for a touchdown. The kick was good, and A&M led. During the rest of a tense battle, the Aggies made three trips deep into Baylor territory, but the stubborn Bear defense held. Late in the game, a desperate Baylor halfback broke loose for an apparent touchdown, but Kyle Elam made a diving tackle and brought

Jack Mahan was a bull of a runner who lettered in 1917, 1919 and 1920. During his three years the Aggies posted a walloping 28–4–1 record. Between the '19 and '20 seasons, he competed in the Olympics on the track team (his event: the javelin). In 1965 he was elected into the Texas A&M Hall of Fame.

the Baylor back down to earth. The game ended shortly thereafter, but only after the Aggies had the battle of their lives.

Ten days later, the Texas Longhorns appeared to have the Aggies in check as they played inspired football to hold A&M scoreless. But R. Higginbotham broke through the Texas line from midfield and appeared to be on his way to a touchdown. A diving tackle stopped Higgy on the twelve-yard line and three tries at the Texas goal line were halted before Rip Collins's field goal attempt went wide. But Texas was off sides on the play giving the Aggies another chance from the five-yard line. Bible pulled Dan McMurrey from his tackle position and the 210-pound McMurrey finally blasted over the goal line on fourth down to give the Aggies a hard-fought 7–0 victory.

This was the seventh straight shutout win for the Aggies, inspiring many of the nation's sportswriters to label them one of the greatest football teams of all time. Famed sportswriter Grantland Rice even echoed these sentiments.

In the final game of the season, the 7–0 Rice Owls, with one of their truly great teams, took the field in Houston against the Aggies and proceeded to march down the field as if they were going to run the Aggies out of the stadium. But A&M held on the twenty-yard line and took over.

Then it was the Aggies' turn, and they proceeded to drive yard-by-yard until they advanced to the Owl's ten-yard line. After three cracks at the Rice line, big Dan McMurrey, behind three blockers, drove over left tackle for a touchdown. The kick was good and it was 7–0 Texas A&M.

In the final period, with five minutes to play, Weir kicked a thirty-five-yard field goal to cap a 10–0 victory and one of the most brilliant records in collegiate football history. A&M had won eight straight games and had not allowed its opponents to score a single point.

In his first season as A&M's head coach, Dana Bible had guided his Aggies to an undefeated, unscored-upon season and won the undisputed championship of the Southwest. It was the Aggies' first championship.

Most of the championship team of 1917 went into the various branches of the military at the end of the season, including Dana Bible, who became a pursuit pilot. Tubby Graves, who had been Bible's assistant, took over, and the few players who returned included Woody Wilson, Mahan, Elan, and Higginbotham. Despite the lack of promising players, the team looked good

Fleet halfback Rosey Higginbotham carrying the ball for the Aggies in A&M's 10–0 victory over Rice in 1917, which capped its perfect season. A week earlier, the Aggies' 7–0 whitewash of Texas had clinched their first SWC championship.

A spirited group of Texas A&M sophomores get the goat of Rice's mascot, which watched the Owls get plucked.

in practice, but suddenly the Students' Army Training Corps canceled the October schedule. Then, just when the schedule was to be resumed, an influenza epidemic hit the campus and football was out for another several weeks.

Late in November, when football was resumed, Higgy went into the Air Corps, Mahan and Woody Wilson were called into their training corps, and A&M was left with a skeleton crew of players.

The opener against Ream Field was a slow, fumble-riddled game, played on a rain-soaked field, but the Aggies pounded out a 6–0 win. Then, in a knock-down drag-out battle with Camp Travis that excited more than 3,000 fans, the Aggies, outweighed by some fifteen pounds per man, scored a touchdown, but missed the extra point. Travis then tied the score, 6–6.

Later, with but three minutes to play, A&M drove fifty yards, with Elam carrying the brunt of the attack, to the three-yard line. Robby Harrison then passed to Scott Alexander for the go-ahead score. Final result: Aggies 12, Camp Travis 6.

At Baylor, the Aggies struggled through a scoreless first half, but Elam and company broke away for three touchdowns in the second half to win 19–0. A&M prepped for its game against Texas by whipping Camp Mabry 19–6 and Southwestern 7–0.

At Austin, the Aggies battled their bitterest foe, the Longhorns, who had an undefeated

Besides a perfect 8–0 record and a conference championship, A&M's 1917 team bludgeoned its way to 270 points while allowing its opposition nary a score of any kind.

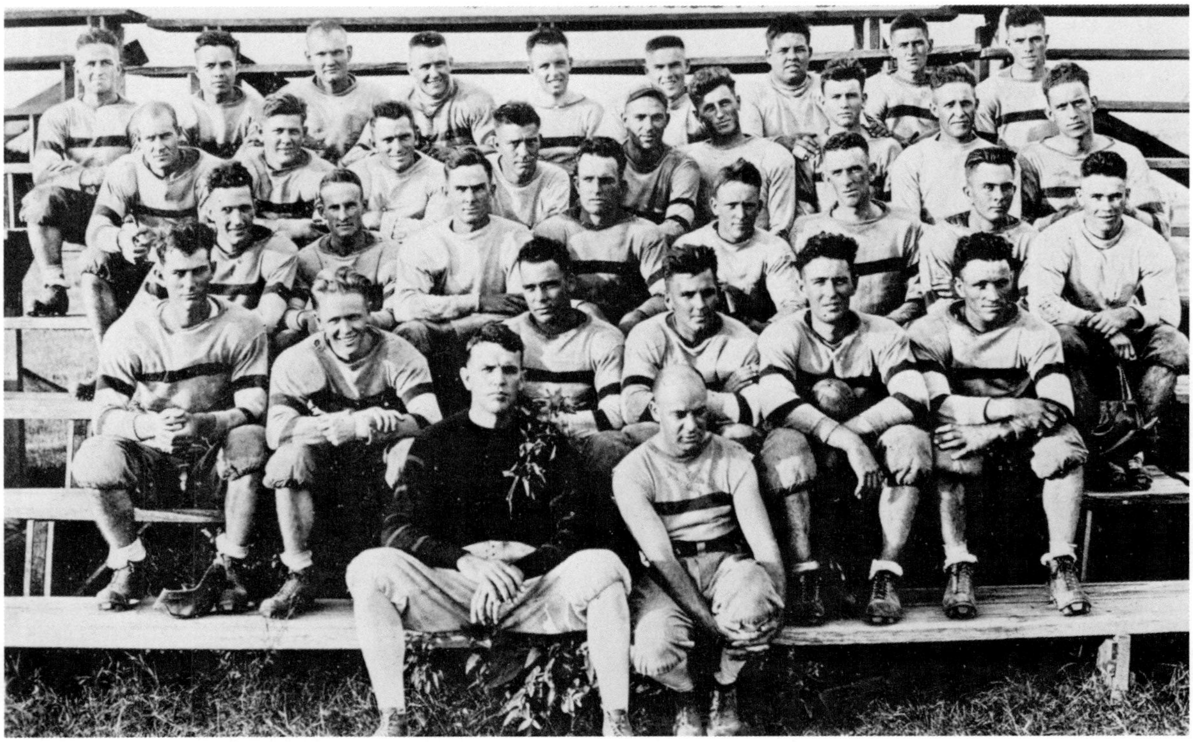

record to match that of the Aggies. Despite the war, more than 10,000 fans were on hand for the game. Texas scored early in the first quarter and held on to win 7–0. It was the first loss in thirteen games for the Aggies, who came back to rout Camp Travis 60–0, before playing Remount Station to a scoreless tie. They finished the season 6–1–1.

On November 11, 1918, the German Army, suffering terrible losses in a great battle on the France-Germany front, asked for a general armistice, and by the end of November, the war was over.

By 1919, hundreds of thousands of young men from Navy installations and the American Expeditionary Forces poured back into schools and colleges all over the nation, and the football coaches found these hardened young men in perfect condition for college football, which had almost been abandoned during the 1917–1918 seasons.

At Texas A&M, the Aggies' Dana Bible returned from his duties as an Air Corps lieutenant and immediately set out to develop another great football team for the 1919 season.

Bible was blessed with a score of veterans who had returned: stars Jack Mahan, Hig Higginbotham, Scotty Alexander, Ed Wilson, Cap Murrah, C. R. Drake, and George Martin were all back and raring to go.

The Athletic Council had scheduled a doubleheader game with the Sam Houston STC and San Marcos STC teams, and A&M routed them both. In the first game, Sam Houston was simply outclassed as the A&M first team romped 77–0. Then, the A&M second stringers defeated San Marcos immediately after the first game ended, 28–0.

Next up was Southern Methodist, which had won its first two games of the season and was eager for the kill against A&M. But the Aggies, with Jack Mahan and Harrison flashing through the Mustang line for two touchdowns, were the standout performers. In addition, Harrison kicked a forty-five-yard field goal to give A&M its third win, 16–0.

Howard Payne, A&M's next foe, played tough. But in the fourth quarter of a scoreless game, A&M drove to Howard Payne's fifteen-yard line. While the 5,000 frantic A&M followers cheered themselves hoarse, Jack Mahan raced in for a touchdown on a reverse. A&M later fell on a fumble in the end zone to ice a 12–0 victory.

Cap Murrah was a gritty three-time All-SWC lineman who opened holes the size of the Gulf of Mexico for All-league performers Higginbotham and Mahan. Together, they were a deadly trio that in two years (1919–1920) helped the Aggies rack up 504 points.

Against Trinity, long runs by Higginbotham, Mahan, and Martin gave the Aggies an easy 42–0 win. Higginbotham's great punting kept Trinity in its half of the field most of the day and gave A&M several good scoring opportunities. Bob Carruthers starred on defense for A&M, blocking three Trinity punts that were turned into scores.

A tough, aggressive Oklahoma A&M team rolled into College Station a week after the Trinity game, confident it could handle A&M. But the Aggies, now on a streak of five straight shutout wins, stunned Oklahoma with two quick scores, then played a cautious game, kicking on first and second downs, in a 28–0 triumph.

Jack Mahan looks for a hole (which he finds for a 15-yard gain) against the Longhorns in the Aggies' 1919 season finale 7–0 victory, A&M's third win against Texas in its last four games.

In the seventh game of the season, against five-time winner Baylor, every member of the A&M starting unit played the entire sixty minutes.

Rosey Higginbotham was the star of the game. He booted a thirty-yard field goal and then in the final period, he surprised the Baylor defense. Rosey lined up for a punt, but at the last moment, he passed the ball to Scott Alexander, who blasted across the goal line for a touchdown to give A&M a 10–0 win.

A week later against TCU, but minus the services of Martin, Jack Mahan, and Knickerbocker, the Aggies took the initiative, and with Rosey Higginbotham playing the game of his life, trounced TCU 48–0. Higgy scored three touchdowns and kicked six extra points for a total of twenty-four points. Jack Pierce at quarterback ran the offense like an all-American, and every member of the team contributed to the eighth consecutive win.

The Aggies were lucky, however, to eke out a 7–0 win over Southwestern, as the team seemed sluggish and out of sorts.

In the final game of the year, on Thanksgiving Day, Texas and A&M battled through a savage first period with neither team having an edge. In the second period, A&M recovered a Texas fumble on the twenty-yard line. Then, in three quick tries, Jack Higginbotham cracked through for a touchdown, made the conversion, and it was 7–0 A&M. Late in the game, Texas managed to drive to the Aggies' five-yard line, but A&M held, took over the ball, and drove upfield as the game ended.

The great win over Texas gave A&M an unprecedented run of ten consecutive shutout victories in 1919, Dana Bible's second SWC championship in three seasons, and an incredible record of 24 wins and 1 loss in the three years since Bible took over the coaching post from E. H. Harlan.

Most important to A&M students and officials were the two victories over Texas in the biggest games of the last three seasons.

A&M's magnificent three seasons, 1917 to 1919, were to be the most significant in Texas

Incredibly, the 1919 Aggies were even more dominant than the 1917 group. Led by a corps of talented players just returning from World War I, they went undefeated in ten games and romped to 275 points, and, oh yes, held their opposition to goose eggs—every single game.

football history, for that record paved the way for a nationally recognized 1921 game against Centre College, victor over Harvard. It was a game that would put A&M football on the front page of every sports section in the nation.

During the 1919–1920 school year, Texas A&M established an intercollegiate football-basketball win streak that still stands as the longest in history for unbeaten teams in the two sports during the same school year. Ten victories in football and 19 in basketball gave A&M an incredible streak of 29 in a row.

Now, in 1920, Coach Bible led a number of the great stars of his 1919 eleven into action. The Aggies opened the season by overwhelming Daniel Baker with the biggest score ever tallied by an Aggie team. They ran up sixteen touchdowns to beat Daniel Baker 110 to 0. Halfback Jack Mahan took the opening kickoff and threaded his way through the entire Baker squad for sixty-five yards and a touchdown. Before it was over, Mahan had scored four touchdowns in a dazzling exhibition of broken-field running.

Two rugged games followed, a 3–0 win over SMU thanks to a thirty-five-yard field goal by Bugs Morris, and a grueling 0–0 tie against LSU. Then, in a complete reversal of form, the Aggies went on a scoring rampage against Phillips University with a 47–0 triumph. Jonnie Pierce directed the team's offense in brilliant style as Mahan and Higgy played well.

Oklahoma A&M's eleven, despite sporting a winning record, proved no match for the aggressive Aggies as the backfield play of Higgy, Pierce, Mahan, Weir, and Morris pounded the Oklahoma line, scoring 35 points while holding the Oklahoma team to a single first down.

The Baylor Bears, who had not scored on the Aggies in four seasons, were confident that 1920 was "their year." But with the exception of their

A posed shot of halfback Rosey Higginbotham, a linchpin on Dana Bible's great teams of 1917, 1919, and 1920.

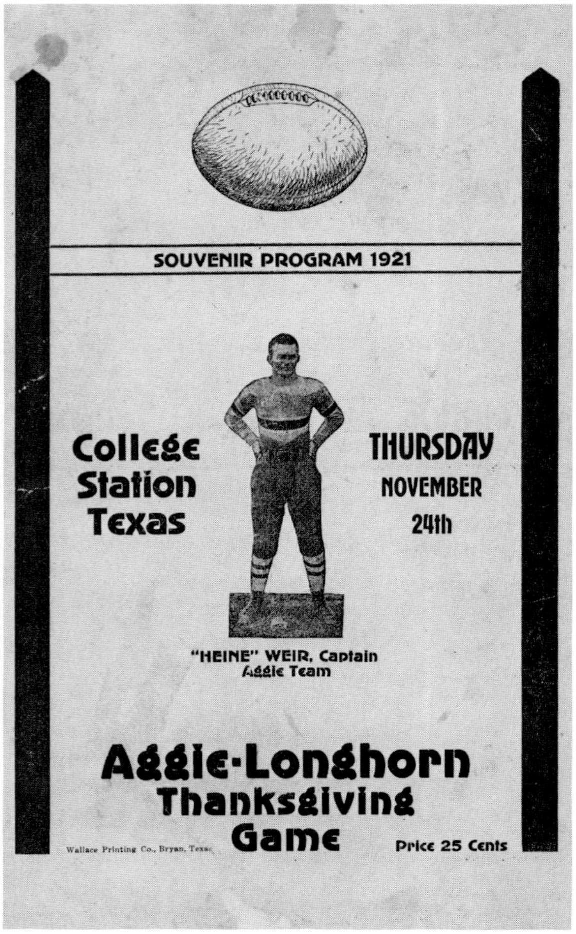

A souvenir from the 1921 A&M–Texas game, which ended 0–0. A tie was all the Aggies needed to clinch the conference crown.

Bodies tumble like dominoes in this action from the 1920 A&M–Texas clash, won by UT 7–3. It was the Aggies' only loss that season and cost them the SWC championship. They would bounce back the next year, however.

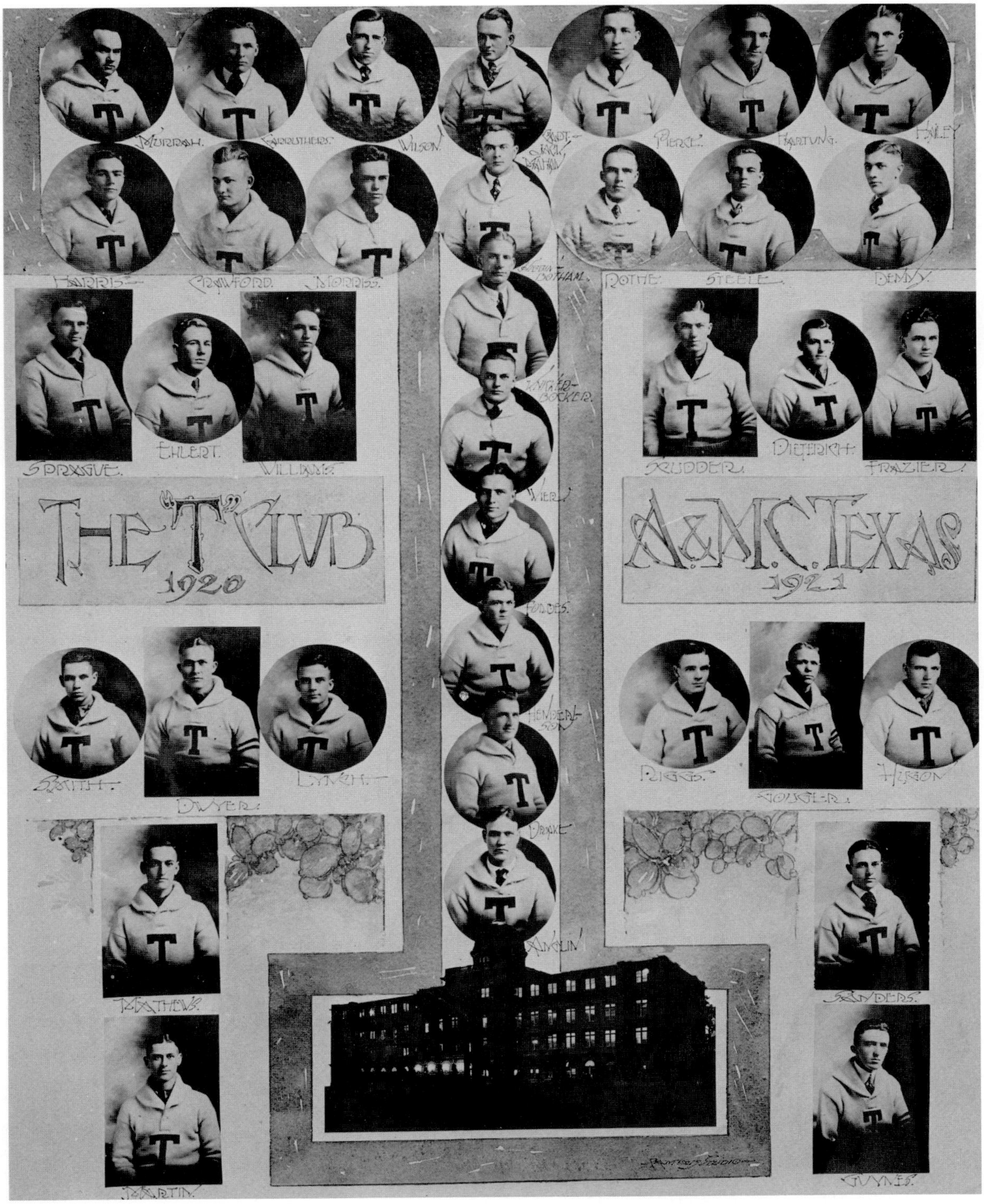

The 1921 Texas Aggies, SWC champs and conquerers of national power Centre College.

great fullback, Joe Dodson, who proved to be difficult to stop, the Aggies had the game well in hand and took a 24–0 win over Baylor. At one point, Dodson thrilled the crowd with a magnificent fifty-yard pass to one of his backs, but Baylor was stopped on the one-yard line and failed to score.

"During this sequence of plays," said Bugs Morris, "we held Baylor for four downs on the one-yard line. Then later in the game, Coach

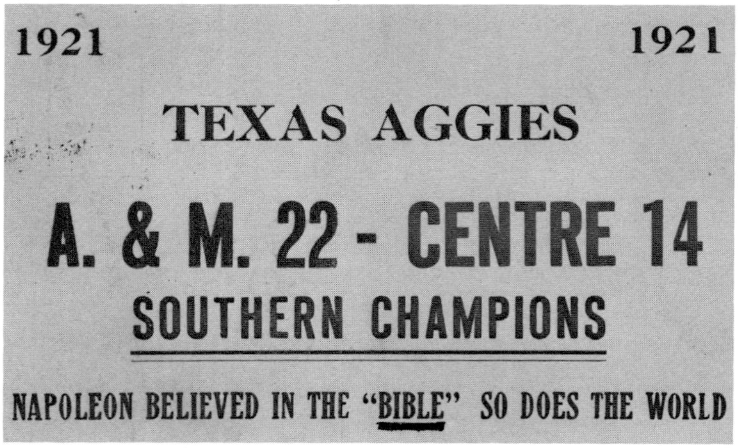
1921 1921

TEXAS AGGIES

A. & M. 22 - CENTRE 14

SOUTHERN CHAMPIONS

NAPOLEON BELIEVED IN THE "BIBLE" SO DOES THE WORLD

A souvenir postcard celebrates the monumental victory over Centre College in 1921.

Bridges of Baylor unveiled a trick play that had all of us guessing who had the ball. We chased every Baylor player on the field before we finally got to the player with the ball, and we nailed him on the one-yard line."

Rice, under the coaching genius of John Heisman, had worked on a slick passing attack in preparation for A&M, but the Aggies worked out an effective defense, stopped the pass, and beat Rice 7–0.

Next up was undefeated Texas.

A&M carried into the contest a streak of twenty-five games without a loss. The Aggies had not been scored on during this streak, and the only tarnish was a scoreless tie with LSU.

Bible pinned his hopes for victory on a strong defense and the punting of Higginbotham, who had averaged forty-nine yards on ten kicks. Bugs Morris booted a twenty-two-yard field goal to put A&M in front, and the Mahan-Higginbotham tandem drove again to the Texas ten-yard line before running out of steam.

The Longhorns began their own drive in the second half, outgaining A&M by a decisive margin, but the Aggies stayed out in front through the third quarter, turning back the 'Horns' attack, stopping them inches from the goal line on the final play of the period. On its next possession, Texas moved to a fourth-and-seven situation on the A&M eleven. A tackle-eligible pass gave Texas a first down by inches on the four, and on the next play, Texas scored, kicked the point to make it 7–3, and owned its first SWC football championship.

"You can understand why it was such a bitter defeat," Bible would say fifty years later, "and it was compounded by the loss coming so late in the game. That loss was the hardest to take of my coaching career."

One of the Texas backfield stars that day was Kyle Elam, a hero for A&M in the 1917 Baylor game, who had lettered also for the Aggies in 1918 before transferring to Texas.

Mahan, one of the mainstays during that great A&M winning streak, also starred in track and field and was a member of the 1920 U.S. Olympic team as a javelin thrower. He was inducted into A&M's Athletic Hall of Fame in 1965. Higginbotham was to return to A&M in 1927 as the freshman coach and baseball coach. He continued as baseball coach through the Matty Bell era (1929-33), then joined Bell at SMU as baseball coach from 1935 until he returned to military service in 1942.

As a lieutenant commander in the Navy, Higginbotham was killed in a fiery plane crash at the Quonset Point, Rhode Island, Naval Base in 1943.

In 1921 the Aggies had to come from behind in several games to post a 6–1–2 record that enabled them to win the SWC crown and earn a post-season berth against Centre College.

Opening the season against Howard Payne, the Aggies were tested, but won 14–7. They followed with a 13–0 win over SMU as Captain Heinie Weir and McMillan starred.

LSU, however, defeated A&M in a rugged battle, 6–0. But the Aggies bounced back to beat Arizona and Oklahoma in close games. Rice won a moral 7–7 "victory," and then the Aggies prepped for their Thanksgiving Day Game against Texas.

The 1921 Aggies-Longhorns clash at Kyle Field not only generated its usual huge share of regional interest, it also set broadcast history. A few weeks earlier, Pittsburgh station KDKA had aired the Pitt-West Virginia game via the wireless—the first radio broadcast of a football game. Now it was the Aggies' turn to make history, airing the first ever play-by-play football broadcast in the Southwestern Conference. Harry Saunders manned the key at Kyle Field with assistance from H. C. Dillingham and Cecil L.

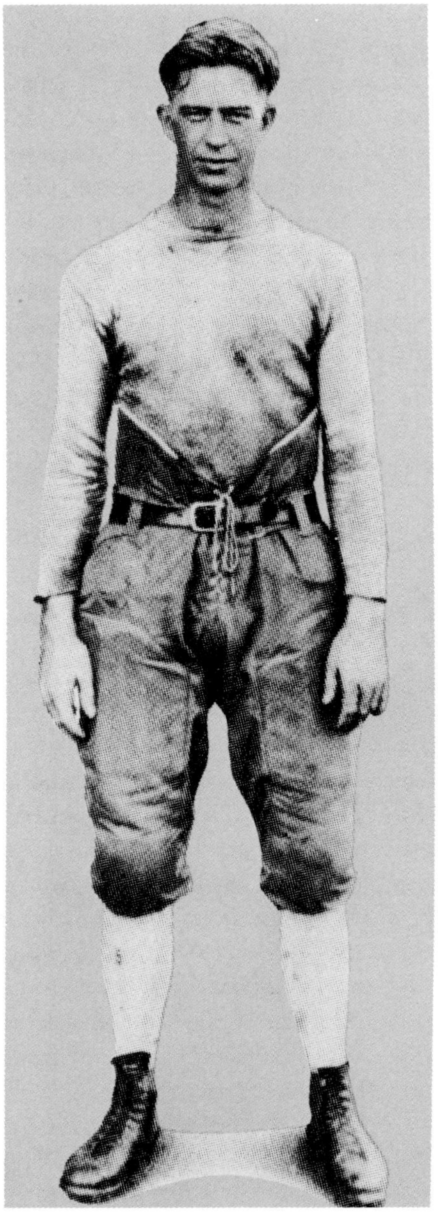

Halfback King Gill, the originator of the Twelfth Man tradition. A statue in front of Kyle Field now immortalizes him.

Matthes. W. A. "Doc" Tolson helped set up the broadcast and then played in the Aggie Band during the game.

The Aggies and 'Horns drove at each other with savage intensity; as the game progressed, the sounds of the blocking and tackling could be heard all over the stadium. Texas tacklers dove into A&M ball carriers with such force that the Aggies fumbled the ball seven times, five times in their own territory. In the last five minutes of the battle, Texas missed two field-goal attempts. The game ended with both teams driving hard, but unable to punch across the line. Final score: 0–0.

After the ding-dong battle, SWC officials agreed that A&M was the choice to oppose Centre College in a post-season game.

In his fifth season as A&M's football coach, Dana Bible had amassed the most remarkable coaching record in A&M history with 30 victories, 2 losses, and 2 ties. It was a record that had brought A&M three SWC championships.

Now, in 1922, Bible was looking forward to another great season. Realizing, of course, that a number of his great stars of the '21 season had departed, he nevertheless felt that his new players would make their mark.

But in the first game of the season, against Howard Payne, the Aggies were taken by surprise as Payne used an outstanding passing attack to defeat A&M 13–7. A week later, Tulsa, evidently noticing the Aggies' weakness, also tossed a number of flashy passes at A&M to eke out a surprising 13–10 win.

Coach Bible and his captain, Puny Wilson, pushed the Aggies hard during the next several practice sessions, and they responded by defeating Southwestern 33–0. However, injuries to key players would hurt the Aggies in subsequent games.

The Aggies defeated LSU 46–0 and Ouichita College 19–6. But Baylor and SMU took turns defeating A&M in successive weeks. Then, in a super effort, A&M defeated Rice 24–0 to climb to 4–4 with Texas looming directly ahead.

In this twenty-third renewal of their classic battle, a 7–1 Texas, a 6 to 1 betting favorite, got the surprise of its life.

"Bugs" Morris recalls the game: "Prior to the game Coach Bible told us the story of David and Goliath. He had been a student of the Bible and his stirring words were a great stimulant to us. I think Coach Bible felt the public thought the odds against A&M were about the same as against David, and when he had finished his tale, we were ready to take on any team in the country."

Bible's underdog Aggies completed two marvelous pass plays that had the crowd roaring. In the first period, quarterback T. L. Miller faked an end run, stopped, and tossed a short pass to King Gill, the fastest man on the A&M team, who raced thirty-five yards for a score. Late in the second period, Jim Marley, the 'Horns fullback, scored a touchdown from the three-yard line for a 7–7 tie.

In the fourth period, Gill, who is responsible for the Twelfth Man A&M tradition, took the ball on a reverse and sped thirty yards to the Texas three-yard line. McMillan then dove in for the touchdown that gave the Aggies one of the biggest upsets of the year, 14–7.

The win cost the Longhorns the SWC title and their coach, Berry Whitaker, who resigned.

For the Aggies it was a 5–4 season, not a good one for Coach Bible. But the win over Texas made the difference.

The 1922 and 1923 seasons were subpar, at least by Bible standards.

The Aggies began the 1923 season with five straight shutout wins over Houston, Howard Payne, Southwestern, Sewanee, and LSU. Then, for some unknown reason, the Aggies slumped badly and dropped games to SMU, Baylor, Rice, and finally, the big game against Texas, 6–0.

The 5–3–1 season, A&M's second straight modest showing, caused some ripples of concern among Aggie faithful. The 1924 season opened brightly, as the Aggies defeated Tarleton, Trinity, Southwestern, Sewanee, Arkansas, TCU, and Rice. But they lost vital SWC games to Baylor and, most important, Texas—for the second year in a row—and the alumni started growling even louder over the losses to hated Texas.

In 1925 Coach Bible breathed a deep sigh of relief as he looked over his players for the first practice session. He still had three members of a great frosh team of 1922, tackle Bones Irvin, fullback Fay Wilson, and husky guard Norm Dansby. The happiest feeling for Bible came when he saw his backfield prospects work out. They were Wilson, an all-SWC fullback in 1924; Bob Berry, a fast-moving, shifty quarterback; and Taro Kishi and Joe McGuire, two rugged halfbacks.

Plus, gangly sophomore, Joel Hunt, who was overlooked at the beginning of the season, soon developed into one of the all-time best Aggie halfbacks.

In the opening game of the season, a strong Trinity eleven got off to a fine start, scoring a touchdown and then a thirty-yard field goal to stun the Aggies by taking a 10–0 lead. But A&M came back to score a touchdown, and then in the third quarter, Joel Hunt and Captain Wilson sparked the attack, pounding out two touchdowns to take a come-from-behind win, 20–10.

Next, Southwestern jumped out in front of A&M with a quick touchdown after recovering an Aggie fumble, and proceeded to take a 6–0 lead. However, in the final period, A&M came to life as Hunt, Claude Watts, and Wilson scored touchdowns to give the Aggies a 23–6 victory.

The Sewanee Tigers always played tough against A&M, and this year they were eager for their third straight win over the Aggies. But they were shipped and packed back to their mountain home in Tennessee as A&M fought the Tigers to a rugged 6–6 tie.

Then, SMU and Baylor were defeated as was Sam Houston, 77–0. TCU, however, provided a stunning surprise, holding the favorite Aggies scoreless, then booting a fourth-quarter field goal to win 3–0. But the Aggies, quickly shaking off the shocking TCU loss, took out all their fury on Rice, shackling them 17–0 prior to their annual Turkey Day battle against Texas.

On Kyle Field the Aggies and Longhorns squared off in one for the ages.

Both teams sported season records of 6–1–1 and were battling to see who would wear the Southwestern Conference championship crown. Some 20,000 fans were up and roaring on every play.

But it was the Aggies, demonstrating a drive and an irresistible attack that was the finest of the season, who showed they couldn't be stopped.

On the opening kickoff Mack Saxon, Texas' fine halfback, fumbled the ball. A&M recovered and pounded upfield, picking up eight, nine, and ten yards on each play. Then a pass from Hunt to Wilson put A&M ahead 6–0. Hunt kicked the extra point and it was 7–0 A&M.

In the second period, Wilson kicked out of bounds on the Texas eighteen-yard line. On the next play, a Texas back fumbled, and Dansby of

The 1925 Aggies won their fourth SWC Championship, their first since 1921. Included in their seven victories was a 28–0 pasting of Texas, the Aggies' biggest margin of victory over the 'Horns to date.

A&M recovered the ball and crashed through the Texas defenders for a touchdown. Texas began to move after recovering an Aggie fumble and got to the Aggies' eight-yard line. But on a pass play, Jules Sikes intercepted the ball and sped ninety-two yards for a third Aggie touchdown.

In the final period, Hunt passed to Bob Berry for another score and the Aggies went on to post a 28–0 victory—and capture their fourth Southwest Conference crown.

The Aggies began their thirty-second year of football as if they were about to repeat as SWC champions. They were impressive in defeating three strong opponents—Trinity, Southwestern, and prickly Sewanee. Then in an amazing show of offensive dynamite, the Aggies blew away New Mexico in a barrage of touchdowns, 63–0. Halfback Jelly Woodman scored seven touchdowns and kicked two extra points for a total of 44 points, a national collegiate record for points in a single game (and still the A&M record for most touchdowns in a game).

However, A&M's dream of retaining its SWC crown was dashed as SMU, outplayed and outfought by the Aggies, scored a touchdown and a safety for nine points, while holding the Aggies to a lone touchdown to upset A&M 9–7. A week later, still smarting from their loss to SMU and hurting from injuries to key players, A&M suffered a 20–9 loss to Baylor. The game was marred by a fight among some cadets and Baylor fans, and one of the cadets, Charles Sessums, later died of the injuries.

Because of this unfortunate incident and general hostile attitude between the schools, no further contests between the two rivals were played for several years.

In the next game, TCU's Bill Washmon and A&M's great back Joel Hunt engaged in a drop-kicking duel. Each kicked two field goals, Washmon's second coming with fifteen seconds remaining to tie the game 13–13.

Against Rice, the Aggie star end S. J. Petty was unstoppable as he caught two nifty TD passes from Hunt in a 20–0 victory.

In the final game of the season, the Longhorns and Aggies squared off in their annual Turkey Day battle. The Aggies quickly broke away as a result of a safety and a field goal by Hunt to take a 5–0 lead. But an inspired Texas filled the air with passes, completing eleven of thirteen for two touchdowns. Bill Ford and Clint Stover of the 'Horns caught the touchdown passes to give Texas a well-earned 14–5 win over a favored Aggie squad.

CAPT.-ELECT HUNT,
All-Southwestern

Joel Hunt led A&M to two SWC championships (1925 and 1927) and a 20–4–1 record in his three years as a letterman and all-SWC performer. His 1927 season was one to remember. He passed, kicked, and ran roughshod over enemy defenses for 19 touchdowns and 128 points, Texas A&M and SWC records. The record stood in the SWC for more than 50 years and remains the standard bearer at A&M. He's a member of three Halls of Fame: National Football, Texas Sports, and Texas A&M.

The loss to Texas closed out a disappointing 5–3–1 season for A&M, a far cry from their championship accomplishment of 1925.

In a book written in 1948 by Weldon Hart, called *Sports' Golden Age*, Hart said: "The Southwest Conference's greatest back and, some say, greatest of all time was not a Ray Morrison protégé, but the name of Joel Hunt led all the rest. Hunt came to A&M from Waco, where he had been a one-year high school sensation on a team that scored 636 points to their opponents' 3. . . ."

All-conference three years in a row, Hunt really blossomed in 1927. He was fully mature, weighed 168 pounds, and had blinding speed. As captain of the team in '27, Hunt scored 128 points, an A&M and NCAA record. He did all of A&M's kicking and most of its running and passing, carrying the ball three out of five times. Furthermore, Hunt was so rugged, he played nearly every minute of every game (he sat out just three minutes of one game).

Although none of these players lettered as Aggies, all played integral roles nonetheless in helping A&M's 1926 team to a 5–3–1 record. Going hard in practice, cheering nonstop during games, and staying prepared should duty call are the thankless but important jobs of those players who see little if any action during their careers. Clockwise: Webb Townsend, Spike Arnold, and Brooks Conover

A flaming, competitive spirit drove Joel Hunt to greatness. He was a natural player who loved practice and scrimmaging and possessed a congenital elusiveness that led a coach to say, "You couldn't tackle him in a telephone booth."

Hunt's biggest day was against defending champion SMU. Coached by the great Jerry Mann, the Mustangs invaded A&M as heavy favorites, for they had defeated Texas, Rice, Missouri, Baylor, and TCU.

All Hunt did that day was score three touchdowns, pass for two more, and punt eight times for an average of forty-four yards without any punt being returned. It was one of the greatest individual performances ever seen in the SWC.

In the opening game of the season against Trinity, Hunt carried the ball four straight times for a touchdown. Hunt and fullback H. Burgess combined to score another touchdown, and from that point on, Trinity never had a chance as Hunt's pinpoint passing and Burgess's aggressive drives piled up five additional scores in a 45–0 win for A&M. One week later, on a field covered with mud, Hunt took the opening kickoff against Southwestern and sped thirty-five yards for a score, sparking A&M to a 31–0 win.

Against a tough rival, Sewanee, and on another rain-soaked field, Hunt ran wild, gaining 177 yards and scoring three times to beat Sewanee 18–0.

Then came a 40–6 win over Arkansas with Hunt once again in amazing form. George Cole handled the kicking for Arkansas in that game and he asked a teammate whom he should kick the ball to. The teammate pointed, "Kick to that No. 8." The ball came right to No. 8, Hunt, and Joel sped ninety-seven yards for a touchdown.

One week later TCU battled the favored Aggies to a scoreless tie in a game that cost the Aggies a possible national championship.

After convincing victories against Texas Tech and SMU, A&M beat Rice 14–0. The Texas game was the final one for Hunt, and he scored two touchdowns, and completed nine passes, one of them for another score, to give the Aggies a brilliant win over Texas, 28–7, and another SWC championship.

The win over Texas gave A&M an 8–0–1 record and six A&M players were named to the All-Conference team.

Joel Hunt, in a letter to Grantland Rice in 1954, talked about his 1927 A&M team: "The 1927 team was a truly great organization, probably second in the conference in all-time rank. It was outstanding in all phases of the game . . . offense, defense, team spirit, blocking, tackling, team speed, a great running offense, and a passing offense that swept SMU, the much heralded 'aerial circus,' right off the field. . . .

"According to modern standards, this team would be short on reserve strength because there were only seventeen lettermen, and at the end of the season there were only twenty-seven players on the squad. Our offense was well-balanced, with great running, passing, punting, place-kicking, and drop-kicking. Also, we introduced the down-the-field pass plus lateral, that is a ten-yard spot pass with the receiver passing the ball back to a teammate. . . .

"My greatest memory of that club is its spirit and team play. For example, I could talk to my downfield blockers and tell them to 'block' or 'go.' And Dana Bible was a great gentleman, a forceful, inspiring leader and a great moral character. He was a man who could have been a success in any profession. I can still hear him say to me, 'Captain, go out there and take charge of your team, take command of the situation.'"

Entering his eleventh year as the head football coach at A&M, Dana Bible could look back on one of college football's great coaching records. He had won five SWC championships, including three undefeated seasons. In 1917 and 1919 Bible's A&M squads won 18 games without allowing opponents a single point. It was a record that to this day stands as one of the great coaching achievements in college football.

Now, in his eleventh year, as he approached the opener against Trinity, Bible was faced with the possibility that this season would be a disaster. When he issued a call for the first practice sessions, not more than a handful of lettermen appeared. That was bad news for Bible, who was facing one of the country's most formidable schedules: the toughest teams in the SWC Conference, including a stronger Rice team, an experienced SMU eleven, and solid teams in Arkansas and the Texas Longhorns, a team with seventeen experienced stars . . . a top player at every post.

"This is going to be a rugged year," Bible said to his new assistant coach, Charlie Bassetts, who was a top assistant to Michigan's Fielding Yost the previous year.

It was somewhere around this time, by the way, that the Aggies' official school colors changed. In the late 1920s—no one is sure exactly when—an order went out from the A&M athletic department for new football jerseys. The manufacturer made an error, and the jerseys arrived maroon and white. Figuring there were too many schools with the color red, department officials shrugged off the mistake and decided to keep the order. The Aggies' official colors have been maroon and white ever since.

If the Aggies weren't wearing red by the 1928 season opener, they were certainly *seeing* it. They whitewashed their first three opponents by a combined score of 111–0. Trinity and Southwestern fell by identical 21–0 scores, and then Sewanee was swamped, 69–0, by a flood of Bill Davis passes to Red Petty and Brooks Conover.

But the Aggies stumbled in the next two games and dropped last-minute contests to Centenary and TCU by 6–0 scores.

Arkansas Coach Francis Schmidt, who had been gunning for the Aggies since the beginning of the season, had his team psyched for the game. And the Porkers responded by drilling the Aggies 27–12. It was the first win by an Arkansas team against A&M since 1910.

The loss to Arkansas brought about a big shakeup. A number of players were dropped or shifted to other positions, while the coaches worked overtime to improve the defense that had bogged down.

The Aggies responded with a new spirit and aggressiveness as they blasted North Texas Teachers 44–0. Quarterback Sheik Davis, who had been injured, ran the team like a field marshal and tossed three TD passes to Carroll "Dick" Tracy.

A determined A&M squad faced the Mustangs of SMU in the eighth game of the season as 5–1 underdogs. But on the first play of the game, R.R. Dorsey took the kickoff, and behind crisp blocking and fancy broken-field running, sped sixty-five yards for a touchdown as the crowd went wild. But the Ponies responded by promptly driving down the field for a touchdown. They missed the extra point, and it was 7–6 A&M.

A frenetic second quarter produced a 13–13 halftime score, but by the start of the fourth, SMU had grabbed a 19–13 lead.

Then with less than two minutes remaining, Captain Z. W. Bartlett blocked a Pony punt, and the Aggies came up with the ball on the SMU seven-yard line. With the fans nearly hysterical, Tom Mills stepped back, feinted a run, stopped, and tossed a high-arching pass to George Zarafonetis, who cradled it for a touchdown. The conversion was missed—by inches—and the game ended 19–19.

Davis completed twelve of twenty-three passes in the next game, against Rice, for more than 180 yards as A&M claimed a 19–0 victory.

Then it was Thanksgiving Day and the great game against a heavier, more experienced Texas team, who outweighed the Aggies by ten to fifteen pounds per man. And for three quarters, the spirited, aggressive play of the Aggies held off the drives and power of the 'Horns and it was 0–0 at the end of the third period. Then an Aggie pass was intercepted, giving the 'Horns good field position. On the first play they drove in for a touchdown. Texas scored on its next two possessions to secure a 19–10 win, clinching the Longhorn's second SWC championship. For the Aggies, it was a sad, lonely ride home as they contemplated their less-than-glittering 5–4–1 record.

5

POST BIBLE

Knute Rockne, architect of Notre Dame's great teams in the 1920s, was offered a number of coaching jobs during his career. Ohio State, Southern California, and Columbia, for instance, offered Rockne coaching jobs at twice his salary at Notre Dame. But Rockne turned down each school. When he received an offer to be the coach at Nebraska, he turned that down, too, but wrote to the Nebraska officials, "I would like to suggest a man for the job that you know very little about. His name is Dana Bible at Texas A&M, and I consider him the finest young coach in America. If you can get him, he's the man to develop your program." Taking Rockne's advice, Nebraska hired Bible, and during the next six years, Bible fielded some of the greatest-ever Cornhusker teams.

Bible was succeeded at A&M by Matty Bell, who had enjoyed success at Texas Christian University. From 1923 to 1928, Matty had given A&M all sorts of trouble, beating and tying the Aggies twice in five games. Perhaps Aggie officials decided, "If you can't lick 'em, join 'em." They offered Matty "more money than I had ever had." Bell hated to leave TCU and debated the offer for several weeks. It was 1929, though, the first year of the Great Depression, and Matty had recently married. He finally decided that the money was the important issue, and so he took the A&M post.

Bell's first coaching job was with the Haskell Indians. "I had no business with a head coaching job at that time," said Matty. "I didn't know anything about coaching." Still, Bell's 1920 team—his first—fared reasonably well, going 8–3. And those three losses were to some stiff foes—Notre Dame, Nebraska, and Marquette.

In 1922 Bell became head coach at Carroll College near Milwaukee, a job which enabled him to cash in on Sundays, when he would play pro football with the Milwaukee franchise of the NFL. He earned $125 per game and felt he had finally hit the jackpot.

But soon Bell would take the reins at TCU for six seasons, before moving to College Station.

Bell's first season was no bed of roses; the great talent that A&M had developed in the past had thinned out. In addition, A&M would offer financial assistance only to those players who made the team. It was not until 1930 that every athlete received financial aid from the Athletic Department. Rival schools in the SWC, meanwhile, offered greater financial assistance and employment, and those benefits were reflected in the team standings.

A tall, rangy, pass-catching end, Walt Ewell played on the 1928 Aggies, Dana Bible's last team at A&M. Lured by a fat contract offer from Nebraska, Bible resurfaced in the thirties with none other than Texas, which offered him $10,000 to return to the state. Depression-gripped Texans were shocked, especially since the salary was more than the governor's.

Bell's 1929 eleven posted a 5–4 record. With luck, they could have gone 7–2, but Tulane prevailed 13–10 in one nail biter and Arkansas in another, 14–13. In the Thanksgiving Day special, A&M whitewashed Texas 13–0 before 20,000 partisan fans.

The following year, the Aggies sagged to 2–7. They defeated Southwestern in the opener 43–0, but then fell to Nebraska, Tulane, Arkansas, and TCU, before squeezing by Centenary 7–6. The Aggies then succumbed to SMU and Rice, with Thanksgiving Day, and Texas, looming. The Longhorns, who had already wrapped up the SWC championship the previous week by beating TCU, were out to avenge their loss to A&M the year before.

And from the opening kickoff, Texas demonstrated its superiority by taking the kickoff and slashing and driving sixty-five yards for a touchdown. In the second period, Pap Perkins, Texas' speedy halfback, sprinted forty-five yards for another score. And Captain Dex Shelley, playing his last game for Texas, scored from the one-yard line and later passed thirty-one yards to Johnny Craig for another touchdown in a 26–0 rout of A&M.

The loss ended one of the most dismal seasons in Texas A&M football; the Aggies were outweighed and outplayed in almost every game.

In 1931 Captain Carl Moulden, one of the leading tackles in the Southwest Conference, led his A&M squad to a 7–3 record. Thanks to Quarterback Jim Aston's passes to halfback Frenchy Dominque and end Charley Malone, the Aggies offense scored more than twice as many points as it did in 1930.

"Moulden was a great inspirational team leader," said Matty Bell. "He had great desire to do well in every game and he inspired his teammates to follow his lead. Carl did not have speed or great size, but he had courage, desire, and leadership."

None of the teams that defeated A&M scored more than a single touchdown. The losses were to TCU, Tulane, and SWC champ SMU.

Texas, coached by 1915 'Horns standout Clyde Littlefield, carried a 6–3 record going into the A&M game.

Texas led 6–0 after one quarter, but Dominque scampered forty yards for a touchdown on a shovel pass from Aston in the second stanza. The PAT gave A&M a lead it would not relinquish.

It was the Aggies' biggest win, and it improved their record to 7–3. Moulden, Dominque, and Charley Malone were named to the all-SWC team.

Matty Bell started the 1932 season with high hopes for a sixth SWC title, but in the early practice sessions, injuries to several key Aggies, including end Charley Malone, guard George Lord, veteran quarterback Jimmy Aston, and several freshmen, dimmed his enthusiasm.

In the opening game of the season, playing in ankle-high mud, the Aggies beat Texas Tech 7–0 before more than 5,000 chilly fans, who were warmed by the play of Frenchy Dominque. On the first drive following the kickoff, Frenchy sprinted upfield for a thirty-five-yard gain, then Aston and R. E. Barfield picked up first downs before Dominque crashed over for the score and a 7–0 A&M lead.

A week later, A&M scored first against Tulane as Aston scored a touchdown and kicked a field goal for a 7–0 lead. Then it was Aston and Dominque picking up big gains through the Green Wave line, setting it up for Jack Stringfellow to burst through the line for another score, making it 14–0 A&M. But Tulane, with great halfback Don Zimmerman leading the way, pounded the Aggies' line for scores in the second, third, and final quarters to win 26–14.

With Aston, Dominque, and Dub Williams leading the way in the next two games, the Aggies beat Houston 26–0 and Texas A&I 14–0. More injuries cost the Aggies dearly, though, and they dropped successive games to TCU, Baylor, and Centenary, before tying SMU. In the only SWC game the Aggies were to win, they barely beat out the Rice Owls 14–7 by scoring an unusual touchdown. With but a few seconds to play in the second period, A&M's Henry Graves tossed a pass to R. E. Connelley on the Rice ten-yard line and frantically called time out to stop the clock. Even though A&M still had two seconds on the clock, the field judge fired his gun ending the half. An argument ensued and play was eventually resumed. Given new life, Graves tossed a pass to Rue Barfield to tie it at the half, 7–7. In the final period, with the score still tied, Sully Woodland and John W. Crow teamed to block a Rice punt, and Crow scooped up the ball and raced into the end zone for a touchdown to win a 14–7 thriller.

On Thanksgiving Day, the Aggies were unable to contain the crushing line smashes by Stafford, Koy, and Hillard, three of the 'Horns' great backs, who pounded the A&M line all afternoon for three touchdowns and a rugged 21–0 win.

For the Aggies, the season of 1932 was one they would like to forget; A&M had dropped games to all their SWC rivals except Rice. They finished a mediocre 4–4–2.

The Texas game marked the end of the wonderful careers of such A&M stars as Jim Aston, Graves, Williams, Hewitt, Wright, Love, Nolan, and Lord.

Undefeated TCU won the SWC crown, while Texas finished second, Rice third, and the Aggies a distant fourth.

Jimmie Aston '33

Quarterback Jimmie Aston lettered from 1930–1932. He led A&M to a riveting 7–6 victory over Texas in 1931, which capped a 7–3 season, the best of new coach Madison Bell's five at the helm. Bell won a little bit more than he lost, which just wasn't enough, so at the end of the 1933 season he was let go.

Coach Matty Bell knew he was under pressure to win in 1933, that his tenure as a football coach was at stake. He had had just one season that could be called successful. That was in 1931, when the Aggies went 7–3. But, of course, one of those wins was the 7–6 conquest of Texas.

With that great pressure on his shoulders, Matty worked harder than he ever had in his life and it looked as if his diligence would pay off as the Aggies opened the 1933 season with easy wins over Trinity 38–0, Tulane 13–6, Sam Houston 34–14, and Texas A&I 17–0.

Led by Captain Charley Cummings, Ted Spencer, John Crow, Bill Jordan, and Red Murray, the Aggies had racked up four straight victories, and a winning season for A&M and Coach Bell was just around the corner. But TCU, coached by the wily Francis Schmidt, took a 13–7 win over the Aggies, before A&M bounced back a week later to defeat Baylor for its fifth win of the year. However, Centenary and SMU defeated the Aggies on successive weeks, and word got around that Bell was on his way out.

The players rallied around their coach, though, and pounded favored Rice 27–0.

In the Thanksgiving Day battle against Texas, the underdog Aggies fought their hearts out and scored a touchdown in the final period to earn a 10–10 tie and a 6–3–1 mark.

After the game, both Coach Bell and Clyde Littlefield of Texas were asked to resign.

Early in 1934, Homer Norton was appointed head football coach at Texas A&M. He brought a remarkable record of achievement with him. Norton was head coach at Centenary College in 1920 and '21 and from 1926 to 1933. His teams of 1927, '32, and '33 had perfect records. His 1930 eleven lost only to the Aggies. In the 1932–1933 seasons, the Centenary "Gentlemen" were *undefeated in twenty games* and *unscored on in fourteen.*

In high school, Norton's love was baseball, and he played with the Columbus team of the American Association before he signed with Centenary as football coach and athletic director. At Birmington–Southern College, Norton won varsity letters in football, baseball, basketball, and track. He was named an all-conference halfback and was awarded a medal as the best all-around athlete in the conference.

A few days after Norton finished his first spring training sessions, he took to the road and appeared at A&M booster clubs throughout the state. He wanted to meet as many alumni as possible, build a good relationship, and set up a program to get jobs for his players during the summer. And, of course, he was laying the groundwork for some recruiting aid.

A quick look at the players he inherited from the 1933 team convinced Norton that 1934 would not be a productive season. He told a group at the Houston A&M Club, "We have players who just don't have the ability to compete in the SWC. We don't have size, speed, ability, or experience."

"Now," said Norton, "This coming season doesn't look too good. We will win a few games and, about next year, I don't know if we'll be any better. We need scholarships. Maybe by 1936 we can offer more scholarships and get some of the better players that Rice, SMU, and Texas are now getting from the high schools. However, it will be 1937 before these new players will be ready to compete."

Before Norton could go any further, one of the more rabid alumni shouted, "Never mind, Homer, telling us about 1937. If you haven't started winning a lot of games by then, you won't be around here to worry about it."

Norton had predicted that his 1934 team would not win many games, and he was right. The Aggies opened the season by defeating Sam Houston 28–0, and then tied Texas A&I 14–14. But they then dropped games to Temple, Centenary, and TCU before beating Baylor 10–7.

Following a 7–7 tie with Arkansas, the Aggies lost four straight to finish at 2–7–2.

There was a decided improvement in the size and speed of the Aggies football team in 1935, including a promising group of sophomores: Johnnie Morrow, Mart Lindsey, Bill Boyd, Fred Wright, Dick Vitek, Pun Schroeder, Bobby Nesrstra, and Jacob Shockey. The left-handed Jacob Shockey was particularly effective. His southpaw passes thrown while running in the opposite direction confounded opponents all season.

In the opening game of the season, Austin scored a touchdown in the first period after A&M's Bobby Nesrstra scored, to make it 6–6. In the final period, with the score still knotted, the Aggies exploded for thirty-one points en route to a 37–6 win.

A week later, the Aggies showed even more power and defense as they defeated Houston Teachers 25–0. Percy Reid, Ed Wicker, and Jacob Shockey scored touchdowns.

But the next several games were against some of the strongest teams in the SWC. A&M also had to face tough Temple, coached by Pop Warner. The Aggies lost to Temple, Centenary,

TCU, Baylor, Arkansas, and Rice in succession, but in the big game of the year, against Texas, the Aggies filled the air with lefty Shockey's passes and defeated the 'Horns 20–6 to finish below .500 again at 3–7.

Homer Norton approached his third season at A&M on the heels of a serious bout with ulcers that sidelined him for a week and a half. However, when he appraised the candidates for the upcoming football season, Norton recovered quickly as he realized he had the horses to go all the way.

With Dick Todd, the most publicized halfback in the Southwest, Norton knew he had the nucleus of an all-star backfield, for in addition to his passing and kicking, Todd was almost impossible to stop once he was in the open field. One of the quarterbacks, Dick Vitek, meanwhile, looked even better in practice than he did the previous season. His sharp, flat passes to end Johnnie Morrow bode well for the season. Big Joe Routt, A&M's first all-American, a guard who single-handedly could shut down an enemy's offense, was back along with Roy Young and Johnny Whitfield at the tackle posts, making the line undoubtedly stronger than any Norton had had at A&M.

The Aggies opened up a twelve-game schedule with wins over Sam Houston 39–6, Hardin-Simmons 3–0, and Rice, also 3–0.

A&M had not defeated TCU in eleven years, but the Aggies were primed for this 1936 matchup. Led by Dick Todd, who scored two touchdowns, and the accurate passing of Jacob Shockey, the Aggies clicked like champions and won 18–7.

TCU's nationally recognized quarterback wiz, Sammy Baugh, filled the air with passes, but could only connect for one touchdown in a game that featured Todd's spectacular seventy-six-yard run in the fourth quarter.

In a game that was slowed by mud and rain that fell throughout, the Aggies and Baylor fought to a scoreless tie. The teams punted a record fifty times, playing conservatively and waiting for that big break that never came.

The Arkansas Razorbacks showed their championship caliber as they defeated A&M 18–0 in a game that featured an outstanding passing attack. Arkansas went on to win the national championship in 1936.

Against a hard-driving SMU eleven, A&M's Bob Nesrsta crashed over for a touchdown in the first period as great line play by the Aggies opened holes on nearly every play. Without Todd (who was injured in the Arkansas game), the Aggie backfield of Shockey, Vitek, and Cummings played inspired football and scored two additional touchdowns. In the final period, Routt and Jones smothered SMU's Bob Finley behind his own goal line for a safety to close out a 22–6 win.

At San Francisco, the Aggies, seemingly awed and fatigued by their first trip to the coast, fumbled the ball twice, and each time an alert San Francisco squad turned the error into a touchdown to take a 14–0 first-half lead. Then, after a scorching talk by Coach Norton, the Aggies played sensationally. In the third period, every backfield man—Chick Manning, Jacob Shockey, Dick Vitek, Bob Nesrsta, and Owens Rogers—scored en route to a 38–14 massacre.

Days later, on a snow-covered gridiron, A&M's fleet backs helped spark the third win in eight days, a 20–7 beating of Utah University. Homer Pitner, the Aggies' tough fullback, battered the Utah line for two touchdowns, and Shockey scored on a ten-yard lateral from Vitek as A&M scored its seventh win of the season.

No doubt feeling the effects of their hectic 2,000-mile road trip, the Aggies a few days later dropped a close battle to Centenary 3–0.

Then, on Thanksgiving Day, the slumping Longhorns, losers of seven games, directed by the ex-Notre Dame star Jack Chevigny, rose to upset weary A&M 7–0.

In the final game of the season, the Aggies met Manhattan College of New York at Tyler, Texas, and defeated the Jaspers as Dick Todd, fully recovered from early-season injuries, led a two-touchdown assault in the third period to overcome a 6–0 Manhattan lead. Todd raced around left end and broke clear for a seventy-six-yard touchdown run, one of the most thrilling plays of the year, to give A&M a victory and bring to an end the greatest football season the Aggies had had since the 1927 team won the SWC championship with an 8–0–1 record.

A&M, 8–3–1 overall, gained a share of third place in the SWC Conference; it was their best finish in five years. Guard Joe Routt became the first A&M player to gain recognition as an

TEXAS AGGIES

COACH HOMER NORTON

BULL MINNOCK

WARRE

JOE ROUTT

GEORGE BRANSON

WALDEN P

H

JOE WHITE

DICK VITEK

JAMES NESRSTA

JIM SHOCKEY

Homer Norton and several of his leading players from the 1937 Aggies, which finished 5–2. Norton (former head coach at Centenary, which had beaten A&M in 1932 and 1933) succeeded Bell in 1934. That first year the Aggies nosedived to 2–7–1, only A&M's second sub-.500 record since 1913. The next year brought little relief as A&M finished 3–7. By 1936, however, Norton had assembled a strong coaching staff and a team of rising young stars that won eight games. The '37 team started slowly, then won three of its last four games (a tie with Rice was the only scar).

In 1936, Norton unleashed a quick, darting halfback named Dick Todd. To date, he, along with Joel Hunt, were A&M's greatest ball carriers. A devastating open field runner, Todd earned all-SWC honors in 1937 and '38. Graduation robbed him of his chance to play on his school's most celebrated team.

all-American (Routt repeated in 1937). Charley DeWare Jr., center and co-captain, and Roy Young, the huge tackle, were named to the all-SWC eleven.

The outstanding winning season no doubt cleared Coach Norton's ulcer attacks, as did the fact most every member of the 1936 squad would be back in 1937.

Everyone expected the 1937 Aggies to have another outstanding season with such stars as co-captain and all-American Joe Routt; Dick Vitek, a smart, aggressive quarterback; Dick Todd, perhaps the deadliest broken-field runner in A&M history; Jacob Shockey, the sensational left-handed passer; and Bob Nesrsta, Virgil Jones, Roy Young, Red Church, and Bill Boyd all returning for another season.

On paper this solid corps of veterans should have come through with a great season. And as the year progressed, the Aggies showed flashes of great offensive power, and in other games, they were able to hold off their opponent. But they seldom put offense and defense together, and the result was a lackluster season.

The Aggies traveled to the Polo Grounds in New York City and a return engagement with Manhattan College. But for fifty-two minutes the Aggies played as if they were in slumberland as the Jaspers got off to an early 7–0 lead and managed to hold on to the lead until late in the fourth period. Suddenly, the Aggies' passes began to hit their mark, and when the Jaspers spread their defense, A&M backs Todd and Nesrsta drove through for consistent gains. Late in the fourth period, it took A&M just three plays to move from the forty-five-yard line to the Manhattan seven, and then Bob Nesrsta drove across for a touchdown. Four minutes later, Mills, Todd, and Rogers broke off gains to move A&M to the Jasper forty-yard line. Then Mills tossed a perfect strike to Rogers, and Owens followed that with a game-breaking touchdown run to give the Aggies a 14–7 win.

In the second game of the season, a Mississippi State eleven that threatened to score only once in the game went down to a 14–0 defeat at Tyler, Texas. Dick Todd almost broke the game open on the initial play as he took the kickoff, sped forty-five yards straight down the middle of the gridiron, and had only one man to beat on the way to pay dirt. He was nailed near midfield, but the Aggies drove downfield and went up 7–0 on a fifteen-yard TD toss from Shockey to Rogers. Then in the second period, Nesrsta drove in for the score and Todd kicked the extra point to ice a 14–0 win.

Late in the fourth period of the next game, against TCU, the Frogs jumped to a 7–0 lead. To make matters worse, Dick Todd was injured and the Aggies attack was stalled. There were just two minutes to play as Ken Mills uncorked a fourth-down pass, a do-or-die attempt. Herb Smith leaped high in the air, caught the ball, and fell into the end zone for a dramatic touchdown that gave A&M a thrilling 7–7 tie.

One week later, the Aggies were jolted in the Baylor game, when the Bears, with a great passing attack, scored two touchdowns to win 13–0. Then an outstanding Arkansas team, in the midst of a great season, raced to a 26–13 win over A&M.

It was up to the now-healthy and dangerous Todd to pick up the falling Aggies. He did—on

Dick Todd, Joe Routt, Joe Boyd, and the rest of the 1937 Aggies experienced a thrill when they traveled across country to play A&M's first game in Gotham City. By a scheduling quirk their opponent was the same as last year's final game opponent, Manhattan College, whom the Aggies had defeated 13–6. Undaunted by the countless distractions of the big city, the country boys of A&M edged Manhattan again, this time 14–7. The win brought added national exposure to the Aggies. Here's the program from that game, played at New York's hallowed Polo Grounds.

Few men in A&M history played the game as well as Joe Routt, a two-time all-American guard in 1936 and '37 and the Aggies' first-ever all-American. An unyielding blocker and fierce defender, Routt met nearly every test on the playing field, clearing lanes for his backfield star Dick Todd and shutting down those of his opponents. World War II whisked him away from Texas and tested him yet again. And once again he didn't back down. Rising to the rank of captain, Routt was killed leading his men on an attack in the Battle of the Bulge in 1944. A member of the National Collegiate Hall of Fame, Routt will forever be remembered by Aggies for his devotion to A&M and—more significantly—to his country.

the opening kickoff against SMU—racing seventy-two yards for the score. Then Joe Turner picked off a desperation pass by SMU and threaded his way down the sideline for sixty-eight yards and a scintillating touchdown as the Aggies won 14–0.

The Aggies had a close battle against Rice seemingly well in hand, when in the final period a series of penalties paved the way for an Owl score and a 6–6 tie, certainly not the outcome A&M needed heading into next week's tussle against their ancient rival.

On a crisp Thanksgiving Day, the Aggies played an inspired brand of football as they attacked the Longhorns on all fronts. It was a game of vicious tackling and blocking by an Aggie line led by Joe Routt. A&M stopped Texas on the ground and in the air to register a bitter 7–0 victory over their chief rival.

The Aggie touchdown came on an interception by Zed Coston, who lateraled to Britt for twenty more yards. Then Shockey tossed a short shovel pass to Todd, who galloped twenty-seven yards to the Texas twelve-yard line. It took Dick Vitek two tries before he busted over for the score.

Against San Francisco, Vitek, Young, Shockey, Church, Boyd, Nesrsta, and Drennan played their last game for A&M; all were outstanding as the Aggies, clicking like a well-oiled, sixteen-cylinder racing car, demolished the Dons to end their season on a memorable note by winning 42–0. The Aggies defense was so tough that it allowed but three first downs, while the offense pounded the Dons for seventeen first downs and 369 total yards. A&M finished at 5–2–2.

"With just a break here and there in the Rice, TCU, and Baylor games, that we should have won, we would have had a marvelous season. But we'll get those breaks soon," Norton said afterward.

As the opening practices began at A&M in 1938, Dean E. J. Kyle announced that Coach Homer Norton's contract would be renewed for an additional five years. Moreover, a local banker provided additional money, which was to be earmarked for a number of football scholarships. With the extra funds, Norton and his assistants were able to visit every town and hamlet in Texas where reports of a local football star had been publicized. Within a four-week period, twenty-three of the leading Texas high school stars had signed an A&M letter of intent.

This enormous financial vote of confidence, along with the veterans and new players assembled, boosted hopes A&M would be among the leading teams in the nation in 1938. The season opened as expected, with A&M knocking off Texas A&I and Tulsa in workmanlike fashion. But Santa Clara and eventual collegiate champ TCU defeated the Aggies, and a week later, a rugged Baylor team withstood three drives by the Aggies, held them late in the game, and forced a 6–6 tie. This game introduced Aggie fans to fullback John Kimbrough, a sophomore substitute, who showed such great driving power that reporters called him "a one-man wrecking crew." The following week, against Arkansas, Kimbrough ran through the Razorback line with such ferocity that several Arkansas players were injured and had to leave the game. Arkansas had a 7–6 lead with about ten seconds left to play, when Kimbrough, Todd, and Owens Rogers battered their way to the one-yard line. As the gun sounded, Kimbrough bulled across for the winning score. Dick Todd kicked the extra point and A&M chalked up a 13–7 victory.

There were only thirty seconds remaining in their next game against SMU when, with the score 7–7, Al Pasqua, an SMU substitute, came off the bench to boot a thirty-five-yard field goal into a swirling wind that beat A&M 10–7 and helped sweep Pasqua into the SMU Hall of Fame.

The annual showdown against Texas was next, and in typical fashion it was a tense, low scoring affair. Texas scored first and held on, despite an A&M score late in the game when guard Al Olbrich recovered a Texas fumble in the end zone. Todd's conversion attempt was blocked, however, and Texas won.

REVEILLE
Mascot of Texas A&M University

Probably no other school mascot is as beloved or as much an integral part of campus life as Reveille. Accompanied by her student handler, Reveille attends classes, athletic games, and Corps military functions. Students eagerly greet her on campus—and Corps freshmen must address her, "Howdy, Miss Reveille, Ma'am." And no one barks louder at sporting events than Reveille.

Reveille's origins are steeped in the traditions of loyalty and compassion between a young man and his dog. One version of several regarding Reveille's origins had some Aggies driving near Navasota in 1931 when their car nicked a black puppy that had dashed in front of the car. The pup was slightly injured. The Aggies brought the puppy, a female, back with them to A&M where they tended to her wounds, then left her alone in their dorm until the next morning. When Reveille was sounded by the bugler, the puppy, startled by the jarring noise of the bugle, started barking incessantly. Her rescuers named her "Reveille" as a result. She then made the Corps area her home, sleeping wherever she wanted.

Reveille was soon participating in the Corps activities and attending football games with the band. She also was taken on Corps trips and shortly after made A&M's mascot. During World War II she was made General in the K-9 Corps of the WAGS, Dogs for Defense. Reveille died January 18, 1944. Buried at the north end of Kyle Field, Reveille was given a formal military funeral.

In 1952 Arthur Weinart ('00) donated a Shetland Shepherd to continue the Reveille tradition. Reveille III was an American Collie, and all have been since. The newest mascot is Reveille VI. She lives with Company E-2. All other Reveilles are buried alongside the original Reveille.

In the final game of a deflating season, the Aggies played outstanding football to defeat Rice 27–0. Todd and Kimbrough starred in the Aggies' best offensive show of the season, scoring two touchdowns in each half, as A&M finished 4–4–1.

Nonetheless, Coach Norton remained optimistic. When he had signed his first coaching contract with the Aggies four years earlier, he had remarked, "I didn't come here to lose." He was now about to make good on that promise.

6

DEPRESSION NO MORE: 1939

Over the years it's occasionally been remarked that John Kimbrough, the slow-talking, chiseled-featured fullback of A&M's 1939 national champions, looked as if he'd stepped right out of a western movie. These folks surely knew their man. After wrapping up his illustrious Aggie career in the 1941 Cotton Bowl, "Jarrin' John" did star in a pair of Zane Grey "B" westerns. *Lone Star Ranger* and *Sundown Jim* were efforts that put him within smoochin' distance of some Hollywood starlets, placed some sorely needed cash in his pockets, and produced this evaluation from film historian Don Miller: "As an actor, Kimbrough was a superb gridiron flash."

Kimbrough, today enjoying retirement in his hometown of Haskell, Texas, can laugh at his abbreviated film career. But if the would-be Gene Autry didn't exactly burn up the back lots of Twentieth Century Fox, he certainly set the hundred-yard fields of the Southwest Conference on fire.

"I never knew anybody better," says Harris Mack Browder, one of the Aggies' unsung "blue boys" who had the unenviable task of practicing against the bruising back every day. "He was a big man, but he could run fast for a man of his size."

Kimbrough scored seventeen touchdowns and intercepted ten passes in the 1939–40 seasons and was twice a first-team All-American. He also received considerable recognition in the Heisman Trophy voting. As a junior in 1939 he finished fifth to Iowa's Nile Kinnick; the following season he was runnerup to Michigan's "Ol' 98," Tom Harmon.

"I always felt he should've gotten the trophy one of those seasons," maintains tailback Cotton Price, who alternated with Marion Pugh in the Aggies' single- and double-wing attack. "Every time we needed short yardage he got it for us. But the Big Ten probably got more publicity than the Southwest Conference did back then, and that has a lot to do with it."

As a matter of fact, Kimbrough, Price & Company were as responsible as anyone in bringing national recognition to Texas A&M and, by extension, the Southwest Conference. Between 1939 and 1941, this talented Aggie squad won twenty-nine of thirty-two games (including a twenty-game win streak), won or shared three straight SWC titles, played in three bowl games, and claimed the 1939 national championship—the first and only in the team's long and storied history. Whenever alumni and lettermen gather around the fire to sip bourbon and discuss the greatest teams ever to represent A&M, this squad more often than not is the one pointed to as perhaps the finest in one hundred years of Aggie football.

This was a team of young men tempered by hard times. While President Roosevelt's New Deal programs had helped restore hope and bailed out hundreds of thousands of American families during the 1930s, the Great Depression continued to linger in the Southwestern states. Besieged by drought, farmers tilted their lean, sun-baked frames into the swirling black dust and began a historic exodus to the cities. Even a small community like College Station was affected, its population quadrupling from about 2,000 in the late 1930s to more than 8,000 a decade later.

Kimbrough had to contend with despair far deeper than seeing tumbleweed blow down main street. While he was in seventh grade, his father, a doctor, died of a heart attack, leaving behind seven children. Already six feet tall and weighing 170 pounds, John played varsity ball for Haskell High School. Three years later, as a sophomore, he teamed with brother Jack to give Haskell High a one-two ball carrying punch that made the school one of the state's prep powerhouses.

After being cut as a freshman at Tulane, Kimbrough transferred to A&M. "Tulane thought I was too tall to be a back, so they tried to make a guard or tackle out of me," he recalls. Norton made the same mistake, until a succession of injuries gave Kimbrough his chance in his sophomore season.

By the middle of the 1938 campaign, Kimbrough had developed into one of the most fearsome, pile-driving fullbacks in college football. When 1939 rolled around, Kimbrough and teammates Joe Boyd, Cotton Price, Herb Smith, and Derace Moser comprised the nucleus of one of the nation's finest scoring machines and its stingiest defense. Boosted immeasurably by the line play of Marshall Robnett, A&M's defense would emerge as the nation's best, allowing only thirty-one points all year and leading the country in rushing defense (41.5 yards per game) and total defense (76.3 yards per game).

In the first game of the season, the Aggies traveled to Oklahoma City to face Oklahoma A&M,

"Jarrin" John Kimbrough succeeded Dick Todd as A&M's number one running back in 1939—and quickly bowled and blazed his way into Aggie lore. Mixing a devastating combination of power and swiftness (he ran the 100–yard dash in 10 flat—extraordinary speed for someone 6–3, 220 pounds) Kimbrough smashed many A&M rushing records and tore through the SWC like a tornado. Named an All-American in 1939 and '40, "Jarrin" John led the Aggies to a combined 20–1 record his last two years, including the coveted national championship. Post-career honors include: induction into the Texas A&M Hall of Fame, Texas Sports Hall of Fame, and Helms Foundation Collegiate Hall of Fame; and named as all-SWC Back from 1920–1968 by Texas Football *magazine.*

and after the opening kickoff and exchange of downs, Oklahoma was never in the game.

First, A&M's Derace Moser reeled off thirty-five yards in a nice runback. Then Cotton Price handed the ball to Kimbrough, and John blasted his way through three Oklahoma A&M tacklers en route to the first Aggie score. After another exchange of downs, Oklahoma kicked to Moser, who returned it all the way for another touchdown. Coach Norton sent in an entirely new eleven and halfback Bill Conatser ripped off a brilliant thirty-yard touchdown sprint behind the fine blocking of Price and Duncan. Bill Dawson kicked the extra point to make it 19–0 at halftime.

In the third period, Conatser took a punt by the Okies' halfback Pete Rivers and threaded his way through the entire Oklahoma team for fifty yards and a touchdown. Audish kicked the extra point, and it was 26–0. Jim Thomason closed out the Aggies' scoring with a touchdown run of thirty yards to cement a 32–0 victory.

The Aggie defense, led by Robnett, Boyd, Chuck Henke, and Smith, held the Oklahoma team to five first downs.

The Centenary game was just three minutes old when Kimbrough broke loose on the Centenary sixteen-yard line and dragged two tacklers across the goal line for a 7–0 lead. In the second period, a Price-to-Kimbrough pass, plus a great run by Thomason and gains by Moser and Price, took the ball to the Centenary five-yard line. Once again, Jarrin' John Kimbrough crashed over for the TD. Final score: 14–0.

A week later in San Francisco, Santa Clara kicked a field goal from the thirty-five-yard line in the third period to take a 3–0 edge. It was the first score against A&M in three games.

Midway in the third period, the Aggies took over and filled the air with short, accurate passes: Marion Pugh to Buchanan, then Pugh to Moser for twenty-nine yards, then another pass to Thomason for a twenty-yard score. Dawson kicked the extra point, making it 7–3, Aggies, and that's how it ended.

The following week, the Villanova Wildcats, boasting an impressive record of twenty-two consecutive victories and led by one of football's most successful coaches, Clipper Smith, rolled into Tyler, Texas, for the annual Rose Festival.

The nation's top sportswriters were on hand for this marquee intersectional battle involving undefeated teams bursting with all-Americans.

On the opening kickoff, the Aggies stunned Villanova as Pugh tossed a surprise lateral to Moser for a big gain. A pass to Herb Smith moved A&M to the five-yard line. Then Kimbrough barreled in for the touchdown.

On their next possession, the Wildcats attempted a first-down pass. But Pugh intercepted and A&M took over. On the first play, Pugh noticed that the Wildcat defensive backs were playing up close to stop Kimbrough, so he quickly changed his signal and lofted a long, high pass to Moser, who caught the ball in full stride for a touchdown. The play covered fifty-five yards and A&M had a 14–0 lead.

After an exchange of downs, Moser took a Villanova punt for a thirty-yard gain. Then Kimbrough and Moser caught passes to take the ball down to the five, where Kimbrough blasted in for another score.

Halfback Bill Conatser took a Villanova punt late in the second period, evaded two tacklers, and raced forty-five yards for another Aggie score. At halftime, Texas A&M had a surprising 33–0 lead.

In the fourth period, with every Aggie player in uniform getting playing time, the Wildcats scored a token touchdown to avert the shutout. The final score was 33–7.

It was the most decisive and impressive win of the year thus far, and more than 250 sports writers reported to their papers across the nation "that Texas A&M had to be seriously considered as one of the nation's top teams."

Facing the 1938 national champions, TCU, in the next game, the Aggies started slow, perhaps playing tentatively because of the Horned Frogs' recent laurels. TCU managed to score a touchdown on a great pass play from Rusty Cowart to Earle Clark in the opening five minutes of the game to take a 6–0 lead. TCU held the lead until the end of the second period, when A&M began to move. On third down, from the eight-yard line, Cotton Price whipped a pass to Kimbrough, who cracked over for a touchdown and a 6–6 tie.

In the third period, Moser intercepted a Cowart pass, then lateraled to Kimbrough. John barreled through for twenty-six yards to the twelve-yard line. Then Moser flashed around end for another touchdown to put A&M on top 13–6. TCU, in desperation, tried several passes. Finally, a long TCU pass was intercepted by Conatser on the A&M eight-yard line, and behind great blocking, Bill galloped ninety-two yards for a touchdown. Dawson made the extra point and A&M had won another battle, 20–6.

Baylor had not beaten the Aggies since 1926 and was thirsting for revenge as it invaded College Station on October 28. The game was but a few minutes old when Baylor's Jack Wilson faded back to pass, only to find that Herb Smith had cracked through his defense. Smith stripped Wilson of the ball at the twenty-five and raced in unmolested for a touchdown. It happened so suddenly that the Bears were dazed by the play. Price kicked the point, and it was 7–0.

In the third period, Jim Thomason pounced on a Baylor fumble on the Bears' thirty-two-yard line. Four plays later it was up to Kimbrough from the eight-yard line, and John just blasted two tacklers away and drove into the end zone for the second touchdown. Price again converted. In the fourth period, Moser broke through the Bears' line for thirty-five yards, Kimbrough hit off tackle for seventeen more, and Moser skirted left end for another touchdown. Final score: A&M 20, Baylor 0.

The Aggies traveled to Fayetteville for a Homecoming Day game against a solid Arkansas team. But A&M proved it was a multifaceted team that could beat you both offensively and defensively. A pass from Jeffrey to Smith gave A&M its first score, and then Robnett intercepted a pass, dashed thirty yards, and lateraled to Kimbrough for another twenty. Bill Conatser followed the interception with a ten-yard touchdown run, before Boyd scored from the eight-yard line on a lateral for another touchdown to make it 21–0.

In the final period, after running for a 38-yard gain, Moser faded back and tossed a perfect rainbow pass for forty-six yards and a touchdown to Conatser to make the final score A&M 27, Arkansas 0.

With the win over Arkansas, the Aggies climbed to 7–0, and only TCU had crossed the Aggie goal line. Their offense was one of the highest scoring in the nation and their defense was just as solid. Now, they were ready to face an outstanding SMU team that had lost but one game, to Notre Dame, by a single point, 20-19.

In a game played on a windy, rainy day, the Aggies and SMU battled each other up and down the gridiron until A&M got a break. The Aggies' Tommie Vaughn recovered a fumble on the SMU nine-yard line and, three plays later, Kimbrough slashed in for what proved to be the only touchdown of the day.

But the biggest break of the day, one that saved the game for A&M, occurred when the Aggies had to punt from their own goal line. SMU's Goss blocked the punt, but Conatser fell on the ball behind the A&M goal line for a safety that gave SMU its two points. But it saved the game for A&M, and the 6–2 victory upped the Aggies' record to 8–0.

In the game against Rice, the Aggies scored in the first period on a Pugh-to-Thomason pass. Then Moser drove to the ten-yard line before Kimbrough bulled in for a touchdown. A Pugh-to-Moser pass, then another to Buck Buchanan, took the ball to the twenty-yard line. Cotton Price then passed seventeen yards to Cowley for the TD. In the final quarter, the Aggies drove to the Rice thirty-four-yard line. On the next play, Price faded back and arched a long, high pass across the field to Bill Conatser, who leaped high into the air, caught the ball, and dashed for the opposite sideline. Then he cut back across the field, cracked through two tacklers, and was out in the clear and across the goal line, untouched. It was a spectacular play and brought a tremendous roar of approval from the delirious crowd. The final count was 19–0.

Texas invaded College Station on Thanksgiving Day for the forty-fourth game of the series between the two schools, and for the first half of the game, neither could overcome stiff defensive pressure. The halftime score was 0–0.

In the third quarter, the Aggies produced a play that was sheer magic. Coach Norton had practiced this very special play for a very special opportunity. Now, here it was. He sent 'Bama Smith to hide along the west sideline. Then on the first play, Cotton Price faked a pass to his right, turned, and passed to Smith, who caught it on the run and made it to the Texas twenty-five-

The Aggies' last game of the 1939 season was a 20–0 whipping of Texas, which clinched A&M's first SWC crown since 1927, preserved its first unblemished season since 1919, and catapulted the Aggies into the Sugar Bowl against Tulane—with a shot at the national championship. Here's the program from that game.

The souvenir program from the sixth annual Sugar Bowl Classic, January 1, 1940. Texas A&M seized its chance and squeezed past Tulane 14–13 to capture its first—and so far only—national championship. It was the culmination of Head Coach Homer Norton's six years of masonry work—and it ended the school's 45-year wait.

yard line before he was stopped. Three plays later, Price connected with Jim Sterling for a touchdown and a 7–0 A&M lead.

On its next possession, A&M again took charge as Price tossed passes to Kimbrough and Smith. Conatser scored on an off-tackle play, and the Aggies led 13–0.

A costly Texas penalty with five minutes left in the game gave the Aggies the ball on the 'Horns' fifteen-yard line. It took Kimbrough two tries before he slammed across for a touchdown, giving the Aggies a 20–0 victory.

The win over Texas gave A&M its tenth consecutive victory, an undefeated season, and the SWC crown for the first time since 1927. Of course, even those riches took a backseat to the thumping of the dreaded Longhorns.

The victory over Texas also assured the Aggies a climactic game in the Sugar Bowl against Tulane, one of the nation's finest teams. It was the first post-season game for the Aggies since they met and defeated Centre College in 1922 in the precursor to the Cotton Bowl game.

Of all the big post-season games held on or about New Year's Day 1940, A&M's 14–13 victory over Tulane was the one all the nation was talking about.

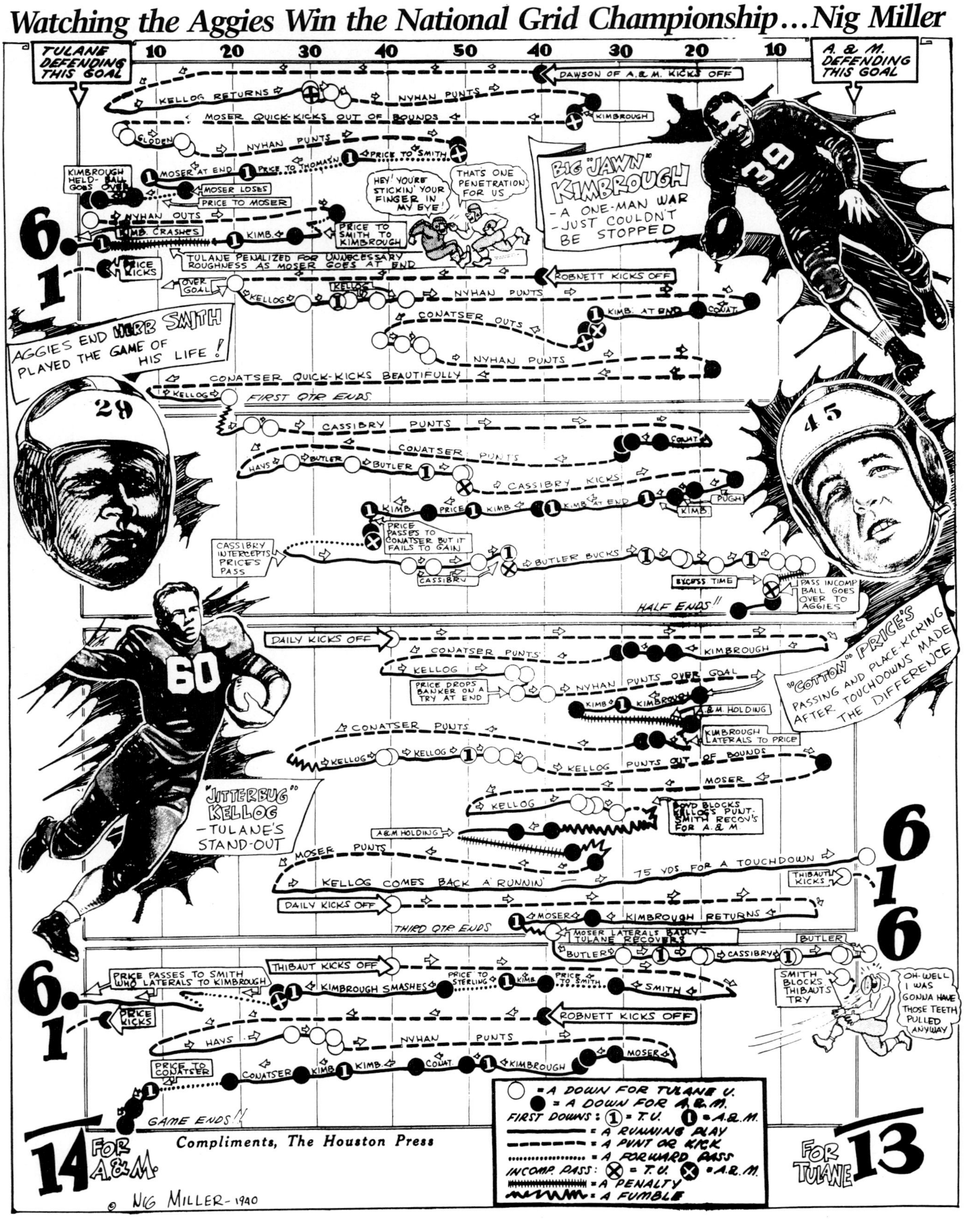

A play-by-play graph of the 1940 Sugar Bowl.

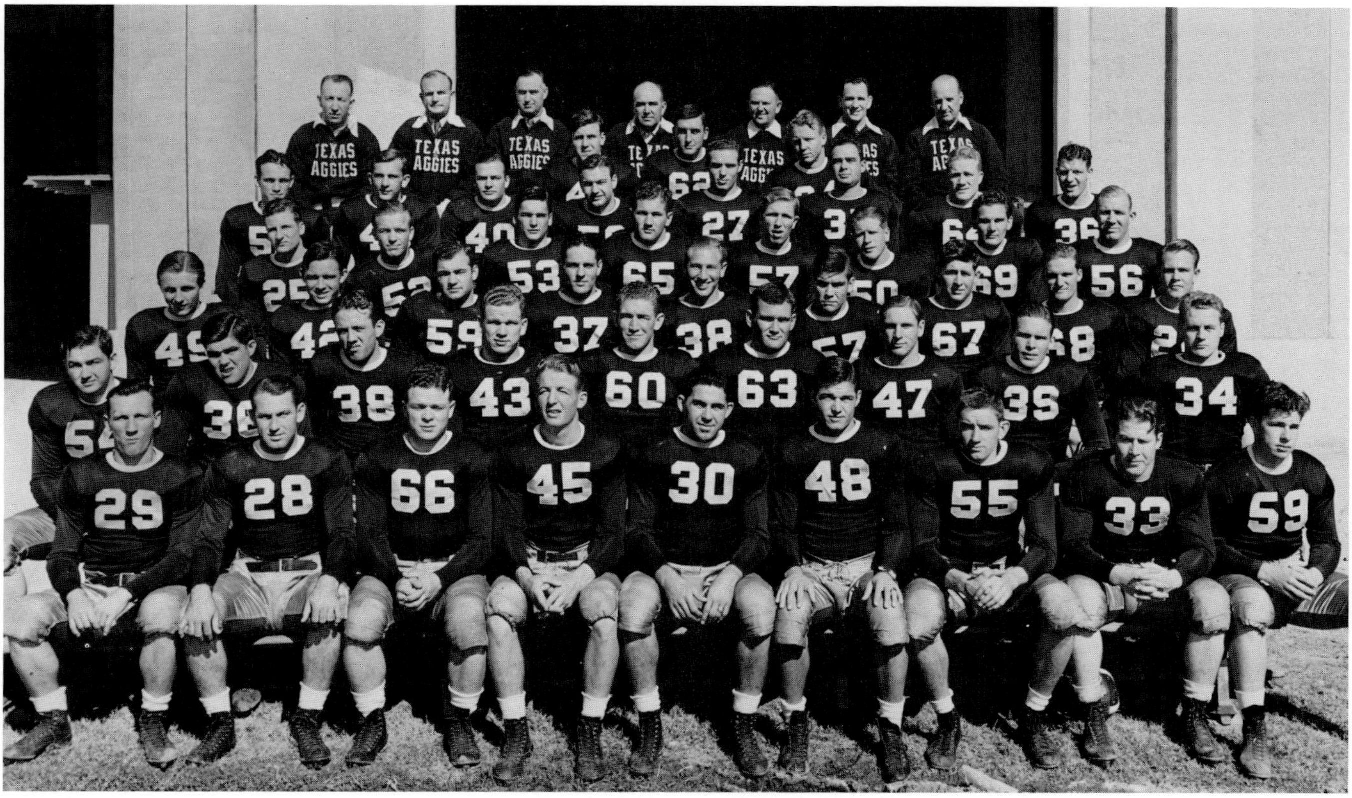

The 1939 National Champions: First row (left to right): *Herbie Smith (tri-captain, all-SWC), Marland Jeffrey, Ed Robnett, Cotton Price, Marion Pugh, Frank Wood, Bill Henderson, Les Richardson, Joe Rothe.* Second row: *Mack Browder, Muley White, Charles Henke, Marshall Robnett (all-SWC), Tommie Vaughn, Euel Wesson, Jim Thomason (all-SWC), John Kimbrough (all-SWC, all-American), Bud Force, 'Bama Smith.* Third row: *Cullen Rogers, Bill Conatser, Derace Moser, Odell Herman, Bill Miller, Hugh Boyd, Bill Buchanan, Jim Sterling, Cotton Williams, Bubba Reeves, Martin Ruby.* Fourth row: *Ernie Pannel, Marshal Spivey, Bill Duncan, John Abbott, Zolus Motley, Bill Blessing, Leon Rahn. Harold Cowley, Dog Dawson, Rock Audish.* Fifth row: *Leonard Joeris, Joe Parish, Howard Shelton, Jo Jo White, Jack Kimbrough, Chip Routt, Carl Greer, Chester Heimann, Joe Boyd (tri-captain, all-SWC, all-American), Gus Bates, Willard Clark.* Sixth row: *Charles Deware, Marty Karow, Bill James, Hub McQuillen, Homer Norton, Lil Dimmitt, Manning Smith, Harry Faulkner, Dough Rollins. (Tri-captain Waleman Price not pictured.)*

Texas A&M received the opening kickoff and began a drive that carried deep into Tulane territory. But Tulane's line stubbornly held fast, and A&M gave up the ball on downs. Tulane did not gain any yardage and kicked back to the Aggies. This time, led by Kimbrough and Moser, A&M punched across a touchdown (a Kimbrough run) after a sustained drive to go up 7–0.

Then Tulane began to move, advancing to the Aggies' eleven-yard line before A&M's band of fighting cadets held, assuring a 7–0 halftime edge.

In the third period, Tulane was caught by surprise as a quick kick by Moser went over the head of Tulane's star back, Bob Kellog. But Kellog raced back, scooped up the ball, and with some great blocking, raced seventy-six yards for a touchdown. The kick was good, and it was a 7–7 game going into the final period.

The Green Wave went ahead on a short touchdown run. But Herbie Smith, playing despite being ill before the game, broke through and blocked the extra-point try. This turned out to be the key play of the game, as A&M took the ensuing kickoff and marched seventy yards for the winning score.

After Kimbrough carried the ball twice to the Tulane twenty-six-yard line, Cotton Price passed to Smith, who took the ball to the ten before lateraling it to the trailing Kimbrough. Big John, who piled up 159 rushing yards on twenty-five attempts for the day, smashed into two defenders, knocked them aside, and stormed into the end zone for his second touchdown. The extra point gave A&M the game and the national championship, 14–13.

It was a glorious moment for A&M, and it solidified Aggie football as a national presence. Even more importantly it gave A&M something its hated rival didn't have, recognition as the greatest team in the land for one season. Sweet music indeed, especially for an Aggie who may at some point find himself in a room full of uters.

When the Aggie coaches, led by Homer Norton, surveyed the field of stars reporting for practice in 1940, they blinked their eyes and congratulated each other. They realized that with all-Americans John Kimbrough and Marsh Robnett, as well as Jim Sterling, Jim Thomason, Ernie Pannell, Derace Moser, Bill Sibley, and Marty Ruby, they would again have an outstanding team that could be in contention for a second straight national title, barring any injuries.

A&M's first test came September 28 against Texas A&I, led by all-American Steve Clarkson. But Kimbrough and company put a dent in the A&I armor quickly. On the first play, Kimbrough raced around end for twenty-five yards and the first touchdown of the year. Several plays later, Big John returned a punt for fifty-seven yards, and on the next play, Bill Conatser sped twelve yards for touchdown no. 2. Then Kimbrough crashed the A&I line for seventeen yards and Marion Pugh passed to Thomason for the final Aggie score in a 26–0 triumph.

At San Antonio's Alamo Stadium the following week, A&M ran through, over, and around Tulsa to score six touchdowns in a 41–6 rout. Kimbrough, Moser, Simmons, Henderson, and Jeffrey scored for the Aggies as every man on the squad got into the game.

A solid UCLA team entertained the Aggies on October 12. Rated the No. 7 team in the nation in 1939, and led by their all-American halfback Jackie Robinson, UCLA gave the Aggies problems in the first period, until the Aggies regained their composure. Kimbrough tore loose for several big gains in the first period and scored a touchdown to give A&M a 67–0 lead, capping a drive that went the length of the field. Conatser kicked the extra point, and that was the end of the scoring as A&M went on to a 7–0 victory. Jackie Robinson, after two nice runs, was injured in the second period and left the game. Kimbrough saved a touchdown when he caught the fleet Robinson from behind.

A&M resorted to an aerial game against TCU after being held scoreless by the Frogs' unorthodox 5–2–3 defense in the first quarter. In the second period, Pugh connected with Simmons on a thirty-five-yard scoring strike. He later hit Thomason on a twenty-five-yard TD pass and then found him later for another tally. TCU scored once more as the game came to a close, A&M 21, TCU 7.

A&M had beaten Baylor in Waco just once since 1920, and from the starting whistle to the final gun, the Bears fought a savage battle. They put two big men on Kimbrough on every play and kept him bottled up fairly well. But Thomason, Pugh, and Henderson gave the Bears trouble. Late in the first period Pugh and Thomason sparked a drive to the Bears' three-yard line. Conatser then faked to Kimbrough, kept the ball, and dove over left tackle for a touchdown. In the third period, Jeffrey threw a long pass to Bill "Jitterbug" Henderson on the twenty-five-yard line, and Henderson broke through a maze of Baylor tacklers for a second A&M score.

Baylor scored late in the game on a pass from Parks to Witt, good for fifteen yards. But it was too late; A&M had their sixteenth consecutive win by a 14–7 margin.

The Arkansas Razorbacks rolled into College Station for their annual tussle with the Aggies, and within the first three minutes of the contest, John Kimbrough cracked through for seventeen yards and a touchdown. Webster kicked a field goal late in the game to give the Aggies their seventeenth straight win, 17–0.

Many of "Jarrin" John's yards came behind All-American guard Marshall Robnett, who earned national honors in 1940.

In 1940, the Aggies squared off against Texas with a 20-game win streak and the SWC championship in the bag. The Horns pinned a 7–0 loss on the Aggies, costing them another national championship. Nonetheless, A&M went on to beat Fordam in the 1941 Cotton Bowl. Here, UT quarterback Pete Layden leaps over Aggie defenders to score the winning touchdown.

The eyes of the nation were focused on Dallas November 9 as the Aggies tangled with SMU. A crowd of more than 27,000 witnessed a thrill-packed game that would be talked about for years.

The game was but four minutes old when A&M got the ball on the Mustangs' thirty-two-yard line. A Pugh-to-Buchanan pass brought the Aggies to the three, and then Bill Conatser dove over the goal line for a touchdown. Pugh converted for a 7–0 A&M lead. Later, a TD pass from Mallouf to Brown boosted SMU into a 7–7 halftime tie.

The big partisan Mustang crowd, expecting a hard fight, was in a frenzy. Could SMU keep it up and upset one of the nation's best teams? The second half would tell.

Bill Conatser answered that question, returning a punt forty-seven yards before Kimbrough bulldozed his way thirty-five yards for a TD. With the score 13–7 in favor of A&M, the Aggies' Bill Routt fell on a blocked punt in the end zone to make the final score 19–7.

Marion Pugh believed that A&M was at its offensive best for the past two seasons when it wiped out a strong Rice team 25–0 for its nineteenth straight win. That was the day Bill Henderson caught eight straight passes to set an A&M record.

In the game against Rice, Moser, Henderson, Jim Sterling, and Kimbrough all scored breakaway touchdowns as A&M drubbed the Owls.

On Thanksgiving Day, before a crowd of 45,000, the Southwest's largest pigskin crowd in history, an inspired Longhorn football squad, backed by a tradition that would not be denied, stopped A&M cold, preventing a twenty-first consecutive victory (counting bowl games), with an astounding 7–0 victory. A touchdown in the first minute of play on two long passes, and an alert defense that throttled the Aggies for the rest of the afternoon, told the story.

In the opening series, with Texas on the move, several long passes from Pete Layden to Crain and Noble Doss put the ball on the one-yard line.

Buoyed by their first trip to the Big Apple, A&M returned in 1941 to meet New York University. Here's the official program.

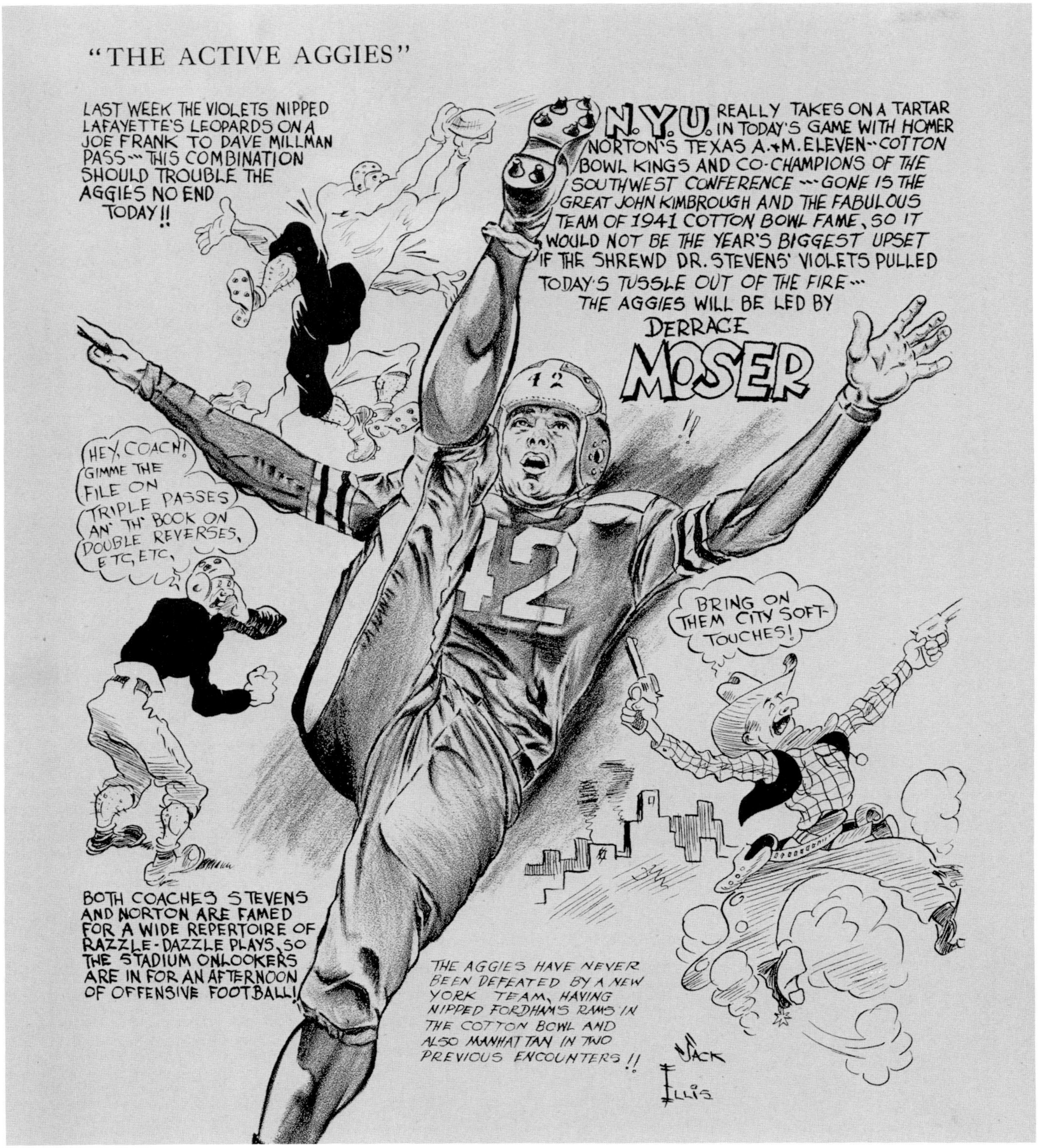

Despite the hopeful tone of this comic, the Aggies, led by all-SWC performer Derace Moser, clobbered NYU 49–7. The seven NYU points were the first allowed by A&M in three games that year.

The 1941 Texas Aggies, led by end James Sterling, center Bill Sibley, backs Cullen Rogers and Leo Daniels, guard Felix Bucek, and co-captain tackle Martin Ruby, rolled to a 9–2 record and captured the school's third consecutive SWC crown. From 1939–1941, the Aggies knifed through the competition for a razor-sharp 29–3 record, including three major bowl appearances, two bowl victories, and a national championship.

Then Layden cracked through for the score. Jack Crain's PAT ended the day's scoring.

John Kimbrough was a virtual one-man rushing crew as he strove with all his strength and speed to cross the Texas chalk line, but each time the Aggies got inside the ten-yard line, Texas' great defense stopped him in his tracks.

The Longhorns' gritty win cost A&M its number one ranking in the polls and an invitation from the Rose Bowl committee (which selected Nebraska instead). With Tennessee and Boston College slated for the Sugar Bowl, the Aggies had a choice of either the Orange Bowl or the Cotton Bowl. After considerable wrangling, players voted at a team meeting to accept a Cotton Bowl bid to play Fordham in Dallas on New Year's Day.

"Not all the boys were happy with the decision," says Kimbrough. "Some of the seniors wanted to skip the bowl games. They wanted to play in the all-star games instead."

Fordham, an eastern powerhouse, was famous for its "Seven Blocks of Granite," which included future Hall-of-Fame coach Vince Lombardi at guard. Coached by former Notre Dame standout Jim Crowley (of Four Horsemen fame), the Rams had lost just once in eight outings and were ranked twelfth in the country.

A&M used one of its trick plays, the "hideout pass," to score its first touchdown. Trailing 6–0 at the start of the third period, Earl "Bama" Smith trotted toward the east sideline while his teammates rushed into their huddle. Smith took off undetected at the snap and hauled in a sixty-two-yard scoring pass from quarterback Marion Pugh to tie the game.

Then in the final period, Kimbrough's eleven-yard TD run and Pugh's conversion gave Texas

A&M a 13–6 lead. Fordham countered with a touchdown, but another blocked PAT gave A&M a narrow 13–12 victory.

Meanwhile, war spread like wildfire as the Nazis occupied Czechoslovakia in 1938, then invaded Poland the following year. France and Britain declared war against Germany. The U.S. Congress enacted the first peacetime selective service act and 900,000 men between the ages of twenty and thirty-six were required to register. Then suddenly, on December 7, 1941, the Japanese bombed Pearl Harbor and President Roosevelt declared war. FDR sent hundreds of merchant ships to Great Britain, while General MacArthur fought off the enemy in the South Pacific. Football coaches and players went off to war and freshmen were called up in all sections of the nation to fill in for the varsity players called to service. Black-out regulations curtailed practice sessions under the lights, while transportation became a major problem for all football teams.

Despite all the restrictions, FDR gave the green light to baseball, football, and other varsity sports.

At College Station, the Aggie cadets were being called up daily to report to various training areas and the A&M football squad—weakened by the loss of all-American John Kimbrough, Marion Pugh, Jim Thomason, and Bill Conatser, who were assigned to an Army All-Star team—opened the 1941 season against the Sam Houston Teachers. The game provided the Aggies with a wonderful "practice" session, for the Sam Houston team was never in the game. A&M, with Henderson, Moser, Daniels, Simmons, and Rogers doing the damage, swept over and through the Sam Houston team for seven touchdowns and a 54–0 win as every man on the squad got an opportunity to play. The following week, A&M played their first night game in Texas and ran over Texas A&I 41 to 0 in another exercise.

A week later, October 11, the Aggies traveled 3,000 miles to New York's great Polo Grounds and faced one of New York University's top teams. But NYU just could not cope with the speedy running game of the Aggies. When the Violets massed to stop the rushing of Moser, Williams, and Spivey, Moser switched to a passing attack and bewildered the Violets with his accurate passes, which gave A&M seven touchdowns and a 49–7 win.

TCU, with an improved team over previous years, again was defeated as the Aggies quickly took command of the game and scored a touchdown on a Moser pass to Spivey, who went over from the six-yard line, making it 7–0 A&M. Then in the final period, the Aggies got the ball on the TCU thirty. Leo Daniel tossed to Sterling and then to Hal Cowley for the second touchdown. Webster kicked the extra point, and it was a 14–0 win for the Aggies.

In 1912 an outstanding Aggie team drubbed the Baylor Bears 53–0 and went on to an 8–1 season. In 1941 the Aggies repeated the 1912 massacre, romping to a 48–0 win over the hapless Bears.

Early in the 1941 game, Moser took a Baylor punt and dashed fifty yards to the Bears' 15. Willie Zapalac then bucked over for the first score. Three minutes later, passes from Jim Sterling and Spivey counted for another touchdown. From that point on, the Aggies racked up five additional scores to win their fifth straight game of the season.

On November 1, the Aggies traveled to Little Rock for their game against an Arkansas team that played better ball against A&M than they had against anyone all season long. The game seesawed back and forth for three periods. Finally, a pass by David Jones of Arkansas was intercepted by A&M's guard Felix Bucek, who scored. Webster kicked the extra point as the Aggies had registered the only score of the game, 7–0.

A&M tallied quickly against SMU as Moser passed to Jim Sterling and Henderson. Moser then faked a pass to Henderson and slicked off tackle for the score. The Mustangs came back, slugging through A&M's line for big gains and then scoring on a Bill Johnston thirty-eight-yard gallop. Johnston kicked the extra point, and it was a 7–7 ball game. Just as the half was coming to an end, Bo Campbell booted a thirty-yard field goal to give SMU a 10–7 lead. But a scrappy A&M team rallied in the final quarter as two great passes from Moser to Spivey resulted in two touchdowns to give the Aggies a tremendous, come-from-behind 21–10 win.

November 15 broke bright and clear and brisk for the Aggies as they defeated Rice 19–6—a win they had to have to clinch the SWC championship for the third successive year. Moser played the game of his young life as he passed, ran, and bucked through the Rice defense to set up three Aggie touchdowns—all this, despite a battered ankle that had to be taped up to his knee. At the half it was 19–0 A&M. Rice came back in the third period with halfback Brumley scoring from the four-yard line. But from then on, it was Webster, Daniels, Rogers, Ruby, and Dickey keeping the Rice Owls from the goal line as the Aggies rang up their ninth straight win.

Then on Thanksgiving Day, a truly inspired Longhorn team that had been defeated just once, by TCU, rolled into College Station and ended A&M's nine-game winning streak 23–0.

It was a ferocious battle until fifty-five seconds before the half ended, when Sanders broke away for fifty yards to the Aggies' two-yard line. Then on fourth down, Jack Crain booted a field goal for a 3–0 Texas lead. As the third period began, Noble Doss of Texas broke loose for eighty-two yards and what seemed certain to be a touchdown. But he was tackled on the eighteen-yard line. Three plays later, Crain scored for Texas. The Longhorns scored a third touchdown in the period to make it 23–0 as the Aggies, desperate to regain ground, filled the air with passes that were intercepted or knocked down. And once again, the Aggies' hopes for an undefeated season and a national championship were ruined for the second successive year by Texas.

In the final game of the 1941 season, the Aggies traveled more than 2500 miles to Tacoma, Washington, and won the "Evergreen Bowl Classic" in a royal battle against Washington State by a 7–0 margin.

Passes from Leo Daniels to Cullen Rogers and Marsh Spivey got the ball to the Washington State eight-yard line. Then Spivey hit Rogers on a pass play and Rogers galloped in for the only score of the day. Webster kicked the extra point, and A&M had won its ninth game of the season.

Both A&M and the Alabama Crimson Tide found themselves with impressive records as they faced each other in the Cotton Bowl matchup, which could conceivably decide the national championship. The Aggies had lost only the one game to Texas en route to the SWC title, while Alabama had dropped games to Mississippi State and Vanderbilt.

A huge, expectant crowd was up and shouting at the opening kickoff as A&M drove to midfield with Leo Daniels, Marsh Spivey, and Jack Webster alternately packing the ball. A fumble gave Alabama the first of several breaks, and they recovered the ball and drove to the Aggies' thirty-yard line. The Aggies held, however, and in the second quarter Hal Cowley scored on a thirty-eight-yard pass from Daniels. Alabama then took the ball right down the field after recovering another A&M fumble and scored to knot the game at 7–7.

In the third period, Nelson fielded a punt, skirted away from three Aggie tacklers, and raced seventy-three yards for an Alabama touchdown. Trailing 13–7, A&M stayed on the ground, couldn't advance, and fumbled the ball away to the Tide, who capitalized with another touchdown by Nelson, this time on a twenty-one-yard run.

Late in the final period, Alabama took a seemingly safe 29–7 lead, but with a few minutes left, A&M caught fire.

With Daniels tossing passes to Sterling and Spivey, the Aggies marched fifty-eight yards for a touchdown. A minute later, A&M struck pay dirt once again. Moser tossed a thirty-five-yard pass to Jim Sterling that Nelson of Alabama deflected and almost intercepted. Luckily for the Aggies, Sterling made an acrobatic catch and dove into the end zone for another Aggie touchdown. The furious comeback fell short, however.

Despite being beaten in every statistical category, the Tide held on to win 29–21 and earn some votes as national champions.

When the gun sounded to end the game, thirteen A&M seniors ended their college football careers. These men had helped bring the Aggies a national championship, two SWC titles, and one co-SWC championship during their three seasons in maroon and white.

During that remarkable period of achievement, the Aggies won 29 games and lost 3, a record unmatched in all of college football.

What made this group so special? "That kind of thing is hard to explain," admits Harris Mack

Browder. "We just had good chemistry, I suppose."

A few years ago, a fifty-year reunion revealed that of the fifty-five or so Aggies who belonged to that team, about half are still alive.

"Most of us have kept in touch over the years," Browder says. "Whenever somebody needed a job or needed some help, we were there for each other. That's the kind of boys we had on that team."

7

FROM A BEAR MARKET TO THE BEAR

Norton and his 1942 Aggies, shattered by the service requirements and the graduation of thirteen varsity lettermen, were hardly ready to face the onslaught of the Tigers of LSU in the opening game of the season. LSU was blessed with two outstanding backfield stars in Steve Van Buren and Alvin Dark. Van Buren would go on to a sensational NFL career and Dark would play shortstop and manage in the major leagues.

Dark and Van Buren were all LSU needed to defeat A&M 16–7 as Dark pitched the football and Van Buren caught several passes to score two touchdowns. For the Aggies, Bill Henderson, Felix Bucek, Leo Daniels, Willie Zapalac, and Big Hank Foldberg were outstanding. The Aggies rebounded in the second game to pound out an impressive 19–0 win over the Texas Tech Red Raiders. Daniels broke out with a great play in the first minute of the game, racing fifty-five yards for a touchdown. Zapalac and Otto Payne also scored touchdowns.

The Corpus Christi Naval team, with numerous college stars in its lineup, was too strong for the Aggies and won 18–7. The Aggies lost to TCU 7–2 and then suffered an ignominious loss to Baylor 6–0.

But a week later, rebounding from those defeats, A&M trounced a highly favored Arkansas team under a barrage of six touchdowns for a 41–0 win. The Aggies then beat SMU 27–20 and played Rice to a scoreless tie.

In the annual Thanksgiving Day game at Austin, Texas scored a touchdown in the second period and held the Aggies scoreless until there were but five minutes left in the game. Then A&M's Barney Welch, behind great blocking, sped seventy-two yards for a touchdown to tie the score 6–6. It was the first Aggie touchdown ever scored at Texas's Memorial Stadium. With two minutes left in the game, Jack Fields and Roy McKay combined on a pass play that covered forty yards to give the 'Horns a touchdown, making the score 12–6.

A&M came back on two pinpoint passes plus a screen play to move the ball to the Texas ten-yard line. But time ran out on A&M.

Washington State, a 2-1 favorite over A&M, was stunned by a forty-five-yard touchdown sprint by Zapalac, and A&M was out in front to stay.

In the second half, A&M quickly opened with a sharp passing attack and two touchdowns to ice a big upset win over the Cougars 21–0.

The win over Washington State ended a flat 4–5–1 season for the Aggies and ended the careers of twenty-two varsity players. Coach Norton and his aides sank into a winter-long funk

With World War II raging, athletic talent was sparse. Many colleges were forced to rely on teenagers to fill their rosters. In 1943, Norton discovered a teenager with grownup talent, 17-year-old Jesse Burditt, who in four seasons at A&M (1943–1946) played both quarterback and running back. In his first season, A&M went 7–2–1 and made its initial appearance in the Orange Bowl, a 19–14 defeat at the hands of LSU.

every time they looked over the roster for the next seasons. They would be long indeed.

Fielding a starting lineup for the 1943 season presented a major problem for Norton. World War II service had taken virtually every veteran player and most of the coaching staff as well. Assistant coaches Dough Rollins, Marty Karow, and Charley DeWare went on active duty as well as the 1942 seniors, juniors, and most sophomores. Consequently, A&M fielded a team that included half a dozen sixteen-year-olds, a large group of seventeen-year-olds, and one or two eighteen- and nineteen-year-olds.

Some local sportswriters referred to the A&M varsity as the Kiddie Korps and the "Beardless Wonders."

Whatever they were called, the kids posted an amazing 7–2–1 record, including surprising wins over top teams LSU, TCU, Arkansas, SMU, and Rice. One of their two losses, however, was a bitter one to Texas.

The youngest player in the '43 starting lineup, seventeen-year-old Jesse Burditt, led the team from his quarterback post. Stan Turner and Butch Burchofsky were the halfbacks and Jim Hallmark was the fullback. Bill Geer and Marion Settegast were the ends, Monte Moncrief and Goble Bryant were the tackles (both received all-American recognition), Harry Turley and Damon Tassos were the guards, and R. C. Wright was the center.

The 27–13 loss to the Longhorns dimmed a bright season, but Norton and his team were delighted to receive an invitation to meet LSU's Tigers in the post-season classic at the Orange Bowl.

Because of the war, co-captain Goble Bryant lettered only one season, but he made the most of it. A punishing blocker from his tackle position, Bryant earned all-SWC honors in 1943.

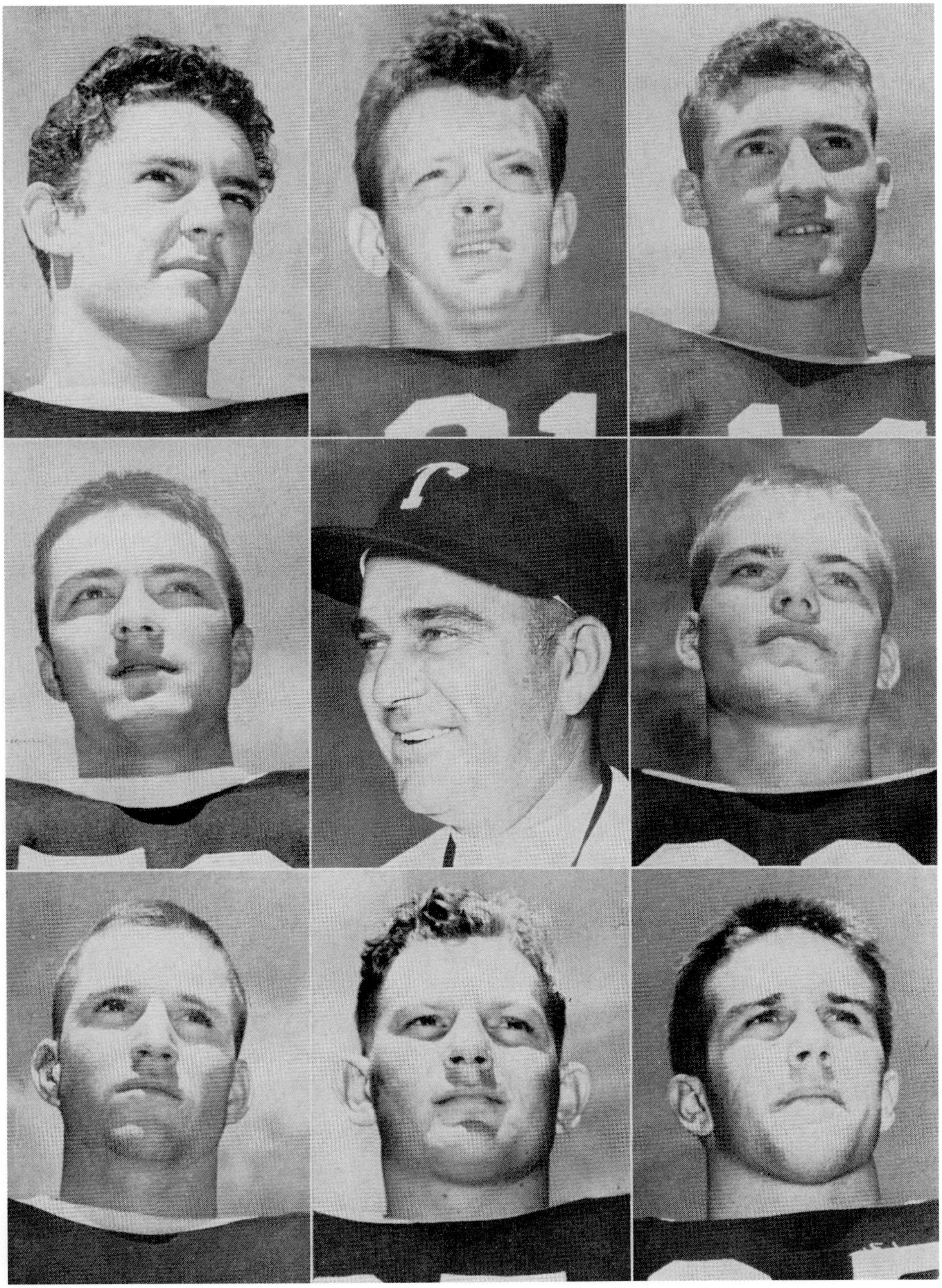

The 1943 Aggies were such a young bunch they were coined the "Kiddie Corps." Here are seven of the young bucks with Heach Coach Norton.

The 1944 Aggies outscored their opponents by a whopping 289–87. None of their seven victories was as lopsided as the 70–14 annihilation of Miami in the season finale. Here's the program from that game.

Earlier in the season, A&M's Kiddie Corps had beaten a star-studded and favored LSU eleven, 28–13, but in the Orange Bowl, all-American Steve Van Buren led his Tigers to a narrow 19–14 victory.

Van Buren scored two touchdowns and led the way to a third score. His sixty-three-yard sprint in the third period clinched the win for LSU. Jim Hallmark's great all-around play, sparked the Aggies' attack.

Working with teenagers had to be one of the most difficult tasks in Norton's career, but he relished it. "This was one of the greatest years in my coaching career," gushed the coach.

Norton was delighted that his "Kiddie Corps" of 1943 was returning in 1944, the fiftieth anniversary of A&M football.

Football turned a corner with the start of the forties. With the new decade came a major development—a fresh style of offensive football that was to become so much the vogue that Notre Dame disciples abandoned their hop-skip shift for it, and even those who remained steadfast to the Warner wingback formation employed features of the new attack.

A mixture of old and new, it took the oldest formation in football, "The Original T," and modernized it by adding a man in motion, which crossed up opposing defenses by adding an element of unpredictability.

Norton explained: "We had what I think were the finest pass patterns of any team in the country. It was my own system and used somewhat differently from most pass patterns, and we also used the T-formation in 1944 instead of the conventional single wing. I switched to the T because the players on our team were so much bigger, stronger, and older than in 1943."

"If I could only find a competent passer," said Norton, "the Aggies would be a tough team to beat." He found that man in Jim Cashion, who was born and brought up on the campus. As the quarterback for the Aggies in '44, the seventeen-year-old Cashion did an admirable job, as did Bob Goff, a great kicker; Butch Burchofsky; and Monte Moncrief, who was voted all-SWC tackle, and all-American honorable mention.

The 1944 Aggies opened the season against Bryan Air Field and raced to a 19–0 halftime lead. After Cashion passed to Goff for a TD in the third quarter, A&M got the ball back and Goff broke off tackle and sprinted seventy-five yards for a touchdown. Several plays later, Cashion scored from the one-yard line after recovering a fumble, and the final score was 39–0.

The Aggies came from behind in the fourth quarter to defeat a stubborn Texas Tech eleven 27–14 in a game that featured Jim Cashion's great passes to Goff and Gene Spires. But injuries were to play havoc with the Aggies for the rest of the season. Most serious was a broken jaw suffered by Butch Burchofsky.

The following week, the Aggies pulled every trick play in their offense, from hideouts to reverses to laterals on punt returns, but it was to no avail as powerful, experienced Oklahoma pulled out a 21–14 nail-biter.

In the game against TCU, the Aggies fumbled nine times, but still had a miracle chance to win or perhaps tie TCU as the final moments of the game ticked off. The score was 13–7 TCU when a pass from Cashion to Joe Scott was tipped out of Scott's hands inside the TCU twenty-yard line to secure the win.

Next, a stubborn, fighting bunch of LSU Tigers playing a tough defensive game, held the Aggies scoreless in a 0–0 battle for three quarters. Then halfback Paul Yates took a reverse from Bobby Goff and swept across the LSU goal line for the only score of the game to pick up win No. 3 by a 7–0 margin. Yates played perhaps the best game of his life.

The North Texas Air Corps team offered little more than a practice session as the Aggies racked up a 61–0 win.

Just a week later, against a strong Arkansas team, it was a twenty-five-yard pass and a series of fumbles that gave Arkansas a tough 7–6 win over A&M. The A&M cadets fumbled the ball seven times, and each time, Arkansas recovered.

Arkansas scored when a pass by halfback Gordy Long to Al Baldwin bounced off the hands of Aggie center Hub Ellis and right into the hands of Baldwin, who scooted twenty yards for a touchdown. Jim Young of Arkansas kicked the extra point, and that made the difference as Arkansas took a 7–6 verdict from A&M.

A&M's passing attack proved devastating against the SMU Mustangs. The Aggies connected for nine of thirteen passes good for five touchdowns and a 39–6 win. Jim Cashion and Jim Palmer were outstanding for the Aggies in this rout of an old rival. Against Rice, a strong A&M line, led by all-SWC tackle Monte Moncrief, bottled up the Owls throughout the game as the Aggies picked up their fifth win of the year, 19–6. The Owls didn't cross beyond midfield until the last five minutes of the game. Texas now loomed.

UT took a 6–0 lead on A&M and then held tough in the late going, stopping four straight Aggie tries from the 'Horns' two-yard line.

In the final game of the 1944 season, A&M throttled the Miami Hurricanes 70–14.

With A&M ahead 25–7 at the half, Norton inserted his second team, then third, and finally, every man on the squad as the Hurricanes proved no match at all. Cashion, Burchofsky, Spires, Jim Parmer, and Joe Scott were outstanding in this game. Scott played the greatest game of his career, scoring four touchdowns and catching five passes.

While the Aggies waged a 100-yard war at Kyle Field, no one forgot that a real war was being fought in Europe and the Pacific. Joe Routt, the school's first all-American selection as a guard on the 1936–37 teams, was an infantry captain caught up in the chaos of the Battle of the Bulge in the closing days of 1944. Advancing on a corps of German tanks during the hottest part of the fighting, Routt was gunned down as he signaled his men into position. Routt, posthumously awarded the Bronze Star for heroism, was one of several former Aggies to pay the ultimate price during four long years of war. Collectively, they left behind an example of service to their school and to their country that A&M cadets continue to find inspiring.

Lineman Monte Moncrief was all-SWC in 1944, '45 and '46. He also was the only Aggie to captain the football team three straight years, from 1944 to 1946.

Homer Norton, beginning his twelfth season as the head coach of the A&M football program, lamented to one of his aides, "We're getting younger and less experienced players since the war. But there's nothing we can do about it. We'll be lucky to win [more than a couple] games this year and the same goes for 1946."

With Butch Burchofsky and Moncrief as co-captains, the Aggies rolled to three straight victories over Ellington Field 54–0, Texas Tech 16–6, and heavily favored Oklahoma 19–14. The Aggies seemingly were on their way to an outstanding season. And with freshman Bob Goode, a rangy, quick-as-a-flash broken-field runner, and Preston Smith and Gene Johnson, the A&M eleven looked more impressive in each game. That is until they were upended by LSU 31–12.

Then in a sluggish demonstration, a week later, TCU scored two quick touchdowns to jump into a 13–0 lead at the end of three quarters. Suddenly, the Aggies caught fire with seven minutes left in the game. They scored a touchdown. Then Burchofsky scooped up a fumble and scampered thirty-five yards for the score, but A&M fell 13–12.

Just one week later, Baylor scored first and took a 13–0 lead. But Aggie guard Grant Darnell stole the ball from a Baylor back and scampered thirty yards for a score. In the third period, teammate Bob Goode swept twenty-five yards for a touchdown, and in the final period, Goode broke through the Bears line for twenty-one yards and a touchdown that gave A&M the win, 19–13.

Arkansas had not heard about the Aggies' touchdown twins, Goode and Smith, but the Razorbacks knew who they were early as the two combined for eighteen points in the first nine minutes of the game. In its finest game of the season, A&M wasted Arkansas 34–0.

On November 10, Bob Goode, the exciting, breakaway artist of the Aggies, bolted fifty-one yards through SMU's tackle and was brought down on the seventeen-yard line. Two plays later, John Ballentine booted a field goal for a 3–0 lead. The Aggies fought off all of SMU's attempts to score and took a brilliant 3–0 win over the Mustangs.

Then with the great war hero, Admiral "Bull" Halsey, in the stands cheering the Aggies on, they completely outplayed Rice, but two costly penalties gave Rice an opportunity to score and the Owls pulled out a hair-tingling 6–0 verdict over A&M.

In the first post World War II Thanksgiving Day Game at College Station, the Longhorns stunned the Aggies early. Fullback Ralph Ellsworth took the ball after a clever fake by Texas' all-American Bobby Layne shot to his left, then, as the Aggie line shifted to stop him, cut across the grain, and in a moment was out in the clear for eighteen yards and a touchdown and a 7–0 lead. The Aggies' Gene Johnson evened the score on a 27-yard touchdown sprint. And in the third period, John Ballentine's seventeen-yard field goal gave A&M a 10–7 lead.

Then Charlie Tatom, a Texas end, pounced on a fumble within the shadows of the Aggies' goal line. On the following play, George Graham blasted through for another Texas touchdown and the 'Horns had a 13–10 lead.

Bobby Layne then tossed a picture-perfect pass to the all-American end Hub Bechtol for a TD. Rooster Andrews, the pint-size extra-point star, kicked the field goal, and Texas had the ball game 20–10 and a Cotton Bowl berth against Missouri.

Norton, upset after the loss to Texas, told his team, "Never have I been as proud of any team in my life as I've been with you guys. I've had great teams here, but none of them gave me more than you men today."

The loss to Texas dropped the Aggies to 6–4, but there was hope that with the war over, a horde of experienced, older, and bigger players would be returning to A&M football for the forthcoming season.

When his two co-captains, fullback Willie Zapalac, a bone-crushing fullback in the style of John Kimbrough, and all-American nominee, tackle Monte Moncrief reported back for the fall practice sessions in 1946, Homer Norton, in his thirteenth year as head coach, greeted his veteran stars with delight. In a short pep talk to the squad before the practice began, he said, "If these two men, Zapalac and Moncrief, are indicative of the kind of men that are going to report for football this year, we'll have a great squad. These two captains are three-year lettermen, and they will lead and inspire this team to what I hope will be a great year."

But to Norton's dismay, there were few additional veterans who came back to school and

Aggie nemesis Bobby Layne, no. 41, a Texas all-American, flips a short pass to halfback Ralph Ellsworth, who scrambles into the end zone in the 1945 game, won by Texas 20–10. It was the Aggies' sixth straight defeat to Texas, which started some grumbling among A&M faithful that perhaps Homer Norton was growing soft.

football. "At this stage of life," Norton told his aides, "they're married, some have children, and some I've talked with aren't that interested in football, after the violence they faced overseas. They want to finish school and get a job."

In the opening game of the season against North Texas State, defending Lone Star Conference champion, the Aggies—with such stalwarts as Zapalac, Moncrief, Barney Welch, Leo Daniels, Babe Hallmark, and Marion Flanagan—all gave a good account of themselves as the Aggies got off to a great start with a 47–0 shutout win over the Eagles. Halfback Barney Welch led the way with three touchdowns.

But a surprisingly strong Texas Tech, which had never beaten A&M, held the Aggies for more than three periods before A&M started to move the ball. But Texas Tech intercepted a pass on the last play of the game and scooted into the end zone to score the lone touchdown and win in a 6–0 thriller.

A week later, a determined bunch of Aggies trekked into Norman, Oklahoma, bent on victory over a strong Oklahoma team. The Aggie line did stop Oklahoma on at least four occasions in the first period, but in the second period, the

Sooners blocked a Barney Welch punt and recovered the ball on the Aggies' five-yard line. Two plays later, they scored, and it was 7–0 Oklahoma.

In the third period, Marion Flanagan took a Sooner punt, broke through two tacklers, and raced out in the clear for seventy-two yards and a touchdown. The PAT made it 7–7.

There was no further scoring until five minutes before the end of the game, when Stan Hollmig's poor kick went out of bounds on the Aggie thirty-four. The Sooners took over and advanced to the A&M ten-yard line. Bob Wallace then kicked a field goal to give Oklahoma a last-minute 10–7 victory.

Some 1,800 wild-eyed A&M rooters traveled to Baton Rouge for the game against LSU. After a thrilling first half, the score was tied 7–7. However, Aggie starters Higgins, Welch, Wright, and Winkler all were sidelined by injuries, and in the second half, the Tigers pounded the weakened Aggie line to shreds as they scored four additional touchdowns to rout A&M 33–9. A week later, with the injured stars in action once more, the Aggies bounced back to take a well-earned 14–0 win over TCU.

In the Baylor game, the Aggies discovered a passing ace in quarterback Buryl Baty. Through the last two periods, Baty twice found receivers for touchdowns as the Aggies flew to a 17–0 victory.

The Aggies then dropped another tight defensive game, this time to Arkansas 7–0.

A Cotton Bowl crowd of 40,000 witnessed one of the Aggies' best games of the year, a 14–0 win over SMU. Moncrief, Ed Dusek, Higgins, and Dickey were outstanding as the Aggies brought their season record to 5–3 with Rice and Texas yet to play.

A charged-up A&M team outplayed SWC champ Rice early, taking a 10–0 halftime lead on a Dusek touchdown and a twenty-five-yard field goal by the sure-footed John Ballentine. But after a spirited halftime talk by their coach, the Owls responded by ringing up four touchdowns and a field goal to swamp A&M 27 to 10.

It was all Bobby Layne as Texas completely outplayed A&M in the Thanksgiving Day battle. Bobby tossed passes until A&M defenders were dizzy as he completed aerials for fifty-one, seventy-five, and forty-seven yards, all for touchdowns in an easy 24–7 win. It was the seventh victory in a row for Texas over A&M, and was one of the chief reasons the Aggie alums were growing uneasy, with many calling for the dismissal of Homer Norton as the Aggies closed out a dismal 4–6 season.

Prior to the 1947 campaign, Norton and his aides worked night and day to develop a team that would rise to the heights that the Aggie supporters wanted.

In the first game of the season against Southwestern, the Aggies played inspired football and ran roughshod over the Pirates 48–0. The offense was sparked by big Ed Dusek, who scored two touchdowns, one on an exciting seventy-one-yard ramble.

Texas Tech had defeated the Aggies in 1946 for their first ever win over A&M and was favored to win its second in a row, but sparkling play by Jim Cashion, Ed Dusek, and Bob Goode paved the way for the Aggies to chalk up win No. 2 by a 29–7 margin. Goode, in particular, was hot. In the first quarter, after a pass from Cashion to Cotton Howell put the ball on the Tech fifteen-yard stripe, Goode sprinted around his right end for a touchdown. In the third period, after A&M's Nort Higgins (who later was killed in the Korean War) tackled Bob Earhart of Tech behind the goal line for a safety, Tech then kicked off to the Aggies. Goode took the ball on his thirty-yard line, skipped past two tacklers, straight-armed a third, then cut to the left sideline and sprinted seventy yards for a touchdown.

Oklahoma snapped the Aggie win streak by scoring a touchdown in each quarter on the way to a 26–14 win. The Aggies had led at the half, 14–13.

Next, the Aggies pushed LSU's Tigers all over the field and scored on the first sequence of plays as they marched steadily upfield. On a double-reverse, Cashion was hit by two tacklers and had to be carried off the field with a broken ankle. Hollmig took over and capped a sixty-five-yard drive by scoring a touchdown from ten yards out. Ballentine's kick was good. But the Tigers came back strong as Y. A. Tittle passed to his ends for two successive touchdowns. LSU led at the half 12–6.

Goode scored for the Aggies in the third period to give A&M a 13–12 lead. But Tittle, who would go on to a great NFL career with the San Francisco 49ers and New York Giants, couldn't be halted. He led LSU on a sixty-five-yard scoring drive to notch a 19–13 come-from-behind victory. To add insult, the Tigers wasted A&M passing ace Jim Cashion, who was lost for the rest of the year.

TCU, coached by Dutch Meyer, used the single wing and double wing, plus numerous spread plays, to easily defeat A&M 26–0 in a listless game. Then against Baylor, the Aggies came to life and played an alert, smart passing game with Buryl Baty, Ed Dusek, and Hollmig sparking the offense in a 24–0 win.

Arkansas and the Aggies played a cautious defensive game after each team scored three touchdowns, and the result was a 21–21 tie in a game at Fayetteville.

Doak Walker, SMU's all-American halfback, simply could not be stopped. It was the Doaker's running and passing that set the stage for the Mustangs' two touchdowns and a 13–0 win over A&M.

In the ninth game of this unhappy season, the Rice Owls pounded the Aggies' defense. When A&M tried to stop the running game of the Owls, their superb quarterback, Tobin Rote, tossed precision-like passes to his ends and backfield mates to ring up a 41–7 rout of the Aggies.

In the final game of the season, the Thanksgiving Day battle against the 8–1 Longhorns, A&M was pulverized by the pinpoint passing of the great Bobby Layne and the sensational running of halfback Tom Landry. The 'Horns scored five touchdowns to win their eighth consecutive game against the Aggies by the convincing score of 32–13.

The loss to Texas gave the Aggies a 3–6–1 season record, and a few days after the season ended, Norton was offered a buyout of his contract, which had two more years to go. Norton accepted the buyout and was out of A&M after a fifteen-year career that was one of the most notable in the nation.

Homer Norton left a legacy at A&M that included a national championship, three SWC titles, and the honor and respect of all his players and the opposing coaches he was associated with during his tenure. And he was heartbroken to leave A&M.

Norton resided and opened a business in College Station and attended all of the home games. In May 1965 he died of a heart attack at his home.

As quarterback for the 1930 Aggies, Harry Stiteler never knew the meaning of the word quit as his Aggies had to battle the best teams in the SWC Conference week after week. But outweighed and outplayed in practically every one of the nine games on the schedule, the Aggies won but two games and lost seven. "There were at least three games that we played, against

After losing seasons in 1946 and 1947, plus two more defeats to Texas, Norton was removed as head coach before the start of the '48 season. Brought in to replace him was Harry Stiteler (center), one of Texas's great high school football coaches and the only coach to win Texas high school football championships with two different schools, Waco and Corpus Christi. Stiteler was offense-minded, but his first two teams just didn't have the horses to take advantage of Harry's imaginative ideas. There was one highlight from the 1948 season, however. After losing their first nine games, the Aggies, behind all-SWC performers Bob Goode (halfback) and Jim Winkler (tackle), stunned heavily favored Texas by fighting to a 14–14 tie. Hired to defeat Texas—Stiteler almost did that very first year. Also in the picture are assistants (left) Bill DuBose and Charles DeWare, the son of the great Aggie end Charles DeWare who starred on the 1905–1908 teams.

Tulane, TCU, Rice, and SMU, that we could have won by scoring one more touchdown, but in every one of those games we were worn down by the pounding as these bigger teams got scores near the end of the game to beat us."

It was Stiteler, a former assistant to Coach Norton, who was named as the Aggies' head coach in 1948.

"Naturally, we had a good recruiting success in my first year," said Stiteler, "I had been a high school coach, and I got a lot of help from coaches who were friends."

Among those new recruits was Bob Smith, who would go on to dizzying heights as one of A&M's great halfbacks and would set running records that would stand for twenty-five years. Also on hand: Glenn Lippman, Yale Lary, Billy Tidwell, Dick Gardemal, Hugh Meyer, Elo Nohavitza, and Jim Fowler.

In the opening game of the season, A&M's inexperienced and lighter squad tangled with a big, tough Villanova team in Philadelphia. The Aggies surprised the Wildcats early on as Wray Whittaker intercepted a Villanova pass and sprinted forty-eight yards for a touchdown. Villanova came back in a hurry to score a touchdown for a 7–7 tie at the half. But the Aggies tired badly in the second half and the Wildcats took advantage by scoring five additional touchdowns to win by a 34–14 margin.

In the game against Texas Tech, the Aggies had a two-touchdown lead, but the Red Raiders scored three touchdowns to win 20–14.

That's the way the entire season went as A&M would take an early lead, then tire. A&M took the lead against Oklahoma and then sagged as the Sooners came back to score a 42–14 win. LSU, TCU, Baylor, and Arkansas all won games from the Aggies. Then, SMU and Rice followed with wins, setting the stage for the Thanksgiving Day battle against Texas.

Texas took a 14–7 lead late in the third period, but then came the big payoff for A&M. Aggie quarterback Buryl Baty fired a pass to Charlie Royalty. Shands rushed Royalty, and batted the ball out of his hands and into the hands of Charlie Wright, who caught the ball and raced twenty-six yards for the touchdown. Turley made the conversion, and that extra point gave the Aggies a 14–14 moral victory.

Thus ended the poorest season in Aggie history, one without any wins and only one tie.

In 1949 the Aggies almost matched the 1948 record as they were only able to beat a weak Texas Tech eleven, 26–7. In this game, halfback Bob Smith came into his own and lived up to all the promise that he showed in his freshman year. Smitty dashed through the Tech line as if it were papier-mâché, scoring three touchdowns and gaining 252 yards. Smith's final touchdown was a thing of beauty as he took a shovel pass from quarterback Baty, broke through left tackle, and outran every Tech player for a spectacular eighty-yard touchdown.

Following the Tech victory, A&M fell to Oklahoma, LSU, TCU, Baylor, and Arkansas.

In the eighth game of the year, against SMU, a team that received national acclaim at the beginning of the season, Bob Smith was unstoppable as he dashed for 175 yards and three touchdowns. But all-American halfback Kyle Rote took a kickoff and sped through the entire Aggie squad for 100 yards in one of the most spectacular runs of the season to tie the Aggies 27–27.

Numerous penalties for rough play characterized the annual battle between Texas and the Aggies. When A&M's Bob Smith was knocked out on a bruising tackle and was carried off the field, the Aggies' play deteriorated and Texas once again prevailed, 42–14, in the most lopsided defeat of A&M since 1901.

The 1–8–1 season was the second disastrous year for Coach Stiteler, the players, and the alumni.

Until the season of 1950, Texas A&M's greatest football hero had been big John Kimbrough, who gained nationwide fame in 1939 and '40 with his all-America play at fullback. In the eleven years since, no Aggie player had been able to dim the memory of the slashing drives and the power-packed smashes of Kimbrough. But this year, a 185-pound, broad-shouldered, strong-legged youngster by the name of Bob Smith, with two varsity years behind him, was taking his place beside "Big John" as one of the greatest backs in A&M history.

No less an authority than SMU's great Sammy Baugh, who watched Smith operate at fullback, announced that Smith was better than

Kimbrough. Baugh's observation was made after Smith's junior year, in which he totaled 1,302 yards—more than such immortals as Red Grange, Glenn Davis, Tommy Harmon, and Frank Sinkwich had gained in a single season.

Although line plunges were a necessary part of Smith's backfield duties, Bob truly was more halfback than fullback. He had speed to burn and the balance of a tightrope walker, a combination that typically left would-be tacklers clutching fistfuls of air. Smith was what some coaches call a "puller;" that is, a back who was always looking for that extra yard and never knew when he was tackled. Even when it appeared that he was finally stopped for good, he was still trying to extricate himself from the pile of arms and legs and head for the goal line.

"He was a fabulous runner," remembers Yale Lary, a former Fort Worth prep star who was Smith's teammate for three years at A&M and then later for a season with the Detroit Lions. "He'd burst through the line . . . hesitate . . . then break loose like a charging bull."

Bob Smith didn't start out his high school career to be a football player. As a prep, the six-foot Lamar High flash was an outstanding sprinter and broad-jump star, but when the grid coach saw Smith's speed and jumping ability, he had him go out for football. In 1946 Smitty led the Houston City Conference in rushing and scoring and was one of the most popular players on the squad.

Smith enrolled at A&M in February 1948 and took part in spring training, but his grades made him ineligible that fall. Throughout the 1948 season, however, Bob was on the "B" team, taking the bruises and blows of the defensive team against the varsity. Bob got another season of spring training in 1949, before he played with the varsity in the fall of 1949. But in 1950, Smith's play sparked the Aggies' victories over Nevada, in the season's opening game by a 48–18 score, and over Texas Tech 34–13.

In each of the games, Smitty broke loose for several big gains and sparked his team to victory over squads that were favored to defeat the Aggies.

Against Oklahoma, rated second to Notre Dame in the 1949 national ranking, the Aggies appeared on the way to their biggest win in five

By 1950, Stiteler had assembled a fleet of talented offensive players who could execute with near deadly precision his sometimes unorthodox, always intricate plays. Led by all-SWC lineman Max Greiner, Andy Hillhouse, and Carl Molberg, and the incomparable All-American fullback Bob Smith, the Aggies amassed 344 points (the most since 1912) en route to a 7–4 mark. A tremendous broken field runner, Smith rambled to 297 yards (plus two runs of more than 70 yards) against SMU that year, still the A&M record. He was often mentioned in the same breath as Red Grange and Tommy Harmon, rarified air indeed!

A quartet of A&M backfield stars who beat Georgia 40–20 in the Presidential Cup Game in Washington D.C. in 1950, A&M's first bowl victory since the 1940 Cotton Bowl. From left: right halfback Billy Tidwell, quarterback Dick Gardemal, fullback Bob Smith, and left halfback Glenn Lippman. To confuse the Georgia defense, Stiteler had Lippman call the signals from his halfback position, a move that clearly worked. Smith punctuated his outstanding season with a 100-yard kickoff return and an 80-yard touchdown run.

years. Tremendous plays by Smitty, Bill Tidwell, and Glenn Lippman had the Aggies in front 28–20 with just four minutes left to play. But within a minute, the Sooners, led by all-American Billy Vessels, scored a touchdown but failed to make the conversion, leaving A&M in front by a point.

The Aggies had to punt with just 1:30 to go in the game, and the Sooners took over. Four great passes put Oklahoma on the fourteen-yard line, where Leon Heath drove across the goal line for the winning score, 34–28.

The Aggies beat Virginia Military Institute 52–0, and the following week, they defeated TCU in a shootout, 42–23.

In the Baylor game, Smith took the ball on the first play from scrimmage, broke through his right tackle, outdistanced three defenders, and

A&M beat Oklahoma 14–7 for its third straight win to open the 1951 season. Here's the game program.

Following the 1950 season, Harry Stiteler resigned as head coach for reasons that were never quite clear. Raymond George (shown here demonstrating to his backfield how to protect the ball) assumed the head coaching job in 1951. Led by Bob Smith, all-conference backs Yale Lary and Glenn Lippman, and tackle Jack Little, George's first team beat Texas in a thriller, 22–21, snapping an 11-game winless streak against the 'Horns.

raced sixty-six yards for the score. In the second period, Smitty was gang-tackled, suffered a broken nose, and was taken out of the game and did not return. The Aggies played the rest of the game as if they were dazed by their misfortune and fumbled the ball five times as Larry Isbell passed Baylor to a 27–20 win.

In the game against SMU, the Aggies were trailing 20–19 when Coach Stiteler told Smith to "saddle up." Smith entered the game with a grotesque black mask to protect his broken nose. With less than five minutes to play in the seesaw battle, Sikes faked a pass and handed the ball to Smith. Smitty—dubbed "the Masked Marvel" by his teammates—took the ball, broke through the secondary, and sped seventy-three yards for a touchdown that gave A&M a sensational 25–20 victory. Smith's rushing record of 297 yards for the day still stands.

A&M had a wonderful opportunity to end the season on a victorious note as they went into the Rice game with a 6–2 record. But losses to Rice, 21–13, and Texas, 17–0, cast a pall of anguish over the Aggie campus and clouded Coach Stiteler's future.

While the Aggies' head coach pondered his fate, the committee handling the inaugural Presidential Cup Game invited Texas A&M to Washington, D.C., to play the Georgia Bulldogs. Today, of course, bowl games are only slightly

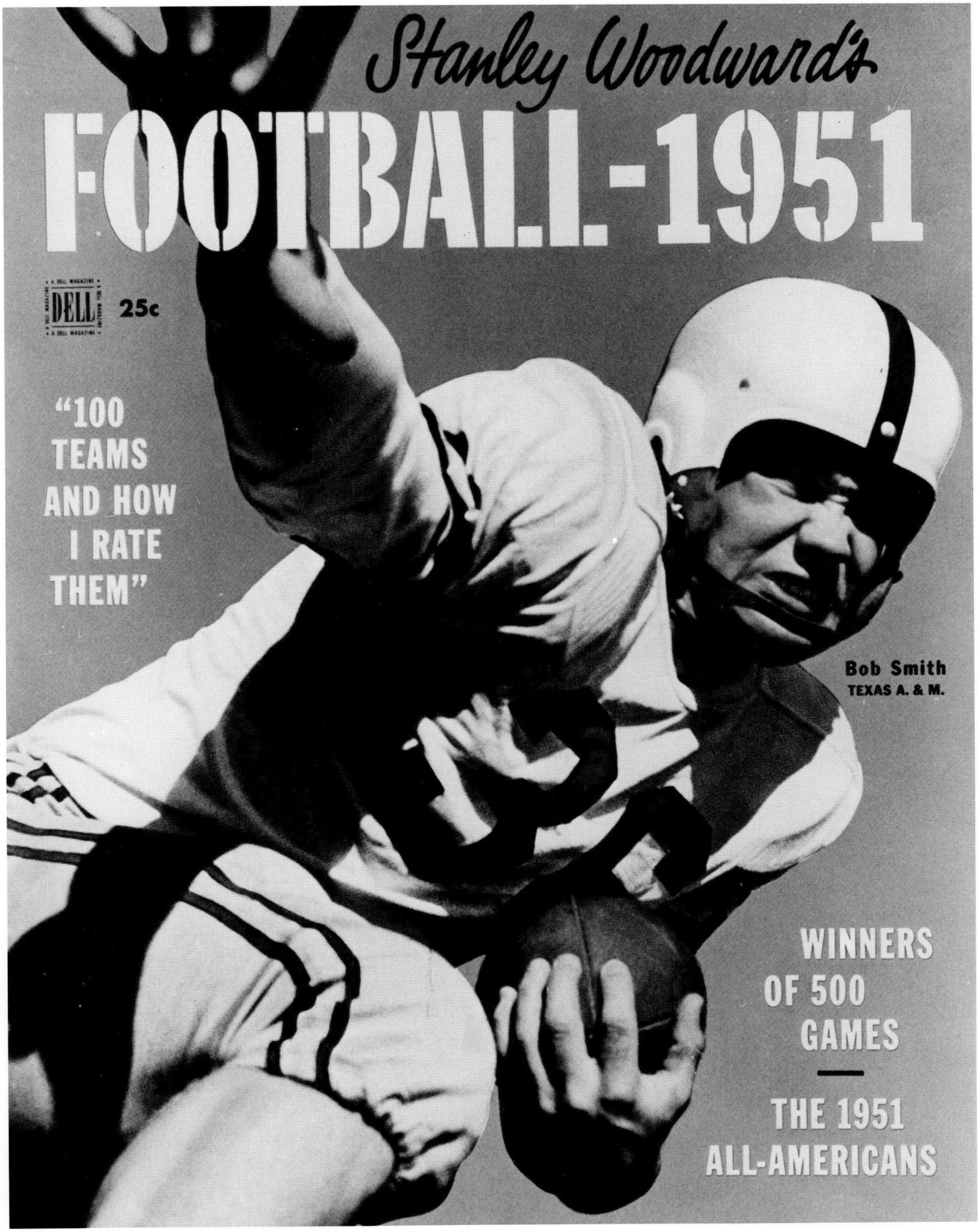

Stan Woodward, one of the nation's top sportswriters, called A&M's Bob Smith the "greatest player in the nation" in this football magazine in 1951.

less plentiful than softball trophies, but in prosperous postwar America the expansion of postseason games was just beginning. The Aggies eagerly accepted.

Georgia opened the contest by kicking off. Smith, playing deep, caught the ball, then dropped it on the three-yard line. The ball rolled behind the goal line, and by the time Smitty had picked up the ball, the Bulldogs were practically on top of him. He managed to extricate himself, though, cut through three tacklers, sped to the sideline, and broke clear. As Aggie blockers paved the way, Smith sprinted 100 yards on one of the most electrifying TD runs of his career. As he returned to the bench after his run, the crowd roared a standing tribute to this great star.

Then with the game but two minutes old, Dick Gardemal tossed a high-arching pass to halfback Glenn Lippman, who scored the Aggies' second touchdown. Then Fowler recovered a Georgia fumble, and on the next play, Smith, from the twenty-yard line, broke into the clear once more, this time for eighty yards and another score for a 20–0 lead. Bill Tidwell added three more touchdowns to give the Aggies a 40–0 lead going into the fourth period. The Bulldogs finally posted 20 points as Stiteler played every member of the A&M squad.

Jack Little earned all-American honors as a tackle in 1951 and 1952, the third two-time all-American in Aggie history. Little went on to star for the Baltimore Colts of the NFL.

Smith, a unanimous All-American choice and the Texas Sportswriters Association's pick as Texas Athlete of the Year, had a huge day. He rushed for 160 yards on twenty carries and added 120 more yards on punt returns. Bill Tidwell played his greatest game as an Aggie, as everything clicked for A&M.

Well, almost everything. As the whooping and hollering Aggies trooped into the dressing room, fresh from a convincing 40–20 victory in the first (and only) Presidential Cup Game, they discovered that somebody had broken into their lockers and rifled through their wallets. Center Hugh Meyer, who had stashed his money in his shoe, was the only Aggie not to get ripped off. Eventually, a soft-hearted congressman saw to it that the players were compensated for their losses.

Coach Stiteler, who had just coached the Aggies to a 7–4 season, their best record since 1944, wasn't as fortunate. He lost his job.

Ray George was born in St. Louis and graduated from Loyola High School in California, where he won four letters in football, developing into one of the best tackles in high school ball. He also won three letters in track and three in baseball as a catcher, and in 1938 was voted University of Southern California's outstanding athlete.

George, who was six-one, 263 pounds, decided to play professional football with Detroit. He later coached a high school football team to an undefeated season. George entered the Navy in 1942, spent time aboard an aircraft carrier in the Pacific, and was discharged in 1945. He played one year with the LA Bulldogs, then joined the USC staff as line coach, and in 1949, was named chief assistant to head coach Jeff Cravath.

George joined the A&M coaching staff in 1950, and in 1951 he was named head coach, succeeding Harry Stiteler, who had two unproductive seasons.

In the opening game of the season at Los Angeles, A&M took to the air against UCLA as quarterbacks Dick Gardemal and Ray Graves completed fifteen of twenty-seven passes for 243 yards and three touchdowns to down UCLA 21–14. Texas Tech was A&M's next victim as Gardemal, Graves, and halfback Glenn Lippman starred to give the Aggies a 20–7 win.

When the Aggies knocked off defending champion Oklahoma 14–7, they commanded national attention and that big win spurred the team on to a 53–14 rout of Trinity the following week.

Glenn Lippman, talking about the win over the Sooners, the 1950 national champions, said: "We had been hoping that they would still be undefeated; however, they had lost to Kentucky after winning thirty-one games in a row. Our team played one of the best games we had played during the three years I've been here, and we were sure that we could go on to a great season.

"But we might have been a bit cocky after the Oklahoma win and the rout of Trinity. We were beaten by TCU, and Baylor held us to a 21–21 tie that was a heartbreaker. Then we lost to Arkansas and tied SMU 14–14. Rice beat us 28–13, and then we got ready to play our big Thanksgiving Day game against Texas. The Longhorns, with a big 7–2 record for the season, were a 4–1 favorite."

BILL "JITTERBUG" HENDERSON '43
Most Versatile Athlete in A&M History
Texas A&M Athletic Hall of Fame
Texas Sports Hall of Fame

The following is a list of the accomplishments of Texas A&M's most extraordinary athlete—Bill "Jitterbug" Henderson. Elected to the Texas Legislature in 1952, Jitterbug, the nickname came from his winning a dance contest, belongs among the pantheons of not only Texas A&M athletes but all athletes in and out of Texas. One opponent he couldn't beat, however, was multiple sclerosis, which took the World War II veteran's life in 1955—a great loss to A&M and all of Texas.

- *Eleven Letters in five sports—football, basketball, baseball, track, swimming. Three freshman letters in addition.*
- *Three football Letters as end on the 1940–1942 teams. All-SWC 1942. The 1941 team was SWC champion, and the 1940 team was SWC co-champion.*
- *Three Letters in track 1941-1943, winning or placing in five events as follows:*

  First place in the discus and javelin at the SWC meet, second place in the shot put, third place tie in the high jump, to lead the Aggies to the 1943 SWC championship. Second place in the 880 and fourth in the javelin in 1941. Third place in the high jump and fourth in the shot put in 1942.

- *Captain of the 1942 basketball team. Three letters.*
- *Intramural boxing and handball champion to fill in his spare time.*
- *Elected in 1964 to Texas A&M Athletic Hall of Fame.*
- *Elected to the Texas Sports Hall of Fame, now in Waco, in 1974.*
- *The first dorm built especially to house athletes in 1958 was named Handerson Hall in honor of Bill "Jitterbug" Henderson.*

On the opening kickoff against Texas, Bob Smith took the ball and attempted to burst through three Longhorn tacklers. He was hit hard, knocked out, and was taken to the sidelines, where it was discovered he had a broken jaw. Lippman came in to play for Smith, and he enjoyed the finest game of his career, gaining 174 yards rushing.

The Aggies scored first, but Texas came storming back to take a 14–7 halftime lead. In the third period, Yale Lary sprinted sixty-eight yards for a score. Later, a thirty-one-yard field goal by Darrow Hooper, plus a brilliant catch by Lary of a tipped pass put the Aggies in front, 22–21.

Then, with thirty seconds to play, Jim Davis of Texas attempted a field goal from the Aggies' twenty-two-yard line. The kick was up, and it looked good—but a gust of wind pulled the ball wide of the post, and the Aggies had at last beaten their bitterest rival for the first time since 1939. And Ray George, thanks to a 5–3–2 season, was asked to return as coach.

Ray George counted a total of twenty-five lettermen reporting for the first fall practice session in 1952, headed by quarterback Ray Graves, halfback Don Ellis, and an all-American nominee in tackle Jack Little. It appeared, on paper at least, that the Aggies would have a solid season.

Against Houston in the opening game of the season, the Graves-to-Ellis combination proved too much for the Cougars as A&M began the game with a sixty-seven-yard TD drive. In the second period, Graves found Ellis for a second touchdown. In the third quarter, with Ellis picking up yardage on the ground and then passing to Graves, the Aggies moved sixty-three yards for another score to finish off the Cougars 21–13.

In the second game of the year, A&M and Oklahoma were stuck in a bruising battle with both teams fighting tooth and nail for any advantage, but the score remained tied at 7–7. In the third period, Don Kachtik broke through for a touchdown to give the Aggies a 14–7 win over a very strong Sooner eleven.

The Kentucky Wildcats surprised A&M by taking a close 10–7 win, and then Michigan State, the number one team in the nation, displayed awesome power and drubbed the Aggies 48–6. TCU then tied A&M, 7–7, and Baylor just managed a 21–20 win over the Aggies.

A&M then regrouped and played its best game of the year, a 31–12 win over Arkansas. The Aggies applied the power to jump ahead at the half, 19–6. But the Razorbacks came back with another touchdown to make the score 19–12 in the third period. However, A&M's Graves passed twice to Ellis for touchdowns to put the game out of reach.

Graves played the best game of his career, completing nineteen of thirty-one passes for three touchdowns—all of them to his favorite receiver, Don Ellis.

In the final game of the season, the SWC champion Longhorns methodically buried the Aggies, rushing for 428 yards and five touchdowns, 32–12.

The loss to Texas gave A&M another losing season, 3–6–1.

The loss to Texas on November 27, 1952, was significant in one respect. The Thanksgiving Day contest marked the first time an Aggies game had been broadcast on that fledgling medium known as television. Technology for bringing the sights and sounds of faraway events into one's living room had existed since the late 1930s, but World War II had temporarily halted its development. Now, in the postwar boom, antennas sprouted like dandelions on rooftops across America. In 1948 the percentage of U.S. homes with at least one television set stood at a meager 1 percent; by 1953 half of all American households were wired into the one-eyed box. Today more than 98 percent of U.S. homes have television. Rather than cut into attendance, as some school officials originally feared, broadcasts have helped spread the popularity of Aggie football, introducing it into corners of the country that just a few decades earlier had never heard of, much less seen, Kyle Field.

Ray George shook up his Aggies for the 1953 season, and it appeared that when he switched halfback Don Ellis to the quarterback spot, it was an outstanding move.

In the first game of the season, against a top-rated Kentucky squad, Ellis's pinpoint passes were on the money on four occasions, but just when the Aggies seemed on the verge of scoring, the Wildcats would keep them at bay—on the four-yard line, then the twenty, then the nine. Late in the fourth period, both teams finally scored touchdowns. The difference was that A&M's Joe Boring converted his extra point as the Aggies won 7–6.

Against Houston in game No. 2, Ellis was red-hot. He completed fifteen of twenty-six pass attempts in a 14–14 tie. Then a week later, against a highly touted Georgia Bulldog squad led by quarterback Zeke Bratkowski, the Bulldogs scored first. A&M tied the game with Ellis scoring a touchdown, and Georgia scored once more to go up 12–7. But Johnny Salyer grabbed a fifteen-yard Ellis pass to score for A&M in the final period to cap a 14–12 victory.

Once again it was Don Ellis pitching passes and Billy Huddleston scoring touchdowns in a 27–14 win over Texas Tech.

Next the Aggies captured their fourth win in five games, 20–7 over TCU.

Don Ellis completed eleven of nineteen passes for 178 yards and a touchdown against a favored Baylor team, but the Bears made good on both extra points, while A&M didn't, in a 14–13 Baylor triumph.

Against the Arkansas Razorbacks, the Aggies were outmanned as halfback Lamar McHan kicked, passed, and ran wild in a 41–14 win.

Next stop was Rice, where a homecoming crowd of 58,000 howled with delight as the Owls intercepted seven Aggie passes and turned them into two touchdowns for a 34–7 win, their ninth straight over A&M.

In the final game of the season, on Thanksgiving Day, Texas, victors over Villanova, Houston, Arkansas, SMU, Baylor, and TCU, rolled into College Station with a heavier, more experienced, and confident squad and managed to outpunch A&M after a rugged afternoon, scoring a 21–12 victory in the annual battle. Don Ellis, A&M's fine quarterback, had a hand in two touchdowns, but in the final period, Texas simply wore down the Aggies.

The loss to Texas gave A&M another losing season and a record of 4–5–1. It also marked the end of Ray George's brief stint as A&M coach. Now, the search was on for a "name" coach, preferably one with a bit of a growl.

8

BEAR ESSENTIALS

It was altogether fitting that the Paul "Bear" Bryant era at Texas A&M was unofficially launched from the stage of the Grove outdoor theater. It was February 8, 1954, and more than 3,000 cadets and Aggie fans had waited patiently for several hours for the school's new football coach and athletic director to arrive at Easterwood Airport. At 8 o'clock in the evening the flight had finally arrived, five hours late, but the crowd didn't care. It cheered like crazy for the man who had been hired to rebuild their crumbled football fortunes, then escorted him to the student center, where he signed the register to another explosion of hurrahs.

Then it was on to center stage to deliver some of that old-time religion to the adoring masses. No fire-and-brimstone preacher ever worked a crowd better than Bear Bryant. He dramatically ripped off his jacket and tie, fired them to the ground, then stomped them into smithereens. The students went wild, the swelling noise sweeping across campus like a prairie fire. Bryant capped his speech: "And we're going to beat those Texas Longhorns this year and every year!" whereupon the crowd raised one final, mighty roar that, if it didn't shatter windows in Austin, wasn't for lack of trying.

"I guess today you could use the word 'theatrical' to describe Coach Bryant," says Charlie Milstead, one of his early recruits. "But back then we just called it motivation."

Paul Bryant was nothing if not motivated. Born September 11, 1913, near Fordyce, Arkansas, he quickly learned that if he wanted to stay ahead of his eleven brothers and sisters, to say nothing of the rest of the world, he had better think, run and act faster than the competition. Ironically, Fordyce's version of a perpetual motion machine never saw a football game until he played in one, the local cobbler putting cleats on his shoes for a high school contest. The young tackle gained considerable notoriety because of his size—6-3, 210 pounds—his enthusiasm, and his aggressiveness. He was eventually recruited for the University of Alabama.

It was at a local circus that Bryant, a girlfriend, and some pals watched a bear wrestle a circus performer. When the promoter offered twenty-five dollars to any person in the audience who would wrestle the bear, Bryant, wanting the prize money, and responding to the taunts of his pals, accepted the challenge and did wrestle the bear.

Bryant threw a football block at the bear and succeeded in flooring it. Then he jumped onto the bear's back and was declared the winner. From that day on, he was named Bear Bryant. But he never collected the prize money, for the

Following back-to-back losing seasons, Raymond George fell into disfavor with the Aggie faithful who yearned for a return to the glory days. A&M officials looked to Kentucky, where they lured the up-and-coming Bear Bryant to College Station. After a miserable 1954 season, Bryant had the Aggies battling for conference and national honors by his second season.

circus promoter promptly left in the middle of the night.

At Alabama, Bryant was known as the "other end," because of the great Don Hutson, who was also a member of those great Alabama teams that went 23–3–2 during a three-year period. Bryant was a prominent member of the 1934 Alabama team that beat Stanford 29–13 in the Rose Bowl.

Upon graduation from Alabama, Bryant served four years as a Tide assistant under Frank Thomas, then went to Vanderbilt and, after the 1941 season, into the Navy.

Following his discharge from the Navy, Bryant took the head coaching post at Maryland, and in his first year in 1945, the Terrapins went 6–2–1—their best season in years. Then Bear went to Kentucky, where in eight seasons his teams went 60–23–5, won the only SEC title in Wildcat history, and played in four post-season bowl games.

In 1954, Texas A&M called and Bryant answered.

Bryant called upon his top-notch staff at Kentucky and brought in as assistants Jerry Claiborne, Pat James, and Phil Cutchin, and as trainer, Smoky Harper. Then he brought in Jim Owen from Oklahoma, along with Tom Tibbs and Elmer Smith, to head his recruiting efforts. Among Smith's recruits was big John David Crow of Springhill, Louisiana, who would go on to become one of the greatest backs in A&M history, an all-American, and a Heisman Award winner in 1957.

Bryant was shocked the first time he gathered his squad together for practice. He thought if there were seventy-five players on scholarship, there had to be at least fifteen first-rate players. He reversed his thinking, however, when he began working with the remnants of a team that had posted a 4–5–1 record in 1953.

"I remember two things about that first spring practice," said Gene Stallings, a freshman at the time, who was destined to be head coach at his alma mater. "It was a tough practice and it was even tougher because we had to practice at night. Coach went to the ROTC authorities in an effort to get us excused from drill in the afternoon, but they refused him and we had to practice after drill and after classes. It was murder.

"When we reported for the regular fall practice, Coach Bryant told us to get a blanket, pillow, and several changes of clothing because we were going on a trip. None of the players had any idea where we were going. We wound up at the Junction camp. We were out on the field each practice day before the sun came up. Then we would go to breakfast. We would practice in the afternoon, then a meeting at night. And pretty soon some of the players began to quit."

The manpower situation became so critical after three centers quit the squad that Bryant promptly issued a uniform to Troy Summerlin, a 150-pound student-manager who had played high school ball. Another example of calling on the Twelfth Man.

Bryant was a contact coach, meaning his practices emphasized the physical. No one was

Coach Bryant and his top-notch staff in 1954. From left, top row: Babe Parilli, Phil Cutchins, Elmer Smith, Willie Zapalac, Jim Owens. Bottom row: Tom Tipps, Jerry Clairborne, Bryant, and Pat James.

exempt from the hitting drills, which undoubtedly contributed to the high attrition rate.

"We had planned to stay at Junction longer," said Stallings, "but we ran out of players. We went out in two buses and came back in one. We never knew how many players we had for practice."

The tough training at the Junction camp established a standard of toughness that all future Aggies could count on. Throughout his career, however, Bryant's methods remained under fire. For example, those players who were injured—allegedly injured, Bear thought—were forced to wear Red Cross shirts. The embarrassment accelerated the healing process. "Coach thought there was a big difference between hurting and actually being hurt," says Charlie Milstead, who played two seasons under Bryant.

Milstead, a star quarterback at Tyler High School, today acknowledges Bryant's reputation as a disciplinarian and a motivator.

"He had a tremendous, unbelievable presence," Milstead marvels. "And he was a great salesman. I remember when he came out to the house to recruit me. My parents were awed by him. You know, I came from a Christian, church-going family. He'd stand up when my mother left or entered the room, and he allowed no cursing on the field. That won my folks over."

A&M's 1955 honorary captains (all seniors). The team posted a 7–2–1 record, the Aggies' best since 1943.

Bryant was true to his word. Any player who cursed was required to drop a dollar into a bucket; assistant coaches paid two dollars. And when Bear slipped up, it cost him five dollars.

"All that money was supposed to go towards a team party at the end of the season," Milstead laughs. "But I don't remember any parties."

There certainly wasn't much celebrating the first season of the Bear Bryant regime. In the opening game of the 1954 campaign, the Aggies scored first against Texas Tech, but didn't have the weight or experience to maintain momentum. A&M was steamrollered, 41–9. The Aggies wound up winning only once, a 6–0 squeaker over Georgia. Less than a year after his fire-breathing speech at the Grove podium, cadets, alumni and media were howling for Bryant's scalp and demanding explanations.

"Come around, see me next year," was his explanation. "We're building a winner here and it will pay off with time."

Bryant was optimistic about his prospects in 1955 because he knew the potential of the great prospects his coaches had recruited. Among them were John David Crow, Charley Krueger, Ken Hall, Loyd Taylor, Jim Wright, Bobby Marks, Roddy Osborne, and Bobby Joe Conrad. They were all future all-stars.

In the opening game at Los Angeles, UCLA, national champ in 1954, used the passing of Ronnie Knox to defeat A&M 21–0.

A&M did manage to recover a Bruin fumble on the twenty-two-yard line, but a penalty stopped the A&M threat, and UCLA was never in trouble after that play. Don Grant, Jack Pardee, and Gene Stallings were standout performers for the Aggies.

Unleashing a furious ground game, the Aggies crushed a strong LSU eleven 28–0 as Jack Pardee scored a touchdown in the first period, then went on a sixty-five-yard jaunt before bulling over from the two-yard line. In the third period, John David Crow sped seventy-seven yards for one TD, then added another.

In the next game, with three minutes to go in the third period and Houston leading the Aggies

John David Crow, carrying the ball against LSU in a 1955 game won by the Aggies 28–0. Crow scored two touchdowns that day, a portend of his greatness.

3–0, A&M struck quickly for three touchdowns and a brilliant 21–3 win.

The following week, the Aggies rolled into nineteenth place in the national team rankings after a convincing 27–0 win over the Nebraska Cornhuskers. Don Grant smashed over from the one-yard line for the first score. Then fullback George Gillar intercepted a pass, sprinted thirty yards to the Nebraska thirty-seven. Four plays later, Gillar sped twenty-six yards for a second tally. Then Don Grant passed eight yards to Ed Dudley with twenty-five seconds left in the half to climax an eighty-seven-yard march for a third A&M touchdown. The Aggie reserves took over late and played Nebraska off their feet. With eight seconds left in the game, Jim Wright blasted across the goal line for another A&M score and another victory.

The following week, the Aggies played their finest game of the season to come from behind and defeat the unbeaten TCU eleven in a 19–16 thriller. One week later, the Aggies upped their winning streak to five games as they battered the Baylor Bears 19–7. Jack Pardee was the big gun for the Aggies as he scored a touchdown and broke off several long runs to put the ball within scoring range.

Arkansas battled A&M tough in their big homecoming game at Fayetteville and played their hearts out, earning a 7–7 tie with the Aggies.

John David Crow remembers that game. "We were miserable," he said. "Everything that we tried went wrong. At halftime our dressing room was like a tomb. Coach Bryant walked in, threw out all the hangers-on and laced each and every one of us. He'd grab me and yell, 'Crow, better get going.' He'd call out a player's name, pick him out, shake him, and tell him what was wrong. We couldn't wait to get out on the field and play again."

Pardee played one of his best games against SMU the following week as he was all over the field on offense and defense. Jack picked up the longest run of the day, a forty-two-yard sprint that was turned into a touchdown and sparked the Aggies to a 13–2 win.

A twisting, turning run by back Bill Denby produces a dramatic touchdown in a 19–16 victory against TCU in 1955.

Next, the Rice Owls had the Aggies on the ropes by a 12–0 margin with only four minutes to play. Then the impossible happened.

First, halfback Loyd Taylor sped fifty-eight yards to the Rice three, then on the next play, Taylor scored a touchdown and made the extra point, and it was 12–7. Then Stallings recovered an onside kick on the Rice forty-three. On the next play, Jim Wright set himself and tossed a perfect strike to Taylor on the five-yard-line, and Taylor drove across for the second score. Taylor made the kick and it was A&M 14–12. Pardee tacked on insurance when he intercepted King Hill's pass to set up a Don Watson touchdown run that capped a great come-from-behind win, 20–12, which moved them up to tenth in the national polls.

In the final game of the season on Thanksgiving Day, A&M went into the big game against Texas needing only a tie with the 'Horns to be assured of a share of the SWC championship.

The Aggies scored first, driving eighty yards just before the half. Wright's pass to Crow for thirty-four yards down to the Texas one set up his own TD plunge. The conversion was missed and the 'Horns began to take charge of the game, scoring to take a 7–6 halftime lead.

In the second half, Texas dominated the game, holding the powerful Aggie offense to one first down the remainder of the game. Texas, meanwhile, scored two touchdowns to win 21–6.

The loss to Texas not withstanding, the Aggies (7–2–1) ended up with their best record in fifteen years. As Bryant told the cadets on his arrival in 1954, "I didn't come here to lose."

"Playing for Coach Bryant was a great experience, an experience that I treasure," Pardee said. "He took that 1954 team that finished with a 1–9 record and built it into a tough, smart, aggressive team, so that by 1956, with players like guard Dennis Goehring, Lloyd Hale, a center, end Bob Drake Keith, tackle Bobby Lockett, guard Dee Powell, Gene Stallings, halfback Don Watson, John David Crow, Roddy Osborne, and myself, and he had us playing like a well-oiled machine. I just knew that in 1956 we were going to have a great club."

The sports experts figured that the SWC race would end with TCU and Texas A&M ranking one-two in that order, just as they stood at the end of the 1955 campaign.

Fittingly, when the season opened, the Aggies ripped apart a strong Villanova squad 19–0. Late in the first period, Wright faked a run, then stopped short and pitched a thirty-yard pass to Taylor, who took the ball on the fifteen-yard line, then stiff-armed a tackler and sped over for a touchdown. In the second period, Murry Trimble recovered a Wildcat fumble on the Aggie forty-two, and in eleven carries, A&M picked up another touchdown as Crow scored from the seven to make it 13–0. In the final period, Crow picked off a Villanova pass. Osborne, Watson, and Gillar then took turns pounding the

Tenacious fullback Jack Pardee, an all-American both on and off the field in 1956, played one of his finest games in a 13–2 win over SMU in 1955. The win moved A&M up to tenth in the national polls.

Wildcat line for yardage, Gillar scoring the final touchdown to ice a 19–0 victory.

The Aggies, showing the same fight and spirit that won seven games for them in 1955, scored early on a touchdown and a field goal and outlasted LSU 9–6.

The next week, end Gene Stallings recovered a Texas Tech fumble on the Raiders' thirteen-yard line. On the next play, Crow smashed across the line for a touchdown, and it was 7–0 with Taylor's extra point. Then Bobby Joe Conrad scored a touchdown in the second period and Jim Wright passed to Don Watson for a third score, and at halftime it was 21–0. Then Pardee and Crow teamed up with runs of twelve and seventeen yards before Crow scored on a pass from Wright to give the Aggies a 40–7 win.

In game No. 4, Houston recovered an Aggie fumble on the twenty, and in six plays took a 7–0 lead. A&M then took the kickoff and drove upfield to the Houston six, but again fumbled the ball. Houston recovered but couldn't move the football. The Cougars punted, but the ball was partially blocked and John Tracey recovered and scored an Aggie touchdown to forge a 7–7 tie at the half.

In the third period, after the Aggies had held on their one-yard line, they moved with savage drives up the field. Then Osborne skirted around left end for a touchdown, and after the conversion, it was 14–7, A&M. But Houston came back to score a touchdown and make the conversion as time ran out and the game ended in a 14–14 tie.

In a game that was played in a driving rain and a wicked windstorm, the Aggies eked out a 7–6 victory over TCU as Watson led the Aggies on an eighty-yard drive in eight plays. On the final play of the drive, Watson passed to Crow for the game winner, the only A&M pass thrown that day.

In the dressing room after the game, sportswriters ganged up on Bryant and asked the question: "Bear, did it go according to plan?"

"No," said the coach, "it went according to prayer."

The next big test for the Aggies was against the Baylor Bears at Waco. "This game was one

All-Americans Charlie Krueger (tackle) and Dennis Goehring (guard) helped A&M end a long dry spell in 1956 when the Aggies won their first SWC title since 1941.

of the bloodiest, meanest I've ever seen," recalled Bryant. "The game was tied 13–13, and we got two great plays that gave us the game. On one of them, Roddy Osborne started an option to his left, but we had blocked for a counter the other way. But he was so quick, he just cut back and made about five yards. Then on fourth down and with all the marbles riding on this play, Crow said, 'Give me that darn ball and I'll put it over.' They did and he scored the touchdown that gave us a great 19–13 win.

"That win over Baylor gave us the impetus to win the next three games over Arkansas, SMU, and Rice, and then we were ready for the Longhorns."

For thirty-two years the Aggies had marched into Memorial Stadium on Thanksgiving Day in a vain attempt to defeat Texas.

But this time, favorites by sixteen points, the Aggies scored first, then added another score to give them a 13–0 lead in the second period. The Longhorns fought back on a forty-three-yard gallop by halfback Walt Fondren, but the Aggies quickly scored again. Again, Texas countered with a TD, this one with just three seconds before halftime to close the gap to 20–14.

The Aggies took the kickoff as the third period began and Jack Pardee scooped up the ball on the goal line. He shot through a huge hole, stiff-armed one tackler, hurdled another, and was away and streaking for another Aggie score when a Texas back tackled Pardee from behind on the Texas fifteen. Pardee's gallop of eighty-five yards had the big crowd screaming with excitement. Three plays later, Pardee went over for another A&M score and a 27–14 lead. One more touch-

"Give me that ball," said John David Crow in a tight game against Baylor in 1956, "and I'll score for you." They gave Crow the ball and he scored the winning touchdown.

down made it 34–14 before Texas came back with a tally of its own to close out the scoring in a 34–21 A&M win.

A&M finished with nineteen first downs and 336 yards rushing and seventy-eight passing. The Longhorns made fourteen first downs and gained a mere 135 yards rushing.

With the win over Texas, the Aggies had won their first SWC championship since 1941 and owned their first undefeated season since their national championship season in 1939.

The star of that 1956 squad was junior halfback John David Crow, who had racked up 561 yards rushing and scored ten touchdowns. A native of Springhill, Louisiana, Crow had been a high school all-American in football, basketball and track. In his junior year he had led the

Gene Stallings was a sure-handed end and captain of the 1956 team. The final chapter in Gene Stallings' association with A&M football would not be written until the late sixties.

Texas A&M Aggies, 1956 SWC champions and first undefeated A&M team since the national champs of 1939.

"I made some lousy moves in 1957," said Coach Bryant. "I should have had John David Crow at fullback, Bobby Joe Conrad at quarterback, and Richard Gay at center. We would have won two to three more games."

Springhill Lumberjacks to the Louisiana state football championship; the following year he led the basketball team to the state title.

Word of Crow's athleticism reached Texas A&M, which happily offered him a scholarship in 1954, the same year Bryant left Kentucky to become the Aggies' twentieth head football coach.

As a freshman, Crow was part of the "cannon fodder" that drilled with the varsity. His football heroics began in 1955, when the sophomore was involved in a play he still calls the greatest thrill of his career. With A&M leading LSU 14–0 in the third period, Crow took a handoff from Jim Wright, broke clear, and thundered seventy-seven yards for a touchdown. It was his first varsity score. The six-two, 215-pound back would go on to register eighteen more touchdowns in his Aggie career, acquiring college football's highest honor in the process.

While the 1956 Aggies were the top-rated team in the nation for most of the season and remain A&M's last undefeated team, Bear Bryant

A pivotal one-point win over TCU (who would finish second in the SWC in '56, one game behind A&M) triggers a wave of jubilation among players and fans. That's Crow (no. 44), Ken Hall (no. 30), and Dennis Goehring (no. 62) being carried off the field on the shoulders of Aggie Cadets.

thought his '57 squad was going to be even better. Bryant blamed himself for it not turning out that way.

"We lost three key players in the summer and I did a lousy job in not making the kind of changes I should have made," he later said. "I should have put John Crow in at fullback, so we could run the option both ways, Rod Osborne at left half, Bobby Joe Conrad at quarterback, and Richard Gay at center. I talked about these supposed changes all summer long, but I was talked out of it."

In the season opener against Maryland, the Aggies took the opening kickoff and marched sixty-four yards in nine plays for a touchdown. Then Maryland came right back and drove fifty-two yards for a score to tie it 7–7.

The second and third quarters were scoreless as both teams battled for position on the field and neither team had an advantage. Crow and Taylor were hurt in the early half of the game, and the Aggies' attack bogged down. But Rod Osborne suddenly found John Tracey alone downfield, fired a thirty-five yard pass to him, and Tracey scored the go-ahead touchdown. Maryland scored a second touchdown, but the try for the extra point was blocked by Osborne, and A&M had a 14–13 lead.

John David Crow hoists his Heisman trophy for photographers shortly after winning the award in 1957. Crow is the only Aggie to win college football's most coveted prize.

Then with five minutes left to play, sophomore back Charlie Milstead raced twenty-two yards, and A&M had its first win of the season, 21–13. In the second game, against Texas Tech, Milstead scored two touchdowns and Osborne scored another to give A&M a 21–0 win over a game, but outclassed, Raider squad.

At Columbia, Missouri, on October 5, the Aggies were held scoreless until the middle of the second period, when they picked up two touchdowns. Two more in the third completed a 28–0 defeat of Missouri. The highlight of the game was a spectacular ninety-one-yard run by Bobby Joe Conrad, who fairly burst off tackle and outdistanced all the Missouri defenders for a TD.

Then in rapid succession, the Aggies defeated TCU 7–0, Baylor 14–0, and Arkansas 7–6.

With only 1:20 left to play in the Arkansas game, Bryant sent in a substitute to tell Osborne to run out the clock. But on the next play, Osborne saw Crow open and tried to pass the ball to John David, but Don Horton of Arkansas intercepted the ball and raced sixty-four yards to the Aggies' twenty-seven before Osborne stopped him. Then, as the Razorbacks attempted a pass, Crow intercepted to save the game for the Aggies as time ran out.

Bryant talked about three plays after the game: "Horton was just running for a touchdown, but that Osborne was running for his life. Then that fella Crow made two of the greatest defensive plays I've ever seen in my life."

The Aggies defeated SMU in a tough showdown 19–6, and then, as A&M fans picked up their morning papers on November 16, they were delighted to find that the nation's sportswriters had voted A&M the number one team in the nation. But that news was overshadowed by the rumors that Bryant was planning to leave A&M to go to Alabama in 1958.

"The story was premature at the time," said Bryant. "Jack Gallagher, a sportswriter from Houston, called me the night before the game regarding a statement Alabama president, Dr. Frank Rose, had made. Rose had said he was going to get a coach with certain qualifications, which pointed to me. I think that story left the team with a letdown feeling and I think that contributed to the kind of game we played against Rice. Rice was very good, but we were down in this game, and Rice beat us 7–6 and went on to win the SWC championship."

Charlie Milstead agrees that Bryant's imminent departure, which he announced at a closed-door team meeting the Wednesday before the Rice game, demoralized the young Aggies. "There was a mixed reaction," he says. "Some didn't like him, but we all knew that as long as he was there we were going to win."

The demoralized Aggies battled rival Texas on the final afternoon of the conference schedule. Midway through a scoreless game, a poor punt gave Texas the ball on the Aggies' 33-yardline. The Longhorns needed eight plays to push the ball across the goal line for a 6–0 lead. A short time later, a field goal gave Texas a 9–0 advantage. The Aggies countered late in the game with a sixty-seven-yard TD drive, but it was too little, too late. The 9–7 loss gave A&M an 8–2 record.

Some good news followed. In the first week of December, Coach Bryant was notified by the Downtown Athletic Club in New York that John David Crow was a finalist for the Heisman Trophy. Playing both ways, the senior back had rushed for 562 yards and intercepted five passes as a linebacker. With more than 1,000 people on hand at the ceremonies, Crow was announced as the winner. His 1,267 votes were twice as many as the runnerup, Iowa tackle Alex Karras, had received.

In accepting the award, A&M's first—and only—Heisman winner said, "The number one person knows how much I thank him. I'll be looking back on this occasion as long as I live, and I hope to set an example for other high school boys who one day will receive the same support I have here tonight."

Then, as Crow fondled the handsome gold-and-black trophy, he added, "It all seems like a dream, and I want to sit down before I make a racket that might wake me up."

The Aggies closed out the year with a loss in the Gator Bowl to Tennessee. A record crowd of 43,709 watched as the two teams struggled on a muddy, rainswept field. With just 5:30 left in the game, Sammy Burklow kicked a seventeen-yard field goal to give Tennessee a narrow 3–0 victory. After being ranked number one earlier in the year, A&M had lost their last three games by a total of six points, dropping them to ninth in the final polls. More significantly, they had lost their coach to Alabama.

After a woeful 1–9 start in his first year, Bryant had guided the Aggies to a combined 24–5–1 record over the next three autumns. While Bryant would go on to cement his legend with the Crimson Tide, winning six national titles in twenty-five seasons, his name still evokes strong emotions at College Station. The ingredients of his success—discipline, dedication, perseverance, hard work—are life lessons for the young men who once suited up in maroon and white for him. Pupils like Crow, Stallings and Pardee went on to enjoy great success after leaving Texas A&M. All are in a position today to look back and, with more fondness than fear, recall their temperamental coach stomping around the field like a bear with a thistle in his paw.

"Anybody who has been around Bear Bryant left with something that you could carry with you," says Charlie Milstead, who played two professional seasons with the Houston Oilers before entering the business world. Not so coincidentally, the Oilers won their only two championships (both in the old AFL) with Milstead in the lineup. "That was the idea that no matter how tough things get in life, you don't allow yourself to get beat. You may lose once in a while, but you're never beaten."

Spoken like a true winner, which is the real legacy Bear Bryant left at A&M.

9

LOST CUBS

Jim Myers turned down the appointment to take over as football coach at A&M after he was told that A&M directors were opposed to him. But when a delegation of students presented him with a telegram that contained more than 2,000 Aggie signatures pleading with him to take the post, Myers accepted, the board agreed, and he became the Aggies' new football coach and athletic director in 1958.

Jim Myers was an outstanding football player at Iowa State in 1940, 1941, and 1942. He then entered the Marine Corps during World War II, played football in the Marine V-12 program and, upon his release from the Marines, finished his senior year at ISU. Upon graduation in 1947, Myers became an assistant coach at Wofford College, then moved up the ladder to Vanderbilt in 1948. Then Jim moved to UCLA, where he was an assistant coach. In 1949, he left UCLA to take over as head coach at Iowa State.

Myers took over at A&M with a group of seventeen solid lettermen led by an outstanding quarterback in Charlie Milstead and a fine pass receiver in John Tracey; fullback Gordon LeBoeuf; Ed Dudley, a fine halfback; and guard Allen Goehring. The Aggies were on track for the opening game of the 1958 season against Texas Tech.

Allen Goehring blocked a Tech punt early in the game and Milstead banged in from the ten-yard line for an Aggie touchdown and a 6–0 lead. In the third period, center Gale Oliver recovered a Tech fumble on the twenty-six-yard line, and a forty-yard drive led by Milstead paved the way to a second score, and Texas A&M had a 14–0 lead.

However, Tech came back, astonishingly, with two fourth-quarter touchdowns to rally for the win, 15–14.

Two conference losses, sandwiched between two nonconference victories, preceded one of the most heart-stopping games of the year.

Baylor was on its way to an easy win in its big homecoming game, leading 21–0 at the half. Then, in the third period, Milstead faked a pass to end John Tracey and drove through right tackle and outran three defenders for a spectacular seventy-seven yard touchdown. Now, it was a 27–7 game.

In the fourth quarter, Milstead began an aerial bombardment that produced three scores. With less than three minutes left the Aggies trailed only by a point, 27–26. With two minutes left, Milstead passed sixty-three yards to Luther Hall. Hall took the ball over his shoulder without breaking stride and galloped for a touchdown to seal a 33–27 victory that had the fans pouring out of their seats and onto the field to carry their heroic Aggies into the dressing room. It was one of those once-in-a-lifetime efforts, and it was a big upset.

Rice, the defending SWC champion, had beaten A&M in 1957, knocking the Aggies out of a Cotton Bowl shot. The 1958 Aggies were out for revenge and they achieved it by defeating the Owls in a thriller, 28–21.

Charlie Milstead was brilliant as he scored two touchdowns, passed for a third, and booted four extra points to give him a personal total of twenty-two points. Gordon LeBouef took a Rice punt and thrilled the huge crowd as he threaded his way fifty-four yards for the touchdown that won the game, thanks to a great last-second block by tackle Ken Beck that cleared the way for LeBouef.

Before a national TV audience on Thanksgiving Day, A&M faced a tough, aggressive Texas team coached by Darrell Royal, which had racked up five straight wins over the top teams in the nation. Texas, led by a young phenom, halfback Rene Ramirez, scored three touchdowns to lead Texas to a 27–0 win.

The loss concluded an unsuccessful 4–6 debut season for Myers.

In 1959 Coach Myers had a number of lettermen back including his passing ace, quarterback Charley Milstead; Gordon LeBouef, a fine running halfback; Randy Sims; Jerry Jenkins; tackle Darrell Dean, and Jack Estes.

The Aggies opened the season by dropping a close encounter to the Texas Tech Raiders 20–14. A week later, though, A&M upset vaunted Michigan State 9–7.

In the first period, A&M's Ralph Smith pounced on a State fumble on the ten-yard line, and in two plays, Milstead punched over for a touchdown. Another State fumble in the second period was recovered by A&M on the twenty. Then Randy Sims, the Aggie field-goal kicker, booted a thirty-one-yarder to give A&M a 9–0 lead they never relinquished.

Mississippi Southern kicked a twenty-two-yard field goal to start the scoring in its battle

The 1957 squad, led by the indomitable John David Crow. Despite Crow's Heisman feats, the Aggies slipped to third in the SWC and 8–3 overall, losing their last three games of the year.

Charlie Milstead, versatile back and captain of the 1959 Aggies.

against A&M, but Milstead scored a TD and A&M won 7–3.

The Aggies then stunned Houston 28–6 as Milstead, Randy Sims, LeBouef, and McGuire scored to give the Aggies their biggest win of the season.

Then, with several key players on the injury list, the Aggies dropped games to TCU, Baylor, Arkansas, SMU, and Texas. The Aggies led 10–0 at halftime, but Texas came back to win 20-17.

The loss to Texas, plus a season record of only three wins against seven losses and three ties, provoked a storm of protest against Myers, and it was only a matter of time that he would be gone . . . unless his next team could beat Texas.

Coach Jim Myers and his staff worked all through the months of January, February, and March, recruiting the top high school players in Texas, players who might step in and strengthen the poor offensive and defensive units of the past two years.

The biggest search by Myers was to find a quarterback to replace Charlie Milstead, who had guided the Aggies offense from 1957 to 1959. Milstead was a solid veteran who could pass, run, and handle his players. But Myers just couldn't find a suitable replacement. Babe Craig, Jack Estes, Daryle Keeling, and Powell Barry were at various times tried at quarterback, but none of the four players solved the problem.

The line was just as much a problem as the quarterback puzzle. Myers tried various sophomore prospects, switching them from position to position, but the defense was just as limited as the Aggies offense.

As a result, the Aggies were able to win but once, against Trinity 14–0, while dropping games to LSU, Houston, Baylor, Arkansas, Rice, and Texas. There were ties with Texas Tech, TCU, and SMU.

The cadets and alumni were now howling for a change as the Aggies ended a dismal 1–6–3 season in 1960.

In 1961 Jim Myers still had a quarterback problem and tried Babe Craig, John Erickson, Jim Keller, Ron Brice, and Jim Linnstaedter during the year at quarterback as they were shuttled in and out of games as the season went on.

Jim Keller started at quarterback in the first game of the season against Houston, rated No. 10 in the nation, and the Aggies surprised even their most fervent admirers by playing the Cougars dead-even. Houston scored in the first period, shortly after recovering an Aggie fumble on their eight-yard line.

The Aggies' score came late in the fourth quarter, after a drive sparked by quarterback Keller. The Aggies went fifty-four yards in eleven plays to score the touchdown. Then, while a large crowd held its breath, Daryle Keeling calmly kicked the extra point to tie the game 7–7 as time ran out.

Texas A&M did not win the game, but its play against a top-rated team boosted the entire squad. LSU dashed the hopes of the Aggies in the second game as the Tigers won 16–7.

Four quarterbacks had a hand in the game against Texas Tech as Erickson, Brice, Linnstaedter, and Jim Keller took turns spearheading the Aggie offense. The four quarterbacks completed twelve of fifteen passes as the Aggies romped in their best effort in five years to post a 38–7 win over Tech. Ron Brice was particularly effective in the second period as he completed five passes for two touchdowns.

In the game against Trinity, the Aggies rolled to their most impressive win since they crushed Miami in 1944 55–0. Every man on the roster got playing time as Travis Reagan sparkled with three touchdowns. Linnstaedter, Murphy, Lee Roy Caffey, Erickson, and Ron Ledbetter each scored a TD, while Daryle Keeling kicked five extra points and Mike Clark added two conversions.

Misfortune plagued the Aggies in their game against TCU as the Frogs came from behind in the final three minutes of play to kick a thirty-yard field goal and squeak past A&M by a 15–14 margin. The Aggies held a 7–0 halftime lead, but TCU scored a touchdown in the third period to make it 7–6. A&M then stormed sixty-seven yards for another touchdown, and it was 14–6. A forty-four-yard TCU TD pass and a field goal gave the Frogs a come-from-behind win.

In the Baylor game, A&M kicked off to the Bears, and when Baylor fumbled the kickoff, A&M recovered the ball, failed to gain yardage, and on fourth down, Erickson kicked a field goal for a 3–0 lead. When the Aggies got possession of the ball on the next exchange of downs, George Hargett passed to Keeling and then to Jerry Rogers, both passes for sixteen yards. Then Erickson went over for a touchdown, and it was 9–0 A&M at halftime. In the third period, Rogers and Lee Roy Caffey sparked a sixty-eight-yard drive for another score. Then in the final moments of the game, the Aggies scored once again and wrapped up a convincing 23–0 win over Baylor.

In the game against Arkansas, the Aggies looked as if they were finally on the move after four wins in the previous five games. They scored quickly against the Hogs to take an 8–7 lead, which they held stubbornly into the fourth period. But the Hogs came back late in the period with a furious attack. They drove ninety yards for a score and took a 15–8 win over A&M as the final gun sounded.

Rebounding from the loss to Arkansas, A&M played its best game of the year as it rallied in the last period to score two touchdowns to defeat SMU 25–12. A&M's three quarterbacks—Keller, Brice, and Erickson—were outstanding as they took turns leading the Aggie offense.

The tough game against SMU resulted in injuries to several players, helping explain losses to Rice and to the Longhorns, and A&M closed out another unhappy season with a record of 4–5–1. As a result of his four losing seasons, Coach Jim Myers was out and a new coach, Hank Foldberg, was in.

An all-American at West Point under Coach Red Blaik, Hank Foldberg had played with A&M during the 1941–42 seasons. He then transferred to Army, where he became a great lineman for the Black Knights.

Hank Foldberg's immediate problem was to come up with a quarterback who could run and pass and lead the team to some wins in 1962. But Foldberg had no more luck than Jim Myers and, although Hank tried out four different men at the quarterback post, the Aggies could not generate a significant offense all year long.

The new coach tried to utilize Jim Keller, John Erickson, Jim Willenborg, and Dan McIlhany at various times during the year, but none of those players had positive leadership qualities.

Consequently, the Aggies dropped the opening game to LSU 21–0, then lost to Houston 6–3. But in the third game, against Texas Tech, Dan McIlhany wrote a storybook ending that was typical of the traditional Aggie fourth quarter.

McIlhany took a Tech kickoff, after Tech had managed a field goal to take a 3–0 lead with less than a minute remaining in the game, and caught the ball two yards behind his own goal line. Dan managed to sidestep two tacklers, break into the clear along the right sideline, and sprint 102 yards for a touchdown. McIlhany's fantastic run got the cadets so excited, they charged out onto the gridiron, carried Dan and other players on their shoulders and paraded about for fifteen minutes before they were ordered off the field. The Aggies had their first win, 7–3.

Three losses followed before the Aggies defeated Baylor 6–3. Mike Clark's two field goals provided the win.

Big Mike Clark and his magic toe provided the weapon that upset SMU in the fourth period of the next game. Clark booted two field goals within minutes of each other, after the Mustangs had taken a 7–6 halftime lead. Clark's two field goals gave A&M a 12–7 victory.

The Rice Owls jogged into Rice Stadium and sprinted out 23–3 winners against A&M in a lackluster game. Clark's thirty-eight-yard field goal was the highlight of a poor Aggies offense that saw A&M reach as far as the Owls' twenty-three-yard line just once.

Three Aggie stars, 1957–1959. Charlie Milstead, receiver John Tracey and Ken Beck, tackle and SWC all-Star.

In the Thanksgiving Day battle against Texas, the Aggies played their finest defensive game of the year and Clark booted a field goal to give A&M a 3–0 lead at halftime. The Aggie offense sputtered all day, though, and in the second half, the Longhorns put two touchdowns on the board to come away with a 13–3 victory.

"We were very close to being a good football team, if our passing was at least average," Foldberg said. "But it wasn't even that. It was a combination of everything, poor blocking, poor passing, and poor receiving."

The 3–7 season in 1962 was the fifth losing year in a row for the Aggies, and it appeared that Coach Foldberg had little to look forward to in 1963.

In spring practice of 1963, Foldberg tried eleven different candidates for the quarterback position before he settled on Jim Keller, who had played that position with the 1961 and '62 teams.

But in the opening game against LSU, Keller sat on the bench as Charlie LaGrange, the sixth-ranked quarterback on the roster, took over in the fourth period to move the Aggies to their lone touchdown with a twenty-three-yard pass to Travis Reagan and a pass to Billy Uzzell, who flipped a lateral to Reagan for the score. It was the Aggies' lone score of the day, but it wasn't enough as LSU ran for two touchdowns and a 14–6 win.

Before a crowd of 81,000, Ohio State ground out a 17–0 win over the Aggies, who were never

The era between Bear Bryant and Gene Stallings was one of struggle: no winning seasons and seven straight defeats to Texas. The '63 contest against t.u. (eventual national champs), however, was a taut battle that ended with the Horns surviving a scare 15–13. Here Travis Reagan makes a dash for the A&M goal line.

JAMES EARL RUDDER '32
Major General, U. S. Army Reserves
President - Texas A&M University

James Earl Rudder played center for Texas A&M in 1931. He was talented enough that years later Sports Illustrated *named him to its first Silver Anniversary All-America team in 1956. Off the field, however, is where Rudder made his greatest contributions.*

After finishing his studies at A&M, Rudder accepted a position at Brady, Texas, high school as a coach and teacher. After a stop at John Tarleton Agricultural College, Rudder was called to serve his country in World War II.

Assigned to the 2nd Ranger Battalion as Commander, Rudder led his forces in an attack on Pointe du Hoc, France, which was between Utah and Omaha Beaches, on June 6, 1944, D-Day. Pointe du Hoc sat, almost impregnably, atop 100-foot cliffs and was occupied by heavily armed Germans. Rudder's hellish mission: to eliminate the Germans' heavy guns that would otherwise be able to rain heavy fire on both beaches. Under murderous fire the Rangers scaled the cliffs only to discover that the guns had been moved about 700 yards inland. Unbowed, they fought through the enemy and successfully put the guns out of commission, thereby saving countless Allied lives below. The price: 135 of the 225 Rangers were either killed or wounded.

For his bravery and decisive leadership in the capture of Pointe du Hoc and other sterling actions during the European campaign, Colonel Rudder was awared the Distinguished Service Cross, the Silver Star, the Bronze Star, the French Croix de Guerre, and the Purple Heart. His actions were remembered 50 years later, when President Clinton cited him as one of the heroes of the D-Day invasion at the 50th anniversay commerations.

When the war ended, Rudder returned to Brady, and from 1946-1952 he served as its mayor. Word of Rudder's spotless reputation and administrative abilities traveled to Austin, where Governor Allan Shivers appointed him Texas Land Commissioner in 1955 to clean up the Veterans' land scandal. The next year he was elected to a full term.

In 1958, James Earl Rudder went home—to Texas A&M. Appointed president in 1959, Rudder transformed A&M, taking it from an all-male, military-oriented school with 7,000 students to a coed institution with more than 14,000. This pattern of growth continued even after his death in 1970. Today, Rudder's legacy lives in the 44,000 students who attend A&M, making it the third largest university in the nation. Tributes on campus include the new conference center adjoining the Memorial Student Center, which in 1989 was named the J. Earl Rudder Conference Center, and a new residence hall, which was named Margaret Rudder Hall in honor of the president's wife in 1989.

in the game. The great State line limited the Aggies to twenty-eight yards rushing and nine passes, while the Buckeyes rolled up 220 yards for an easy win.

A brilliant diving catch in the end zone by all-conference end Dave Parks and a thirty-seven-yard field goal by Harry Daniels gave Texas Tech ten points in the first half of the Aggies' next game, enough to ensure a Red Raider win. There was no scoring in the entire second half as the game turned into a defensive struggle.

Jim Keller made his first start of the season and led A&M to a convincing 23–13 win over a tough Houston team on a Saturday night at Kyle Field. Keller took advantage of four Cougar fumbles that produced three touchdowns, a field goal, and the first Aggie victory of the season. And for the first time, the Aggies' 6–2 defense held. The Cougars managed only forty-three yards rushing. Keller, used primarily as a safety in A&M's three previous games, scored two touchdowns, and his key runs on fourth down kept the A&M offense moving throughout the game.

TCU was up next. The Aggies jumped out to an early lead but the Horned Frogs fought back in the second period to pull into a 14–14 tie, and that's how the game ended. But the all-out effort against TCU and a couple of injuries cost the Aggies against Baylor, Arkansas, and SMU.

In the game against Rice, the Owls' Gene Fleming took the ball on the opening kickoff and sped ninety-eight yards for a touchdown, and before the fans were seated, Rice had a 7–0 lead. But the Aggies recovered and fought back with two field goals by Bob Lee and a third-period scoring drive engineered by Jim Keller to gain a magnificent 13–6 win over a highly favored Rice eleven.

On Thanksgiving Day, 1963, the Texas Longhorns, riding the crest of a nine-game winning streak, rolled into Kyle Field ranked No. 1 in the nation.

On paper, the Aggies didn't have a prayer, and as the game began, Texas quickly marched downfield. The 'Horns got to the twenty-five, then after failing to gain a first down, kicked a field goal and jumped into a 3–0 lead.

The field goal by Texas seemed only to add some fighting spirit to the Aggies' attack and they quickly began a drive into Longhorn territory. On a third-down play, quarterback Jim Keller faked a run, then stopped and threw a fifty-four-yard bomb to Travis Reagan. Running at full speed, Reagan dashed across the goal line, and it was a brand-new ball game with A&M in front 7–3.

In the third period, an unstoppable Aggie team moved further out in front as Bill Moore recovered a Texas fumble at the A&M forty-five. A&M scored on a forty-yard pass to George Hargett to make it 13–3.

However, the Longhorns were still alive, and in the fourth period, they scored a touchdown to narrow the gap to 13–9.

As the game wound down to the four-minute mark, the Aggies began to flounder. John Brotherton intercepted a Texas pass, but as he attempted to lateral to a teammate, he fumbled the ball and the Longhorns recovered on the Aggies' forty-five-yard line.

With 2:30 left to play and with Texas on the Aggies' twenty, Tommy Wade attempted to pass to George Sauer in the end zone, but Jim Willenborg of A&M picked it off, and fell in the end zone for an apparent interception. But the referee ruled that Willenborg did not have possession of the ball when he slid out of the end zone.

Texas drove downfield and scored in the closing seconds when Duke Carlisle burst through the Aggies' line and crashed over for the touchdown to secure the Texas win and keep alive the Longhorn's national championship hopes.

For Texas A&M, it was a tremendous battle and probably the highlight of the Myers-Foldberg era. But almost-wins don't count for a coach like Hank Foldberg, who had had two losing seasons in a row, plus two losses to Texas. Now, in 1964, it would be a do-or-die year for Foldberg. He simply had to win, or else he would be gone.

In 1964, the Aggies dropped their first seven games, and then in the surprise of the year, they beat out a tough SMU eleven by a 23–0 margin. The loss to A&M was the worst conference beating inflicted on SMU in three years as the Aggies held the Mustangs to thirty-eight yards rushing. Sophomore Eddie McKaughan was the spark that ignited the Aggies attack, completing eight of sixteen passes for three touchdowns.

But the Aggies dropped their last two games to Rice and Texas, and Foldberg, 6–23–1 in three years as coach, was gone.

10

"MAKE SOMETHING HAPPEN"

Gene Stallings, A&M's new football coach, was born in Paris, Texas, March 2, 1935, and he never wanted to be anything else than a football coach.

At Paris High School, Stallings played under Coach Ray Berry, and early on, he proved he had the leadership and ability to become a great athlete and a leader of men. When Gene was a sophomore at Paris, he was an end on an outstanding football team. The other end was Ray Berry Jr., who was destined to be one of the great Southwest Conference stars and one of the greatest pass receivers in professional football.

At Paris High, Stallings was captain of the football, baseball, and golf teams in his senior year, and in 1953 was recruited by Ray George and Texas A&M, where he eventually signed.

In 1954, Stallings was a sophomore under Bear Bryant. Gene learned much from the legend—about handling athletes, about game preparation, about strategy. He soaked it all in. By 1956, Stallings was a star end and one of the tri-captains of the A&M squad that went 9–0–1 and captured the SWC championship, the first since 1939.

When Bryant left A&M for Alabama, he took Stallings with him. Stallings was to serve seven seasons as an assistant to Bryant on the Alabama staff before Texas A&M named him head football coach.

Gene Stallings's portrait, if you were to sketch it, would be red, white, and blue. He's a ramrod straight Texan, a man of sharp beliefs and principles. He does not smoke, rarely drinks, keeps his language clean, and rises every morning at 5:30. He espouses down-home family values, loves his family, his ranch, and his football team.

"I'm this kind of person," said Stallings. "If I go into a restaurant ten times, I'm liable to order the very same food ten times."

When Stallings was appointed to "his dream job" at A&M, he told the A&M Board of Directors, "We will win the championship within three years, or you can have the job back."

Just one day after he was appointed head coach at A&M, Stallings appointed a group of assistants who had played with him on the 1956 A&M championship team. They were Jack Pardee, Loyd Taylor, Dee Powell, and Don Watson.

The enthusiastic Stallings, employing the slogan "make something happen," canvassed the Southwest for the best in high school talent. He signed sixty-three players that winter, the core of his eventual conference champions.

In the first game of the 1965 season, the Aggies met LSU, rated the No. 7 team in the nation, and they gave a fine account of themselves as they battled the Tigers throughout a fierce defensive game that resulted in a 10–0 loss. LSU scored the 10 points in the first half, but were held scoreless by the Aggies defensive unit in the last two periods of a purely defensive struggle.

A determined A&M evened its season record when it upset an outstanding Georgia Tech squad in a come-from-behind 14–10 win.

A&M's passing attack, plus a bruising defense, paid off in the first half against Texas Tech, and the Aggies had a 10–0 halftime lead. In the second half, it was a brand-new game as Tech's quarterback, Tommy Wilson, began to find his receivers with unerring accuracy and managed to score three times to eke out a 20–16 win over the Aggies.

Against Houston, an alert, rugged defense and a twenty-six-yard field goal provided the 10–7 margin of victory for the Aggies. With the score tied at 7–7, Glynn Lindsey, the Aggies' great kicker, booted the game winner.

TCU, another top team in the SWC, had built a 10–3 lead over the Aggies at the end of the third quarter. Then in a blazing drive, the Frogs drove down to the Aggie sixteen. On fourth down they attempted a field goal that was partially blocked by Ted Nelson. (Nelson is now the head track coach at A&M, after serving twenty-four years as an assistant.) The Aggies recovered the ball and drove upfield as Harry Ledbetter passed to Ken McLean for a touchdown to make the score 10–9. Then the Aggies attempted to try for two points on the PAT, but the pass was intercepted and TCU maintained a 10–9 lead. In the final two minutes, the Frogs scored a touchdown to give them a decisive 17–9 win.

Coach Gene Stallings and his staff, 1965.

The heartbreaking loss to TCU in the last minute of the game took a toll on the Aggies, for they lost successive games to Baylor, SMU, and Arkansas without scoring a single point.

But surprisingly, A&M bounced back to score a dramatic 14–13 win over another highly rated team, the Rice Owls, as Ed McKaughan sparked A&M's two scoring drives. He tossed passes to Jim Stabler for one score, then another nineteen yards to Johnny Poss for the second score. Glenn Lindsay made the two important PATs to win the game.

In the final game of the season against Texas, the Aggies almost pulled the game out of the fire with one of the most unusual plays ever attempted. When Stallings was at Alabama, he had his quarterback bounce a lateral to a halfback, who would then grab the ball and race downfield for a huge gain. The play was tried only two or three times at Alabama. Now, in this game Stallings called for quarterback Harry Ledbetter and signaled him to use this play, called "The Texas Special."

The score was 0–0 in the second period, when, with the Aggies backed up to their own nine-yard line, Ledbetter threw what looked like a poor pass to Jim Kauffmann. Ledbetter acted out his disgust for what looked like a poor pass. He banged his fist in his hands and shook his head in disgust. Kauffmann kicked the ground and started back into the huddle. All this time, Dude McLean, who had been racing downfield, slowed up and headed back toward the huddle. Suddenly, Kauffman turned and fired the ball as far as he could, connecting with Dude, who was now racing downfield all alone.

Texas linemen were just standing there with amazement, while the Aggie players were shouting and jumping for joy as McLean raced over the goal line for a touchdown. The Kauffmann-to-McLean pass still ranks as one of the longest-scoring aerial plays in the SWC—ninety-one yards.

After that sensational touchdown play, the Aggies scored again as Bubba Collins raced thirteen yards for a second touchdown and A&M had what looked like a safe 17–0 lead.

But Texas came shooting from the hip, scored twice in the third period, and once more in the fourth to pull out a remarkable come-from-behind 21–17 stunner.

Gene Stallings's first year at Texas A&M was not impressive, for his team won but three games and lost seven. What was impressive was the number of top prospects recruited for the next few years.

The next season, 1966, was to be another rebuilding year for Gene Stallings as he and his aides worked around the clock to put together a team that could compete with an improved SWC. TCU, Baylor, Rice, SMU, and Arkansas looked as impressive in their spring training sessions as any teams in any conference in the nation.

The biggest problem facing the previous two A&M coaches, Jim Myers and Hank Foldberg, was filling the quarterback spot. At one time, Foldberg had tried eleven different players and Myers three or four. But there was not one standout performer.

In 1966, sophomore Edd Hargett took over as the starting quarterback and quickly demonstrated his ability to take charge of his team. He threw two touchdown passes in each win over Texas Tech and TCU, then led the Aggies to a share of the conference lead by upsetting Baylor 17–13.

In the Baylor game, the Bears had cut A&M's early 17–0 lead to 17–13, and the Aggies were holed up inside their own twenty-yard line. Hargett entered the huddle and told his mates, "Let's get the hell out of here, now." The Aggies quickly moved.

Losses in three of their next four games dropped the Aggies to 4–5–1. Hargett had enjoyed a banner year, establishing five A&M records in passing and offense.

But in 1967, Hargett really came into his own.

A record-setting crowd of more than 48,000 fans saw a once-in-a-lifetime football game on October 14, 1967, in Lubbock, Texas. Hargett plunged a dagger into the hearts of Texas Tech with a spine-tingling run after the final gun had sounded to vault A&M past the Red Raiders. It was an unforgettable dash by the strapping quarterback.

The Red Raiders had already beaten Texas 19–13, and had been confident that they could easily beat the Aggies, who were on the losing end of their first four games of the season.

Tech took an early 3–0 lead and held that margin until a second field-goal attempt blew up in their face with less than three minutes to go before the half.

Then Hargett unleashed his great right arm and began tossing passes all over the field, connecting for two touchdowns to give the Aggies a 14–3 lead over a stunned Tech team.

In the third period, Tech regained its composure, stayed on the ground, and scored on its first two possessions with Leinert Baker and Freeman providing the muscle. Baker then scored a second touchdown, and now, it was a 17–14 game as Baker converted just as the third period ended.

Then Hargett went back to work and moved the Aggies eighty yards, all in the air. He passed to Sallee for twenty-three, then to Tommy Maxwell for fifteen, again to Maxwell for sixteen, and then across the middle for Harris for thirteen yards. Then Stegent grabbed Hargett's thirteen-yard pass and fell over the goal line to give A&M a 21–17 lead.

But Tech scored again to take a 24–21 lead with less than a minute left.

A&M took possession after Tech attempted an on-side kickoff. Then Hargett went to work again. He tossed a bullet pass to Stegent, another to Maxwell.

On the next play, Long grabbed Hargett's desperation pass at the fifteen with only fifteen seconds left to play.

Hargett took the snap from center, faded back to try to get a pass away, but three Tech tacklers were in on him. Then Hargett slipped away, angled toward the left sideline, and scurried for pay dirt. Riggs made the conversion to give

Quarterback Edd Hargett and halfback Larry Stegent led A&M to numerous big wins in 1967, '68, and '69. Hargett captained the 1968 team; Stegent was captain of the '69 squad.

Bill Hobbs earned all-American honors in 1967, the year the Aggies broke a ten-year drought and won the SWC. One of the most sensational plays of the year was Hobbs' 102 yard interception-return for a touchdown against TCU.

A&M a 28–24 victory in one of the most miraculous comebacks of all time.

The win over Tech to snap a season-opening four-game losing streak was the sports story of the week. Cadets and alums were bubbling over with confidence and hope. And as it turned out those hopes weren't false.

A week later, the Aggies took a 7–0 lead over TCU until the final period. Then Bill Hobbs, junior linebacker, intercepted a TCU pass deep in the end zone and streaked 102 yards for a TD as A&M chalked up a 20–0 shutout of the Horned Frogs. Then A&M beat Baylor, Arkansas, and Rice, giving it five wins in a row, with Texas up next.

The Aggies hadn't beaten the Longhorns since Bear Bryant's 1956 SWC champions took the measure of the 'Horns by a 34–21 score.

Now with a Cotton Bowl and an SWC title on the line, the Aggies couldn't be contained.

Edd Hargett tossed 20 passes, completing ten for two touchdowns against Alabama in the 1968 Cotton Bowl.

The 1967 Aggies were Stallings' only winning team, but oh, what a team it was. After losing its first four games, A&M streaked to seven consecutive victories, including a 10–7 win over Texas, A&M's first since 1956.

Outstanding defensive back Curley Hallman made a key interception of a Kenny Stabler pass in A&M's 20–16 win over Alabama in the 1968 Cotton Bowl.

The stage was now set for a bitter showdown. The Aggies had to win for a Cotton Bowl berth, while Texas had to win for a chance to remain in the race for the SWC crown.

The first half of the game was played so cautiously, so defensively that both teams looked strangely out of place. But late in the second period, Charlie Riggs kicked a field goal to give A&M a 3–0 lead.

Late in the fourth period, Texas quarterback Bill Bradley mounted a telling drive and scored on a keeper to give Texas a 7–3 lead.

Then seconds later, Hargett—a giant-killer all season long—threw eighty yards to Bob Long, who had made big plays all season. Long got under the ball, caught it, tucked it under his arm, and outran a host of Texas tacklers for a touchdown. The Aggies had broken the Texas jinx, had beaten the 'Horns 10–7 for the first time in ten long years.

Now they were on their way to the Cotton Bowl and a meeting with Bear Bryant's powerful Alabama team.

The storyline was a marketing director's dream. This was Bryant's first game against A&M since he left the school in 1957, so all the hype centered around the "Old Master" matching wits with his former disciple, Gene Stallings. Nearly 75,000 fans turned out on a cold, drizzly day to see who would prevail.

The Aggies moved the ball well in the first half, as Hargett completed 10 of 20 passes for two touchdowns and a 13–10 lead.

It was a different story in the second half, as Stallings rewrote the game plan. The Aggies stuck to the running game, passing the ball just once. The decisive score came in the third period when Wendell Housley bowled over several defenders en route to a twenty-yard touchdown run. The Tide's Kenny Stabler countered with his second touchdown run, but that closed out the scoring. A&M had capped their Cinderella season with a 20–16 victory. After the game Bryant crossed the field and wrapped Stallings in—what else?—a Bear hug.

The series of dramatic victories made Stallings the toast of the town and the Aggies preseason picks to win a second straight SWC crown. After all, reasoned the sportswriters, all but five of the stars who fashioned the seven-game win streak were returning.

And it looked as if the experts were correct when the Aggies opened a 12–0 lead over a strong LSU in the opening game of the '68 season. However, in the second half, the Tigers suddenly began to roar, scored two touchdowns, converted one of the extra points, and eked out a 13–12 win over A&M. When the Aggies shocked a strong Tulane team with a 35–3 beating, though, they once again emerged as title contenders.

But A&M was to win just two more, over TCU 27–7 and Rice 24–14. Hargett threw touchdown passes in nine of the next ten games, and on at least five occasions, he threw two or more touchdown passes. No one in the league could come close to Hargett in 1968. Barney Harris again led the Aggies in pass receptions with forty-nine, and Bob Long pulled in eight passes for touchdowns to wind up with a school record of nineteen.

But the Aggies' 2–5 record in conference play and 3–7 for the season did not delight Aggie fans. Nor did the 35–14 defeat at the hands of Texas. It was not a happy period for Stallings and his coaches, who could not wait to begin a new season in 1969.

The 1969 edition of the Texas Aggies returned to the campus early in August to begin their season workouts. And for most observers, there seemed to be four questions left unanswered after spring practice.

The first of these questions was: "Who would be the Aggies quarterback?" The position had been vacated by three-year starter Edd Hargett, who had been drafted by the New Orleans Saints. During spring practice, Jim Sheffield, junior letterman from Houston, and Rocky Self, a sophomore redshirt, had both looked like possible starters.

The second question had to do with the health of Larry Stegent, a two-year junior letterman from Houston, who was the leading ground-gainer in '68, and had turned in an outstanding performance in the Cotton Bowl. The coaches agreed that if Stegent could recover from a shoulder operation, it would mean a big boost to the Aggie ground game.

Questions three and four were the offensive line and the defensive backfield. How good would they be? Coach Stallings seemed to feel that the offensive line problems had been solved. In the defensive secondary, only one experienced letterman returned, safety Dave Elmendorf, who would go on to become a great one.

That's how the Aggies shaped up as they gathered forces and left for the opening game of the season with LSU in Tiger Stadium.

A capacity crowd of more than 69,500 fans saw LSU break a scoreless tie with two TDs in the second quarter. In the second half, the Tigers added 21 points to bring the score to 35–0. A&M wound up losing 35–6.

After this disappointing showing, the Aggies pulled themselves together, with the help of a series of lineup changes by Stallings, and were ready for the Nebraska Cornhuskers at Lincoln. But once again the Aggies seemed to be in a trance as the game began, picking up just thirty-six yards in the first half, while Nebraska picked up two touchdowns and had a 14–0 lead.

In the second half, Rocky Self came into the game and began to fill the air with passes. He completed sixteen of thirty-one tosses for 136 yards. Larry Stegent also returned to the lineup, but even with these two stars playing well, the Aggies could not score and the game ended with Nebraska still on top 14–0.

A&M faced an undefeated Army eleven at West Point and behind the brilliant play of Rocky Self, who started his first collegiate game at quarterback, and Larry Stegent, who carried thirty-two times for 120 yards, the Aggies won 20–13.

In its first SWC game, A&M lost a thriller to Texas Tech 13–9 as Tech pulled the game out, thanks to pass interference.

Unable to stop the TCU running attack, the Aggies lost to the Frogs 16–6. A&M did not mount an effective attack until the final ten minutes of play, when it scored its lone touchdown.

Playing their first home game of the season, against Baylor, A&M took a 10–0 halftime lead.

It took only five plays in the third period for A&M to pick up another touchdown as Rocky Self exploded on a brilliant forty-yard TD sprint. The last Aggie score came as sophomore Ed Ebrom returned an interception forty-three yards. A&M had its first SWC victory, 24–0.

Facing an Arkansas team that was undefeated in six games, A&M easily picked up a touchdown in the first period. But two questionable calls by the officials ruined two possible Aggie scores and Arkansas rolled to a 35–13 win over A&M. Larry Stegent and Rocky Self were outstanding, while Barney Harris grabbed his eighty-fourth reception in three years to set a new A&M pass-reception record.

SMU came to Kyle Field and brought with it the nation's leading passer in Chuck Hixson, but for the second time on their home turf, the Aggies played as if they were Cotton Bowl bent. They scored on two of their first three possessions with drives of seventy-eight and seventy-six yards. Rocky passed to Ross Brupbacher for twenty-eight yards and the first touchdown.

All-American safety Dave Elmendorf anchored the Aggie defensive backfield in '69 and '70.

Hixson managed to complete twenty-two passes for a total of 240 yards, but was unable to score a touchdown as A&M won 20–10.

After a cliff-hanger loss to Rice, 7–6, the Aggies prepped to face their annual Turkey Day rivals, the Texas Longhorns, in what everyone hoped would be another thrilling battle.

Texas, on the verge of another national championship, played as though it wanted it badly. The Longhorns blew out A&M 39–0 in the first half en route to a 49–12 pasting. For A&M and Stallings, it was the second straight 3–7 season.

The blowout concluded the Aggies' least successful decade. Overall, the team had compiled a 31–64–6 record during the 1960s, a .337 winning percentage. There was little joy in Aggieland. The unsettling situation was of a piece with the social upheaval taking place on campuses across the nation. Vietnam, America's longest and costliest war, also was its most controversial and unpopular. A&M was painted with the same brush applied to the service academies, making recruiting difficult. At least this was one reason offered by apologists.

Another reason was a "nearly unbelievable" string of injuries to key players, particularly in 1968, says Dave Elmendorf, who was a sophomore jack-of-all-trades that disappointing season. "Wendell Housley and Larry Stegent both went down," he recalls, as did several linemen. The situation got so bad Elmendorf played five different positions before settling into the safety spot as a junior. By his senior year the 6-2, 195-pound native of Westbury, Texas was playing at an all-American level. The same couldn't be said of the team as a whole, however.

In 1970, under rainy, mud-caked conditions, the Aggies opened the season against Wichita State. However, State soon realized that it would take more than wet skies and a muddy field to dampen the spirit of the Aggies, who went to work at the opening kickoff.

State received the kick, failed to gain a first down, and punted to A&M. Dave Elmendorf took the kick and scooted forty yards to give A&M a first down on the State thirty-four-yard line.

Lex James, the sophomore quarterback, sparked A&M on a drive down to the twenty-four. A field-goal try was wide and State took

Quarterback Lex James gets set to toss a 79–yard scoring pass to Hugh McElroy to give A&M a 20–18 lead with just 13 seconds left in the game vs LSU in 1970. It was one of only two victories that season.

over. Again they had to kick to A&M, and this time the Aggies went to work with a vengeance. They worked it to the ten, before Steve Burks went in for the score. On its next possession, A&M drove eighty-three yards, with Brad Dusek taking it in for the TD.

Wichita then came back with a well-planned passing attack and scored to make it 14–7. Just before halftime, Pat McDermott, A&M's classy field-goal kicker, booted one from the twenty-five-yard line, and it was a 17–7 lead for A&M at the half.

The Aggies kept up their attack with a fifty-yard drive that culminated in a touchdown as James, on a keeper play, scored from the twelve to give A&M a 24–7 lead. McDermott began the fourth period by kicking a thirty-five-yard field goal to boost the Aggie lead to 27–7.

Then the reserves took over for Texas A&M and engineered two scoring drives of fifty-five and fifty-two yards, with Tommy Goodwin crossing the goal line after receiving a forty-nine-yard aerial bomb from James. Wichita then took over in the final minutes and scored again to make the final score A&M 41, Wichita State 14.

Three weeks later, the Wichita State team, on its way to a game, suffered the loss of every player and coach as the plane carrying the squad crashed. The Texas Aggies football team voted to forgo its traditional year-end football banquet and donated the money to the Wichita State Football Fund.

Third-string quarterback Joe Mac King directs the Aggies to a spine-tingling 10–9 win over Baylor in 1971. The loss snapped an 11–game SWC losing streak and spurred A&M on to four consecutive victories. Nonetheless, Stallings was replaced at the end of the year by Emory Bellard.

On Saturday, October 17, the Aggies faced the powerhouse LSU Tigers, ranked No. 12 nationally and coming off a 9–1 season. The Tigers started as though they would run the young Aggies out of the stadium, scoring a touchdown on the first play from scrimmage as

---

THE TEXAS SPECIAL

Longest Trick Play in Southwest Conference History

Gene Stallings struggled to rebuild A&M in his first year, 1965. But it was tough going. Entering the '65 Thanksgiving Day game with Texas the Aggies had posted a 3–6 record. Texas' record under Darrell Royal was a subpar 5–4, but with All-American Tommy Nobis and All-SWC Diron Talbert, the Longhorns expected to mop up A&M as they had since 1956, the last A&M win.

Texas had A&M backed up to its nine-yard line in the first quarter of a scoreless tie and it looked as though the dam was about to burst. And it did! On first down Harry Ledbetter, the Aggie quarterback, on instructions from Coach Stallings, called for "The Texas Special." On the snap, he stood up and threw a low spiral that hit the ground in front of the wingback on the left side (Jim Kauffman), and skittered into his hands. Kauffman stomped the ground in disgust, and Harry Ledbetter threw down his hands in frustration. EVERYBODY on the field and in the stands relaxed, as the play was apparently over and the pass incomplete. But then Kauffman suddenly turned and threw a long pass to Ken "Dude" McLean, who was running alone down the right center of the field, and across the goal line, with no defenders anywhere close. When the referee signaled a touchdown, the stunned crowd slowly realized that the bounced pass was actually a lateral thrown slightly backwards to Kauffman, who had lined up two to three yards back of the line of scrimmage.

It was a 91-yard touchdown pass that had been put in the playbook just for Texas. The field judge had been tipped off before the game by Stallings so that an inadvertent whistle would not be blown when the lateral hit the ground. Texas had been "city slicked" by the Farmers—on national television! It was the only pass Jim Kaufman ever threw in his career.

The momentum of the play spurred the Aggies to a 17–0 halftime lead, but an embarrassed Texas regrouped at halftime and came back with three touchdown passes to win 21–17.

The "Texas Special" has been shown on national television many times—usually before the annual Thanksgiving Day game with Texas. Although such records are not kept, it is believed this is the longest successful trick play for a touchdown in NCAA history!

No trick was necessary to complete this pass to Ken McLean in the Aggies' famous 1965 contest against Texas. Ledbetter's pass set up A&M's first score.

quarterback Bud Lee found Andy Hamilton on a seventy-three-yard scoring play. On the exchange of downs, the Tigers added to their score with a field goal and a safety to give them a 12–0 margin at the half.

But the Aggies, after receiving a verbal scalding from Stallings, roared back in the third period with two field goals by McDermott. Then Homer May grabbed a bullet pass from James for a touchdown, and the Aggies were out in front of a thriller, 13–12.

LSU managed two more field goals to take an 18–13 lead in the waning minutes of the fourth period. But with less than a minute to play, the Aggies got the ball on their twenty-one-yard line and James began to pepper receivers with passes. Finally, James dropped back and found his man, Hugh McElroy, who was out in the clear at midfield. James took a couple of steps back, then fired a high arching pass to McElroy, who took the ball over his shoulder and—behind a great block by Homer May—raced down the sideline for fifty yards and the winning touchdown as 1,500 Aggies in the stands went berserk. Final score: A&M 20, LSU 18. The Aggies had done it again.

Then something happened to the Aggies: They dropped games to Ohio State 56–13, Michigan 14–10, Texas Tech, TCU, Baylor, Arkansas, SMU, Rice, and then to Texas, 52–14.

The season was a disaster for Stallings and A&M, for this was the first Aggie team in sixteen years that did not win a single SWC game all season. It would be a long winter for Coach Stallings.

For the past several years, it had been "Wait till next year" for the Aggies. Next year was here once again as Coach Gene Stallings took the Aggies into battle for his seventh season. The Aggies were determined to get revenge on all the teams they had lost to in 1970, and in their first start of the new campaign, they dominated the Wichita State Shockers 41–7.

The following week, the Aggies returned to Baton Rouge, but the Tigers of LSU were out for a bit of revenge themselves. The Aggies couldn't do anything right and dropped a humiliating loss to the Tigers by a whopping 37–0 score. Then, unable to shake off the LSU loss, the Aggies dropped games to Nebraska 34–7, Cincinnati 17–0, Texas Tech 28–2, and TCU 14–3.

Stallings, constantly searching for a winning combination, finally came up with third-string quarterback Joe Mac King, who directed the team to a thrilling 10–9 upset victory over Baylor. The biggest play of the game was a fifty-three-yard field goal by Pat McDermott to win the game. That kick of McDermott's broke the school record.

The nationally ranked Arkansas Razorbacks came into the game against A&M confident they would chalk up another win over a Texas team. They had previously beaten the Longhorns and were about to set their chart for a Cotton Bowl game.

But to their utter dismay, the Aggies, primed for this vital matchup, simply would not be beaten this day and ran over and through Arkansas for a 17–9 victory as sophomore halfback Mark Green scored two touchdowns to lead the Aggies to their biggest win of the year.

The following week, Green again led the Aggies in another outstanding game as he carried the ball forty-one times for 158 yards and scored two touchdowns to give the Aggies their third straight win over highly touted SMU.

In one of the most exciting games of the year, the Aggies continued on their winning ways to again come from behind to defeat Rice in a seesaw battle by an 18–13 score. Green's touchdown and McDermott's field goal gave A&M a 9–6 halftime lead. Then Rice went ahead in the third period 13–12. But in an incredible last period, Joe Mac King went to work, sparking A&M on a sixty-seven-yard drive as he completed all four of his passes for sixty-seven yards and the winning score.

The victory, the fourth in a row for the fast-moving Aggies, brought them back to the .500 mark in the SWC title race and set the scene for a Thanksgiving Day showdown against Texas to settle who would go to the Cotton Bowl.

But Texas routed A&M 34–14 as the Longhorns held A&M to three first downs in the game. The 'Horns wrapped up the game in the second period as they scored three touchdowns. A&M fell to 5–6.

"Shortly after the Texas game," said Stallings, "I was summoned to the president's house and was told that I was through."

In his seven seasons, Stallings won one SWC title, lost to Texas six out of seven tries, and had but one winning season.

Looking back, the Aggies "probably just didn't have the talent" during this period, says Dave Elmendorf. And while Stallings' dismissal was unfortunate, he asks rhetorically: "What other yardstick can you use for a coach except his record?"

Elmendorf and Stallings both moved into the NFL—Elmendorf as an all-Pro safety with Los Angeles and Stallings as an assistant coach with Dallas. The teams met each other frequently during the 1970s, affording teacher and student opportunities to gab for a few minutes after the final gun.

"I felt like Stallings might have been a little young when we were at A&M," Elmendorf says today. "I had the sense that, after having been a Bear Bryant disciple, he was searching for his own identity. But at Dallas and now with Alabama, where he's won a national championship, he's proven that he can win consistently. And that's the name of the game."

11

THE WISHBONE COMES TO COLLEGE STATION

The new football coach, Emory Bellard, had established himself as a highly successful Texas high school coach. During fifteen years at three different high schools—Ingleside, Breckenridge, Central High of San Angelo—he compiled a record of 139–34–3. His teams won eleven district titles, two regionals, and two state titles and a share of another.

Bellard left San Angelo and spent five seasons at the University of Texas. While at Texas, Bellard invented the wishbone formation, which the Longhorns used to achieve a record six straight SWC championships.

A native of Luling, Texas, Bellard graduated from Southwest Texas State. He was named athletic director of A&M in addition to head coach.

In the opening game of the 1972 season, Wichita State stunned the Aggies, almost running them out of the stadium, by scoring two quick touchdowns. But A&M woke up to win 36–13. The next outing was embarrassing, though, as Nebraska pummeled A&M 37–7.

The Aggies, now 1–1, embarked on their third consecutive road trip to the unfriendly confines of Tiger Stadium to tangle with LSU, and to the surprise of practically everyone, the Aggies dominated the first half. But the Aggies dropped three potential TD passes, and at the half, it was a 14–10 game with LSU in front. The Aggies fell apart in the second half and lost 42–17. The one bright ray of sunshine for the Aggies came when halfback Carl Roaches took an LSU kickoff and returned it ninety-seven yards for an Aggie touchdown.

Mistakes and turnovers plagued the Aggies through the next several games and they lost to Army 24–14, Texas Tech 17–14, TCU 13–10, and Baylor 15–13. Then in a complete turnaround, the Aggies bounced back to upset favored Arkansas 10–7. It marked the first time in fifteen years that A&M had beaten the Razorbacks twice in successive seasons. Against Arkansas, Bob Murski and Larry Ellis each intercepted Razorback passes. Ellis scored the Aggies' lone touchdown on one of those intercepted passes after a twenty-six-yard sprint.

A&M then beat SMU 27–17 as Skip Walker scored two touchdowns and Pat McDermott broke his field-goal record of fifty-three yards with a fifty-four-yarder.

In the final two games of the year, Rice took a 20–14 verdict and Texas outgunned and outplayed A&M by ringing up a 38–3 win over the Aggies in the season's finale.

After a first-season record of 3–8 Coach Emory Bellard said, "We aren't there yet, but we're headed in the right direction. And for next year we have a group of ten freshmen who can

The Aggies' new coach, Emory Bellard, originated the intricate, successful wishbone offense while at Texas. Here he talks with his troops before their first game vs Wichita State in 1972, a 36–12 victory. Bellard's first A&M team struggled to a 3–8 record while learning the new offense.

run the 100 in ten seconds. That ought to give our next year's opponents something to worry about."

The 1973 season saw fifteen outstanding freshmen of the past season on the varsity squad and a new offense devised by Bellard. It certainly paid off in the opening game of the season. The new offense, called the T-Bone, was led by a new quarterback, Mike Jay, just out of the U.S. Marine Corps, and Mike guided his team to a 48–0 win over Wichita State in the opener. It was A&M's most lopsided win in years and featured a seventy-seven-yard dash by halfback Alvin Bowers, a fifty-one-yard interception return for a touchdown by Pat Thomas, and three touchdowns by Skip Walker of twenty-eight, nineteen, and seven yards. In the second game against LSU, the Aggies threatened to upset the Tigers in a contest that was close until the final minutes, when LSU scored a touchdown to win a 28–23 squeaker. Randy Haddox, the Aggies' kicker, set a record when he booted three field goals.

Next, a strong Boston College team, favored to win by three touchdowns, was tested. Following a BC touchdown that tied the score, Carl Roaches took the kickoff and out-sped BC's tacklers. He cut to the sideline, where he raced 100 yards, aided by several great blocks, to score and give A&M a 24–17 lead. But in the fourth period, Boston College exploded for two touchdowns and came up with a 32–24 victory.

The following week, a tough, experienced Clemson squad, facing the Aggies for the first time, jumped out to a 9–0 lead. Then with seventeen-year-old David Walker subbing for Mike Jay at quarterback and Bubba Bean breaking off a seventy-eight-yard touchdown sprint, A&M surprised even its most ardent cadet followers with a 30–15 victory. It looked at long last as if the Aggies were on their way to Cotton Bowl heaven.

But once again, their hopes were dashed. The following week Texas Tech intercepted four passes and recovered two fumbles to win 28–16.

Quarterback David Walker led the Aggies against TCU in his first start at that position and was so impressive in this game that Coach Bellard installed him as the regular for the remainder of the season. The two Walker boys, David, who gained eighty-one yards, and Skip, who gained 122 yards rushing, were the stars in a 35–16 Aggie win over TCU.

With Walker directing the Aggies from his quarterback post, the Aggies rolled to an impressive win over the Baylor Bears 28–22. But the Aggies fell to Rice 24–20 and lost to SMU 45–10. In the final game of the year, they dropped another game to Texas by a 42–13 margin.

Fullback Bubba Bean carries the ball against Rice in the Aggies' 37–7 romp over the Owls in 1974. Bean would star on Bellard's '74 and '75 teams, earning all-SWC honors both years.

Carl Roaches was one of the best return men in A&M history. He electrified crowds from 1972–1975.

Quarterback David Walker was so impressive in a 1973 game against a tough TCU that Coach Bellard installed him as the regular quarterback—as a freshman. Here he is in the 1974 17–0 whitewash of TCU.

And once again, it was, "Wait until next year."

Bellard, looking back on the season, said, "In retrospect of the 1973 season, it was a season upon which a solid foundation was laid for a very promising future for a talented, aggressive, inexperienced squad. I believe that this squad is on the threshold of proving to be an outstanding football team and I am looking forward to big things."

In 1974, after a sluggish first half that gave A&M a touchdown and a field goal against a rugged Clemson Tiger team, the Aggies opened up an attack that completely stunned Clemson and paved the way for 434 yards and an impressive 24–0 win. The victory gave the Aggies a shot in the arm and they rolled to another win over an outstanding LSU team 21–14, only their second over LSU since 1960. Skip Walker, Bubba Bean, and Bucky Sams each scored a touchdown for the Aggies. As the game ended, the thousands of Aggie fans, cadets, and alumni began a chant: "Cotton Bowl, Cotton Bowl."

After the Aggies traveled to Seattle and beat Washington 28–15, they jumped to No. 5 in the national rankings.

But something went wrong in the game against the Kansas Jayhawks. Despite the great passing of Walker, who completed eight straight passes at one point in the game, the Aggies were outplayed 28–10.

Then the following week, before a national TV audience, the Aggies played their best game of the season to roll to a 28–7 win over Texas Tech before a sellout crowd at Kyle Field.

In the second period, halfback Skip Walker set an Aggie record as he scored three touchdowns, while the Aggies' solid defensive unit shut down the highly regarded Tech offense to win 28–7.

In the game against a powerful TCU, the Aggies came out throwing passes all over the field to stun the Toads 17–0. David Walker hit on seven of nine passes to run up a total of 220 yards for the victory, one of the most impressive of the year.

The following week against Baylor, the Aggies scored in every period, to post a 20–0 shutout over the Bears. The loss to A&M was the first of the season for the highly regarded Bears and ran the Aggies' season mark to 6–1. College Stadium was aglow.

Arkansas strutted into College Station and left with a stunning 20–10 loss to the Aggies, who were voted the No. 3 team in the nation after the win.

After such stellar recognition, A&M got a rude awakening against SMU.

The Mustangs, eager to knock off the high-riding Aggies, rolled up 16 points in the first half and a dazed A&M never recovered, falling 18–14. The Aggies' offense started to click in the second half, but it was too little and too late.

A week later, A&M, still shell-shocked by their loss to SMU the previous week, managed to shake themselves out of the doldrums and pound Rice 37–7.

All season long, the Aggies were top contenders for a shot at the Cotton Bowl and maybe a national title. But on a dismal day in Austin, it all disappeared as Texas won 32–3.

At game's end, Bellard said, "We just got a good ol' country licking. We gave them those quick scoring opportunities, and you get down by 17 points in the first minute and you just can't untrack yourself."

In 1975 Dave Shipman took over as the Aggies' quarterback and led A&M to eight straight wins and an SWC title, the first since 1967. Here's Shipman engineering the wishbone against Illinois, who fell 43–13 to the Aggies.

Bellard's third season was a highly successful one. Although the Aggies failed to win the SWC title, they did compile an impressive 8–3 season and were ranked nationally throughout most of the season. "But we'll get better," he promised.

The 1975 Aggies faced an incredible challenge when they reported for two-a-day workouts in mid-August. They were selected as the overwhelming favorite to win the SWC and began the season ranked No. 8 in the nation.

There were forty-one lettermen returning—by far the most experienced group of players that Bellard had at A&M. The group included sixteen starters, two established all-Americans (cornerback Pat thomas and linebacker Ed Simonini), and several all-SWC nominees.

The season opened a week earlier than usual, but it didn't faze the Aggies as they scored a quick touchdown and then played possession ball to take a thrill-packed 7–0 win over a tough, aggressive Mississippi squad, which was rated one of the South's best teams.

The Aggies then traveled to Baton Rouge, where they opened up a bag of tricks to dazzle LSU 39–8. Returning home, A&M faced an Illinois team regarded as one of the best in the Big Ten. But the Aggies went about their business, turned on the offense, and came away with a 43–13 win.

Voted the best defensive team in the nation, they embarked on a three-week travel program—three games on the road. First, A&M knocked off Kansas State 10–0. Then they beat Tech 38–9 and TCU 14–6.

Against Tech, Bubba Bean set an A&M record with a 94-yard touchdown run from scrimmage. In the Aggies' 19–10 win over Baylor (which followed the victory over TCU), safety Lester Hayes intercepted a pitchout and took it 77 yards for a touchdown.

Second-string quarterback Mike Jay took over when David Shipman was injured and led the Aggies to a 33–14 win over the Rice Owls for their ninth win as the Aggies were voted the No. 2 team in the nation. As the Texas Longhorns rolled into town, the State of Texas was in an uproar, for the 'Horns were hot, too, having gone 9–1. Tickets for this great battle of Texas teams were impossible to get, and a crowd of more than 57,000 fans jammed every inch of the stadium at College Station.

Texas brought to this battle a fine quarterback in Marty Akins and a Heisman star in Earl Campbell, leading rusher in the Southwest Conference.

But when Akins was hurt on the first play from scrimmage and had to leave the game with a bad knee, the 'Horns were in big trouble. Campbell was stopped time after time. He carried the ball fifteen times and picked up just forty yards rushing for a season's low.

Quarterback Mike Jay had his Aggies in front 10–7, but he was slammed to the turf by two Texas defenders and had to leave the game in the second period. Shipman replaced him and did an adequate job.

1975 all-SWC performer Richard Osborne played tight end for the Aggies from 1972–1975. In the 1975 Texas game, Osborne made a spectacular grab for a touchdown that propelled the Aggies to a 20–10 triumph.

In the first quarter, the teams played cautiously. Then the Aggies took over and moved steadily for sixty-six yards before the 'Horns stopped them. Then Tony Franklin, A&M's ace kicker, made a thirty-one-yarder to give A&M a 3–0 lead. Three minutes later, in the second period, A&M fullback George Woodard softened the Texas defense before Jay passed to Richard Osborne for a TD and a 10–0 lead.

Aggie fans were beginning to chant, "We're No. 1," when Texas began to march. But they fizzled and had to punt. It was on the next A&M punt that Raymond Clayborn raced sixty-six yards for a Texas touchdown as the crowd went absolutely wild. Now it was a 10–7 battle.

Barefoot kicker and all-American Tony Franklin booted two monster field goals against Baylor in the 1976 24–0 victory. One kick was good for 64 yards; he followed that with a 65 yarder to break all NCAA kicking records.

A workhorse, all-SWC running back George Woodard scored four touchdowns for A&M against Rice in a 57–14 thrashing in 1976.

In the fourth period, with the score still 10–7, Shipman began to utilize the big freshman fullback, Woodard, all 245 pounds, and he slowly battered the Texas line for yardage every time he carried the ball. He scored early in the fourth quarter to make it 14–10 in favor of A&M.

Stopping the 'Horns the rest of the way, A&M won 20–10 (Tony Franklin, who had missed on four tries, finished the scoring with a field goal).

A&M had just one more game to play, Arkansas.

But the Aggies fell hard, 31–6, and had to share the SWC title with Arkansas and Texas.

In their first post-season bowl game since 1967, A&M met the University of Southern California and lost 20–0 in the Liberty Bowl.

The 10–2 season was Coach Bellard's best, and represented the most wins for A&M since the championship of 1939. The defense was the best in the nation.

Nine A&M players were selected in the NFL draft of 1976. They were Ed Simonini, Bubba Bean, Pat Thomas, Jackie Williams, Skip Walker, Bruce Welch, Carl Roaches, Richard Osborne, and Glenn Bujnoch.

With a proven starter or talented newcomer at nearly every position, the Aggies were the odds-on favorites to end up in the 1977 Cotton Bowl. The defense was nearly as solid as the group that was ranked number one in the nation a year earlier, and the dynamic wishbone offense appeared to have the punch of a heavyweight champion.

Texas A&M opened the season by blanking the Virginia Tech Gobblers 19–0. However, the offense was sluggish and off-key and would be a portent of things to come during the rest of the season.

"The big thing in their offense is their fullback."

Those were the words which many opposing coaches echoed about the Aggies' massive, 245-pound fullback, George Woodard, who piled up 177 yards in twenty-nine carries as the Aggies defeated a strong Kansas State eleven 34–14. Kansas State Coach Ellis Rainsberger, speaking of Woodard, said, "We set up a special three-man defense to sit on Woodard's tail throughout the game, but he still managed to put on a good show. He's a great player."

As the game opened, it was apparent that quarterback Dave Shipman was not able to spark the team's offense as A&M fell behind 7–0. But when Coach Bellard inserted David Walker at quarterback, the Aggies began to roll and piled up five touchdowns.

The game against the Wildcats was a preview of the roller-coaster ride the Aggies would take during the season. While they were to reach impressive heights, they first would sink to some incredible depths.

If A&M was the preseason choice to win the SWC, then somebody forgot to tell Bill Yeoman's Houston Cougars, who completely dominated the Aggie offense. The Cougars' offense unleashed three touchdown passes in the first half and had A&M reeling in the turf. The Aggies played a much better game in the second half, shut out the Cougars, and managed to score two touchdowns, but the damage had been done and Houston came away with a deserved 21–10 victory.

Just a week later, against the Fighting Illini, the Aggies won a close defensive battle 14–7. Linebacker Robert Jackson was the Aggies' defensive star as he made ten tackles and was all over the field, always threatening the Illini backs. Kevin Monk and Willie Thompson intercepted two Illini passes each, with Thompson's being the key theft. He deciphered some Illini trickery, picked off the pass, and carried the ball deep into Illinois territory. On the next play, Woodard smashed in for the wining score.

Coach Steve Sloan of Texas Tech said his team had to pass to beat A&M, and it did just that as Tech handed A&M its first home loss since 1973, 27–16.

A&M's secondary was victimized by three scoring passes as Tech jumped into a 21–0 lead before A&M could cross midfield. However, a second-half rally led by Walker almost pulled the game out for A&M. Walker completed a seventy-six-yard bomb to Curtis Dickey on one play and also rushed for 127 yards.

After they built their lead, Tech stacked the middle of the line and, time after time, stopped the bull-like charges of George Woodard, who was able to generate only fifteen yards rushing.

Next, in another form reversal, A&M's defensive team put on a great show as it shut out Baylor 24–0. Dave Walker started his first game of the year at quarterback and gave the offense the spark that had been lacking in previous games. Tony Franklin broke the NCAA field-goal record as he kicked one for sixty-four yards, then followed with a sixty-five-yarder. His field goals took the steam out of the Bears, and they simply folded in the stretch. Woodard continued his march toward the 1,000-yard mark with sixty-two yards on eighteen carries.

The Rice Owls flew into College Station October 23 with their artistic aerial circus led by QB Tommy Kramer. Kramer's passes had the A&M secondary in fits as he put the ball in the air a remarkable fifty-nine times, completing twenty-four for 376 yards. Fortunately, the Aggies offense was also in rare form and was able to muster considerable yardage in return. The Aggies put points on the scoreboard in pinball-machine rapidity and won 57–34.

Together, both teams amassed more than 1,000 yards of total offense. Woodard was again a workhorse for A&M as he collected 188 yards and four touchdowns. Tony Franklin booted five field goals to set an SWC record.

The following week, a tough A&M defense smothered SMU, holding the Ponies to a mere ninety-seven total yards. Just as tough as the Aggie defense, the A&M offense was having a field day at the expense of SMU, running over and through the Mustangs in a 36–0 victory march. Led by David Walker and Woodard, the Aggies pushed SMU all over the field and could

Quarterback Mike Mosely hands off to George Woodard as a blocking wall begins to develop in this 1979 duel against Rice, won 41–15 by the Aggies.

have really piled it on, but Bellard inserted every man on the squad and the Aggies coasted the rest of the way.

It didn't take much to remind the A&M players about the 1975 Arkansas game, an embarrassment that had been witnessed by a nationwide TV audience. This year the roles were reversed. A&M—not Arkansas—was cast as the spoiler. Thus, with the fateful score of 31–6 pounded into their angry brains all week, the Aggies did to Arkansas what the Razorbacks did to the Aggies only a year before.

Curtis Dickey, A&M's slashing halfback, was the big hero as he rushed for ninety-two yards on twenty carries.

A&M then punished TCU 59–10 as Woodard topped the 1,000-yard mark for the season and Curtis Dickey scored twice.

Keith Baker, a sub quarterback, proved that he could play with the regulars as he pitched two magnificent passes, one for fifty-one yards, another for ninety yards, both for touchdowns.

In the annual Turkey Day shootout, Texas A&M rolled to a 27–3 victory over the Longhorns. The win was the first in Austin since 1956, the Bear Bryant and John David Crow era. It marked the first time since World War I that A&M had defeated Texas two years in a row. It was also the first time Texas was held without a touchdown since 1939.

David Walker, Woodard, and Tony Franklin were outstanding in this all-important game for A&M as it clinched a post-season test with the Florida Gators in the Sun Bowl on January 1.

The win over Texas gave A&M a 9–2 season, one of the finest in A&M history. It was Bellard's second winning season, and every indication pointed to his remaining at A&M for as long as he wished.

In a dazzling display of offensive execution, the Aggies trounced Florida 37–14 as they racked up 365 yards of total offense, with Woodard gaining 125 yards on twenty-five carries. Walker kept the Gator defense off guard throughout the game, hitting eleven of eighteen passes. Tony Franklin was voted the game's MVP as he kicked three field goals, one a sixty-two-yarder that set a national bowl game record.

A&M's great defensive unit was superb, holding the Gators to just twenty-seven yards and no first downs in the first half.

For A&M (10–2), it was a great year. The 327 points scored by the high-flying offense generated by Coach Bellard was one of the most potent in A&M history.

The 1977 football campaign was disappointing for Coach Emory Bellard and company. Pre-season polls had the Aggies finishing either first or second in the SWC. But when it was over, A&M found itself with an 8–4 record and a third-place conference finish behind rivals Texas and Arkansas.

The temperature was over 100 degrees as the Aggies prepared to kick off to the Kansas Jayhawks in the opening game of the season at College Station. The heat, however, didn't slow the Aggies, who were led by running backs George Woodard and Curtis Dickey. The Aggies defeated the Jayhawks, 28–14 as Woodard, who now weighed in at 285 pounds, broke the game wide open with a fifty-one-yard touchdown sprint.

But after the Kansas game, it would be a while before Woodard would run again at Kyle Field, for the Aggies packed their bags and headed east to Virginia. This would be the first of five stops for the A&M Road Show, which included games at Virginia Tech, Texas Tech, Michigan, Baylor, and Rice.

In the first road game, A&M defeated Virginia Tech 27–6 in a contest that enabled Coach Bellard to use every man on his traveling squad. Tech offered little resistance and Bellard kept the score down by using his second- and third-string players from the first period.

If Texas A&M was to win the SWC title, then most experts figured the Aggies would have to beat Texas Tech. The Raiders were led by quarterback Rod Allison. Sportswriters around the nation thought that Allison had an excellent chance of winning the Heisman Award. But Rod never got that chance.

Early in the second quarter against A&M, Allison was tackled by A&M safety Carl Grulich and a couple of other Aggie huskies, and when he was taken out of the game, the team's physician discovered that Allison had a broken bone in his left foot. It was an injury that Tech could not overcome. Led by four field goals by A&M's incredible kicker, Tony Franklin, in the fourth period, the Aggies picked up 21 additional points to ramble home 33–17. Curtis Dickey also was in great form in this game; his sixty-eight-yard TD run gave A&M much-needed momentum to outscore Tech and take a hard-fought game. Now it was on to Ann Arbor to tangle with the nation's No. 1 team, the Michigan Wolverines.

"It was the most embarrassing game for A&M since Coach Bellard took over in 1972, for the Aggies played like a bunch of high school kids," said an assistant coach. And when the rousing cheers of 105,000 fans who packed the stadium had ended, A&M found itself on the short end of a 41–3 score.

The first half was an even ball game as Tony Franklin uncorked a long field goal to give A&M a short-lived 3–0 edge. Then the sky began to fall in as the Wolverines picked up a touchdown in the second period.

In the second half, Michigan let loose and ran up a total of 34 points, thanks to fumbles and interceptions as everything A&M tried turned to ashes.

The Wolves converted seven Aggie turnovers as Coach Bo Schembechler defensed A&M's attack almost to perfection. David Walker completed just one pass and was intercepted three times. It was the first loss for A&M since Walker had become the No. 1 quarterback. But it was a big one, for the game was seen on nationwide television and many major sportswriters and commentators were on hand to witness the Aggies' poor exhibition.

Against Baylor a week later, Walker was nigh perfect. He sparked the A&M offense to a 35–14 halftime lead and threw three touchdown passes. A vital interception by Kenneth Taylor late in the fourth period assured an Aggie win, 38–31, after a wild second half that saw Baylor pick up 27 points, while holding A&M to a single field goal. But Taylor's touchdown clinched the game for A&M.

The Rice Owls this year were without their magical quarterback Tommy Kramer, and they were no match for the Aggies, who clubbed out a 28–14 win.

The Aggies made one mistake after another in their game against SMU and trailed the men from Dallas 21–7 at the half. But on the first play of the second half, Walker tossed a touchdown pass to Darrell Smith, good for twenty-nine yards. On the next possession Walker sped twenty-nine yards for a score as the Aggies kept rolling to a 38–21 win.

Time ran out on A&M's great comeback attempt against Arkansas as the Razorbacks intercepted a desperation pass by David Walker and grabbed a last-minute 26–20 victory.

Arkansas jumped out in front of A&M at the start of the game and led 19–6 at halftime. But Woodard and Curtis Dickey scored touchdowns to give A&M a 20–19 lead as the big crowd stood and roared at every play.

Then with two minutes left to play, Ron Calcagni coolly dropped back and completed a fifty-eight-yard TD pass to give Arkansas a touchdown and a 26–20 lead. The Aggies were down, but not out. They got the ball back and, behind the running of Dickey and Woodard and Walker, advanced to the Hogs' fourteen-yard line. But Arkansas held on to secure the win.

Against the TCU Horned Frogs, the Aggies amassed a total of 687 yards for a new SWC record as the touchdown twins, Woodard and Dickey, performed spectacularly. But the spotlight was on a newcomer, freshman quarterback Mike Mosley, who was subbing for the injured David Walker. Mosley rushed for ninety-eight yards, tossed two touchdown passes, and directed the offense with the confidence of a four-star general. The victory over the Frogs, 52–23, assured the Aggies of another post-season contest. It would be either in the Cotton Bowl or the Bluebonnet Bowl. The game with Texas would decide that.

On a tragic November afternoon, Texas stormed into College Station and blasted the Aggies. Earl Campbell scored three touchdowns and rushed for 222 yards, proving that he deserved the Heisman Trophy. The final was 57–28.

But Campbell wasn't the only show in town. A&M's four touchdowns against Texas were the most scored against the 'Horns by a conference team. For A&M, George Woodard was outstanding as he broke the 1,000-yard mark for the second year in a row. Curtis Dickey again sparkled, but the two were not enough to overcome Texas.

In the final game of the regular season, quarterback Mike Mosley led the Aggies to a 27–7 win over Houston. Mike scored two touchdowns, rushed for 109 yards, and completed five of seven passes as the Aggies began to think about their opponent in the Bluebonnet Bowl Game on December 31.

In the Bluebonnet Bowl, A&M faced the University of Southern California in a battle that turned out to be the best offensive game in the history of the event. One would need a calculator to add up all the records that were broken as the Trojans defeated the Aggies 47–28.

Mosley had a wonderful first half, but had problems in the second half. Five A&M turnovers enabled USC to win easily. Coach Bellard's wishbone offense gained more than 500 yards, but his defense yielded 600 yards.

USC quarterback Rob Hertel was unstoppable as he threw four touchdown passes, and

Dwight Ford, USC's classy halfback, set a school record with a ninety-four-yard TD scamper.

For A&M, George Woodard bulled for 185 yards and two touchdowns, while Mosley rushed for 185 yards and one touchdown. Five Aggie fumbles helped USC gain control of the game after the Aggies had run up a 14–0 lead in the first period. Southern California picked up two touchdowns in each of the last three quarters.

For Emory Bellard, his 8–4 Aggies had given him his fourth winning season in his six years at the helm.

On September 8, 1978, the Texas Aggies opened their eighty-fourth football season with an impressive 37–10 win over Kansas in a game played at Lawrence.

The win catapulted the Aggies into tenth place in the national polls. But the most interesting aspect of this first win of the new season was the manner in which Mike Mosley, the young sophomore, handled and directed his team from his quarterback post. Mosley completed seven of eleven passes for two touchdowns as the team rolled up 444 yards of total offense.

"This was one of the best opening days that I can recall," said Bellard.

A week later, the Aggies traveled to Boston to meet the aggressive Boston College Eagles, and for the second week in a row, the Aggies overwhelmed their opponents with a powerful offense, 37–2.

In the first home game, the Aggies showed why they were now ranked No. 7 in the polls as they completely demolished Memphis State 58–0. The following week, the Aggies mashed Texas Tech 38–9. Suddenly, the Texas Aggies were the No. 4-ranked team with the No. 1 defense.

But it wasn't meant to be. They dropped successive games to Houston (33–0) and Baylor (24–6). The bubble had burst and the alumni were screaming for Bellard's scalp.

On the morning of October 24, a chalk-faced Emory Bellard told a packed horde of news and television commentators that he could no longer remain at Texas A&M and would resign immediately.

Bellard said that he came to his office on a Tuesday morning, a few days after the Baylor game, and was informed by a reliable source that he would be asked to resign by the Aggie boss, Dr. Jarvis Miller, although he would be asked to stay on as athletic director.

After a quick visit to Miller's office that morning, Bellard became convinced that he would also be asked to resign as athletic director at the end of the year.

Then, the coach who had restored some of the glory to A&M during his six and a half years at A&M, sent this statement to the press:

> I asked Mr. Tate, our assistant A.D., to read this because I would not be able to keep my composure. Therefore under existing circumstances, I feel that I must resign my post as athletic director and head football coach, immediately, at Texas A&M University.

Later, the explanation was given that Bellard's failure to please the highly vocal Aggie alumni had done him in.

After the Bellard statement was read, Assistant Athletic Director Tate commented:

"For a long, long time, Emory put his mind, his heart and soul and body into this job, but it seems like it wasn't enough for some people and I think he just got good and tired of it all."

A few days later, Offensive Coordinator Tom Wilson was named to replace Emory Bellard as head coach.

Under Wilson's direction, the crippled Aggies defeated Rice and SMU, dropped games to Arkansas and Texas, and beat TCU to wind up the season with an invitation to play Iowa State in the Hall of Fame Bowl.

The Aggies defeated Iowa State 28–12 to end the season at 8–4.

It was the task of Tom Wilson to put together the remains of an A&M team that had started the 1978 season on a high note and ended on a sad one. Wilson's first test was against an old and testy rival, Rice.

Incredibly, the team was able to overcome Bellard's resignation and defeat the Owls 38–21. The win raised A&M's record to 5–2.

In the four days Wilson had to prepare for the game, he introduced some new twists to the Aggie offense. On the first play of the game, end Doug Teague was sent in motion in a formation never used by Bellard. Quarterback Mike Mosley took the snap from center, dropped back, and passed fifty-two yards to Gerry Carter for a touchdown. It was a play that Wilson had thought about for five years, but was never able to call.

Just one week later, against SMU, the Aggies battled the Mustangs for fifty-five minutes, and the score stood 17–17.

Kicker Tony Franklin, who dreamed of kicking a field goal that would win an important game, saw his fantasy become reality against SMU. With a minute left on the clock, Tony, who kicked barefooted, calmly wiped his feet and then booted a game-winning twenty-nine-yarder. The final was 20–17.

The kick was worth more than the victory for Franklin. With the boot, Franklin broke the NCAA record for the most field goals (fifty-four), most field-goal attempts (ninety-six), and most career kick-scoring points (282).

Next, with representatives from four major bowls looking on, the Aggies lost a vital game to Arkansas 26–7.

Following the game, A&M officials accepted a bid to face Iowa State in the Hall of Fame Bowl to be played in Birmingham, Alabama, on December 20. It was the fourth straight year that a Texas A&M team would appear in a post-season bowl game.

Before the Iowa State game, A&M had to battle its bitter Texas rival on December 1 at

Tom Wilson replaced Emory Bellard in mid-season of 1978 and went 4–2 the rest of the season, including a 28–12 Hall of Fame Bowl victory over Iowa State. Wilson's teams enjoyed moderate success and beat Texas in back-to-back years, 1979 and 1980. Despite a 33–16 Independence Bowl victory over Oklahoma State in 1981, Wilson was removed as head coach following the game.

Curtis Dickey fights off a Longhorn and breaks away for a big gain. Dickey was an all-SWC tailback who ran for 276 yards against Iowa State in the '78 Hall of Fame.

Austin. Texas had been invited to the Sun Bowl to meet a championship Maryland team.

The Longhorns proved to be superior in this eighty-fifth meeting between the teams and defeated A&M 22–7 before a national TV audience. With the loss, the Aggies ended the season 7–4, the first time since 1973 that a Texas A&M team had lost more than three games in a regular season.

On December 20, 1978, halfback Curtis Dickey took a giant stride toward the 1979 Heisman Trophy with a spectacular performance against Iowa State in the second Hall of Fame Bowl. Dickey ran for 276 yards on thirty-four carries, scored one touchdown, and sparked the Aggies to a convincing 28–12 win.

With the victory, the Aggies finished the season with an 8–4 record, a new football coach, and the promise of a bright future.

Brigham Young, one of the nation's top passing teams, opened the 1979 season with its all-American quarterback Marc Wilson at the height of his career. But the Aggies' strong defensive unit corralled Wilson and his mates and seemingly had the game well in hand.

Leading 17–10 with just three minutes left to play in the game, the Aggies were content to run out the clock.

But Wilson quickly moved the ball downfield to the Aggies' two-yard line. Then on fourth down, Wilson lobbed a short pass to his tight end, Clay Brown, for the touchdown that moved the Cougars to within one point of the Aggies. With the score 17–16 A&M, Wilson hit on a two-point conversion pass to give Brigham Young a thrilling 18–17 win.

The Baylor Bears held A&M scoreless for three quarters, piling up a 17–0 advantage as the game entered the final stages. Texas A&M woke up, though, and scored a quick touchdown before succumbing 17–7.

Tom Wilson had listened all week long to dozens of angry callers telling him what was wrong with the A&M football team. Aggie armchair critics blamed the team's two losses on everything from racial unrest to a lack of commitment. But on this day at State College, Pennsylvania, where the Aggies faced sixth-ranked Penn State, the Aggies played an inspired game and upset the Nittany Lions 27–14.

"It's probably the greatest win that I can remember," said Wilson, as he rode off the field on the arms of his ecstatic players.

Quarterback Mike Mosley and halfback Curtis Dickey played the best games of their lives as they ran, passed, and out-fought Penn State from the opening gun. It was Dickey who used his great speed to score three touchdowns and set up a fourth with 184 yards rushing to become the season's fourth-leading rusher in the SWC.

Gary Kubiak, a freshman, started at quarterback for A&M, but on the very first play suffered a bruised left elbow. Mosley came in and fumbled the ball on the first play, leading to a Penn State score.

But then Dickey got untracked. His first TD run was a sixty-nine-yard thing of beauty. He also scored on runs of eleven and twenty-one yards.

Full of confidence and desire, the Aggies looked toward the Cotton Bowl. But losses to Memphis State, then Texas Tech, Houston, and Arkansas ended those dreams (victories over Memphis State, Rice, SMU, and TCU helped take out some of the sting).

In a season full of more frustration than fulfillment, the Aggies ended it in the best way possible, with a stunning upset win over Texas 13–7.

Texas came into Kyle Field ranked No. 5 in the nation with a 9–1 record. A win over the Aggies would clinch a Sugar Bowl matchup against Alabama and Bear Bryant.

Instead, the Aggies sent the 'Horns to El Paso and the Sun Bowl as they sideswiped Texas with their shocking win.

The Aggies totaled thirteen points on two David Hardy field goals of twenty-two and twenty-three yards and a second-period touchdown by Curtis Dickey.

Mike Mosley called a special "Dickey" option play in the second quarter. On this play, Mosley tossed the ball to Curtis Dickey and raced for the left corner of the end zone. Dickey, who was supposed to throw a pass back to Mosley, found he was covered and then spotted an opening and took off. He sprinted into the end zone.

In the locker room after the Texas game, Coach Wilson said: "We're a hell of a lot better than a 6–5 team. There were at least three games we lost that we had in the bag. We beat Texas, and they're going to a Bowl game. We beat Penn State, and they're going to a bowl. I think we're better than both those clubs. And next year we're going to be a lot better."

The 1980 season began auspiciously with a superb victory over Mississippi and ended with another win over bitter rival Texas, second in a row for the Aggies over the 'Horns. But in between those outstanding games, victories were few and far between.

The Aggies were only able to defeat Texas Tech and TCU in addition to Texas and Ole Miss, and the season ended with just four victories and seven losses. (One such loss was 17–13 to Houston that didn't start until 11:33 P.M. Saturday night. The gun sounded at 2:41 A.M. on Sunday. All this to accommodate the Houston Astros, who were in the playoffs.) The howls of anguish by cadets, alumni, and officials mounted and Coach Tom Wilson knew that he had to turn the football program around and win an invitation to a national bowl game, or else.

In 1981, for the first time in more than a decade, the Aggies were not considered major contenders for the SWC crown. Instead, they were selected by such publications as *Texas Football* to compete for the conference cellar. Excluded from both AP and UPI honor rolls, the Aggies were ranked eighteenth in the twenty-team poll which lists the worst teams in the nation.

Coach Tom Wilson and his staff had combed every corner of Texas high school football in an effort to recruit the most promising players, and they did snatch five or six of the top prep gridders. But these youngsters would not be able to break into the lineup until their sophomore year.

The Aggies began their eighty-seventh football year with an important intersectional game against a strong California–Berkeley team in Los Angeles.

California–Berkeley scored quickly, and it appeared that the Aggies were in for a disastrous afternoon.

In the 1981 Independence Bowl quarterback Gary Kubiak passed for 255 yards and three touchdowns to lead the Aggies to victory.

The Golden Bears continued to dominate the first quarter, scoring a second touchdown, while the only offense the Aggies could muster came on a twenty-nine-yard field goal by David Hardy.

In the second period, quarterback Gary Kubiak sparked the Aggies as they showed flashes of power, but could not score. Meanwhile Cal–Berkeley racked up another fourteen points to lead 28–16.

A blistering talk by Coach Wilson during halftime motivated the Aggies and they came out fighting mad. The offense began to roll, and behind the fine efforts of halfback Johnny Hector (eighteen carries for 128 yards), the Aggies picked up steam. But they still needed another score to tie or win the game because they trailed 28–26 with less than five minutes to play.

It was up to the trusty right leg of David Hardy. With the ball on the California thirty-five-yard line, Hardy booted a field goal that just hit the crossbar and bounced in to give A&M a 29–28 victory.

The following Monday morning, Texas A&M was no longer listed on the poll of the nation's bottom twenty and began to prep for its next game against a sturdy Boston College team.

The Aggies waited two weeks and traveled 2,000 miles for a chance to repeat their great second-half performance, which gave them a comeback win over California–Berkeley.

But on this night in September, the Boston College Eagles had a chance to come back themselves, for they had lost previous games to A&M and were hell-bent on getting even.

A&M made it easy for BC by botching up plays, fumbling the ball, and being penalized. Still, A&M led 12–6 in the fourth quarter. But another fumble turned the ball over, and the Eagles converted the TD and the PAT to win 13–12.

Louisiana Tech came into the game against A&M hoping it could stop the Aggies' potent running game.

But the Aggies were not to be denied this day, and they quickly ran up one touchdown after another as flanker Don Jones scored two touchdowns on pass completions of thirty-two and ninety-two yards in a 43–7 shellacking.

Oddly, the Texas A&M football program began going through an unstable period as rumors started circulating that someone high up in the A&M Athletic Department would be fired because of the Aggies' poor performances. Later the prophecy was realized as Athletic Director Marv Tate announced he would resign effective within the month. Who had ordered his firing

---

YELL PRACTICE and THE AGGIE BONFIRE
The First Televised Yell Practice
The World's Largest Annual Bonfire

Most schools cheer, but Aggies—YELL—! And have Yell Practices each week to boot. And at midnight.

Most schools have cheerleaders, but Aggies—have YELL LEADERS —!

Most schools use megaphones and sound systems with amplifiers. Aggie YELL LEADERS use signals passed through the stands. No sound systems are used—none are needed. Aggies take pride in their loud yells, done while in a "hump" position (bent over with hands on knees).

Most schools' cheerleaders perform gymnastics and cartwheels. Aggies strut, give hand signals, and stay on the ground.

Most schools' cheerleaders dress in shorts and skirts. Aggie YELL LEADERS wear white shirts and pants. This is serious, down-to-earth business.

Aggies stand throughout the games in the Twelfth Man tradition to show their support. Yet Aggies have more fun due to the camraderie and the knowledge that they are an integral part of the game.

The Aggie Bonfire is the world's largest annual bonfire. The bonfire symbolizes Aggies' love for Texas A&M and their burning desire to Beat t.u. Its height usually reached 100 feet, before safety concerns restricted it to 55 feet. The bonfire is held the week of the annual Thanksgiving game with t.u. and is located on the Polo Field. Months of planning and effort by the Corps and student body go into construction of the bonfire. The cuttings for timber are regulated to ensure environmental protection. The bonfire is actually one large yell practice, with attendance estimated to be in excess of 40,000. It is televised over HSE sports cable network—probably the only yell practice and/or bonfire on television.

remains unclear, but the official reason for his dismissal was that the athletic program suffered from a "lack of direction." At any rate, this heightened Wilson's anxiety about his job security.

The situation looked better after the Aggies took games from Texas Tech and Houston, each by a single point. A loss to Baylor followed, but a rousing 51–26 win over Rice made everyone on the team and coaching staff begin to feel better. Gary Kubiak threw for an A&M record six touchdown passes in the win over Rice.

But losses to SMU and Arkansas, followed by a 37–7 win over TCU, left A&M with a record of 6–4 as it began to ready itself for the crucial game against Texas.

It was a game that would decide the fate of Coach Wilson.

After Texas A&M's loss to Arkansas, powerful Aggie alumni meeting across the state began screaming for the dismissal of Wilson. The meetings continued into the day of the game between Texas and A&M, and it seemed to be a foregone conclusion that unless Wilson defeated Texas, he would be out.

At any rate, the A&M players gave every indication that they knew how important this final game of the season could be for their coach and pledged they would win.

On Thanksgiving Day, a record crowd of more than 71,000 fans saw a Texas Longhorn team that was too big and strong for A&M. Texas scored three touchdowns in the second period to win 21–13.

In the Independence Bowl against Oklahoma State, it was the brilliant play of A&M quarterback Gary Kubiak, who passed for 255 yards, that led to a 33–16 win. Kubiak teamed with flanker Jim Williams on scoring passes of fifty and thirty-eight yards and tailback Johnny Hector scored on a five-yard jaunt. Another offensive standout, David Hardy, connected on four field goals, including a fifty-yard shot to round out the scoring in a game that concluded Coach Tom Wilson's career at A&M.

Aggie seniors who played their last game for their alma mater included Kent Adams, Temple Aday, Keith Baldwin, Dave Bandy, Dan Davis, John Dawson, Larry Edmondson, David Hill, Mike Little, and Ricky Lopez.

12

JACKIE SHERRILL SPELLS SUCCESS

Success: It's what every football coach wants, yet most find highly elusive. But not the new Texas A&M athletic director and head football coach Jackie Sherrill.

Success and Sherrill have known each other for quite some years. And to Sherrill, there's only one form of football: successful football.

He's known nothing but. Ever since his playing days at Alabama when the Tide and fabled coach Bear Bryant won two national championships and played in three major bowls, success has been his best friend. And his long association with success didn't end at Alabama. It continued when Jackie moved to Arkansas, Iowa State, Pittsburgh, Washington State, and Texas A&M.

Jackie Sherrill's head-coaching record was dazzling. His first job was with Washington State, where he guided the Cougars to a point where they became a major player in the highly competitive Pacific 10 Conference. Then he moved over to Pittsburgh, where the Panthers went 9–2–1 and were ranked sixth in the nation. In 1978, Jackie led Pitt to an 8–4 mark. In 1979, Pitt was 11–1 and won the Fiesta Bowl as Sherrill was named Eastern Coach of the Year. The Panthers went 11–1 again in 1980 and they defeated South Carolina in the Gator Bowl.

Jackie Wayne Sherrill was born November 28, 1943, in Duncan, Oklahoma, the youngest of eight children.

Jackie's dream had been to play football for his native state's university—Oklahoma. At Biloxi High (he'd moved to Mississippi), Jackie was an all-American fullback and his mind was made up that he'd be a Sooner, until Bear Bryant entered the picture, met Jackie, and discussed football for several hours. At the end of the meeting, Jackie enrolled at Alabama on a scholarship.

Sherrill played seven different positions for the Tide and teamed with Joe Namath, Ken Stabler, and Steve Sloan to win the national title in 1964 and 1965. Deciding to give up an earlier goal of becoming a doctor, Jackie became an assistant coach at Alabama. The following year, he worked with the varsity linemen.

He then moved to Arkansas and then Iowa State, before joining Johnny Majors at Pitt as an assistant head coach.

In his debut as A&M's head coach, Jackie Sherrill's team was bothered by defensive flaws and Boston College's Doug Flutie, one of those rare quarterbacks who could pass and run and fake and run. Doug was so successful against A&M that he passed for 356 yards and three touchdowns to easily take the opener 38–16.

In 1982 the new head coach, Jackie Sherrill, discusses a pass route with tight end Mark Lewis. Sherrill would revive A&M's status as a national power before his untimely departure in 1988. He also added a new twist to the Twelfth Man tradition, recruiting members of the student body to play on the kickoff team (below).

In a complete reversal of form, the Aggies, led by quarterback Gary Kubiak's three touchdown passes and David Hardy's four field goals, ran roughshod over Texas–Arlington 61–22. UTA, the Southland Conference champ a year earlier, looked impressive as the teams lined up to start the game. However, once Kubiak unleashed his trusty rifle arm, UT–Arlington was never in the game.

Once again, the Aggies put on an incredible aerial display as quarterback Gary Kubiak filled the air with passes in a romp over Louisiana Tech, a Division II school, by a whopping 38–27 margin. Although the score indicates a rather close contest, Tech was never in the ball game, and only sloppy work by A&M's defensive unit allowed Tech to pile up 27 points. "Altogether, it was a very poor performance by us," said Sherrill, after the game.

In the first SWC game of the season, Texas Tech outscored A&M in another aerial battle. This time, A&M defense allowed Tech's passing attack 21 points in the third period to give the Red Raiders a 24–15 win. "This was a game where one player could have won for us," said Sherrill. "That player was Kubiak, and he should have thrown the ball fifty, fifty-five times instead of the thirty-five I allowed."

Once again, the Aggies fumbled their way to defeat as they dropped an important SWC game to Houston 24–20. The Aggies fumbled the ball three times, threw two interceptions, and that was the ball game and the second loss to an SWC team. The loss knocked the Aggies out of the SWC title race after just two games.

In the next two games against Baylor and Rice, the Aggies looked like a championship team. They beat the Bears 28–23 and routed the Owls, 49–7, as Kubiak threw for five touchdowns. Kubiak was named Associated Press Player of the Week. Wide receiver Don Jones tied a record by catching three touchdown passes.

When Kubiak was injured in the first period of a game against SMU, it was all over for the Aggies as substitute John Elkins, an untried sophomore, was rushed into the game. But he was not equal to the task as he fumbled the ball several times, overthrew his receivers on pass plays, and just didn't function well as the Ponies romped to a 47–9 win.

Arkansas shut out the Aggies 35–0, then Texas blew their annual Thanksgiving Day game wide open in the first period, running up a 27–0 lead. The game finally ended with the Longhorns piling on one of the highest scores in this rivalry, 53–16, dropping the Aggies to 5–6.

"Give me a couple of years and pray that my quarterback can stay healthy and I'll promise a winner," said Jackie Sherrill.

Few traditions at Texas A&M are as revered as the Twelfth Man, the Aggie who stands ready at all times to go into the football game if needed. Still, it is a historical fact that no Twelfth Man, including the 1922 original, had ever been called into action.

But that would be changed, Sherrill told the corps of cadets at the Aggies' first practice of the 1983 season.

Billy Cannon Jr. (the son of the former Heisman winner Billy Cannon) was an outstanding defensive back and kick returner from 1980–1983. Here he is returning a punt against Baylor in Sherrill's first year. A&M slipped by the Bears 28–23.

Sherrill said he would choose twelve students—ten regulars and two alternates—to serve as the A&M kickoff team at all home games.

"I have a very strong feeling about these students," Sherrill said, "I want to endorse what they're doing. They've been standing ready at games for a long time. Now they will be actually helping us out."

Sherrill's announcement sparked pandemonium on campus.

He said the students selected for the Twelfth Man program would wear jersey numbers one through twelve with a "Twelfth Man" insignia on the sleeve. "The students will handle kickoff coverage duties at all seven A&M home games," Sherrill said. "They will be treated as nonrecruited walk-ons and will be required to practice with the team on Fridays, but with their dedication and desire, I would expect most would show up for practice as often as they could."

However, the Twelfth Man Kickoff team debut was marred in the opening game against California, when an unsuccessful on-side-kick attempt to open the game turned into a California touchdown two plays later. In the second half, however, the Twelfth Man fulfilled its mission.

The score was tied 17–17 with just 1:20 left to play, when Cal fumbled the ball and A&M recovered on its own three-yard line.

Coach Sherrill called time and spoke briefly to his players on the sidelines. Then on the next play, an A&M halfback was tackled behind his own goal line and California had two points and the ball game as the gun sounded to end the battle with California in front 19–17 over the Aggies.

The Aggies beat Arkansas State 38–17 the following week as A&M kicker Alan Smith booted a record six field goals.

Meanwhile, safety Billy Cannon, the six-four, 225-pound speedster, took an Arkansas punt, raced upfield sixty yards, and wiped out two Arkansas tacklers with a tremendous stiff-arm as he scored.

Coach Sherrill utilized every man on the squad as the Aggies rolled up 38 points, scoring six touchdowns in the first win of the season. It was their first shutout in five years.

At Kyle Field the following week, Oklahoma State outplayed the Aggies in every department to come away with a 34–15 win.

A&M jumped out to a 6–0 lead in the opening minutes of the game, but frequent fumbles led to one Oklahoma score after another as the Cowboys' defense toughened each time the Aggies moved into scoring position.

A&M followed with a loss to Texas Tech 3–0, a win over Houston 30–7, a thriller of a game against Baylor that ended in a 13–13 tie, a loss to Rice and SMU, and then wins over Arkansas and TCU. On Thanksgiving Day, the Aggies stood 5–4–1 as they prepared to play 10–0 Texas, the nation's top team.

A&M played a remarkable first half against Texas as the Aggies scored two quick touchdowns. But something happened to the Aggies on their way to a stunning upset, for with just two minutes left in the half, Texas quarterback Rick McIvor tossed six passes for two touchdowns, and as the half ended, it was Texas 14, Texas A&M 13.

Then in the third period, the Longhorns really began to move. They blocked an Aggie punt and converted it into a touchdown. Then a few plays later, the 'Horns kicked a field goal.

As the Aggies attempted to move the ball, their attack stalled and they tried a kick into a harsh wind. The punt traveled about fifteen yards and Texas took over. McIvor promptly tossed a beauty of a screen pass for thirty-five yards and a TD. Two additional McIvor passes gave Texas two more scores, and it was Texas 45, A&M 13 as the ordeal ended. Needless to say, the alumni were not pleased.

But in 1984 the Aggies began the year with wins over Texas–El Paso, Iowa State, and Arkansas State. The 3–0 start was the best for an Aggie team since 1978.

His Aggies down 19–3 in the second period against Arkansas State, quarterback Kevin Murray sparked A&M's comeback with a twenty-seven-yard touchdown sprint. Then a few plays later, he completed a forty-two-yard pass to Jimmy Teal for another score, and it was 19–16.

But later, Murray, attempting to carry off tackle, was hit hard by three tacklers and had to be carried off the field. His replacement, Craig Stump, then completed three passes in a row, then a fourth pass to Jim Teal, who caught the ball on the dead run and sprinted over the goal line for another touchdown. The kick was good and Texas A&M had a thriller of a win, 22–21.

Texas Tech spoiled A&M's 3–0 record by hanging a 30–12 win over the unhappy Aggies in a game played on a wet, muddy field. A&M's Alan Smith kicked four field goals, and that was all the offense that A&M was able to generate. As a result, Tech took its fourth straight win over the Aggies.

A strictly defensive battle waged between Houston's Cougars and the Aggies resulted in a 9–7 win for the Cougars. Houston was unable to cross the goal line, but managed three field goals for the points necessary to win.

Baylor then managed to defeat A&M on a muddy field, 20–16.

Next, the Aggies picked up touchdowns by Roger Vick, Mark Lewis, and Craig Stump to beat Rice 38–14. Jim Hawkins, A&M's great runner, stole the show when he took a Rice punt and cut down the sideline, hurdled a tackler, got good blocking, and then sped sixty-eight yards for a touchdown.

But once again, the Aggies reverted to their up-and-down play as they looked ragged against SMU and went down to another defeat, 28–20. A week later, traveling to Fayetteville, Arkansas, the Aggies dropped another game to the Razorbacks 28–0. Arkansas intercepted two passes thrown by Craig Stump for touchdowns. The Hogs also recovered five Aggie fumbles that led to two more scores. Stump was relieved in the third period by reserve quarterback John Mazur, but John fumbled twice and did not key any offense for the Aggies. Ray Childress, a giant all season on defense, made thirteen tackles and recovered two Arkansas fumbles.

The Aggie offense, sputtering all season long, finally came to life in the game against TCU, ranked No. 17 in the country.

Roger Vick, an outstanding fullback for four seasons, 1983–1986, was hard to bring down. Here a Baylor tackler is dragged for ten more yards. Vick earned all-SWC honors in 1986.

Ray Childress, an all-American end in 1983 and '84, was a defensive giant for A&M. Ray captained the 1984 team which won this game against Iowa State 38–17. It was Sherrill's first team to finish over .500 as the Aggies won six and lost five.

In the very first minute of the game, the Aggie crowd of 39,000 had something to cheer about when James Flowers picked off a TCU pass and returned the ball fifty-three yards for a touchdown. Aggie halfback Anthony Toney rushed for ninety-seven yards and three touchdowns and sophomore Eric Franklin, brother of the great Tony Franklin, kicked field goals of fifty and forty-three yards to add to the Aggies' 35–21 victory. The entire Aggie squad played like champions of the past, and it looked as if they were prepared for the game of their lives the following week against Texas.

In a game played before one of the largest crowds in Memorial Stadium history, the Aggies played the finest game of their three years under Coach Jackie Sherrill to demolish the Texas Longhorns 37–12.

A&M stunned the 'Horns with a swarming defense that gave the Texas offense trouble throughout the game. Ray Childress, Rod Saddler, and Johnny Holland spent more time in the Texas backfield than some of the Longhorns. The result was the Aggies completely shut down the Texas running game.

A&M running backs Roger Vick, Anthony Toney, and Thomas Sanders came up with big plays and were aided by quarterback Craig Stump's passing to Jimmy Teal. The Aggies scored three touchdowns in the first half and had a cheering crowd on its feet as it led 20–0.

In the third period, the 'Horns responded, got to the twenty-eight-yard line, and then attempted a field goal, which was blocked by linebacker Domingo Bryant. Scott Polk scooped up the ball and, helped by great downfield blocking, scooted seventy-six yards to the Texas seven-yard line. UT held, but Franklin booted one of his three field goals.

Texas put on a two-touchdown spurt in the final minutes of the game, but it was Texas A&M all the way with a brilliant 37–12 win.

The victory gave the Aggies a 6–5 record and the first winning season of the Sherrill era.

Jackie Sherrill became an instant hero when his team ended the season with tremendous wins over TCU and Texas. The games were won with an exciting, wide-open offense, something that the fans had not seen all year.

"This is only the beginning." Sherrill said. "Wait until I get my quarterback set and a couple of good receivers and, I tell you, we're going to be tough to beat next year."

The first look at the 1985 Texas Aggies was available Saturday, April 13, during the Maroon-White spring scrimmage. Head Coach Jackie Sherrill had moved away from the Alumni-Varsity-game format as the game featured only those players hoping to see action in the fall.

Speaking of action, this game featured very little in the way of any new offense that had been sought by A&M fans. The Aggies' new "run and shoot" offense was kept under cover to prevent opposing scouts from learning too much.

John Holland, an all-SWC linebacker, impressed Coach Sherrill the most with his top-notch play in this game.

"Holland is as good as anybody in the nation," Sherrill said. "He has the potential to be an all-American this year."

A crowd of more than 74,000 fans jammed the Crimson Tide Stadium at Birmingham on a chilly, frosty September night to watch the season opener. The game was a matchup between two former teammates, Jackie Sherrill and Ray

Two-time all-American linebacker John Holland was the key to the touted Aggies defense of 1985 and 1986.

Perkins of Alabama. Sherrill and Perkins played together at Alabama under the direction of Coach Bear Bryant.

As the game began, the Alabama defense kept the Aggies out of the end zone, although A&M managed to gain more total yards than the Tide. It was one of those games that either team could have won as the teams battled each other up and down the gridiron.

Toward the end of the fourth period, Alabama had a 16–10 lead as quarterback Kevin Murray began to move the Aggies. But Alabama pounced on a fumble and with two minutes to play, scored another touchdown to lock up the victory 23–10.

Aggies senior halfback Anthony Toney, who scored the Aggies' lone touchdown, summed up the game: "We played a better game than they did; we should have won. The penalties hurt us, cost us the game."

The first home game gave the Aggies a chance to patch up the holes they found in the game plan in the loss to Alabama. The Aggies made few mistakes against Northeast Louisiana and defeated the Indians 31–17 in a smartly played game. Soph quarterback Kevin Murray, despite off-field problems, played brilliantly, leading the Aggies on all three touchdown drives. Murray passed ten times for 140 yards. The spotlight, however, was on Anthony Toney, who rushed for 106 yards and had touchdown runs of two, one, and four yards. Toney and Eric Franklin, who kicked three field goals for the day, combined for a total of 29 points.

A&M put on an incredible offensive display against Tulsa, gaining a total of 702 yards, second highest in the SWC, as the Aggie scoring machine buried Tulsa 45–10.

Texas Tech had defeated A&M three years in a row and Coach Sherrill had determined this was one game that the Aggies "must" win for a successful season. With that in mind, the A&M offense was in top form, rolling up 200 yards on the ground and 181 yards passing, and just managed to eke out a 28–27 win over the Red Raiders. Murray completed fourteen of twenty passes and Roger Vick carried the brunt of the rushing game as he gained 125 yards.

A&M picked up its fourth win in a row as it scored the most points ever against Houston and rolled over the Cougars 43–16. Murray sparked the offense with fourteen pass completions, while fullbacks Vick and Toney combined for 141 yards rushing. The win improved the Aggies' overall record to 4–1.

Quarterback Craig Stump, a freshman, was the starting quarterback for the final eight games of the '84 season, then played through '85 and '86.

Just when it appeared as if the Aggie scoring machine was set for a top national ranking, the Baylor Bears, playing the best football in the SWC, stopped the onrushing Aggies with a stunning 20–15 victory. A&M played its poorest game of the season, fumbling the ball, missing tackles, and dropping passes that could have meant a couple of touchdowns.

A few big plays by the Aggies dominated the game against Rice. A&M intercepted four passes and recovered two fumbles in a 43–28 rout. Anthony Toney and Roger Vick scored two touchdowns each, while Kevin Murray completed

Quarterback Kevin Murray was a brilliant player throughout the 1985 and '86 seasons. Under his leadership A&M played dominant offensive football, scoring 747 points over two seasons and winning 19 games.

sixteen passes, including a forty-yarder to Shea Walker for a touchdown.

SMU had a six-year winning streak against A&M, and at long last, the Mustangs were rated among the nation's top twenty teams. But all of that evaporated in the big game at College Station.

There was only 1:46 left to play in the game and SMU led 17–16, when Coach Sherrill gave Eric Franklin the "field goal sign" and Eric instantly complied. He brushed his toe, shot forward as the ball came to his holder, and drove his right foot into the ball . . . and it rose and rose more than forty-eight yards, true as an arrow, and as the ball went over the crossbar, the gun went off to end the game and A&M had a thriller of a win, 19–17.

The victory over SMU gave A&M a 6–2 record as it rose to the top of the conference. The victory guaranteed a post-season bowl bid for the Aggies.

The Arkansas Razorbacks visited Kyle Field with a No. 9 national ranking and one of the best, and trickiest, wishbone offenses in the land. However, they left town making other plans for New Year's Day as the Aggies, playing their best game thus far, defeated Arkansas 10–6.

The A&M defense stonewalled every move by the Razorback offense. Domingo Bryant recovered an Arkansas fumble and the Aggies turned the misplay into a touchdown. Then Eric Franklin booted another three-pointer, and the Aggies had their seventh win of the year.

In another must-win situation, A&M combined a wide-open attack with a stubborn defense to easily down TCU 53–6. Murray completed fifteen of twenty-two passes as he picked the TCU defense to shreds. Murray picked up 246 passing yards, including passes to Keith Woodside, Jeff Nelson, and Shea Walker for touchdowns. Toney scored twice, and Ira Valentine also scored a touchdown as every man on the roster, including the "Twelfth Man" crew, got into the game.

Coach Sherrill celebrated his forty-second birthday on Thanksgiving Day. As a gift from his players, the Aggies scored a 42–10 win over Texas. After the game, Sherrill said, "This was the best gift I've ever received on my birthday."

The win over Texas gave A&M a trip to the Cotton Bowl and a game against the star-studded Auburn University team.

The dream came true and the big day finally arrived.

The entire nation had its eyes on the Aggies and their Cotton Bowl rivals, the Auburn Tigers, led by Heisman Trophy winner Bo Jackson. The Las Vegas oddsmakers favored Auburn 2–1.

The game began at a slow pace, but then A&M came on strong with two quick scores plus a field goal by Franklin in the second period to take a 15–13 lead over the Tigers.

Fullback Anthony Toney (all-SWC in 1985) runs for daylight behind the blocking of Louis Cheek (no. 78) and halfback Keith Woodside. A&M captured its first SWC crown under Sherrill in 1985—its first since 1975. The Aggies would win the next two titles and rack up 29 victories over three years.

Late in the third quarter and into the fourth, A&M picked up the pace, outscored the Tigers 21–3, and ran away with the game 36–16.

Murray set a Cotton Bowl record with 292 passing yards, while Toney, Vick, Rod Bernstine, and Woodside piled up rushing and receiving records.

The Aggie defense, meanwhile, was unyielding. Late in the fourth period, they stopped Jackson on four tries at the goal line to keep Auburn out of the end zone. Domingo Bryant contributed two interceptions, robbing Auburn of scoring opportunities.

A&M, with a 10–2 season record, captured the SWC crown and was voted the No. 5 team in the nation.

Coach Jackie Sherrill called the Cotton Bowl win the "biggest of my life," and the season "one of the greatest."

If Jackie Sherrill had any hopes of a national title in 1986, they ended abruptly when the Aggies came up short in their opening game of the season against LSU, losing 35–17.

The game marked a renewal of the series that originated in 1899 between these two great Southern powers. LSU led in the series 23–14 with 3 tie games and the rivalry was rekindled at that year's game as 79,713 people jammed every inch of Tiger Stadium.

The Aggies began the game as if they were going to blow LSU right out of the ball park. They moved the ball effortlessly seventy-five yards within the first few minutes for a touchdown. But the Aggies took themselves out of the game in the second period with key turnovers and a porous defense that allowed LSU a number of big plays. The Tigers scored on a beautiful pass play that went for sixty-five yards, then followed with touchdown drives of thirty-one and thirty-four yards for two additional scores to win going away.

The following week, the Aggies rebounded from the LSU loss and trounced North Texas

In the 1986 Cotton Bowl (A&M's first since 1968) against Auburn and Bo Jackson, the Aggies, led by Kevin Murray, Roger Vick, Rod Bernstine, and Keith Woodside piled up rushing and receiving records. Here Bernstine (no. 29) is ready to ramble as Rod Harris (no. 17) and Keith Woodside (no. 33) clear his path. A&M won 36–16.

State 48–28 in a game that gave playing time to every man on the team, including the players on the Twelfth Man squad.

For the seventh consecutive year, A&M opened its SWC title defense against the Texas Tech Raiders, and for the first time in eighteen years, the Aggies were the defending SWC and Cotton Bowl champs.

After a shaky first period, the Aggies took command of the game, picking up six straight first downs at one point in a drive that covered fifty-five yards. Roger Vick drove over for the first touchdown; from that point on, the Aggie offense couldn't miss. Murray passed for 285 yards as the Aggies rolled to a 45–8 win.

A week later, the Aggies snuffed out Houston 19–7 as Scott Slater kicked four field goals. The win brought A&M's record to 4–1.

Baylor opened its game with A&M with a bang, and before the stunned Aggies knew what was happening, the Bears led 17–0.

But Murray saved A&M from oblivion by streaking eighteen yards for a score, then throwing for three additional touchdowns.

Baylor, however, held a six-point lead going into the final four minutes of the game. But Murray faked a pass to his left, dodged two tacklers, and lobbed a pass to Tony Thompson, who caught it to claim a 31–30 victory.

Afterward, Jackie Sherrill praised his players and said: "I've been around the game a long time, and I've never seen a comeback like that ever."

Despite injuries to four key players, A&M continued on its winning ways with a smashing 45–10 victory over Rice as Kevin Murray took advantage of the Owls' defensive mistakes to pass for 215 yards and a touchdown, giving him the school's record for career yardage. Murray also moved into fifth place on the all-time SWC yardage list with 5,542 yards.

The following week, SMU scored 21 points and gained 250 yards in the first half to take a 21–0 lead. Then the Aggies uncorked their offensive bag of tricks, ran up 17 points, and trailed 21–17 at halftime.

Each team took turns going into the lead in the third and fourth periods. Then with 2:35 left in the game, the Aggies got the ball on their forty-nine-yard line. Keith Woodside snared a pass that looked as if he had no chance at all to catch. After outjumping two defenders for the ball, Woodside came down to earth in the end zone and A&M had a 39–35 victory.

The seventh-ranked Aggies ran out of game-winning comebacks against Arkansas as the Hogs upset them 14–10. Arkansas used a ball-control offense and quick defense to overtake A&M as the Aggies showed little resemblance to the team that had rallied for a last-minute win over SMU two weeks before.

Arkansas scored its first touchdown with a nice mixture of running and passing plays and A&M charged back with a touchdown to tie the score at 7–7. Then Arkansas answered to take a 14–7 lead.

Scott Slater kicked a forty-yard field goal with just six and a half minutes left to play in the game to bring the score to 14–10. With just three minutes remaining, A&M took control of the ball and got to the Arkansas sixteen-yard line, where Murray tried in vain to score, tossing four incompletions.

A week later, in a complete reversal of form, the Aggies trounced TCU in an amazing offensive display as they racked up a 74–10 win. The Aggies scored on eleven of their first twelve possessions as Kevin Murray rang up a total of 508 passing yards to break Gary Kubiak's single-game mark.

A&M's 16–3 win over the Longhorns wasn't the prettiest exhibition of football, but it did fulfill two goals: The Aggies beat Texas for the third time in a row and the victory assured them of a Cotton Bowl berth against the outstanding champions of the Big Ten, Ohio State.

Against Ohio State, the powerful Aggie offense never got started and at halftime it was a 7–6 game with Ohio State in front. But in the third period, all-American Chris Spielman of Ohio State intercepted two Murray passes, and returned one for a touchdown. Another interception, by Michael Kee, gave the Buckeyes another score in the third period, dashing A&M's hopes. The Buckeyes played a cautious, defensive battle the rest of the game to take the Cotton Bowl title. Final score: Ohio State 28, Texas A&M 12.

The sports programs at Texas A&M during 1987–88 were linked by a common characteristic. In just about every major sport, A&M squads were in a rebuilding situation and forced to rely on newcomers and replacements for the important contributions.

Perhaps nowhere was this more apparent than in the football program in 1987 as Coach Jackie Sherrill prepared to face one of the most difficult schedules in his six years as football coach.

Sherrill dealt with the loss of his star quarterback, Kevin Murray, who in his three years at A&M had broken all sorts of passing records and led the team to three outstanding seasons. Sherrill dealt with this problem for 1987 by using a three-man rotation consisting of Craig Stump, freshman Lance Pavlas, and another outstanding frosh, Bucky Richardson.

One would have to search long and hard to find a more rags-to-riches story than the Bucky Richardson saga. After leaving Louisiana to come to A&M, Bucky was not expected to see much action because he had learned the quarterback position in high school in an option offense.

But when the passing game sputtered in A&M's first game of the season and LSU defeated A&M 17–3, Bucky was installed as the quarterback in the game against Southern Mississippi. Late in the fourth quarter, he sped eighty-two yards for a touchdown as the Aggies scored an impressive 27–14 win. Bucky's touchdown run was the third longest in A&M history.

In the game against Texas Tech, nothing went right for the Aggies as their offense sputtered and stopped as the Red Raiders scored on two long plays in the first period to take a 14–0 lead. Then Keith Woodside scored on a fifty-six-yard scamper after recovering a Tech fumble. Two minutes later, freshman sprinter Darren Lewis scored after intercepting a Tech pass and the score was tied 14–14.

Tech picked up another score and a field goal to go ahead 24–14 at the half and late in the game, a Tech field goal gave the Raiders a substantial 27–14 edge.

Late in the game, fullback Matt Gurley of A&M dashed eight yards for an Aggie score to make it 27–21 as time ran out in the third quarter.

Quarterback Craig Stump played an inconsistent first period against the Houston Cougars and Coach Sherrill replaced him in the second period

From 1987 to '91, halfback Darren Lewis was a sensation. A 10 second sprinter in the 100-yard dash, Darren was a threat to score every time he got the ball. He tallied almost twenty 100-yard games. In 1988 and 1990 Lewis was an all-American.

Freshman Bucky Richardson was installed at quarterback in the first game of the 1987 season against LSU.

with rookie quarterback Bucky Richardson, who had been playing well in practice sessions. On the Aggies' first possession, Bucky had the Aggies moving and quickly drove to a touchdown en route to a 22–17 victory.

It was a bittersweet win for A&M because the victim was Houston coach Jack Pardee, the former Aggies great.

Richardson again sparked A&M in its 34–10 bruising of Baylor.

After the game, Sherrill said, "I told our guys that not only did we become an average football team, but we had become a very good one, and we moved in the direction to become a great one."

A&M trounced Louisiana Tech 32–3 as the Aggies' great defensive unit limited Tech to 103 yards. A&M compiled 620 yards on the ground as Richardson keyed the attack with 108 yards himself and his direction of the Aggies offense was perfect.

In the game against Rice, Richardson took a pass from his center on the second play from scrimmage and scooted through tackle and was off on a spectacular fifty-six-yard touchdown sprint. But Rice scored a TD and it was 7–6 A&M.

Larry Horton and Darren Lewis teamed up on a seventy-five-yard play, and the next time A&M

had the ball, Scott Slater kicked a forty-one-yard field goal. Five minutes later, Slater booted a twenty-eight-yarder and it was 20–13 A&M. In the third and fourth periods, A&M added two touchdowns, one by Lewis and another by Gary Oliver, to wrap up an outstanding 34–21 victory.

A&M's defense stifled the Arkansas offense as the Aggies moved out in front of the SWC race with a 14–0 win over the Hogs. The victory at Kyle Field came before a record-breaking crowd of 73,511.

It was the first shutout for an A&M team since 1978, and the first time an Arkansas team had been held scoreless since 1983.

Early in the first period, Arkansas kicked the ball after failing to move on three downs, and Rod Harris put the Aggies in front by taking the punt and racing away from three Hog tacklers, speeding for sixty-six yards and a touchdown.

Then with both teams battling each other, neither having an advantage until late in the fourth period, Craig Stump directed an A&M drive for seventy-eight yards to the five-yard line and then shot a pass to Gary Oliver and Oliver hit pay dirt to give A&M a 14–0 win.

The day was cold, windy, and wet, but that didn't seem to bother running back Darren Lewis, who took a pitchout from quarterback Craig Stump, fumbled the ball, but quickly scooped it up, and dashed eighty yards for the first touchdown against TCU.

The Frogs came back with a terrific burst of scoring and forged in front 24–23 at the half. But in the second half, A&M picked up nineteen points on touchdowns by Lewis and Harris and a field goal by Slater to win going away 42–24.

A record crowd of more than 78,000 fans enjoyed a great Thanksgiving party at Kyle Field as Texas A&M outplayed Texas to win the annual holiday battle 20–13.

Texas took an early lead as A&M fumbled the ball on its first possession on the A&M twenty-nine-yard line and Texas recovered the ball. But the Aggies stopped Texas on three downs and the Longhorns' Wayne Clements booted a forty-seven-yarder to give the 'Horns a 3–0 lead.

Late in the second period, with both teams playing a strictly defensive battle, A&M took the ball on its own ten-yard line. Stump faked a pass, then pivoted and handed the ball to halfback Keith Woodside, playing his last game for the Aggies, and all Keith did was drive off tackle, reverse his field, and gallop ninety yards for the spectacular touchdown to give the Aggies a 7–3 lead.

But Texas was not through. On the very next play, Texas caught the Aggies on a blitz and Eric Metcalf took a screen pass and dashed fifty-five yards for a Texas score. It was 10–7, Texas.

Scott Slater then booted the longest field goal of his A&M career—a beautiful fifty-three-yarder—and it was a 10–10 game at halftime.

Then Bucky Richardson, in at quarterback for Stump, managed to break loose for twenty-five yards and a touchdown to win the game for A&M 20–13 just as the gun sounded.

The victory gave A&M the SWC crown and a Cotton Bowl date.

Once again, the Aggies traveled to Dallas to meet a Heisman Trophy winner. This time it was Notre Dame's great flanker, Tim Brown, a sprinter, who could run the 100-yard dash in his football uniform in ten seconds. Brown sped seventeen yards for Notre Dame's first score against the Aggies in the first period. Then A&M's Scott Slater promptly came back with a field goal from the twenty-six-yard line, and it was a 7–3 game. But Notre Dame's Jack Graedel kicked a thirty-six-yard field goal to up the lead to 10–3.

The Aggies then scored on a trick play set up by halfback Darren Lewis, who took a pitchout, then shot a twenty-five-yard pass to Tony Thompson, who just walked in for the touchdown.

With the ball in Notre Dame's possession, the Irish fumbled on their twenty-one-yard line. Moments later, A&M's Larry Horton cracked through the Irish line for a touchdown. The two-point conversion made it Texas A&M 18, Notre Dame 10.

Quarterback Bucky Richardson guided the Aggies on another drive in the third quarter, with Pavlas and Horton carrying the ball. Richardson then scored the touchdown from the six-yard line. The Aggies then poured it on for a 35–10 win.

Jackie Sherrill and his Aggies were sitting atop the football world and looking for new worlds to conquer.

From 1979 to 1988 Texas A&M had one of the most successful football programs in the nation, chalking up three SWC titles, two Cotton Bowl victories, seven winning seasons and, best of all, four straight lickings of Texas. Defense was the hallmark of these teams, and the following Aggies, all of them all-Americans, were key performers during that period. Clockwise from top: Jacob Green, 1979, defensive end; Ray Childress, 1983, '84, defensive end (no. 53); Johnny Holland, 1985, '86, linebacker; Doug Williams, 1985, tackle; John Roper, 1987, linebacker.

Texas A&M's sensational victory over Notre Dame in the Cotton Bowl marked the end of an era in Aggie football as sixteen seniors ended their college football careers on a high note.

This senior class was one of the most successful ever to perform on Kyle Field. Under coach Jackie Sherrill, the Aggies collected three SWC crowns, two Cotton Bowl titles, and won 31 of their last 38 games, including their fourth straight over Texas.

In 1988, the Aggies looked forward to another successful season, but they dropped an unheard of three straight opening games to Nebraska, LSU, and Oklahoma State. To make matters worse, A&M was placed on probation by the NCAA after a former player, George Smith, made allegations of a payoff to him by Coach Sherrill and an assistant coach.

The Smith bombshell was a national front-page sports story which finally led to Sherrill relinquishing his dual posts as athletic director and football coach. R. C. Slocum, an assistant, replaced Sherrill for one game (TCU), an 18–0 A&M victory.

Then to the astonishment of the experts, the Aggies, playing like the championship team of '87, went on to beat Texas Tech, Houston, Baylor, and Louisiana Tech, before losing to Arkansas and Alabama. The annual battle with the Longhorns would be Sherrill's next to last game at A&M.

Perhaps as a present for their coach of the past seven years, the Aggies outplayed the 'Horns and their defense shut down Texas in a close 28–24 triumph.

In the opening twenty-five minutes of play, the Aggies were full of pep and vinegar and jumped off to a 28–0 lead. The Longhorns were asleep at the switch.

A&M scored after eleven minutes of play in the first period as Lewis, the Aggie speedster, broke away for a fifteen-yard TD. Slater added the first of his four extra-point kicks, and it was 7–0.

Then on the next possession, Bucky Richardson, A&M's great quarterback, sparked the team on a forty-eight-yard drive to the Texas seven. Bucky was hit hard, fumbled the ball, and had to leave the game with an injury. Chris Osgood replaced Bucky and engineered a TD drive. The A&M special team got a chance to play, and the "Blitz Brothers," John Roper and Aaron Wallace, combined to block a field goal and turn it into another Aggie score. Now it was 21–0.

Osgood then led the Aggies on a sixty-eight-yard drive, and capped it with a ten-yard keeper.

At halftime, the Longhorns had made only four first downs and ninety-eight total yards. Sherrill, back after the TCU game, credited the Aggie seniors for their leadership and play.

In the second half, A&M relaxed, and in so doing, almost lost the ball game as Texas mounted a furious drive, intercepted two passes for touchdowns, and recovered two A&M fumbles for two more scores to climb to within 28–24.

A&M was holding on for dear life. Fortunately for the Aggies, however, A&M held off the 'Horns, and the game finally ended with A&M in front of Texas for the fifth straight time under Coach Jackie Sherrill. The Aggies' 500th win in their history proved to be Sherrill's last.

Alabama ended Sherrill's reign at A&M with a merciless 30–10 victory.

On December 12, Sherrill formally handed in his resignation as football coach and athletic director and R. C. Slocum was named to replace him.

John David Crow, former Aggie Heisman Trophy winner, was named athletic director as a new era in Texas A&M football was at hand.

13

A RENEWAL OF FAITH WITH COACH R. C. SLOCUM

Replacing one of the winningest coaches in A&M history was a formidable task, but Richard Copeland (R. C.) Slocum immediately proved that he had the experience and background to handle the toughest head coaching job in the Southwest Conference. In his five seasons at the helm, Slocum—an assistant to Emory Bellard, Tom Wilson and Jackie Sherrill from 1972 until 1988—has stockpiled a dazzling 49–12–1 record (including Cotton Bowl loss to Notre Dame) and established a wheelbarrow of A&M and SWC records. Most impressive of all his accomplishments is his winning percentage, the highest of all active Division I coaches with at least five years' service.

Making Slocum's record more remarkable is the fact that he inherited a squad shocked over the controversy surrounding the dismissal of Jackie Sherrill. Slocum was able to handle these unfortunate problems because he was well-acquainted with Aggie football. He knew the players, he knew the schedule, and he knew all the problems associated with the NCAA's probe into the A&M program. The rookie head coach assembled the players, calmed their fears, and pointed out that they had to face all kinds of problems in life. This one was just one more that had to be solved.

Slocum's low-key, straight-shooting manner won over his players. According to quarterback Bucky Richardson, "Coach Slocum is one of the guys. You don't get nervous about him. It's never, 'Uh-oh, here comes the coach, better look out.' We could go to his office and talk to him any time."

One of the favorite topics of discussion is motivation. According to Slocum, the best motivation is self-motivation. It had led Slocum from Oakdale, Louisiana, where he was born in 1944, to Orange, Texas, where he was an all-District end on a team that reached the semifinals his senior year.

Slocum attended McNeese State College, where he set several receiving records and earned a graduate degree in education administration. Slocum took over as defensive coordinator at Lake Charles High School in 1968–69 before moving on to the collegiate ranks. He served two years at Kansas State, then joined the Aggies' staff in 1972. Except for one season, 1981, when John Robinson called him to head his defensive staff at Southern Cal, Slocum was an Aggie assistant coach until being hired to replace Jackie Sherrill.

Along the way Slocum acquired a reputation for building rock-solid defenses around hard-hitting, aggressive, enthusiastic young men.

Texas A&M's new head coach, R. C. Slocum, an assistant at A&M since 1972, produced a solid first year in 1989, winning eight games and losing four.

Fullback Bob Wilson sparkled in the opening game against Hawaii in 1990, scoring two touchdowns.

"You like to lead a person to the point where he is excited about being the best he can be and aspires to get the most out of himself in every thing he pursues," he explains. "We try to create an atmosphere where the players believe in themselves. You encourage a person to work at it, set goals and you can accomplish anything you set out to achieve and be something special."

The 1989 edition of the Aggies was something special right out of the chute. In Slocum's head coaching debut, Larry Horton hauled the opening kickoff back ninety-two yards for a touchdown to spark a 28–16 upset win over seventh-ranked Louisiana State. It was the Aggies' first victory over the Tigers since 1975.

In his rookie season, Slocum turned out an A&M team that won eight games and lost four. With luck, though, R. C. could have had an 11–1 season. But A&M dropped a wild and woolly 27–24 game to Texas Tech, lost to a top-ranked Arkansas team by a point, 23–22, and then fell to Pitt in the John Hancock Bowl, 33–28.

On Thanksgiving Day, however, Slocum's Aggies surprised 76,803 fans with a 21–10 upset win over Texas. It marked the sixth consecutive time the Aggies had defeated their archrival. Moreover, the confident manner in which A&M won the game indicated that this team would be a contender for national honors in the near future.

In 1990, the Texas A&M team began the season recognized by the AP as No. 13 in the nation. But five time zones and an island atmosphere had Slocum worrying as the Aggies traveled to Hawaii for the opening game against the Rainbow Warriors.

Slocum's fears proved unfounded as the Aggies cruised to a 28–13 win. Running back Darren Lewis rushed for 117 yards on twenty-four carries for a touchdown. It was Lewis's eighteenth 100-yard game, breaking Curtis Dickey's A&M record of seventeen. Fullback Robert Wilson scored two touchdowns and quarterback Lance Pavlas handled the team flawlessly and threw for a touchdown to Wilson.

A&M then set a school record, gaining 774 yards in routing Southwest Louisiana 63–14. The Aggies so dominated the game that punter Sean Williams never got a chance to kick the ball.

Quarterback Lance Pavlas passed for ten completions and scored three touchdowns to lead the Aggies to an easy win.

Next, North Texas was ambushed 40–8, but the overconfident Aggies were beaten in a thriller of a battle by LSU 17–8.

The turning point in the LSU game occurred in the second period, when the Aggie halfback Darren Lewis was ejected from the game for tossing an elbow at an LSU player. With their star running back out of the game, the Aggies had little in the way of an offense and dropped the game by the score of 17–8.

A&M's running game led the way next as the Aggies defeated Texas Tech 28–24 in a nail biter that was not decided until the final moments.

Heisman Award candidate Darren Lewis rushed for 232 yards in thirty-four carries, his first 200-yard game of the season.

The most dramatic moment of the game came as time expired in the second period. A&M had just driven seventy-three yards in nine plays to take a 7–6 lead. But on the ensuing kickoff, Tech's Rod Blackshear took the kick, banged through two A&M tacklers, cut to the sideline, and raced ninety-two yards for a touchdown, the first ever scored against the Twelfth Man kickoff team. After the TD, Slocum benched the Twelfth Man for the rest of the game.

Houston defeated the Aggies in a come-from-behind thriller, scoring a touchdown in the final minute for a 36–31 victory.

Quarterback Bucky Richardson, who had injured a knee in 1988, started his first game in two years, but Bucky couldn't rouse the Aggies from their lethargy. As a result, Baylor and A&M played to a dull 20–20 tie.

Successive wins over SMU 38–17 and Rice 41–15, plus a surprise upset win over the two-time defending conference champion Arkansas Razorbacks, gave the Aggies a 7–2–1 season mark and a shot at another Cotton Bowl game, if they could defeat TCU and Texas.

A&M did win over TCU in convincing fashion, 56–10, and the representatives from the Holiday Bowl offered A&M a game against Brigham Young. Texas A&M officials approved the game.

However, the Aggies had to meet Texas before the Brigham Young game, and they had just one week to prepare for the Longhorns, who had clinched the SWC crown, prior to the Thanksgiving Day game against A&M.

On Thanksgiving Day, the Aggies jumped out to an early 14–0 lead as Darren Lewis sprinted for two touchdowns. But Texas, just as determined, ran for three scores and took the lead 21–14. The Aggies scored again, but Texas came right back to lead 28–21 with just four minutes left to play.

A&M drove eighty yards for another score to pull within one point of the 'Horns. But Texas stopped Darren Lewis on the two-point conversion as time ran out, and the 'Horns had a 28–27 thriller.

Three weeks later in San Diego, the Aggies stampeded ninth-ranked Brigham Young in the

Bucky Richardson rejoices after adding another touchdown in A&M's 65–14 rout of Brigham Young in the 1990 Holiday Bowl.

Running back Greg Hill rushed for 212 yards and two touchdowns against LSU in 1991. The Aggies coasted to a 45–7 opening victory en route to a 10–2 record and their first SWC title since '87.

Holiday Bowl, 65–14. The 51-point margin of victory was the greatest in collegiate bowl history.

This was a tale of two quarterbacks. Ty Detmer, BYU's Heisman Trophy winner, was knocked out in the first quarter and never returned. Meanwhile, Bucky Richardson had a day too good even for dreams. He accounted for 322 yards of total offense, passing for 203 and rushing for another 119. He tossed one touchdown pass and scored three more himself, including a twenty-two-yard reception from Darren Lewis on a trick play in the second quarter. All told, the Aggies outgained the Cougars by nearly 500 yards.

The Holiday Bowl win put the Aggies at 9–3–1 for the season, and they finished fifteenth in the final Associated Press rating for college football teams.

In the final game of the year, twenty-four Aggie seniors said goodbye to their college football years at Texas A&M, and they all got a chance against BYU and played their level best.

It was more than eight months after the Aggies had routed Brigham Young in the Holiday Bowl, and the Aggies were still in stride, rolling over Louisiana State 45–7 in the opening game of the 1991 season.

Minus the services of their crack quarterback Bucky Richardson and fullback Doug Carter, the Aggies looked as if they were still capable of beating any team in the nation as freshman tailback Greg Hill exploded for two touchdowns and 212 rushing yards. In this, his first game in an Aggie uniform, Hill broke the rushing record for a freshman in his first game. Redshirt freshman Jeff Granger had a huge day, throwing for four TD passes.

Critics say a young, inexperienced team is supposed to make mistakes in a football game,

Quarterback Bucky Richardson leads the Aggies over Baylor. He passed for 182 yards and scored two touchdowns as A&M pounded out a 34–12 win in the 1991 game. Baylor was ranked 16th in the nation at the time.

Texas A&M wide receiver Tony Harrison leaps high in the air to take the ball away from two Rice defenders in a game. A&M won 38–21 in 1991.

but in the game against the Tulsa Hurricanes, the Aggies made all the mistakes—and they were costly.

As a result, A&M dropped a hair-raising thriller to Tulsa 35–34.

The Aggies thundered to a big 28–10 halftime lead, and it looked as if they were going to coast in for another win.

But the unrated, unranked Tulsa team jumped all over the Aggies in the third period, scoring nineteen points to take a 29–28 lead. Then in the final period, A&M scored a touchdown to go in front 34–29. With five minutes left in the game, Tulsa pulled out the victory with a last-minute score.

Next, the Aggies took good care of Southwestern Louisiana 34–7 in a game that was dedicated to the U.S. troops in Operation Desert Storm as Bucky Richardson, Greg Hill, Tony Harrison, and Kevin Smith all played well.

One week later, the Aggies played like champions as they demolished Texas Tech in the first Aggie win at Tech's Jones Field since 1985.

It was all Bucky Richardson in the first half. All he did was score three touchdowns, rush for seventy-nine yards, and pass for 121 yards. Richardson was named player of the game after guiding A&M to a near-perfect 37–14 victory.

The nation's sportswriters and commentators realized that the Texas Aggies were a team to be reckoned with after they pounded out a 34–12 win over the fifteenth-ranked Baylor Bears in a game that saw the Aggies' two touchdown stars, Richardson and Greg Hill, dominate the game. Richardson set the tempo by scoring two touchdowns, passing for 182 yards, and rushing for forty-two more as he played the finest game of his young career. Bucky keyed the win by tossing a beautiful pass of twenty-five yards to Tony Harrison on the first play of the game for a touchdown; the stunned Bears looked on in frozen silence as Tony sped in for the score. From that point in the game, the Bears never recovered their poise and the Aggies easily beat them.

For the third straight week, Bucky Richardson was the key to the Aggies' offense. Richardson scored A&M's only touchdown in the third quarter as he bulled his way into the end zone from fifteen yards out, carrying three defenders on his back.

The Aggies then churned out a 21–3 lead over Houston and began to coast in the third period before the Cougars rang up fifteen unanswered points to close to 21–18.

But Aggie Greg Hill sped twenty-seven yards for a touchdown late in the third period to guarantee a 27–18 win for A&M.

The victory brought the Aggies to a 5–1 overall record and 3–0 in SWC games.

All the Aggies now needed was to defeat SMU to clinch the SWC crown. The Aggies roared out of their dressing room, tore into the Mustangs from the start, scored two quick touchdowns within six minutes, and continued to pour in fresh troops, including The Twelfth Man group, in a 65–6 rout. A&M was simply a powerhouse as it captured its first SWC title in four years.

Texas A&M had won the SWC title, and the next stop was the Cotton Bowl. But Coach Slocum would not accept a bowl bid until the Aggies met and defeated the Texas Longhorns.

The Aggie players were so anxious for a postseason bowl game that they made certain they would beat their ancient rivals, the Longhorns.

On Thanksgiving Day, the eager Aggies tore out after the 'Horns. A&M linebacker Marcus Buckley leaped high in the air, intercepted a Texas pass, and sped nineteen yards for a touchdown.

Later in the third period, cornerback Kevin Smith returned a Texas punt seventy-three yards for another score. Greg Hill scored after A&M drove upfield for eighty yards, then he ran two yards for another Aggie touchdown as A&M rolled over Texas 31–14.

The Aggies' winning streak of nine in a row came to a quick and sudden end in the Cotton Bowl as Florida State, alert enough to recover a total of eight Aggie fumbles, scored just one touchdown to defeat the Aggies 10–2 in a game that displayed little offense.

The Aggies drove through the Seminoles' defense with ease as the game opened and Greg Hill sped off tackle and got into the open field. But as he reached the end zone, Hill fumbled the ball and the Seminoles recovered on the two-yard line. Florida State then tried to move the ball, but A&M's great linebacker, Quentin Coryatt, sacked FSU quarterback Casey Weldon for a safety. But A&M could not generate any offense as Florida scored a touchdown in the first period and a field goal in the fourth to take a 10–2 victory.

The bowl loss to Florida State, while disappointing, couldn't really diminish another marvelous season. Slocum praised his team for its superior play, particularly on defense. The '91 Aggies had led the nation in total defense, surrendering but 222 yards a game, and the '92 squad had built on that excellence, once again leading the Southwest Conference in all four major defensive categories (total defense, rushing defense, scoring defense and pass efficiency defense).

Slocum had made hard-hitting defense a trademark of A&M football, first as defensive coordinator and now as head coach. The Aggies' blitzing style can be likened to ants swarming on a candy bar. The "Wrecking Crew's" basic scheme, a 3–4–4 alignment, puts a premium on fast, aggressive defenders. Penn State may have the title of "Linebacker U.," but it's Texas A&M that has provided the NFL with such linebackers as Quentin Coryatt, Johnny Holland, Larry Kelm, Aaron Wallace, William Thomas, and Marcus Buckley over the last decade.

"Our style is just to play with reckless abandon so that we measure up to the guys who came before us," said Coryatt, 1991 SWC defensive player of the year and a first-round pick of the Indianapolis Colts. "Guys like Dana Batiste and Adam Bob (both NFL picks in 1988) played

Linebacker Quentin Coryatt ("The Terminator") was the leader on the 1991 Wrecking Crew defense that led the nation in total defense.

the way I like to play—run to the ball and hit hard. Once we put pressure on the quarterback, our secondary was so good he didn't have time to look very long for a receiver. He had to pull it down and run."

When R. C. Slocum took over the reins of the Texas A&M football program in 1989, he said he wanted the Aggies to become one of the nation's elite teams, perenially mentioned as contenders for the national championship.

But that was not quite possible during the past three seasons, for the A&M roster had been dominated by underclassmen. The previous season, the Aggies had only nine seniors on their entire roster.

In 1992, with perhaps one of the best groups of starters ever to return, Coach Slocum said he expected another great year and a "clear shot" at the national championship.

In the opening game of the season, at Anaheim Stadium in California, the Aggies faced an imposing Stanford team with a reputation as a clever, shifty, tricky team.

The game was supposed to be a battle between the Stanford smarts and the Aggie brawn. Instead, the game turned into a slow-moving, cautious defensive battle with no scoring in the first period. In the second period, Stanford scored on a short run by J. Lasely from the A&M seven-yard line.

Three quarters passed without any further scoring, and then A&M began to key its offense until it reached the Indians' twenty-one-yard line. Quarterback Jeff Granger hit end Greg

Above: Running back Greg Hill leans for the end zone in the Aggies' 31–14 win over Texas in 1991.

Below: Cornerback Kevin Smith, a future No. 1 draft pick of the Dallas Cowboys, broke open the 1991 game against the Longhorns with a 73-yard punt return for a touchdown.

Schorp for a touchdown, and it was a 7–7 game.

Then with four and a half minutes left to play, Terry Venetoulias kicked a thirty-nine-yard field goal, and A&M had a hard-earned 10–7 win.

Next stop on the Aggie Express was a trip to Baton Rouge and the annual LSU game. For three quarters, the game was a seesaw affair, with one team in front, then the other.

At the end of three periods, A&M had a 17–14 lead.

Tight end Greg Schorp celebrates with offensive lineman John Ellisor after grabbing a 21-yard touchdown pass against Stanford in the 1992 Disneyland Pigskin Classic III. The Aggies went on to a 10–7 victory over the Cardinal in Stanford coach Bill Walsh's return to the college ranks.

Fullback Doug Carter hurdles an LSU defender during the Aggies' 1992 31–22 victory over the Tigers, A&M's first win in Baton Rouge since 1975.

On the first play of the fourth period, cornerback Derrick Frazier intercepted an LSU pass on the twenty-two-yard line. On the next play, running back Rodney Thomas sped over left end for a touchdown and a 24–14 lead. Then with less than five minutes to play, fullback Clif Groce capped an eighty-yard Aggie drive with a touchdown from the twelve-yard line to ice the game 31–22.

At home for the first time this season, against Tulsa, the Aggies were held to a single field goal in the first half, while Tulsa scored a touchdown.

In the second half, running back Greg Hill scored a touchdown on a short dash from the eight-yard line. He also caught a TD pass as the Aggies rolled to their third straight win of the season 19–9.

Trailing 10–3 at halftime against Missouri, the Aggies suddenly spurted for twenty-three second-half points to storm over the Tigers 26–13. The key play of the game was a remarkable screen pass, Granger to Tony Harrison. Harrison broke into the clear, cut to the sideline, and raced seventy-three yards for the score. A touchdown by Hill in the third period, another by Hill in the fourth session, and a field goal by Terry Venetoulias clinched the game for A&M.

Texas Tech took a 17–16 lead over A&M late in their memorable battle on October 3. With less than five minutes to play, it looked as if A&M's victory string of four straight games was all but over.

But the Aggies were not done just yet.

With a third down and eight yards to go on the Tech forty-two-yard line, Granger went back to pass, but Tech's huge tackle, Dusty Beavers, had him in his grasp. Somehow Granger shook loose and tossed a fifteen-yard pass to Greg

The Wrecking Crew defense swarmed over the LSU Tigers in 1992 as the Aggies rolled 31–22.

Schorp for a first down on the four-yard line. Then in came A&M's Terry Venetoulias, who booted a perfect three-pointer, and A&M had a hair-raising 19–17 thriller of a win.

A&M picked up its sixth straight victory as it stunned Rice with two quick touchdowns in the first period, another in the third, and two more in the final period to win going away 35–9. Corey Pullig, a highly rated young quarterback, relieved regular Jeff Granger in the third period and completed a fifty-eight-yard pass play to Tony Harrison for the Aggies' final touchdown of the game.

The Baylor Bears took a 13–7 lead over A&M going into the third period, but Greg Hill's forty-yard touchdown sprint, Terry Venetoulias's field goal, and a safety gave the Aggies a 19–13 victory, their seventh straight of the season.

A&M's running back Greg Hill scored two touchdowns and his running mate Rodney Thomas scored three times as Texas A&M had too much offense and defense for SMU in a 41–7 laugher.

Louisville coach Howard Schnellenberger brought one of his best teams to Kyle Field for the game against A&M. But maybe they should have stayed home, for they had to contend with freshman quarterback Corey Pullig, at his best. Pullig completed fourteen of twenty-two passes for one touchdown and 128 yards, while Greg Hill ran wild, scoring three touchdowns. Rodney Thomas picked up another touchdown as the Aggies rolled over the Cardinals 40–18.

The Houston Cougars took a 17–10 lead over A&M at halftime, but the Aggies exploded for three touchdowns by Greg Hill, all in the third period, to take a 31–17 lead. Houston came back with a seventy-three-yard TD run by Ron Peters. A&M came right back when Billy

Linebackers Larry Jackson (left) and Steve Solari keep tabs on wily Baylor quarterback J. J. Joe in 1992's 19–13 victory over the Bears.

Mitchell ran a kickoff back ninety-five yards to the two-yard line. Then Rodney Thomas scored on the next play, and it was A&M, 38–23. The final score was 38–30.

Texas A&M took a 13–7 lead into the third period in its game against TCU, then exploded for twenty-four additional points in the third and fourth periods, en route to a 37–10 win.

Before a record crowd of howling fans, Texas jumped to a 3–0 lead over A&M in their Thanksgiving Day battle. But an aroused bunch of fightin' Aggies came back to run up seventeen points in the second period and take a 17–3 lead at halftime. Once again, Hill and Thomas starred, both scoring touchdowns.

Greg Hill rambles for a 40-yard touchdown against Baylor in 1992. Hill finished the day with 119 yards on 19 carries. During Hill's three-year A&M career, the Aggies compiled a 17–1 record when he rushed for over 100 yards.

Linebacker Jason Atkinson wraps up Longhorn quarterback Peter Gardere in 1992's 34–13 win over the 'Horns in Austin.

A&M added 17 more points as it pounded out another win over Texas, 34–13. It was A&M's twelfth straight win of the season and only the second time in SWC history that a team won as many as twelve games during the regular season.

In the Cotton Bowl in Dallas (Texas A&M's seventh appearance), the Aggies met Notre Dame. The Irish, with one of their finest teams in years, gave a demonstration of defense as they held the rough-riding Aggies at bay and led 7–0 at halftime.

The Irish carried their momentum into the third period, picking up touchdowns by Jerome Bettis, Notre Dame's great fullback. Bettis scored two touchdowns to give Notre Dame a lead too big to overcome. Final score: Notre Dame 28, Texas A&M 3.

For Coach R. C. Slocum, who was to begin his fifth year as head coach in 1993, this had to be one of his most satisfying years, for he had

Marcus Buckley (no. 9) knocks Rice quarterback Bert Emanuel off his feet in 1992.

Bottom: Defensive back Aaron Glenn iced the Aggies' 34–13 victory over Texas in 1992 with this 95-yard interception return for a touchdown. Patrick Bates (no. 29) runs interference for Glenn.

Coach R. C. Slocum leads the Aggies into the 100th Anniversary of Texas A&M Football. Under his leadership the Aggies posted a 39–10–1 record through 1992.

The Wrecking Crew swarms over Louisiana State running back David Butler in 1993's 24–0 win over the Tigers.

won two successive SWC titles, had his team in two Cotton Bowl games, and was about to enter Texas A&M's 100th year of football with a corps of outstanding veterans, including a potential all-American quarterback in Pullig, and a pair of great running backs in Hill and Thomas, and one of the top defensive units in college football.

When Jackie Sherrill left Texas A&M in 1988, Aggie fans and alumni had serious doubts about A&M's future as a perennial power in the SWC and nationally. But R. C. Slocum, a longtime defensive assistant at A&M, was named head coach and Slocum erased all doubts about his ability.

Beginning Texas A&M's 100th anniversary of football in 1993 and his twenty-second year as a coach at A&M, R. C. Slocum has the longest tenure of any football coach in Aggies history.

Aggie teams under Coach Slocum had won 39 games, lost 10, and tied 1 from 1989 to 1992,

Shifty Leeland McElroy cuts off the block of offensive lineman Tyler Harrison in the Aggies' 1993 victory over LSU.

Offensive lineman Dexter Wesley (no. 75) leads interference for running back Rodney Thomas (no. 20) in the Aggies' 73–0 shellacking of Missouri in 1993.

Linebacker Keith Mitchell (no. 23) blocked this punt against Oklahoma in 1993.

Defensive lineman Sam Adams was a first-team all-American and a finalist for the Lombardi Award in 1993.

and with one of the most outstanding groups of veterans returning for the 100th season, R. C. believed that the Aggies of 1993 would be a team of destiny.

And when the first practice sessions began in the fall of '93, Slocum and his aides, Bob Davie, assistant head coach; Bob Toledo, quarterback coach; David Culley, wide receiver coach; Kirk Doll, linebacker coach; Bill Johnson, defensive line coach; and Gary Kubiak, running backs coach; along with Mike Sherman, Shawn Slocum, and Trent Walters, were delighted as they looked over the 1992 returnees. They included the six-three quarterback, Corey Pullig, one of the nation's finest passers; those sensational touchdown twins, Greg Hill and Rod Thomas; fullback Clif Groce; ends Greg Schorp and Tony Harrison; guards Jason Matthews and Dexter Wesley; a pair of fine guards in Tyler Harrison and Calvin Collins; and Chris Dausin at center. Additionally, there were sparkling alternates at every position.

And when the Aggies opened the season at College Station against the LSU Tigers, Coach Slocum was all smiles after watching the Aggies' performance as they looked unbeatable with a 24–0 shutout of LSU. The first half saw both teams playing a strictly defensive game, each team exploring, searching for a weakness as the half ended in a 0–0 tie.

A&M's explosive running back Rodney Thomas took off on an eighty-yard run, then the redshirt freshman Leeland McElroy blasted for two touchdowns as quarterback Corey Pullig called a great game, completing fourteen of twenty-four passes and scoring two touchdowns. The A&M "Wrecking Crew" (the defense) was magnificent, allowing the Tigers just 200 yards rushing.

Oklahoma and Texas A&M met at Norman, Oklahoma, on September 11, but the Aggies would just as soon forget all about the game and Oklahoma, for the Sooners booted a field goal in the first period, scored ten points in the second,

Leeland McElroy set an NCAA record by returning two kickoffs for touchdowns against Rice in 1993. McElroy brought three kickoffs back for touchdowns in 1993 to set another NCAA record and led the nation in kickoff return average.

1994 quarterback Corey Pullig's passing ability gave the Aggies balance on offense.

seven more in the third, and then buried A&M with four touchdowns in the final period to rout the Aggies 44–14.

Tailbacks Rodney Thomas and Leeland McElroy set a Texas A&M scoring record as each scored three touchdowns in A&M's 73–0 bludgeoning of Missouri. Corey Pullig had an easy day, scoring two touchdowns, as every player on the squad, including the "Twelfth Man" crew, got playing time.

Texas Tech, always a troublemaker against A&M, fell 31–6. Once again Corey Pullig called a smart game for the Aggies, scored two touchdowns, and completed fourteen of twenty-seven passes. Rodney Thomas continued his sensational running with two touchdowns, while the

Defensive back Aaron Glenn was a first-team all-American and a finalist for the Jim Thorpe Award in 1993.

"Wrecking Crew" limited the Tech Raiders to just two field goals.

The Aggies exploded for seventeen points in the second period against Houston as Greg Hill played his first game of the year and picked up 128 yards rushing. His backfield mates, Rodney Thomas and Leeland McElroy, also did damage in a 34–10 win over Houston.

At Waco, Texas, the Aggies and Baylor battled to a 10–10 tie at halftime, but A&M spurted in the second half to outscore Baylor 24–7 and defeat the Bears 34–17.

The freshman sensation, Leeland McElroy, returned two kickoffs for two touchdowns in the first quarter against Rice, including a ninety-three-yard runback, as the Aggies raced to a 38–10 win over the Rice Owls.

Defensive end Eric England puts pressurc on TCU's quarterback in 1993.

On a cold, windy, blustery day, the Aggies and SMU battled the elements as well as each other, and in a rough defensive battle, the Aggies won 37–13.

At College Station, the Aggies and the Cardinals of Louisville engaged in a quarterback duel, with two of the nation's finest young players, Jeff Brohm of Louisville and Corey Pullig of A&M, battling each other for honors. But the Aggies scored on their first two possessions in the first period and then scored in each period to easily defeat Coach Howard Schnellenberger's

Head coach R. C. Slocum, with his Cotton Bowl hat on proudly, "saws varsity's horns off" in the A&M locker room after the 18–9 win over Texas in 1993.

Kyle Field—Texas A&M University. Home of the Fightin' Texas Aggies, Kyle Field has been home sweet home for the Aggies, and sweet it is. They have posted a 41–3–1 home record since 1985.

team 42–7. Pullig completed fourteen of twenty passes for three touchdowns, while Brohm completed twelve of thirty-two passes.

At Fort Worth, A&M scored on its first two possessions and then romped over TCU 59–3. In the second period, A&M's sensational Greg Hill took a short screen pass and raced ninety-four yards for a touchdown, one of the longest in A&M history. It was the eighth straight win for A&M and the ninth in ten games as the Aggies prepped for their annual Thanksgiving Day battle against the Texas Longhorns.

True to form, A&M won its ninth game in the last ten against the Longhorns by an 18–9 score. Leeland McElroy's 102-yard kickoff return for a touchdown was the longest of the year in all of college football.

The victory gave the Aggies their third straight SWC title and closed out a sensational 10–1 season.

In their third straight Cotton Bowl appearance, the Aggies took an early lead against Notre Dame but then committed costly turnovers in the second half that helped Notre Dame to a 24–21 victory.

Under Slocum's tutelage, the Aggies seem to have a head start on a successful second century of football at Kyle Field. But there are always the vagaries of fate—fumbles, tipped passes, blown knees, failed exams—to contend with. The only certainty is that, come what may, Coach Slocum will maintain his even-keel philosophy.

"For us to get anything done on the football field we have to learn to work together and to care for each other," he says. "Our society is the same way. Nothing goes totally the way you want it to in football, and in life you have to deal with disappointments.

"There are times when you have great success, but other times when things are going so bad you can't understand it. You have to deal with both ends. Don't get too carried away when things are going well, and don't get so depressed when things go poorly. That's one of the main lessons learned from football."

Wise words from a wise man. To which one hundred years' worth of lettermen, alumni, coaches and fans can only add:

Gig 'em!

APPENDIX

ALL-TIME COACHING RECORDS
1894–1993

PERIOD	NAME	YEARS COACHED	OVERALL W	OVERALL L	OVERALL T	OVERALL PCT.	SWC W	SWC L	SWC T	SWC PCT.
1894	F. D. Perkins	1	1	1	0	.500	—	—	—	—
1896	A. M. Soule/H. W. South	1	2	0	1	.833	—	—	—	—
1897	C. W. Taylor	1	1	2	0	.333	—	—	—	—
1898	H. W. Williams	1	4	2	0	.667	—	—	—	—
1899–1901	W. A. Murray	3	7	8	1	.469	—	—	—	—
1902–1904	J. E. Platt	3	18	5	1	.771	—	—	—	—
1905–1906	W. E. Bachman	2	13	3	0	.813	—	—	—	—
1907	L. L. Larson	1	6	1	1	.813	—	—	—	—
1908	N. A. Merriam	1	3	5	0	.375	—	—	—	—
1909–1914	Charles B. Moran	6	38	8	4	.800	—	—	—	—
1915–1916	E. H. Harlan	2	12	5	0	.706	3	2	0	.600
1917; 1928	D. X. Bible	11	72	19	8	.768	28	15	7	.630
1918	D. V. Graves	1	6	1	0	.857	1	1	0	.500
1929–1933	Madison Bell	5	24	21	3	.531	8	14	3	.380
1934–1947	Homer Norton	14	82	53	9	.601	42	35	6	.542
1948–1950	Harry Stiteler	3	8	21	2	.274	3	13	2	.222
1951–1953	Raymond George	3	12	14	4	.467	3	12	3	.250
1954–1957	Paul "Bear" Bryant	4	25	14	2	.622	14	9	1	.604
1958–1961	Jim Myers	4	12	24	4	.333	5	18	3	.250
1962–1964	Hank Foldberg	3	6	23	1	.217	5	15	1	.262
1965–1971	Gene Stallings	7	27	45	1	.377	19	30	0	.388
1972–1978	Emory Bellard	6	48	27	0	.640	29	18	0	.617
1978–1981	Tom Wilson	3	21	19	0	.525	14	15	0	.483
1982–1988	Jackie Sherrill	7	52	28	1	.648	36	17	1	.676
1989–	R. C. Slocum	5	49	12	1	.803	33	4	1	.892

A&M FOOTBALL, YEAR-BY-YEAR

1894
Coach F. D. Perkins

AGGIES		OPP
14	Galveston HS (Ball)	6
0	at Texas	38
14	**(1–1)**	**44**

1895
No Team

1896
Coach A. M. Soule & Coach H. W. South

AGGIES		OPP
0	Galveston HS (Ball)	0
22	Austin College	4
28	Houston HS	0
50	**(2–0–1)**	**4**

1897
Coach C. W. Taylor

AGGIES		OPP
0	Houston HS	10
6	TCU	30
4	Austin College	0
10	**(1–2)**	**40**

1898
Coach H. W. Williams

AGGIES		OPP
51	Houston HS	0
0	at Texas	48
0	Houston HS	6
16	at TCU (W)	0
22	Austin College	6
28	Fort Worth U.	0
117	**(4–2)**	**60**

1899
Coach W. A. Murray

AGGIES		OPP
43	Houston HS	0
0	Sewanee	10
22	Tulane	0
52	LSU	0
33	Baylor	0
0	at Texas (SA)	6
150	**(4–2)**	**16**

1900
Coach W. A. Murray

AGGIES		OPP
6	Kan. City Medics	6
0	at Texas (SA)	5
0	at Texas	11
11	Waxahachie Ath. Club	0
44	Henry College	0
61	**(2–2–1)**	**22**

1901
Coach W. A. Murray

AGGIES		OPP
6	Baylor	0
6	Baylor	17
0	at Texas (SA)	17
0	at Texas	32
0	Baylor	46
12	**(1–4)**	**112**

1902
Coach J. E. Platt

AGGIES		OPP
11	St. Edwards	0
0	Trinity	0
11	Baylor	6
22	Baylor	0
0	Texas (SA)	0
17	Tulane	5
22	at TCU (W)	0
34	Trinity	0
11	at Texas	0
128	**(7–0–2)**	**11**

1903
Coach J. E. Platt

AGGIES		OPP
16	Trinity	0
11	at TCU (W)	0
6	Arkansas	0
0	Oklahoma	6
0	Baylor	0
18	Baylor	0
16	TCU	0
0	Trinity	18
5	Baylor	0
6	at Texas	29
14	TCU	6
92	**(7–3–1)**	**59**

1904
Coach J. E. Platt

AGGIES		OPP
49	Deaf & Dumb Inst.	0
5	Baylor	0
29	TCU	0
5	Sewanee	17
6	at Texas	34
10	Baylor	0
104	**(4–2)**	**51**

1905
Coach W. E. Bachman

AGGIES		OPP
29	Houston	0
20	TCU	0
42	Baylor	0
24	Trinity	0
18	Austin College	11
24	at TCU (W)	11
6	Transylvania, Ky.	29
17	Baylor	5
0	at Texas	27
180	**(7–2)**	**83**

1906
Coach W. E. Bachman

AGGIES		OPP
42	TCU	0
34	Daniel Baker	0
22	at TCU (W)	0
18	Tulane	0
32	Haskell Institute	6
22	LSU	12
0	at Texas	24
170	**(6–1)**	**42**

1907
Coach L. L. Larson

AGGIES		OPP
34	Fort Worth Univ.	0
0	at Texas (D)	0
11	LSU	5
5	Haskell Institute	0
32	TCU	5
18	Tulane	6
19	Oklahoma	0
6	at Texas	11
125	**(6–1–1)**	**27**

1908
Coach N. A. Merriam

AGGIES		OPP
6	Trinity	0
5	Baylor	6
0	LSU	26
13	at TCU (W)	10
8	Texas (H)	24
0	Haskell Institute	23
32	Southwestern	0
12	at Texas	28
76	**(3–5)**	**117**

1909
Coach C. B. Moran

AGGIES		OPP
17	Austin College	0
0	TCU	0
15	Haskell Institute	0
9	Baylor	6
23	Texas (H)	0
47	Trinity	0
14	Oklahoma	8
5	at Texas	0
130	**(7–0–1)**	**14**

1910
Coach C. B. Moran

AGGIES		OPP
48	Marshall School	0
27	Austin College	5
35	TCU	0
33	Transylvania, Ky.	0
0	at Arkansas	5
23	at TCU	6
14	Texas (H)	8
6	Southwestern	0
17	Tulane	0
203	**(8–1)**	**24**

1911
Coach C. B. Moran

AGGIES		OPP
22	Southwestern	0
33	Austin College	0
16	Auburn	0
17	Mississippi	0
0	Texas (H)	6
22	Baylor	11
24	Dallas U.	0
134	**(6–1)**	**17**

1912
Coach C. B. Moran

AGGIES		OPP
50	Daniel Baker	0
59	Trinity	0
27	Arkansas (D)	0
57	Austin College	0
28	Oklahoma	6
41	Miss. State	7
41	Tulane	0
10	Kansas State	13
53	Baylor	0
366	**(8–1)**	**26**

1913
Coach C. B. Moran

AGGIES		OPP
7	Trinity	0
6	Austin College	0
19	Polytechnic College	6
0	Miss. State	6
0	Kansas State	12
0	Oklahoma A&M	3
0	Haskell Insitute	28
14	Baylor	14
7	LSU	7
53	**(3–4–2)**	**76**

LEGEND: A = Amarillo H = Houston B = Beaumont LR = Little Rock, AR D = Dallas J = Jackson, MS SA = San Antonio FW = Fort Worth W = Waco G = Galveston T = Tacoma

1914
Coach C. B. Moran

AGGIES		OPP
32	Austin College	0
0	Trinity	0
40	TCU	0
0	Haskell Insitute (FW)	10
63	LSU (D)	9
32	Rice	7
24	Oklahoma A&M	0
14	Mississippi (D)	7
205	**(6–1–1)**	**33**

1915
Coach E. H. Harlan

AGGIES		OPP
40	Austin College	0
62	Trinity	0
13	at TCU	10
33	Missouri School of Mines	3
21	Haskell Institute (D)	7
0	at Rice	7
13	Texas	0
0	Miss. State	7
182	**(6–2)**	**34**

1916
Coach E. H. Harlan

AGGIES		OPP
6	Southwestern	0
20	Dallas U.	6
0	LSU (G)	13
62	SMU	0
13	Haskell Institute (D)	6
0	at Rice	20
3	at Baylor	0
77	Missouri School of Mines	0
7	at Texas	21
188	**(6–3)**	**66**

1917
SWC CHAMPIONS
Coach D. X. Bible

AGGIES		OPP
66	Austin College	0
98	Dallas U.	0
20	Southwestern	0
27	LSU (B)	0
35	Tulane	0
7	at Baylor	0
7	Texas	0
10	at Rice	0
270	**(8–0)**	**0**

1918
Coach D. V. Graves

AGGIES		OPP
6	Ream Field	0
12	Camp Travis	6
19	at Baylor	0
7	Southwestern	0
19	Camp Mabry	6
0	at Texas	7
60	Camp Travis	0
0	Remount Sta.	0
123	**(6–1)**	**19**

1919
SWC CHAMPIONS
Coach D. X. Bible

AGGIES		OPP
77	Sam Houston STC	0
28	San Marcos STC	0
16	at SMU	0
12	Howard Payne	0
42	Trinity	0
28	Oklahoma A&M	0
10	at Baylor	0
48	TCU	0
7	Southwestern	0
7	Texas	0
275	**(10–0)**	**0**

1920
Coach D. X. Bible

AGGIES		OPP
110	Daniel Baker	0
3	at SMU	0
0	LSU	0
47	Phillips U.	0
35	at Oklahoma A&M	0
24	at Baylor	0
7	Rice	0
3	at Texas	7
229	**(6–1–1)**	**7**

1921
SWC CHAMPIONS
Coach D. X. Bible

AGGIES		OPP
14	Howard Payne	7
13	at SMU	0
0	at LSU	6
17	Arizona	13
23	Oklahoma A&M	7
14	at Baylor	3
7	at Rice	7
0	Texas	0
22	Centre College (Dixie Classic)	14
110	**(6–1–2)**	**57**

1922
Coach D. X. Bible

AGGIES		OPP
7	Howard Payne	13
10	Tulsa U. (D)	13
33	Southwestern	0
46	at LSU	0
19	Ouichita College	6
7	at Baylor	13
6	at SMU	17
24	Rice	0
14	at Texas	7
166	**(5–4)**	**69**

1923
Coach D. X. Bible

AGGIES		OPP
53	Sam Houston STC	0
21	Howard Payne	0
13	Southwestern	0
14	Sewanee (D)	0
28	at LSU	0
0	SMU	10
0	at Baylor	0
6	at Rice	7
0	Texas	6
135	**(5–3–1)**	**23**

1924
Coach D. X. Bible

AGGIES		OPP
40	John Tarleton SC	0
33	Trinity	0
54	Southwestern	0
7	Sewanee (D)	0
40	Arkansas A&M	0
7	at SMU	7
7	at Baylor	15
28	TCU	0
13	Rice	6
0	at Texas	7
229	**(7–2–1)**	**35**

1925
SWC CHAMPIONS
Coach D. X. Bible

AGGIES		OPP
20	Trinity	10
23	Southwestern	6
6	Sewanee (D)	6
7	SMU	0
77	Sam Houston STC	0
13	at Baylor	0
0	at TCU	3
17	at Rice	0
28	Texas	0
191	**(7–1–1)**	**25**

1926
Coach D. X. Bible

AGGIES		OPP
26	Trinity	0
35	Southwestern	0
6	Sewanee (D)	3
63	New Mexico	0
7	at SMU	9
9	at Baylor	20
13	TCU	13
20	Rice	0
5	at Texas	14
184	**(5–3–1)**	**59**

1927
SWC CHAMPIONS
Coach D. X. Bible

AGGIES		OPP
45	Trinity	0
31	Southwestern	0
18	Sewanee (D)	0
40	Arkansas	6
0	at TCU	0
47	Texas Tech	6
39	at SMU	13
14	at Rice	0
28	Texas	7
262	**(8–0–1)**	**32**

1928
Coach D. X. Bible

AGGIES		OPP
21	Trinity	0
21	Southwestern	0
69	Sewanee (D)	0
0	Centenary	6
0	TCU	6
12	at Arkansas	27
44	North Texas STC	0
19	at SMU	19
19	Rice	0
0	at Texas	19
205	**(5–4–1)**	**77**

1929
Coach Madison Bell

AGGIES		OPP
54	Southwestern	7
10	at Tulane	13
19	Kansas State (D)	0
7	at TCU	13
13	Arkansas	14
54	SF Austin STC	0
7	SMU	12
26	at Rice	6
13	Texas	0
203	**(5–4)**	**65**

1930
Coach Madison Bell

AGGIES		OPP
43	Southwestern	0
0	at Nebraska	13
9	Tulane (D)	19
0	at Arkansas (LR)	13
0	TCU	3
7	Centenary	6
7	at SMU	13
0	Rice	7
0	at Texas	26
66	**(2–7)**	**100**

1931
Coach Madison Bell

AGGIES		OPP
33	Southwestern	0
21	John Tarleton SC	0
0	at Tulane	7
29	Iowa U. (D)	0
0	at TCU	6
33	Baylor	7
7	at Centenary	0
0	SMU	8
7	at Rice	0
7	Texas	6
137	**(7–3)**	**34**

1932
Coach Madison Bell

AGGIES		OPP
7	Texas Tech (A)	0
14	at Tulane	26
26	Sam Houston STC	0
14	Texas A&I	0
0	TCU	17
0	at Baylor	0
0	at Centenary	7
0	at SMU	0
14	at Rice	7
0	at Texas	21
75	**(4–4–2)**	**78**

1933
Coach Madison Bell

AGGIES		OPP
38	Trinity	0
13	at Tulane	6
34	Sam Houston STC	14
17	Texas A&I	0
7	at TCU	13
14	Baylor	7
0	at Centenary	20
0	SMU	19
27	at Rice	0
10	Texas	10
160	**(6–3–1)**	**89**

1934
Coach H. H. Norton

AGGIES		OPP
28	Sam Houston STC	0
14	Texas A&I	14
6	at Temple	40
0	Centenary (B)	13
0	TCU	13
10	at Baylor	7
7	Arkansas	7
0	at SMU	28
6	Rice	25
0	at Texas	13
13	Michigan State (SA)	26
84	**(2–7–2)**	**186**

1935
Coach H. H. Norton

AGGIES		OPP
37	SF Austin STC	6
25	at Sam Houston STC	0
0	Temple	14
6	at Centenary	7
14	at TCU	19
6	Baylor	14
7	at Arkansas (LR)	14
10	at Rice	17
20	Texas	6
0	SMU	24
125	**(3–7)**	**121**

1936
Coach H. H. Norton

AGGIES		OPP
39	Sam Houston STC	6
3	at Hardin-Simmons	0
3	at Rice	0
18	TCU	7
0	at Baylor	0
0	Arkansas	18
22	at SMU	6
38	at U. of San Francisco	14
20	Utah	7
0	at Centenary	3
0	Texas	7
13	Manhattan College	6
156	**(8–3–1)**	**74**

1937
Coach H. H. Norton

AGGIES		OPP
14	at Manhattan College	7
14	Miss. State	0
7	at TCU	7
0	Baylor	13
13	at Arkansas	26
14	SMU	0
6	at Rice	6
7	Texas	0
42	at U. of San Francisco	0
117	**(5–2–2)**	**59**

1938
Coach H. H. Norton

AGGIES		OPP
52	Texas A&I	0
20	Tulsa	0
0	Santa Clara	7
6	TCU	34
6	at Baylor	6
13	Arkansas	7
7	at SMU	10
6	at Texas	7
27	Rice	0
137	**(4–4–1)**	**71**

1939
NATIONAL CHAMPIONS
Coach H. H. Norton

AGGIES		OPP
32	at Oklahoma A&M	0
14	Centenary	0
7	at Santa Clara	3
33	Villanova	7
20	at TCU	6
20	Baylor	0
27	at Arkansas	0
6	SMU	2
19	at Rice	0
20	Texas	0
14	Tulane (Sugar Bowl)	13
212	**(11–0)**	**31**

1940
SWC CO-CHAMPIONS
Coach H. H. Norton

AGGIES		OPP
26	Texas A&I	0
41	Tulsa (SA)	6
7	at UCLA	0
21	TCU	7
14	at Baylor	7
17	Arkansas	0
19	at SMU	7
25	Rice	0
0	at Texas	7
13	Fordham (Cotton Bowl)	12
183	**(9–1)**	**46**

1941
SWC CHAMPIONS
Coach H. H. Norton

AGGIES		OPP
54	Sam Houston STC	0
41	Texas A&I (SA)	0
49	at New York U.	7
14	at TCU	0
48	Baylor	0
7	at Arkansas (LR)	0
21	SMU	10
19	at Rice	6
0	Texas	23
7	Wash. State (T)	0
21	Alabama (Cotton Bowl)	29
281	**(9–2)**	**75**

1942
Coach H. H. Norton

AGGIES		OPP
7	at LSU	16
19	Texas Tech	0
7	at Corpus Christi NAS	18
2	TCU	7
0	at Baylor	6
41	Arkansas	0
27	at SMU	20
0	at Rice	0
6	at Texas	12
21	Wash. State	0
130	**(4–5–1)**	**79**

1943
Coach H. H. Norton

AGGIES		OPP
48	Bryan AFB	6
13	at Texas Tech	0
28	at LSU	13
13	at TCU	0
0	North Texas AC (Arlington)	0
13	at Arkansas	0
22	SMU	0
20	at Rice	0
13	Texas	27
14	LSU (Orange Bowl)	19
184	**(7–2–1)**	**65**

1944
Coach H. H. Norton

AGGIES		OPP
39	Bryan AFB	0
27	Texas Tech (SA)	14
14	at Oklahoma	21
7	TCU	13
7	at LSU	0
61	North Texas AC (Arlington)	0
6	Arkansas	7
39	at SMU	6
19	at Rice	6
0	at Texas	6
70	at Miami U.	14
289	**(7–4)**	**87**

1945
Coach H. H. Norton

AGGIES		OPP
54	Ellington Field	0
16	at Texas Tech	6
19	Oklahoma	14
12	LSU	31
12	at TCU	13
19	Baylor	13
34	at Arkansas	0
3	SMU	0
0	at Rice	6
10	Texas	20
179	**(6–4)**	**103**

1946
Coach H. H. Norton

AGGIES		OPP
47	North Texas State	0
0	Texas Tech (SA)	6
7	at Oklahoma	10
9	at LSU	33
14	TCU	0
17	at Baylor	0
0	Arkansas	7
14	at SMU	0
10	Rice	27
7	at Texas	24
125	**(4–6)**	**107**

1947
Coach H. H. Norton

AGGIES		OPP
48	Southwestern	0
29	Texas Tech (SA)	7
14	at Oklahoma	26
13	at LSU	19
0	at TCU	26
24	Baylor	0
21	at Arkansas	21
0	SMU	13
7	at Rice	41
13	Texas	32
169	**(3–6–1)**	**185**

1948
Coach H. Stiteler

AGGIES		OPP
14	at Villanova	34
14	Texas Tech (SA)	20
14	at Oklahoma U.	42
13	at LSU	14
14	TCU	27
14	at Baylor	20
6	Arkansas	28
14	at SMU	20
6	Rice	28
14	at Texas	14
123	**(0–9–1)**	**247**

1949
Coach H. Stiteler

AGGIES		OPP
0	Villanova	35
26	Texas Tech (SA)	7
13	at Oklahoma	33
0	at LSU	34
6	at TCU	28
0	Baylor	21
6	at Arkansas	27
27	SMU	27
0	at Rice	13
14	Texas	42
92	**(1–8–1)**	**267**

1950
Coach H. Stiteler

AGGIES		OPP
48	Nevada (SA)	18
34	at Texas Tech (SA)	13
28	at Oklahoma U.	34
52	Virginia Mil. Ins.	0
42	TCU	23
20	at Baylor	27
42	Arkansas	13
25	at SMU	20
13	Rice	21
0	at Texas	17
40	Georgia (Presidential Cup)	20
344	**(7–4)**	**206**

1951
Coach R. George

AGGIES		OPP
21	at UCLA	14
20	Texas Tech (D)	7
14	Oklahoma U.	7
53	at Trinity	14
14	at TCU	20
21	Baylor	21
21	at Arkansas	33
14	SMU	14
13	at Rice	28
22	Texas	21
213	**(5–3–2)**	**179**

1952
Coach R. George

AGGIES		OPP
21	at Houston	13
14	Oklahoma A&M (D)	7
7	Kentucky	10
6	at Mich. State	48
7	TCU	7
20	at Baylor	21
31	Arkansas	12
13	at SMU	21
6	Rice	16
12	at Texas	32
137	**(3–6–1)**	**187**

1953
Coach R. George

AGGIES		OPP
7	at Kentucky	6
14	Houston	14
14	Georgia (D)	12
27	at Texas Tech	14
20	at TCU	7
13	Baylor	14
14	Arkansas (LR)	41
0	SMU	23
7	at Rice	34
12	Texas	21
128	**(4–5–1)**	**186**

1954
Coach Paul Bryant

AGGIES		OPP
9	Texas Tech	41
6	Oklahoma A&M (D)	14
6	at Georgia	0
7	at Houston	10
20	TCU	21
7	at Baylor	20
7	Arkansas	14
3	at SMU	6
19	Rice	29
13	at Texas	22
97	**(1–9)**	**177**

1955
Coach Paul Bryant

AGGIES		OPP
0	at UCLA	21
28	LSU (D)	0
21	Houston	3
27	at Nebraska	0
19	at TCU	16
19	Baylor	7
7	at Arkansas	7
13	SMU	2
20	at Rice	12
6	Texas	21
160	**(7–2–1)**	**89**

1956
SWC CHAMPIONS
Coach Paul Bryant

AGGIES		OPP
19	Villanova	0
9	at LSU	6
40	Texas Tech (D)	7
14	at Houston	14
7	TCU	6
19	at Baylor	13
27	Arkansas	0
33	at SMU	7
21	Rice	7
34	at Texas	21
223	**(9–0–1)**	**81**

1957
Coach Paul Bryant

AGGIES		OPP
21	Maryland (D)	13
21	at Texas Tech	0
28	Missouri	0
28	Houston	6
7	at TCU	0
14	Baylor	0
7	at Arkansas	6
19	SMU	6
6	at Rice	7
7	Texas	9
0	Tennessee (Gator Bowl)	3
158	**(8–3)**	**50**

1958
Coach Jim Myers

AGGIES		OPP
14	Texas Tech (D)	15
7	at Houston	39
12	Missouri	0
14	at Maryland	10
8	TCU	24
33	at Baylor	27
8	Arkansas	21
0	at SMU	33
28	at Rice	21
0	at Texas	27
124	**(4–6)**	**217**

1959
Coach Jim Myers

AGGIES		OPP
14	Texas Tech (D)	20
9	at Michigan State	7
7	at Miss. Southern	3
28	Houston	6
6	at TCU	39
0	Baylor	13
7	at Arkansas	12
11	SMU	14
2	at Rice	7
17	Texas	20
101	**(3–7)**	**141**

1960
Coach Jim Myers

AGGIES		OPP
0	at LSU	9
14	Texas Tech	14
14	at Trinity	0
0	at Houston	17
14	TCU	14
0	at Baylor	14
3	Arkansas	7
0	at SMU	0
14	at Rice	21
14	at Texas	21
73	**(1–6–3)**	**117**

1961
Coach Jim Myers

AGGIES		OPP
7	Houston	7
7	at LSU	16
38	at Texas Tech	7
55	at Trinity	0
14	at TCU	15
23	Baylor	0
8	at Arkansas	15
25	SMU	12
7	at Rice	21
0	Texas	25
184	**(4–5–1)**	**118**

1962
Coach H. Foldberg

AGGIES		OPP
0	at LSU	21
3	at Houston	6
7	Texas Tech	3
6	at Florida	42
14	TCU	20
6	at Baylor	3
7	Arkansas	17
12	at SMU	7
3	at Rice	23
3	at Texas	13
61	**(3–7)**	**155**

1963
Coach H. Foldberg

AGGIES		OPP
6	at LSU	14
0	at Ohio State	17
0	at Texas Tech	10
23	Houston	13
14	at TCU	14
7	Baylor	34
7	at Arkansas (LR)	21
7	SMU	9
13	at Rice	6
13	Texas	15
90	**(2–7–1)**	**153**

1964
Coach H. Foldberg

AGGIES		OPP
6	at LSU	9
0	at Houston	10
12	at Texas Tech	16
7	at Southern Cal.	31
9	TCU	14
16	at Baylor	20
0	Arkansas	17
23	at SMU	0
8	at Rice	19
7	at Texas	26
88	**(1–9)**	**162**

1965
Coach G. Stallings

AGGIES		OPP
0	at LSU	10
14	at Georgia Tech	10
16	at Texas Tech	20
10	Houston	7
9	at TCU	17
0	Baylor	31
0	at Arkansas (LR)	31
0	SMU	10
14	at Rice	13
17	Texas	21
80	**(3–7)**	**170**

1966
Coach G. Stallings

AGGIES		OPP
3	at Georgia Tech	38
13	at Tulane	21
35	Texas Tech	14
7	at LSU	7
35	TCU	7
17	at Baylor	13
0	Arkansas	34
14	at SMU	21
7	at Rice	6
14	at Texas	22
145	**(4–5–1)**	**183**

1967
SWC CHAMPIONS
Coach G. Stallings

AGGIES		OPP
17	SMU	20
20	Purdue (D)	24
6	at LSU	17
18	Florida State	19
28	at Texas Tech	24
20	at TCU	0
21	Baylor	3
33	Arkansas	21
18	at Rice	3
10	Texas	7
20	Alabama (Cotton Bowl)	16
211	**(7–4)**	**154**

1968
Coach G. Stallings

AGGIES		OPP
12	at LSU	13
35	at Tulane	3
14	at Florida State	20
16	Texas Tech	21
27	TCU	7
9	at Baylor	10
22	Arkansas	25
23	at SMU	36
24	Rice	14
14	at Texas	35
196	**(3–7)**	**184**

1969
Coach G. Stallings

AGGIES		OPP
6	at LSU	35
0	at Nebraska	14
20	at Army	13
9	at Texas Tech	13
6	at TCU	16
24	Baylor	0
13	at Arkansas	35
20	SMU	10
6	at Rice	7
12	Texas	49
116	**(3–7)**	**192**

1970
Coach G. Stallings

AGGIES		OPP
41	Wichita State	14
20	at LSU	18
13	at Ohio State	56
10	at Michigan	14
7	Texas Tech	21
15	TCU	31
24	at Baylor	29
6	Arkansas	45
3	at SMU	6
17	Rice	18
14	at Texas	52
170	**(2–9)**	**304**

1971
Coach G. Stallings

AGGIES		OPP
41	Wichita State	7
0	at LSU	37
7	at Nebraska	34
0	Cincinnati	17
7	at Texas Tech	28
3	at TCU	14
10	Baylor	9
17	at Arkansas (LR)	9
27	SMU	10
18	at Rice	13
14	Texas	34
144	**(5–6)**	**212**

1972
Coach E. Bellard

AGGIES		OPP
36	at Wichita State	13
7	at Nebraska	37
17	at LSU	42
14	Army	24
14	Texas Tech	17
10	TCU	13
13	at Baylor	15
10	Arkansas	7
27	at SMU	17
14	Rice	20
3	at Texas	38
165	**(3–8)**	**243**

1973
Coach E. Bellard

AGGIES		OPP
48	Wichita State	0
23	at LSU	28
24	Boston College	32
30	at Clemson	15
16	at Texas Tech	28
35	at TCU	16
28	Baylor	22
10	at Arkansas	14
45	SMU	10
20	at Rice	24
13	Texas	42
292	**(5–6)**	**231**

1974
Coach E. Bellard

AGGIES		OPP
24	Clemson	0
21	at LSU	14
28	at Washington	15
10	at Kansas	28
28	Texas Tech	7
17	TCU	0
20	at Baylor	0
20	Arkansas	10
14	at SMU	18
37	Rice	7
3	at Texas	32
222	**(8–3)**	**131**

1975
SWC TRI-CHAMPIONS
Coach E. Bellard

AGGIES		OPP
7	Mississippi	0
39	at LSU	8
43	Illinois	13
10	at Kansas State	0
38	at Texas Tech	9
14	at TCU	6
19	Baylor	10
36	SMU	3
33	at Rice	14
20	Texas	10
6	at Arkansas (LR)	31
0	So. California (Liberty Bowl)	20
265	**(10–2)**	**124**

1976
Coach E. Bellard

AGGIES		OPP
19	Virginia Tech	0
34	Kansas State	14
10	at Houston	21
14	at Illinois	7
16	Texas Tech	27
24	Baylor	0
57	Rice	34
36	at SMU	0
31	at Arkansas (LR)	10
59	TCU	10
27	at Texas	3
37	Florida (Sun Bowl)	14
327	**(10–2)**	**126**

1977
Coach E. Bellard

AGGIES		OPP
28	Kansas	14
27	at Virginia Tech	6
33	at Texas Tech	17
3	at Michigan	41
38	at Baylor	31
28	at Rice	14
38	SMU	21
20	Arkansas	26
52	at TCU	23
28	Texas	57
27	Houston	7
28	USC (Bluebonnet Bowl)	47
350	**(8–4)**	**304**

1978
Coach E. Bellard (4–2)

AGGIES		OPP
37	at Kansas	10
27	at Boston College	2
58	Memphis State	0
38	Texas Tech	9
0	at Houston	33
6	Baylor	24

1978
Coach Tom Wilson (4–2)

AGGIES		OPP
38	Rice	21
20	at SMU	17
7	at Arkansas (LR)	26
15	TCU	7
7	at Texas	22
28	Iowa State (Hall of Fame Bowl)	12
291	**(8–4)**	**183**

1979
Coach Tom Wilson

AGGIES		OPP
17	Brigham Young (H)	18
7	at Baylor	17
27	at Penn State	14
17	at Memphis State	7
20	at Texas Tech	21
14	Houston	17
41	at Rice	15
47	SMU	14
10	Arkansas	22
30	at TCU	7
13	Texas	7
243	**(6–5)**	**159**

1980
Coach Tom Wilson

AGGIES		OPP
23	at Mississippi	20
0	at Georgia	42
9	Penn State	25
41	Texas Tech	21
13	at Houston	17
7	Baylor	46
6	Rice	10
0	at SMU	27
24	at Arkansas	27
13	TCU	10
24	at Texas	14
169	**(4–7)**	**259**

1981
Coach Tom Wilson

AGGIES		OPP
29	at California–Berkeley	28
12	at Boston College	13
43	Louisiana Tech	7
24	at Texas Tech	23
7	Houston	6
17	at Baylor	19
51	at Rice	26
7	SMU	27
7	Arkansas	10
37	TCU	7
13	Texas	21
33	Oklahoma State (Independence Bowl)	16
280	**(7–5)**	**203**

1982
Coach J. Sherrill

AGGIES		OPP
16	Boston College	38
61	UT-Arlington	22
38	Louisiana Tech	27
15	Texas Tech	24
20	at Houston	24
28	Baylor	23
49	Rice	7
9	at SMU	47
0	at Arkansas (LR)	35
34	TCU	14
16	at Texas	53
286	**(5–6)**	**314**

1983
Coach J. Sherrill

AGGIES		OPP
17	California	19
38	Arkansas State	17
15	Oklahoma State	34
0	at Texas Tech	3
30	Houston	7
13	at Baylor	13
29	at Rice	10
7	SMU	10
36	Arkansas	23
20	at TCU	10
13	Texas	45
218	**(5–5–1)**	**174**

1984
Coach J. Sherrill

AGGIES		OPP
20	Texas-El Paso	17
38	Iowa State	17
22	Arkansas State	21
12	Texas Tech	30
7	at Houston	9
16	Baylor	20
38	Rice	14
20	at SMU	28
0	at Arkansas	28
35	TCU	21
37	at Texas	12
245	**(6–5)**	**217**

1985
SWC CHAMPIONS
Coach J. Sherrill

AGGIES		OPP
10	at Alabama (B)	23
31	Northeast Louisiana	17
45	Tulsa	10
28	at Texas Tech	27
43	Houston	16
15	at Baylor	20
43	at Rice	28
19	SMU	17
10	Arkansas	6
53	at TCU	6
42	Texas	10
36	Auburn (Cotton Bowl)	16
375	**(10–2)**	**186**

1986
SWC CHAMPIONS
Coach J. Sherrill

AGGIES		OPP
17	at LSU	35
48	North Texas State	28
16	So. Mississippi	7
45	Texas Tech	8
19	at Houston	7
31	Baylor	30
45	Rice	10
39	at SMU	35
10	at Arkansas	14
74	TCU	10
16	at Texas	3
12	Ohio State (Cotton Bowl)	28
372	**(9–3)**	**215**

1987
SWC CHAMPIONS
Coach J. Sherrill

AGGIES		OPP
3	LSU	17
29	Washington	12
27	at So. Mississippi (J)	14
21	at Texas Tech	27
22	Houston	17
34	at Baylor	10
34	at Rice	21
32	Louisiana Tech	3
14	Arkansas	0
42	at TCU	24
20	Texas	13
35	Notre Dame (Cotton Bowl)	10
273	**(10–2)**	**158**

1988

Coach J. Sherrill

AGGIES		OPP
14	Nebraska (E)	23
0	at LSU	27
15	at Oklahoma State	52
50	Texas Tech	15
30	at Houston	16
28	Baylor	14
24	Rice	10
56	Louisiana Tech	17
20	at Arkansas	25
18	TCU	0
28	at Texas	24
10	Alabama	30
293	**(7–5)**	**253**

1989

Coach R. C. Slocum

AGGIES		OPP
28	LSU	16
6	at Washington	19
44	at TCU	7
31	Southern Mississippi	14
24	at Texas Tech	27
17	Houston	13
14	at Baylor	11
45	at Rice	7
63	SMU	14
22	Arkansas	23
21	Texas	10
28	Pittsburg (John Hancock Bowl)	31
343	**(8–4)**	**192**

1990

Coach R. C. Slocum

AGGIES		OPP
28	at Hawwaii	13
63	at Southwestern La.	14
40	North Texas	8
8	at LSU	17
28	Texas Tech	24
31	at Houston	36
20	Baylor	20
41	Rice	15
38	at SMU	17
20	at Arkansas	16
56	TCU	10
27	at Texas	28
65	Brigham Young (Holiday Bowl)	14
400	**(9–3–1)**	**218**

1991
SWC CHAMPIONS

Coach R. C. Slocum

AGGIES		OPP
45	LSU	7
34	at Tulsa	35
34	at Southwestern La.	7
37	at Texas Tech	14
34	at Baylor	12
27	Houston	18
38	at Rice	21
44	at TCU	7
13	Arkansas	3
65	SMU	6
31	Texas	14
2	Florida State (Cotton Bowl)	10
404	**(10–2)**	**154**

1992
SWC CHAMPIONS

Coach R. C. Slocum

AGGIES		OPP
10	Stanford (A)	7
31	at LSU	22
19	Tulsa	9
26	at Missouri	13
19	Texas Tech	17
35	Rice	9
19	Baylor	13
41	at SMU (CB)	7
40	Louisville	18
38	at Houston	30
37	TCU	10
34	at Texas	13
3	Notre Dame (Cotton Bowl)	28
352	**(12–1)**	**196**

1993
SWC CHAMPIONS

Coach R. C. Slocum

AGGIES		OPP
24	LSU	0
14	at Oklahoma	44
73	Missouri	0
31	at Texas Tech	6
34	Houston	10
34	at Baylor	17
38	at Rice	10
37	SMU	13
42	Louisville	7
59	at TCU	3
18	Texas	9
21	Notre Dame (Cotton Bowl)	24
425	**(10–2)**	**143**

SOUTHWEST CONFERENCE STANDINGS BY YEARS

1915

TEAM	WON	LOST	TIED	PCT
Baylor	3	0	0	1.000
Oklahoma	3	0	0	1.000
Arkansas	1	1	0	.500
Texas	2	2	0	.500
Texas A&M	1	1	0	.500
Rice	1	2	0	.333
Southwestern	0	2	0	.000
Okla. A&M	0	3	0	.000

1916

TEAM	WON	LOST	TIED	PCT
Texas	5	1	0	.833
Baylor	3	1	0	.750
Oklahoma	2	1	0	.666
Texas A&M	2	1	0	.666
Arkansas	0	2	0	.000
Okla. A&M	0	3	0	.000
Southwestern	0	3	0	.000

1917

TEAM	WON	LOST	TIED	PCT
Texas A&M	2	0	0	1.000
Baylor	2	1	0	.666
Oklahoma	1	1	1	.500
Texas	2	3	0	.400
Okla. A&M	1	2	0	.333
Arkansas	0	1	1	.000

1918

TEAM	WON	LOST	TIED	PCT
Texas	4	0	0	1.000
Oklahoma	2	0	0	1.000
Texas A&M	1	1	0	.500
Rice	1	1	0	.500
SMU	1	2	0	.333
Arkansas	0	1	0	.000
Baylor	0	2	0	.000
Okla. A&M	0	2	0	.000

1919

TEAM	WON	LOST	TIED	PCT
Texas A&M	4	0	0	1.000
Rice	3	1	0	.750
Oklahoma	2	1	0	.667
Texas	3	2	0	.600
Arkansas	1	2	0	.333
SMU	0	2	1	.000
Baylor	0	3	1	.000
Okla. A&M	0	2	0	.000

1920

TEAM	WON	LOST	TIED	PCT
Texas	5	0	0	1.000
Arkansas	2	0	1	1.000
Texas A&M	5	1	0	.833
Rice	2	2	1	.500
Baylor	1	2	1	.333
Phillips	0	3	0	.000
Okla. A&M	0	3	0	.000
SMU	0	4	1	.000

1921

TEAM	WON	LOST	TIED	PCT
Texas A&M	3	0	2	1.000
Texas	1	0	1	1.000
Arkansas	2	1	0	.667
Baylor	2	2	0	.500
Okla. A&M	1	1	0	.500
Rice	1	2	1	.333
SMU	0	4	0	.000

1922

TEAM	WON	LOST	TIED	PCT
Baylor	5	0	0	1.000
Texas	2	1	0	.667
Texas A&M	2	2	0	.500
SMU	2	2	0	.500
Okla. A&M	2	3	0	.400
Arkansas	1	3	0	.250
Rice	1	4	0	.200

1923

TEAM	WON	LOST	TIED	PCT
SMU	5	0	0	1.000
Texas	2	0	1	1.000
TCU	2	1	0	.667
Arkansas	2	2	0	.500
Baylor	1	1	2	.500
Okla. A&M	1	3	0	.250
Rice	1	4	0	.200
Texas A&M	0	3	1	.000

1924

TEAM	WON	LOST	TIED	PCT
Baylor	4	0	1	1.000
SMU	2	0	4	1.000
Rice	2	2	0	.500
Texas A&M	2	2	1	.500
Okla. A&M	1	1	1	.500
Texas	2	3	0	.400
Arkansas	1	2	1	.333
TCU	1	5	0	.167

1925

TEAM	WON	LOST	TIED	PCT
Texas A&M	4	1	0	.800
Texas	2	1	1	.625
TCU	2	1	1	.625
SMU	1	1	2	.500
Arkansas	2	2	1	.500
Rice	1	2	1	.375
Baylor	0	3	2	.200

1926

TEAM	WON	LOST	TIED	PCT
SMU	5	0	0	1.000
Baylor	3	1	1	.700
Texas	2	2	0	.500
Arkansas	2	2	0	.500
TCU	1	1	2	.300
Texas A&M	1	3	1	.300
Rice	0	4	0	.000

1927

TEAM	WON	LOST	TIED	PCT
Texas A&M	4	0	1	.900
SMU	4	1	0	.800
Arkansas	3	1	0	.750
Texas	2	2	1	.500
TCU	1	3	0	.400
Baylor	0	5	0	.000

1928

TEAM	WON	LOST	TIED	PCT
Texas	5	1	0	.833
Baylor	3	2	0	.600
TCU	3	2	0	.600
SMU	2	2	1	.300
Texas A&M	1	3	1	.300
Rice	0	5	0	.000

1929

TEAM	WON	LOST	TIED	PCT
TCU	4	0	1	.900
SMU	3	0	2	.800
Arkansas	3	2	0	.600
Texas	2	2	2	.500
Baylor	2	2	1	.500
Texas A&M	2	3	0	.400
Rice	0	5	0	.000

1930

TEAM	WON	LOST	TIED	PCT
Texas	4	1	0	.800
Baylor	3	1	1	.700
TCU	4	2	0	.667
SMU	2	2	1	.500
Arkansas	2	2	0	.500
Rice	2	4	0	.333
Texas A&M	0	5	0	.000

1931

SMU	5	0	1	.917
TCU	4	1	1	.750
Texas A&M	3	2	0	.600
Rice	3	3	0	.500
Texas	2	3	0	.400
Baylor	1	5	0	.167
Arkansas	0	4	0	.000

1932

TCU	6	0	0	1.000
Texas	5	1	0	.833
Rice	3	3	0	.500
Texas A&M	1	2	2	.400
Baylor	1	4	1	.250
SMU	1	4	1	.250
Arkansas	1	4	0	.200

1933

Arkansas	4	1	0	.800
Baylor	4	2	0	.667
TCU	4	2	0	.667
Texas A&M	2	2	1	.500
Texas	2	3	1	.418
SMU	2	4	0	.333
Rice	1	5	0	.167

1934

Rice	5	1	0	.833
Texas	4	1	1	.750
SMU	3	2	1	.583
TCU	3	3	0	.500
Arkansas	2	3	1	.417
Texas A&M	1	4	1	.250
Baylor	1	5	0	.167

1935

SMU	6	0	0	1.000
TCU	5	1	0	.833
Rice	3	3	0	.500
Baylor	3	3	0	.500
Arkansas	2	4	0	.333
Texas	1	5	0	.167
Texas A&M	1	5	0	.167

1936

Arkansas	5	1	0	.833
TCU	4	1	1	.750
Texas A&M	3	2	1	.583
Baylor	3	2	1	.583
SMU	2	3	1	.417
Texas	1	5	0	.167
Rice	1	5	0	.167

1937

Rice	4	1	1	.750
TCU	3	1	2	.667
Arkansas	3	2	1	.583
Baylor	3	3	0	.500
Texas A&M	2	2	2	.500
SMU	2	4	0	.333
Texas	1	5	0	.167

1938

TCU	6	0	0	1.000
SMU	4	2	0	.667
Baylor	3	2	1	.583
Rice	3	3	0	.500
Texas A&M	2	5	1	.417
Texas	1	5	0	.167
Arkansas	1	5	0	.167

1939

Texas A&M	6	0	0	1.000
SMU	4	2	0	.667
Baylor	4	2	0	.667
Texas	3	3	0	.500
Arkansas	2	3	1	.417
TCU	1	5	0	.167
Rice	0	5	1	.083

1940

Texas A&M	5	1	0	.833
SMU	5	1	0	.833
Rice	4	2	0	.667
Texas	4	2	0	.667
TCU	2	4	0	.333
Arkansas	1	5	0	.167
Baylor	0	6	0	.000

1941

Texas A&M	5	1	0	.833
Texas	4	1	1	.750
TCU	4	1	1	.750
Rice	3	2	1	.583
SMU	2	4	0	.333
Baylor	1	4	1	.250
Arkansas	0	6	0	.000

1942

Texas	5	1	0	.833
Rice	4	1	1	.750
TCU	4	2	0	.667
Baylor	3	2	1	.583
Texas A&M	2	3	1	.417
SMU	1	4	1	.250
Arkansas	0	6	0	.000

1943

Texas	5	0	0	1.000
Texas A&M	4	1	0	.800
SMU	2	3	0	.400
Rice	2	3	0	.400
TCU	1	4	0	.200
Arkansas	1	4	0	.200

(Baylor did not field team in 1943 because of war)

1944

TCU	3	1	1	.700
Texas	3	2	0	.600
Arkansas	2	2	1	.500
Texas A&M	2	3	0	.400
Rice	2	3	0	.400
SMU	2	3	0	.400

(Baylor did not field team in 1944 because of war)

1945

Texas	5	1	0	.833
SMU	4	2	0	.667
Rice	3	3	0	.500
Texas A&M	3	3	0	.500
TCU	3	3	0	.500
Baylor	2	4	0	.333
Arkansas	1	5	0	.167

1946

Rice	5	1	0	.833
Arkansas	5	1	0	.833
Texas	4	2	0	.667
Texas A&M	3	3	0	.500
SMU	2	4	0	.333
TCU	2	4	0	.333
Baylor	0	6	0	.000

1947

SMU	5	0	1	.917
Texas	5	1	0	.833
Rice	4	2	0	.667
TCU	2	3	1	.417
Texas A&M	1	4	1	.250
Arkansas	1	4	1	.240
Baylor	1	5	0	.167

1948

SMU	5	0	1	.917
Texas	4	1	1	.750
Rice	3	2	1	.583
Baylor	3	2	1	.583
Arkansas	2	4	0	.333
TCU	1	4	1	.250
Texas A&M	0	5	1	.083

1949

Rice	6	0	0	1.000
Baylor	4	2	0	.667
Texas	3	3	0	.500
TCU	3	3	0	.500
SMU	2	3	1	.417
Arkansas	2	4	0	.333
Texas A&M	0	5	1	.083

1950

Texas	6	0	0	1.000
Baylor	4	2	0	.667
Texas A&M	3	3	0	.500
TCU	3	3	0	.500
Rice	2	4	0	.333
SMU	2	4	0	.333
Arkansas	1	5	0	.167

1951

TCU	5	1	0	.833
Baylor	4	1	1	.750
Texas	3	3	0	.500
Rice	3	3	0	.500
Texas A&M	1	3	2	.333
Arkansas	2	4	0	.333
SMU	1	4	1	.250

1952

Texas	6	0	0	1.000
Rice	4	2	0	.667
SMU	3	2	1	.583
TCU	2	2	2	.500
Baylor	1	3	2	.333
Texas A&M	1	4	1	.250
Arkansas	1	5	0	.167

1953

Texas	5	1	0	.833
Rice	5	1	0	.833
Baylor	4	2	0	.667
SMU	3	3	0	.500
Arkansas	2	4	0	.333
Texas A&M	1	5	0	.167
TCU	1	5	0	.167

1954

Arkansas	5	1	0	.833
SMU	4	1	1	.750
Baylor	4	2	0	.667
Rice	4	2	0	.667
Texas	2	3	1	.417
TCU	1	5	0	.167
Texas A&M	0	6	0	.000

1955

TCU	5	1	0	.833
Texas A&M	4	1	1	.750
Texas	4	2	0	.667
Arkansas	3	2	1	.583
Baylor	2	4	0	.333
SMU	2	4	0	.333
Rice	0	6	0	.000

1956

Texas A&M	6	0	0	1.000
TCU	5	1	0	.833
Baylor	4	2	0	.667
Arkansas	3	3	0	.500
SMU	2	4	0	.333
Rice	21	5	0	.167
Texas	0	6	0	.000

1957

Rice	5	1	0	.833
Texas	4	1	1	.750
Texas A&M	4	2	0	.667
SMU	3	3	0	.500
Arkansas	2	4	0	.333
TCU	2	4	0	.333
Baylor	0	5	1	.083

1958

TCU	5	1	0	.833
Rice	4	2	0	.667
SMU	4	2	0	.667
Texas	3	3	0	.500
Texas A&M	2	4	0	.333
Arkansas	2	4	0	.333
Baylor	1	5	0	.167

1959

Texas	5	1	0	.833
Arkansas	5	1	0	.833
TCU	5	1	0	.833
SMU	2	3	1	.417
Baylor	2	4	0	.333
Rice	1	4	1	.250
Texas A&M	0	6	0	.000

1960

Arkansas	6	1	0	.857
Texas	5	2	0	.714
Baylor	5	2	0	.714
Rice	5	2	0	.714
TCU	3	3	1	.500
Texas Tech	1	5	1	.214
Texas A&M	0	4	3	.214
SMU	0	6	1	.071

1961

Texas	6	1	0	.857
Arkansas	6	1	0	.857
Rice	5	2	0	.714
Texas A&M	3	4	0	.429
TCU	2	4	1	.357
Baylor	2	5	0	.286
Texas Tech	2	5	0	.286
SMU	1	5	1	.214

1962

Texas	6	0	1	.929
Arkansas	6	1	0	.857
TCU	5	2	0	.714
Texas A&M	3	4	0	.429
Baylor	3	4	0	.429
Rice	2	4	1	.357
SMU	2	5	0	.286
Texas Tech	0	7	0	.000

1963

Texas	7	0	0	1.000
Baylor	6	1	0	.857
Rice	4	3	0	.571
Arkansas	3	4	0	.429
TCU	2	4	1	.357
SMU	2	5	0	.286
Texas Tech	2	5	0	.286
Texas A&M	1	5	1	.214

1964

Arkansas	7	0	0	1.000
Texas	6	1	0	.857
Baylor	4	3	0	.571
Rice	3	3	1	.500
Texas Tech	3	3	1	.500
TCU	3	4	0	.429
Texas A&M	1	6	0	.143
SMU	0	7	0	.000

1965

Arkansas	7	0	0	1.000
Texas Tech	5	2	0	.714
TCU	5	2	0	.714
Baylor	3	4	0	.429
SMU	3	4	0	.429
Texas	3	4	0	.429
Texas A&M	1	6	0	.143
Rice	1	6	0	.143

1966

SMU	6	1	0	.857
Arkansas	5	2	0	.714
Texas	5	2	0	.714
Texas A&M	4	3	0	.571
Baylor	3	4	0	.429
TCU	2	5	0	.286
Texas Tech	2	5	0	.286
Rice	1	6	0	.143

1967

Texas A&M	6	1	0	.857
Texas Tech	5	2	0	.714
TCU	4	3	0	.571
Texas	4	3	0	.571
Arkansas	3	3	1	.500
SMU	3	4	0	.429
Rice	2	5	0	.286
Baylor	0	6	1	.071

1968

Texas	6	1	0	.857
Arkansas	6	1	0	.857
SMU	5	2	0	.714
Texas Tech	4	3	0	.571
Baylor	3	4	0	.429
Texas A&M	2	5	0	.286
TCU	2	5	0	.286
Rice	0	7	0	.000

1969

Texas	7	0	0	1.000
Arkansas	6	1	0	.857
Texas Tech	4	3	0	.571
TCU	4	3	0	.571
SMU	4	3	0	.571
Texas A&M	2	5	0	.286
Rice	2	5	0	.286
Baylor	0	7	0	.000

1970

Texas	7	0	0	1.000
Arkansas	6	1	0	.857
Texas Tech	5	2	0	.714
TCU	3	4	0	.429
Rice	3	4	0	.429
SMU	3	4	0	.429
Baylor	1	6	0	.143
Texas A&M	0	7	0	.000

1971

Texas	6	1	0	.857
Arkansas	5	1	1	.833
TCU	5	2	0	.714
Texas A&M	4	3	0	.571
SMU	3	4	0	.429
Rice	2	4	1	.357
Texas Tech	2	5	0	.286
Baylor	0	7	0	.000

1972

Texas	7	0	0	1.000
Texas Tech	4	3	0	.571
SMU	4	3	0	.571
Rice	3	4	0	.429
Baylor	3	4	0	.429
Arkansas	3	4	0	.429
Texas A&M	2	5	0	.286
TCU	2	5	0	.286

1973

Texas	7	0	0	1.000
Texas Tech	6	1	0	.857
Rice	4	3	0	.571
SMU	3	3	1	.500
Arkansas	3	3	1	.500
Texas A&M	3	4	0	.429
TCU	1	6	0	.143
Baylor	0	7	0	.000

1974

Baylor	6	1	0	.857
Texas A&M	5	2	0	.714
Texas	5	2	0	.714
Arkansas	3	3	1	.500
SMU	3	3	1	.500
Texas Tech	3	4	0	.429
Rice	2	5	0	.286
TCU	0	7	0	.000

1975

Texas A&M	6	1	0	.857
Arkansas	6	1	0	.857
Texas	6	1	0	.857
Texas Tech	4	3	0	.571
SMU	2	5	0	.286
Baylor	2	5	0	.286
TCU	1	6	0	.143
Rice	1	6	0	.143

1976

Texas Tech	7	1	0	.875
Houston	7	1	0	.875
Texas A&M	6	2	0	.750
Baylor	4	3	1	.625
Texas	4	4	0	.500
Arkansas	3	4	1	.438
Rice	2	6	0	.250
SMU	2	6	0	.250
TCU	0	8	0	.000

1977

Texas	8	0	0	1.000
Arkansas	7	1	0	.875
Texas A&M	6	2	0	.750
Houston	4	4	0	.500
Texas Tech	4	4	0	.500
Baylor	3	5	0	.375
SMU	3	5	0	.375
TCU	1	7	0	.125
Rice	0	8	0	.000

1978

Houston	7	1	0	.875
Texas	6	2	0	.750
Arkansas	6	2	0	.750
Texas Tech	5	3	0	.625
Texas A&M	4	4	0	.500
SMU	3	5	0	.375
Baylor	3	5	0	.375
Rice	2	6	0	.250
TCU	0	8	0	.000

1979

Arkansas	7	1	0	.875
Houston	7	1	0	.875
Texas	6	2	0	.750
Baylor	5	3	0	.625
Texas A&M	4	4	0	.500
SMU	3	5	0	.375
Texas Tech	2	5	1	.313
TCU	1	6	1	.188
Rice	0	8	0	.000

1980

Baylor	8	0	0	1.000
SMU	5	3	0	.625
Houston	5	3	0	.625
Rice	4	4	0	.500
Texas	4	4	0	.500
Texas A&M	3	5	0	.375
Arkansas	3	5	0	.375
Texas Tech	3	5	0	.375
TCU	1	7	0	.125

1981

SMU	7	1	0	.875
Texas	6	1	1	.813
Houston	5	2	1	.688
Arkansas	5	3	0	.625
Texas A&M	4	4	0	.500
Rice	3	5	0	.375
Baylor	3	5	0	.375
TCU	1	6	1	.188
Texas Tech	0	7	1	.062

1982

SMU	7	0	1	.938
Texas	7	1	0	.875
Arkansas	5	2	1	.688
Houston	4	3	1	.563
Baylor	3	4	1	.438
Texas Tech	3	5	0	.375
Texas A&M	3	5	0	.375
TCU	2	6	0	.250
Rice	0	8	0	.000

1983

Texas	8	0	0	1.000
SMU	7	1	0	.875
Baylor	4	3	1	.563
Texas A&M	4	3	1	.563
Arkansas	4	4	0	.500
Texas Tech	3	4	1	.438
Houston	3	5	0	.375
TCU	1	6	1	.188
Rice	0	8	0	.000

1984

Houston	6	2	0	.750
SMU	6	2	0	.750
Texas	5	3	0	.625
TCU	5	3	0	.625
Arkansas	5	3	0	.625
Baylor	4	4	0	.500
Texas A&M	3	5	0	.375
Texas Tech	2	6	0	.250
Rice	0	8	0	.000

1985

Texas A&M	7	1	0	.875
Arkansas	6	2	0	.750
Baylor	6	2	0	.750
Texas	6	2	0	.750
Houston	3	5	0	.375
Rice	2	6	0	.250
Texas Tech	1	7	0	.125
TCU	0	8	0	.000
*SMU	5	3	0	.625

1986

Texas A&M	7	1	0	.875
Arkansas	6	2	0	.750
Baylor	6	2	0	.750
Texas Tech	5	3	0	.625
Texas	4	4	0	.500
Rice	2	6	0	.250
Houston	0	8	0	.000
*SMU	5	3	0	.625
*TCU	1	7	0	.125

1987

Texas A&M	6	1	0	.857
Texas	5	2	0	.714
Arkansas	5	2	0	.714
Texas Tech	3	3	1	.500
Baylor	3	4	0	.429
TCU	3	4	1	.429
Houston	2	4	1	.357
Rice	0	7	0	.000
§SMU	0	0	0	.000

1988

Arkansas	7	0	0	1.000
*Texas A&M	6	1	0	.857
Houston	5	2	0	.714
Texas Tech	4	3	0	.571
Baylor	2	5	0	.286
Texas	2	5	0	.286
TCU	2	5	0	.286
Rice	0	7	0	.000
§SMU	0	0	0	.000

1989

Arkansas	7	1	0	.875
Texas A&M	6	2	0	.750
*Houston	6	2	0	.750
Texas Tech	5	3	0	.625
Baylor	4	4	0	.500
Texas	4	4	0	.500
TCU	2	6	0	.250
Rice	2	6	0	.250
SMU	0	8	0	.000

1990

Texas	8	0	0	1.000
Texas A&M	5	2	1	.808
Baylor	5	2	1	.688
Rice	3	5	0	.375
TCU	3	5	0	.375
Texas Tech	3	5	0	.375
Arkansas	1	7	0	.125
SMU	0	8	0	.000
*Houston	7	1	0	.875

1991

Texas A&M	8	0	0	1.000
Baylor	5	3	0	.625
Arkansas	5	3	0	.625
Texas Tech	4	4	0	.500
TCU	4	4	0	.500
Texas	4	4	0	.500
Houston	3	5	0	.375
Rice	3	5	0	.375
SMU	0	8	0	.000

1992

Texas A&M	7	0	0	1.000
Baylor	4	3	0	.571
Rice	4	3	0	.571
Texas	4	3	0	.571
Texas Tech	4	3	0	.571
SMU	2	5	0	.286
Houston	2	5	0	.286
TCU	1	6	0	.143

1993

Texas A&M	7	0	0	1.000
Texas Tech	5	2	0	.714
Texas	5	2	0	.714
Rice	3	4	0	.429
Baylor	3	4	0	.429
TCU	2	5	0	.286
SMU	1	5	1	.214
Houston	1	5	1	.214

* ineligible for SWC Championship
§ Did not field a team: NCAA sanctions

A&M IN FINAL WIRE SERVICE POLLS

YEAR	AP	UPI
1939	1	no poll
1940	6	no poll
1941	9	no poll
1955	17	14
1956	5	5
1957	9	10
1974	16	15
1975	11	12
1976	7	8
1978	19	18
1985	6	7
1986	13	12
1987	10	9
1989	20	NR
1990	15	13

YEAR	AP	USA TODAY
1991	12	13
1992	7	6
1993	9	8

TEAM OFFENSIVE RECORDS

RUSHING

MOST RUSHES, GAME: 85 vs. TCU, 1977

MOST RUSHES, SEASON: 709, 1977

FEWEST RUSHES, GAME: 16 vs. Arkansas, 1966

MOST YARDS, GAME: 606 vs. TCU, 1977

MOST YARDS, SEASON: 3829 (661 att.), 1990 (12 games)

FEWEST YARDS, SEASON: 731, 1965

BEST AVERAGE PER RUSH, SEASON: 5.8 (661-3829), 1990

BEST AVERAGE PER GAME: 319.1, 1990

MOST FIRST DOWNS, GAME: 28, SMU, 1990

MOST FIRST DOWNS, SEASON: 196, 1990

PASSING

MOST PASSES COMPLETED, GAME: 33 vs. TCU, 1982

MOST PASSES COMPETED, SEASON: 230, 1986

MOST PASSES ATTEMPTED, GAME: 58 vs. SMU, 1968

MOST PASSES ATTEMPTED, SEASON: 400, 1982

FEWEST PASSES ATTEMPTED, SEASON: 70, 1956 (SWC record)

MOST YARDS, GAME: 376 vs. SMU, 1968

MOST YARDS, SEASON: 2691, 1986

FEWEST YARDS, SEASON: 336, 1960 (SWC record)

MOST TD PASSES, GAME: 6 vs. Rice, 1981; 6 vs. Rice, 1982

MOST TD PASSES, SEASON: 21, 1982

FEWEST PASSES INTERCEPTED, SEASON: 5, 1992 (100 att.)

MOST PASSES HAD INTERCEPTED, GAME: 7 vs. Texas, 1943; 7 vs. Rice, 1953

MOST PASSES HAD INTERCEPTED, SEASON: 30, 1941

BEST COMPLETION PERCENTAGE, GAME: (min. 10 att.) 90.5 vs. Arkansas, 1981 (19 of 21)

BEST COMPLETION PERCENTAGE, SEASON: 60.4, 1986 (230 of 381)

BEST AVERAGE YARDS PER GAME, SEASON: 244.6, 1986

MOST FIRST DOWNS, GAME: 22 vs. SMU, 1968

MOST FIRST DOWNS, SEASON: 145, 1986

TOTAL OFFENSE

MOST PLAYS, GAME: 103 vs. TCU, 1986 (65 run, 38 pass, 705 yards)

MOST PLAYS, SEASON: 895, 1986 (514 run, 381 pass); 897, 1988 (653 run, 244 pass), (12 game season)

MOST YARDS, GAME: 774 vs. SW Louisiana, 1990

MOST YARDS, SEASON: 5653, 1990

BEST AVERAGE YARDS PER GAME, SEASON: 471.1, 1990

MOST FIRST DOWNS, GAME: 38 vs. TCU, 1986 (SWC record)

MOST FIRST DOWNS, SEASON: 291, 1990

PUNTING

MOST PUNTS, GAME: 17 vs. SMU, 1945

MOST PUNTS, SEASON: 92, 1946

BEST AVERAGE, GAME: (min. five) 53.6 vs. Houston, 1977

BEST AVERAGE, SEASON: 43.6, 1965

PUNT RETURNS

MOST RETURNS, GAME: 13 vs. LSU, 1975 (SWC record)

MOST RETURNS, SEASON: 69, 1943 (9 games) (SWC record)

MOST YARDS, GAME: 319 vs. NATC, Arlington, 1943 (SWC record)

MOST YARDS, SEASON: 933, 1941 (SWC record)

BEST AVERAGE RETURN, SEASON: 17.6, 1950

KICKOFF RETURNS

MOST YARDS, GAME: 226 vs. Boston College, 1973 (six returns)

MOST RETURNS, GAME: 8 vs. Ohio State, 1970; 8 vs. LSU, 1971

BEST AVERAGE RETURN, SEASON: 24.8, 1992

SCORING

MOST POINTS, GAME: 110 vs. Daniel Baker, 1920

MOST POINTS, SWC GAME: 74 vs. TCU, 1986

MOST POINTS, SEASON: 402, 1991

MOST FIELD GOALS, GAME: 6 vs. Arkansas State, 1983 (SWC record)

MOST FIELD GOALS, SEASON: 21, 1986

FUMBLES

MOST FUMBLES, GAME: 10 vs. Ellington Field, 1945; 10 vs. Texas, 1954

MOST FUMBLES LOST, GAME: 9 vs. Ellington Field, 1945 (SWC record)

MOST FUMBLES, SEASON: 50, 1973

MOST FUMBLES LOST, SEASON: 31, 1974

PENALTIES

MOST PENALTIES, GAME: 16 vs. Texas Tech, 1986; 16 vs. TCU, 1990

MOST PENALTIES, SEASON: 104, 1991

MOST YARDS PENALIZED, GAME: 167 vs. Texas Tech, 1949 (14 penalties)

MOST YARDS PENALIZED, SEASON: 895, 1991

FEWEST PENALTIES, SEASON: 27, 1937

FEWEST YARDS PENALIZED, SEASON: 200, 1948 (31 penalties)

MISCELLANEOUS TEAM RECORDS

MOST CONSECUTIVE GAMES WON: 19, 1939–40

MOST CONSECUTIVE GAMES UNBEATEN, INCLUDING TIES: 19, 1939–40 (all wins)

UNBEATEN SWC SEASONS: 9—1917, 1919, 1921, 1927, 1939, 1956, 1991, 1992, 1993

UNTIED, UNBEATEN SEASONS: 3—1917, 1919, 1939

UNBEATEN SEASONS (WITH TIES): 2—1927, 1956

NATIONAL CHAMPIONSHIP TEAMS: 1—1939

SWC TITLES WON OR SHARED: 17

CONSECUTIVE SHUTOUTS: 18, 1918–1920 (SWC record)

BOWL APPEARANCES: 21 (11–10)

WORST DEFEAT: 48–0 vs. Texas, 1898 (non-conference)

WORST DEFEAT, SWC: 52–14 vs. Texas, 1970

TEAM DEFENSIVE RECORDS

RUSHING

FEWEST RUSHES ALLOWED, GAME: 14, Houston, 1992

FEWEST RUSHES ALLOWED, SEASON: 272, 1939

FEWEST YARDS ALLOWED, GAME: -58, TCU, 1974

FEWEST YARDS ALLOWED, SEASON: 399, 1940 (9 games) (SWC record)

LOWEST AVERAGE ALLOWED PER RUSH, SEASON: 1.3, 1940

LOWEST AVERAGE ALLOWED PER GAME: 41.5, 1939

PASSING

FEWEST COMPLETIONS ALLOWED, GAME: 0, Ellington Field, 1945; Oklahoma A&M, 1954; Arkansas, 1956; Texas, 1973; SMU, 1974; Arkansas, 1991

FEWEST COMPLETIONS ALLOWED, SEASON: 33, 1943 (138 att.) (SWC record)

FEWEST YARDS ALLOWED, GAME: 0, same six opponents as above

FEWEST YARDS ALLOWED, SEASON: 348, 1939 (SWC record)

FEWEST TD PASSES ALLOWED, SEASON: 0, 1957 (SWC record)

LOWEST COMPLETION PERCENTAGE ALLOWED: 23.9, 1943 (33 of 138)

LOWEST AVERAGE ALLOWED PER GAME: 34.8, 1939

TOTAL DEFENSE

FEWEST PLAYS ALLOWED, GAME: 38 vs. Ellington Field, 1945

FEWEST PLAYS ALLOWED, SEASON: 447, 1939 (SWC record)

FEWEST AVERAGE YARDS ALLOWED, PLAY: 1.71, 1939 (447-763) (NCAA record)

FEWEST YARDS ALLOWED, GAME: -19 vs. Ellington Field, 1945

FEWEST YARDS ALLOWED, SEASON: 763, 1939

LOWEST AVERAGE ALLOWED, SEASON: 76.3, 1939

FEWEST FIRST DOWNS ALLOWED, GAME: 0 vs. Ellington Field, 1945

FEWEST FIRST DOWNS ALLOWED, SEASON: 54, 1939 (SWC record)

PUNTING

MOST PUNTS FORCED, GAME: 17 by Texas Tech, 1943 (SWC record)

MOST PUNTS FORCED, SEASON: 114, 1939

LOWEST AVERAGE PUNT, GAME: (min. five) 22.1, TCU, 1944 (9 for 199)

LOWEST AVERAGE PUNT, SEASON: 34.4, 1949

MOST PUNTS BLOCKED, SEASON: 5, 1941

LOWEST PUNT RETURN AVERAGE ALLOWED, SEASON: 1.3, 1973

FEWEST PUNT RETURNS ALLOWED, SEASON: 11, 1978 (52 punts)

FEWEST PUNT RETURN YARDS ALLOWED, SEASON: 57, 1978 (11 returns)

KICKOFF RETURNS

LOWEST AVERAGE RETURN ALLOWED, SEASON: 13.9, 1955; 13.1, 1983 (12th Man Kickoff Team)

SCORING

FEWEST POINTS ALLOWED, SEASON: 0, 1917 (eight games); 0, 1919 (10 games) (SWC record)

FUMBLES

MOST FUMBLES RECOVERED, GAME: 7 vs. Baylor, 1982

MOST FUMBLES RECOVERED, SEASON: 29, 1952 (SWC record)

INDIVIDUAL OFFENSIVE RECORDS

RUSHING

LONGEST RUN

PLAYER	YARDS	OPP./YEAR
Bubba Bean	94	T. Tech/'75
Keith Woodside	90	Texas/'87
Darrell Smith	90	TCU/'76
Vic "Choc" Kelley	85	Oklahoma/'07
P. C. Colgin	85	§SHTC/'25
Rodney Thomas	84	Baylor/'92
Darren Lewis	84	Houston/'89
Bucky Richardson	82	So. Miss/'87
Bob Smith	81	Georgia/'50
Darren Lewis	80	TCU/'87
Bob Smith	80	T. Tech/'49
Earnest Jackson	80	TCU/'81
Curtis Dickey	80	TCU/'77
David Beal	80	Kansas/'78
Glenn Lippman	80	Nevada/'50

§ Sam Houston Teachers College

SEASON YARDS

PLAYER	YEAR	YARDS
Darren Lewis	1988	1692
Darren Lewis	1990	1691
Greg Hill	1992	1339
Bob Smith	1950	1302
Greg Hill	1991	1216
George Woodard	1976	1153
Curtis Dickey	1978	1146
George Woodard	1977	1107
Curtis Dickey	1977	978
Darren Lewis	1989	961
Roger Vick	1986	960
Bubba Bean	1975	944
Bubba Bean	1974	938

CAREER YARDS

PLAYER	YEARS	YARDS
Darren Lewis	1987–90	5012*
Curtis Dickey	1976-79	3703
George Woodard	1975–77; '79	2911
Bubba Bean	1972–75	2846
Johnny Hector	1979–82	2587
Greg Hill	1991–92	2555
Roger Vick	1983–86	2471
Bob Smith	1949–51	2415
Bucky Richardson	1987–91	2095
Skip Walker	1972–75	1878

SINGLE GAME RUSHES

PLAYER	ATT.	OPP./YEAR
Roger Vick	41	Texas/'86
Mark Green	41	SMU/'71
Darren Lewis	40	Houston/'88
George Woodard	39	Michigan/'77
George Woodard	39	Kansas St./'76
Darren Lewis	38	Texas/'88
Johnny Hector	37	TCU/'80
Roger Vick	37	T. Tech/'85
Darren Lewis	34	Arkansas/'88
Darren Lewis	34	La. Tech/'88
Curtis Dickey	34	TCU/'78
George Woodard	34	SMU/'76
Darren Lewis	34	T. Tech/'90
Darren Lewis	34	Baylor/'90

SINGLE GAME YARDS

PLAYER	YARDS	OPP./YEAR
Bob Smith	297	SMU/'50
Darren Lewis	232	T. Tech/'90
Curtis Dickey	230	TCU/'78
Earnest Jackson	219	TCU/'81
Bob Smith	215	T. Tech/'49
Greg Hill	212	LSU/'91
Darren Lewis	212	Texas/'88
Bubba Bean	204	Clemson/'73
Darren Lewis	201	Houston/'88
Darren Lewis	201	Rice/'89
Darren Lewis	194	TCU/'87
Darren Lewis	192	Arkansas/'88
Johnny Hector	191	TCU/'80

SEASON RUSHES

PLAYER	ATT.	YEAR
Darren Lewis	306	1988
Darren Lewis	291	1990
Greg Hill	267	1992
George Woodard	245	1977
Greg Hill	240	1991
George Woodard	239	1976
Roger Vick	220	1986
Anthony Toney	208	1985
Curtis Dickey	205	1978
Bob Smith	199	1950
Larry Stegent	197	1969
Darren Lewis	185	1989

*Data incomplete before 1950

CAREER RUSHES

PLAYER	ATT.	YEARS
Darren Lewis	909	1987–90
Curtis Dickey	697	1976–79
George Woodard	625	1975–77; '79
Roger Vick	598	1983–86
Johnny Hector	550	1979–82
Greg Hill	507	1991–92
Bubba Bean	482	1972–75
Larry Stegent	463	1967–69
Bob Smith	439	1949–51
Skip Walker	371	1972–75

OTHER RUSHING RECORDS

MOST TOUCHDOWNS, GAME:
Jelly Woodman, 7 vs. New Mexico, 1926

BEST AVERAGE PER CARRY, SEASON:
Bucky Richardson, 6.9, 1990

BEST AVERAGE PER CARRY, CAREER:
Bucky Richardson, 5.7, 1987–91

SINGLE SEASON 100-YARD GAMES:
Darren Lewis, 10 (1988)

CAREER 100-YARD GAMES:
Darren Lewis, 27 (1987–90)

SINGLE SEASON 200-YARD GAMES:
Darren Lewis, 2 (1988); Darren Lewis, 2 (1990)

CAREER 200-YARD GAMES:
Darren Lewis, 5 (1987–90) (SWC Record)

CONSECUTIVE 100-YARD GAMES:
Darren Lewis, 10 (Last 10 Games of 1988)

SEASON TOUCHDOWNS

PLAYER	YEAR	TD
Joel Hunt	1927	19
Darren Lewis	1990	18
George Woodard	1976	17
Greg Hill	1992	15
Jelly Woodman	1926	14
Bob Smith	1950	14
George Woodard	1977	13
Rodney Thomas	1992	13
Anthony Toney	1985	12
Greg Hill	1991	12
Bob Goode	1945	11
Darren Lewis	1989	11
John Kimbrough	1939	10
John David Crow	1956	10
Robert Wilson	1988	10
Roger Vick	1986	10
Bucky Richardson	1991	10

CAREER TOUCHDOWNS

PLAYER	YEARS	TD
Darren Lewis	1987–90	44
George Woodard	1975–77	35
Curtis Dickey	1976–79	34
Joel Hunt	1925–27	30
Bucky Richardson	1987–91	30
Greg Hill	1991–92	27
Skip Walker	1972–75	25
Bob Smith	1949–51	23
Roger Vick	1983–86	23
Johnny Hector	1979–82	20
John David Crow	1955–57	19
Bob Long	1966–68	19
Bubba Bean	1972–75	19

RUSHING YARDAGE RECORDS BY CLASS

CLASS	PLAYER	YARDS	YEAR
Freshman	Greg Hill	1216	1991
Sophomore	Darren Lewis	1692	1988
Junior	Bob Smith	1302	1950
Senior	Darren Lewis	1691	1990

FRESHMAN RUSHING

PLAYER	YARDS	YEAR
Greg Hill	1216	1991
Curtis Dickey	726	1976
Darren Lewis	668	1987
George Woodard	604	1975
Robert Wilson	425	1988
Roger Vick	425	1983

PASSING

LONGEST PASS PLAY

PLAYERS	YDS	OPP./YEAR
Gary Kubiak to Don Jones	92	La. Tech/'81
Jim Kaufmann to Dude McLean	91	Texas/'65
Edd Hargett to Barney Harris	84	TCU/'68
Chris Osgood to Shane Garrett	84	SMU/'89
David Shipman to Skip Walker	84	SMU/'75
Jacob Shockley to Waylon Manning	83	USF/'36
Edd Hargett to Bob Long	80	Texas/'67

SINGLE GAME YARDS

PLAYER	YARDS	OPP./YEAR
Edd Hargett	376	SMU/'68
Bucky Richardson	321	TCU/'91
Edd Hargett	309	TCU/'66
Kevin Murray	309	Tulsa/'85
Kevin Murray	308	Baylor/'86
Gary Kubiak	306	Rice/'82

SEASON YARDS

PLAYER	YEAR	YARDS
Kevin Murray	1986	2463
Edd Hargett	1968	2321
Kevin Murray	1985	1965
Gary Kubiak	1982	1948
Gary Kubiak	1981	1808
Lance Pavlas	1989	1681
Lex James	1970	1662
Kevin Murray	1983	1544
Edd Hargett	1966	1532
Edd Hargett	1967	1526

CAREER YARDS

PLAYER	YEARS	YARDS
Kevin Murray	1983–86	6506
Edd Hargett	1966–68	5379
Gary Kubiak	1979–82	4078
Lance Pavlas	1987–90	3185
Bucky Richardson	1987–91	3039
Mike Mosley	1977–80	2545
David Walker	1973–77	2517
Lex James	1970–72	2297
Craig Stump	1984–87	2182
Charles Milstead	1957–59	2072
Ray Graves	1951–52	1610

SINGLE GAME COMPLETIONS

PLAYER	COMP.	OPP./YEAR
Edd Hargett	32	SMU/'68
Gary Kubiak	32	TCU/'82
Gary Kubiak	25	Texas Tech/'82
Kevin Murray	25	Baylor/'86
Kevin Murray	25	Texas/'86
Kevin Murray	25	Rice/'83

SINGLE GAME TOUCHDOWN PASSES

PLAYER	TDS	OPP./YEAR
Gary Kubiak	6	Rice/'81
Gary Kubiak	5	Rice/'82
Kevin Murray	4	Tulsa/'85
Kevin Murray	4	Arkansas/'83
Jeff Granger	4	Tulsa/'91

SEASON COMPLETIONS

PLAYER	COMP.	YEAR
Kevin Murray	212	1987
Gary Kubiak	181	1982
Edd Hargett	169	1968
Kevin Murray	147	1985
Lance Pavlas	134	1989
Kevin Murray	132	1983
Edd Hargett	132	1966
Gary Kubiak	111	1981
Lex James	111	1970
Edd Hargett	99	1967

CAREER COMPLETIONS

PLAYER	COMP.	YEARS
Kevin Murray	534	1983–86
Edd Hargett	400	1966–68
Gary Kubiak	315	1979–82
Lance Pavlas	248	1987–90
Mike Mosley	204	1977–80
Bucky Richardson	196	1987–91
David Walker	177	1973–77
Craig Stump	174	1984–87
Charles Milstead	164	1957–59
Lex James	162	1970–72
Ray Graves	138	1951–52

SINGLE GAME ATTEMPTS

PLAYER	ATT.	OPP./YEAR
Edd Hargett	58	SMU/'68
Edd Hargett	55	Arkansas/'68
Kevin Murray	48	Rice/'83
Gary Kubiak	46	TCU/'82
Edd Hargett	44	Arkansas/'66
Gary Kubiak	41	La. Tech/'82
Gary Kubiak	40	Texas Tech/'82
Kevin Murray	40	Baylor/'86

SEASON ATTEMPTS

PLAYER	ATT.	YEAR
Kevin Murray	349	1986
Edd Hargett	348	1968
Gary Kubiak	324	1982
Edd Hargett	265	1966
Kevin Murray	251	1985
Kevin Murray	249	1983
Lance Pavlas	227	1989
Lex James	225	1970
Gary Kubiak	209	1981
Edd Hargett	208	1967
Rocky Self	199	1969

CAREER ATTEMPTS

PLAYER	ATT.	YEARS
Kevin Murray	926	1983–86
Ed Hargett	821	1966–68
Gary Kubiak	594	1979–82
Lance Pavlas	439	1987–90
Bucky Richardson	405	1987–91
David Walker	374	1973–77
Mike Mosley	368	1977–80
Craig Stump	363	1984–87
Lex James	346	1970–72
Charles Milstead	319	1957–59
Ray Graves	262	1951–52

SEASON TD PASSES

PLAYER	TDS	YEAR
Gary Kubiak	19	1982
Kevin Murray	17	1986
Edd Hargett	16	1968
Kevin Murray	14	1983
Kevin Murray	13	1985
Gary Kubiak	11	1981
Lance Pavlas	10	1989
Edd Hargett	10	1966
Craig Stump	10	1984

CAREER TD PASSES

PLAYER	TD	YEARS
Kevin Murray	48	1983–86
Edd Hargett	40	1966–68
Gary Kubiak	31	1979–82
Lance Pavlas	18	1987–90
David Walker	14	1973–77
Craig Stump	14	1984–87
Bucky Richardson	14	1987–91

SEASON COMPLETION PERCENTAGE

(min. 100 attempts)

PLAYER	COMP.-ATT.	PCT.	YEAR
Kevin Murray	212-349	.607	1986
Lance Pavlas	134-227	.590	1989
Kevin Murray	147-251	.586	1985
Mike Mosley	82-142	.578	1979
Ray Graves	93-164	.567	1952
Gary Kubiak	181-324	.559	1982

CAREER COMPLETION PERCENTAGE

(min. 200 attempts)

PLAYER	COMP.-ATT.	PCT.	YEAR
Kevin Murray	534-926	.577	1983–86
Lance Pavlas	248-439	.565	1987–90
Mike Mosley	204-368	.554	1977–80
Gary Kubiak	314-595	.527	1979–82
Ray Graves	141-271	.520	1950–52

PASSING YARDAGE RECORDS BY CLASS

CLASS	PLAYER	YARDS	YEAR
Freshman	Kevin Murray	1544	1983
Sophomore	Kevin Murray	1965	1985
Junior	Kevin Murray	2463	1986
Senior	Ed Hargett	2321	1968

RECEIVING

SINGLE GAME RECEPTIONS

PLAYER	REC.	OPP./YEAR
Ken McLean	13	Texas/'65
Barney Harris	13	SMU/'68
Keith Woodside	12	Arkansas/'86
Rod Harris	9	Okla. St./'88
Don Ellis	8	Arkansas/'52
Rod Bernstine	8	So. Miss./'86
Keith Woodside	8	Houston/'86
Rod Bernstine	8	TCU/'86
Keith Woodside	8	Texas/'86
Jeff Nelson	8	Tulsa/'85
Johnny Hector	8	Houston/'82
Gary Oliver	8	Arkansas/'90
Greg Schorp	8	Louisville/'92

SEASON RECEPTIONS

PLAYER	REC.	YEAR
Rod Bernstine	65	1986
Ken McLean	60	1965
Keith Woodside	52	1986
Jeff Nelson	51	1985
Barney Harris	49	1968
Shea Walker	40	1986
Rich Siler	40	1983
Gerald Carter	39	1979
Rod Harris	37	1988
John Tracey	37	1958
Mike Jones	36	1989
Percy Waddle	36	1989

CAREER RECEPTIONS

PLAYER	REC.	YEARS
Keith Woodside	110	1983–87
Rod Bernstine	105	1983–86
Shea Walker	98	1983–86
Jeff Nelson	92	1982–85
Barney Harris	91	1967–69
Tony Harrison	89	1990–93
Rod Harris	87	1985–88
Richard Osborne	86	1972–75
Bob Long	79	1966–68
Jimmy Teal	74	1982–84
Ken McLean	73	1962–65

RECEPTION RECORDS BY CLASS

CLASS	PLAYER	NO.	YEAR
Freshman	Rod Bernstine	24	1983
Sophomore	Rich Siler	40	1983
Junior	Keith Woodside	57	1986
Senior	Rod Bernstine	65	1986

SINGLE GAME YARDS

PLAYER	YDS	OPP./YEAR
Ken McLean	*250	Texas/'65
Hugh McIlroy	180	LSU/'70
Jimmy Teal	173	SMU/'84
Barney Harris	162	SMU/'68

SEASON YARDS

PLAYER	YDS	YEAR
Ken McLean	835	1965
Mike Whitwell	731	1981
Rod Bernstine	710	1986
Barney Harris	745	1968
Jeff Nelson	651	1985
Jimmy Teal	631	1984
Mike Whitwell	603	1980
Percy Waddle	600	1989
Rod Harris	592	1988
Tony Harrison	577	1991
Bob Long	541	1967
Gerald Carter	528	1979

CAREER YARDS

PLAYER	YDS	YEARS
Tony Harrison	1576	1990–93
Shea Walker	1411	1983–86
Rod Harris	1395	1985–88
Mike Whitwell	1372	1978–81
Barney Harris	1298	1967–69
Bob Long	1298	1966–68
Jimmy Teal	1258	1982–84
Richard Osborne	1181	1972–75
Jeff Nelson	1167	1982–85
Keith Woodside	1156	1983–87

SINGLE GAME TOUCHDOWNS

PLAYER	TDS	OPP./YEAR
Don Ellis	3	Arkansas/'52
Don Jones	3	Rice/'82

SEASON TOUCHDOWNS

PLAYER	TDS	YEAR
Bob Long	8	1968
Bob Long	8	1967
Jimmy Teal	6	1984
Don Jones	6	1981
Ross Brupbacher	6	1969
Andy Hillhouse	6	1950
Tony Harrison	6	1991
Rod Bernstine	5	1986
Keith Woodside	5	1986
Don Jones	5	1982
Homer May	5	1970
Percy Waddle	5	1989

CAREER TOUCHDOWNS

PLAYER	TDS	YEARS
Bob Long	19	1966–68
Tony Harrison	14	1990–93
Don Jones	11	1980–83
Jeff Nelson	10	1982–85
Rod Bernstine	8	1983–86
Jimmy Teal	8	1982–84
Shea Walker	8	1983–86
Homer May	8	1970–72
Rod Harris	7	1985–87

TOTAL OFFENSE

SINGLE GAME

PLAYER	RUN/PASS/ TOTAL	OPP./ YEAR
Edd Hargett	42/376/418	SMU/'68
Bucky Richardson	120/231/359	Rice/'91
Bucky Richardson	27/321/348	TCU/'91
Gary Kubiak	7/306/313	Rice/'82
Edd Hargett	-3/309/306	TCU/'66
Kevin Murray	-7/309/302	Tulsa/'85
Bob Smith	297/0/297	SMU/'50

SEASON

PLAYER	RUN/PASS/ TOTAL	YEAR
Kevin Murray	-115/2463/2348	1986
Edd Hargett	9/2321/2330	1968
Gary Kubiak	178/1808/1986	1981
Bucky Richardson	448/1492/1940	1991
Kevin Murray	-72/1965/1892	1985
Gary Kubiak	-63/1948/1885	1982
Darren Lewis	1691/ 57/1748	1990
Darren Lewis	1692/ 0/1692	1988
Lance Pavlas	-2/1681/1679	1989
Kevin Murray	99/1544/1643	1983
Edd Hargett	17/1532/1549	1966

CAREER

PLAYER	RUN/PASS/ TOTAL	YEARS
Kevin Murray	-51/6506/6455	1983–86
Edd Hargett	32/5379/5411	1966–68
Darren Lewis	5012/ 150/5162	1987–90
Bucky Richardson	2095/3039/5134	1987–91
Gary Kubiak	188/4078/4266	1979–82
Mike Mosley	1396/2545/3941	1977–80
Curtis Dickey	3703/ 0/3703	1976–79
David Walker	912/2517/3429	1973–77
Lance Pavlas	-97/3212/3115	1987–90
George Woodard	2911/ 0/2911	1975–79

PUNT RETURNS

LONGEST

PLAYER	YARDS	OPP./YEAR
Bob Goode	98	Ellington Field/'45
Charlie Royalty	93	Villanova/'48
Carl Roaches	84	Rice/'72
Preston Smith	74	Arkansas/'45
Kevin Smith	73	Texas/'91
Marion Flanagan	72	Oklahoma/'46
Dick Todd	72	SMU/'37
Kevin Smith	71	Rice/'91
Carl Roaches	71	SMU/'73
Barney Welch	71	Texas/'42
Yale Lary	69	SMU/'50

SINGLE GAME YARDS

PLAYER	RT-YDS	OPP./YEAR
Rod Harris	8-123	La. Tech/'87
Rod Harris	7-108	Arkansas/'87
Bob Goode	1-98	Ellington Field/'45
Charlie Royalty	1-93	Villanova/'48
Barney Welch	2-93	Arkansas/'46

SEASON YARDS

PLAYER	RT-YDS	AVG.	YEAR
Marion Flanagan	49-475	9.7	1943
Rod Harris	37-391	10.6	1987
Yale Lary	24-388	16.2	1951
Rod Harris	42-345	8.2	1986
Jimmie Hawkins	39-331	8.5	1985
David Scott	46-318	6.9	1979
Derrick Frazier	29-301	10.4	1992
Jimmie Hawkins	33-298	9.0	1984
Carl Roaches	38-238	6.3	1975
Billy Cannon	31-280	9.0	1982

CAREER YARDS

PLAYER	YEARS	RT-YDS	AVG.
Rod Harris	1985–88	116-971	8.4
Carl Roaches	1972–75	115-924	8.0
Jimmie Hawkins	1982–85	87-749	8.6
Billy Cannon	1980–83	86-649	7.6
Yale Lary	1949–51	33-597	18.1
David Scott	1979–80	79-439	9.3
Dave Elmendorf	1968–70	37-345	4.4
Shane Garrett	1988–90	45-344	7.6
George Hargett	1961–63	37-341	9.2

KICKOFF RETURNS

LONGEST RETURNS

PLAYER	YARDS	OPP./YEAR
Carl Roaches	*100	Boston College/'73
Dan McIlhany	*100	Texas Tech/'62
Bob Smith	*100	Georgia/'50
Joel Hunt	97	Arkansas/'27
Carl Roaches	97	LSU/'72
Billy Mitchell	95	Houston/'92
Hugh McIlroy	94	Nebraska/'71
Larry Horton	92	LSU/'89
Bob Goode	90	Oklahoma/'48

SINGLE GAME YARDS

PLAYER	YARDS	OPP./YEAR
Carl Roaches	*193	Boston College/'73
Jack Pardee	139	Texas/'56
Billy Mitchell	133	Houston/'92

SEASON YARDS

PLAYER	YEAR	RT-YDS	AVG.
Dave Elmendorf	1970	23-457	19.4
Hugh McIlroy	1971	17-439	25.8
Carl Roaches	1973	15-426	28.4
Carl Roaches	1972	18-426	23.7
Larry Horton	1989	17-420	24.7
Don Ellis	1952	17-413	24.2
Bob Goode	1948	16-407	25.4
Rod Harris	1988	22-388	17.6
Billy Mitchell	1992	11-336	30.5
Rod Harris	1987	15-329	21.9

CAREER YARDS

PLAYER	YEARS	RT-YDS	AVG.
Rod Harris	1985–88	59-1209	20.5
Carl Roaches	1972–75	43-1087	25.3
Larry Stegent	1967–69	39-814	20.9
Dave Elmendorf	1969–70	35–689	19.7
Don Ellis	1952–53	26-566	21.8

PUNTING

LONGEST

PLAYER	YARDS	OPP./YEAR
Bobby Goff	86	Texas Tech/'44
Wilbert Randow	85	Texas/'33
Kyle Stuard	81	La. Tech/'81
Todd Tschantz	80	Rice/'85
David Davis	75	Tulsa/'92
Stan Hollmig	74	LSU/'47
Derace Moser	74	TCU/'41
Mitch Robertson	74	Rice/'71
Phil Scoggin	74	Texas/'65
Steve O'Neal	73	Baylor/'66
Phil Scoggin	73	SMU/'64

SEASON AVERAGE

(min. two punts per game)

PLAYER	NO-YDS	AVG.	YEAR
David Davis	70-3067	43.8	1992
Phil Scoggin	88-3833	43.6	1965
David Appleby	57-2466	43.3	1977
Todd Tschantz	33-1406	42.6	1985
Sean Wilson	45-1906	42.4	1990
Steve O'Neal	67-2836	42.3	1966
Steve O'Neal	81-3402	42.0	1967
Mark Stanley	59-2479	42.0	1974
Kyle Stuard	67-2806	41.9	1983
Sean Wilson	36-1500	41.7	1989
Jim Keller	66-2738	41.5	1963

CAREER AVERAGE

(min. 100 punts)

PLAYER	YEARS	NO-YDS	AVG.
Todd Tschantz	1984–86	106-4498	42.4
Phil Scoggin	1964–65	161-6739	41.9
Steve O'Neal	1966–68	212-8854	41.8
Kyle Stuard	1980–83	205-8472	41.3
Sean Wilson	1987–90	185–7577	41.0
David Davis	1991–92	122-4983	40.8
David Appleby	1976–79	226-9222	40.8
Mark Stanley	1973–75	166-6580	39.6

FIELD GOALS

SEASON

PLAYER	YEAR	FG-ATT.	PCT.
Scott Slater	1986	21-27	.778
Alan Smith	1983	18-26	.692
Tony Franklin	1976	17-26	.654
David Hardy	1982	16-22	.727
Terry Venetoulias	1992	16-23	.696
Tony Franklin	1977	16-28	.571
Eric Franklin	1985	15-27	.556
Scott Slater	1987	15-22	.682
Terry Venetoulias	1991	13-18	.722
David Hardy	1981	13-19	.684
Alan Smith	1984	12-20	.600
Tony Franklin	1975	12-28	.429

SINGLE GAME

PLAYER	NO.	OPP./YEAR
Alan Smith	6	Arkansas St./'83
Tony Franklin	5	Rice/'76
David Hardy	4	UTA/'82
Scott Slater	4	Houston/'86
Scott Slater	4	TCU/'87

CAREER

PLAYER	YEARS	FG-ATT.	PCT.
Tony Franklin	1975–78	56-101	.554
David Hardy	1979–82	43-63	.683
Scott Slater	1986–88	42-61	.689
Alan Smith	1980–84	32-51	.627
Terry Venetoulias	1991–92	29–41	.707
Layne Talbot	1987–90	21-32	.656
Eric Franklin	1984–86	20-32	.625
Pat McDermott	1970–72	20-38	.526
Randy Haddox	1973–74	19-40	.475

LONGEST

PLAYER	YARDS	OPP./YEAR
Tony Franklin	65	Baylor/'76
Tony Franklin	64	Baylor/'76
Tony Franklin	62	Florida/'77
Tony Franklin	59	Rice/'75
Layne Talbot	59	Baylor/'90
Alan Smith	59	Arkansas St./'83
David Hardy	57	UTA/'82
Tony Franklin	57	Texas/'76
Randy Haddox	57	Arkansas/'74
Alan Smith	57	Arkansas St./'83
David Hardy	56	La. Tech/'82
Tony Franklin	56	SMU/'76

INDIVIDUAL DEFENSIVE RECORDS

TACKLES

SINGLE SEASON TACKLES

PLAYER	TACKLES	YEAR
Doug Carr	157	1978
Johnny Holland	155	1984
Larry Kelm	152	1986
Grady Hoermann	151	1971
Johnny Holland	150	1985

CAREER TACKLES

PLAYER	YEARS	TACKLES
Johnny Holland	1983–86	455
Mike Little	1978–81	448
Ed Simonini	1972–75	425
Ray Childress	1981–84	360
Doug Carr	1977–80	359

SINGLE GAME TACKLES

PLAYER	TACKLES	OPP./YEAR
Larry Horton	24	Baylor/'90
Larry Kelm	24	SMU/'85
Johnny Holland	22	Alabama/'85
Johnny Holland	20	S. Miss./'86
Jay Muller	19	Arkansas/'85
Larry Kelm	19	S. Miss./'86

TOTAL TACKLES ANNUAL LEADERS

YEAR	PLAYER (POS.)	NO.
1992	Patrick Bates, lb	95
1991	Jason Atkinson lb	95
1990	Larry Horton, ss	117
1989	Larry Horton, ss	102
1988	Dana Batiste, lb	110
1987	John Roper, lb	104
1986	Johnny Holland, lb	147
1985	Larry Kelm, lb	152
1984	Johnny Holland, lb	155
1983	Ray Childress, de	117
1982	Jeff Fuller, db	90
	Bobby Strogen, lb	90
1981	Bobby Strogen, lb	133
1980	Mike Little, lb	116
1979	Doug Carr, lb	136
1978	Doug Carr, lb	157
1977	Carl Grulich, ss	132
1976	Robert Jackson, lb	143
1975	Ed Simonini, lb	101
1974	Ed Simonini, lb	98
1973	Ed Simonini, lb	130
1972	Grady Hoermann, lb	130
1971	Grady Hoermann, lb	151

TOTAL TACKLE RECORDS BY CLASS

CLASS	PLAYER	NO.	YEAR
Freshman	Ed Simonini	98	1972
Sophomore	Doug Carr	157	1978
Junior	Grady Hoermann	151	1971
Senior	Larry Kelm	152	1986

SINGLE SEASON

PLAYER	SACKS	YEAR
Jacob Green	20	1979
John Roper	15	1988
John Roper	15	1987
Ray Childress	15	1983
Aaron Wallace	14.5	1988
Jacob Green	13	1978
William Thomas	13	1990
Marcus Buckley	13	1991
Marcus Buckley	12	1992

CAREER

PLAYER	YEARS	SACKS
Aaron Wallace	1986–89	42
Jacob Green	1977–79	37
John Roper	1985–88	36
Marcus Buckley	1990–92	29
Ray Childress	1981–84	25

SCORING

SINGLE GAME

PLAYER	YEAR	TD	PTS	OPPONENT
Jelly Woodman	1926	7	44	N. Mex./'26
Preston Smith	1945	4	25	Ell. Fld/'45

SEASON

PLAYER	YEAR	TD	PAT	FG	TP
Joel Hunt	1927	19	n/a	n/a	128
Darren Lewis	1990	19	0	0	114
George Woodard	1976	17	0	0	102
Greg Hill	1992	17	0	0	102
Scott Slater	1986	0	37	21	100
Terry Venetoulias	1991	0	49	13	88
Terry Venetoulias	1992	0	39	16	87
Tony Franklin	1977	0	38	16	86
Bob Smith	1950	14	0	0	84
Jelly Woodman	1926	14	0	0	84

CAREER

PLAYER	YEARS	TD	PAT	FG	TP
Tony Franklin	1975–78	0	123	56	291
Darren Lewis	1987–90	45	0	0	270
Joel Hunt	1925–27	30	29	5	224
Scott Slater	1985–88	0	96	42	222
David Hardy	1979–82	0	90	43	219
George Woodard	1975–77	35	0	0	210
Curtis Dickey	1976–79	34	0	0	206

*(Incomplete before 1977)

OTHER DEFENSIVE RECORDS

CAREER FUMBLES CAUSED: Jacob Green, 12 (1977–78)
SEASON FUMBLES CAUSED: Jacob Green, 6 (1978); Aaron Wallace, 6 (1987)
CAREER FUMBLE RECOVERIES: Marcus Buckley, 10 (1990–92)
SEASON FUMBLE RECOVERIES: Lester Hayes, 5 (1975); Domingo Bryant, 5 (1985)
CAREER PASSES BROKEN UP: Derrick Frazier, 36 (1989–92)
SEASON PASSES BROKEN UP: Aaron Glenn, 20 (1992)
CAREER QB PRESSURES: Aaron Wallace, 48 (1986–89)
SEASON QB PRESSURES: William Thomas, 30 (1990)
§CAREER TACKLES FOR LOSSES: John Roper, 32 (1985–88)
§SEASON TACKLES FOR LOSSES: John Roper, 13 (1988)
§ sacks are not included

PASS INTERCEPTIONS

SINGLE GAME

PLAYER	INT.	OPP./YEAR
Joe Boring	4	Arkansas/'52

SEASON

PLAYER	YEAR	INT
Bill Sibley	1941	10
Kevin Smith	1989	9
Lester Hayes	1976	8
Joe Boring	1952	8
Bill Hobbs	1967	7
Kevin Smith	1990	7
Lester Hayes	1975	6
Pat Thomas	1974	6
Dave Elmendorf	1970	6
Lee Hitt	1971	6
David Hoot	1970	6
Aaron Glenn	1992	6

CAREER

PLAYER	YEARS	INT
Kevin Smith	1988–91	20
Lester Hayes	1973–76	14
Pat Thomas	1972–75	13
Dave Elmendorf	1968–70	12
Kip Corrington	1983–87	11
Bill Hobbs	1966–68	11
Joe Boring	1952–53	11
Domingo Bryant	1982–85	9
James Flowers	1983–86	8
Derrick Frazier	1989–92	8
Jeff Fuller	1980–83	8

LONGEST RETURNS

PLAYER	YARDS	OPP./YEAR
Bill Hobbs	100	TCU/'67
Cullen Rogers	99	Arkansas/'42
Aaron Glenn	95	Texas/'92
Bill Conatser	92	TCU/'39
J. V. Sikes	92	Texas/'25
Ramsey Bradberry	89	SMU/'89
Ross Brupbacher	80	Tulane/'68
Kevin Smith	78	Rice/'90
Lester Hayes	77	Baylor/'75

INTERCEPTION RECORDS BY CLASS

CLASS	PLAYER	NO.	YEAR
Freshman	Several players with two		
Sophomore	Kevin Smith	9	1989
Junior	Bill Sibley	10	1941
Senior	Lester Hayes	8	1976

OTHER PASS INTERCEPTION RECORDS

MOST YARDS INTERCEPTION RETURNS, GAME: Bill Hobbs, 132 vs. TCU, 1967 (SWC record)
MOST YARDS INTERCEPTION RETURNS, SEASON: Ross Brupbacher, 167, 1967
MOST YARDS INTERCEPTION RETURNS, CAREER: Kevin Smith, 289, 1988–91

TEXAS A&M ALL AMERICANS

YEAR	PLAYER	POSITION
1936	Joe Routt	Guard
1937	Joe Routt	Guard
1939	Joe Boyd	Tackle
1939	John Kimbrough	Fullback
1940	John Kimbrough	Fullback
1940	Marshall Robnett	Guard
1950	Bob Smith	Fullback
1951	Jack Little	Tackle
1952	Jack Little	Tackle
1956	Jack Pardee	Fullback
1956	Charles Krueger	Tackle
1956	Dennis Goehring	Guard
1957	Charles Krueger	Tackle
1957	John David Crow *(Crow won the Heisman Trophy in 1957)*	Halfback
1966	Maurice Moorman	Tackle
1967	Bill Hobbs	Linebacker
1968	Bill Hobbs	Linebacker
1968	Rolf Krueger	Tackle
1968	Tommy Maxwell	Safety
1968	Steve O'Neal	Punter
1970	Dave Elmendorf	Safety
1974	Pat Thomas	Cornerback
1975	Pat Thomas	Cornerback
1975	Ed Simonini	Linebacker
1975	Garth Ten Napel	Linebacker
1976	Robert Jackson	Linebacker
1976	Lester Hayes	Safety
1976	Tony Franklin	Kicker
1978	Tony Franklin	Kicker
1979	Jacob Green	Def. End
1983	Ray Childress	Def. End
1984	Ray Childress	Def. End
1985	Johnny Holland	Linebacker
1985	Doug Williams	Offensive Tackle
1986	Johnny Holland	Linebacker
1987	John Roper	Linebacker
1988	Darren Lewis	Running Back
1990	Darren Lewis	Running Back
1991	Kevin Smith	Cornerback
1992	Marcus Buckley	Linebacker
1992	Patrick Bates	Safety
1993	Sam Adams	Def. End
1993	Aaron Glenn	Cornerback

A&M's ALL-SOUTHWEST CONFERENCE PLAYERS

(First Team Only, AP and/or UPI)

1915
John Garrity, end
N. M. Braumiller, guard

1916
Newt Settegast, tackle
Jim Crow, tackle

1917
Tim Griesenbeck, end
Ox Ford, tackle
E. S. Wilson, guard
Rip Collins, back
Jack Mahan, back

1919
E. S. Wilson, guard
W. E. Murrah, guard
C. R. Drake, tackle
R. G. Higginbotham, halfback
Jack Mahan, fullback
Scott Alexander, end

1920
W. E. Murrah, end
C. R. Drake, tackle
R. G. Higginbotham, halfback
Jack Mahan, fullback
T. F. Wilson, end

1921
Sam Sanders, back
T. F. Wilson, end
W. E. Murrah, guard

1922
W. D. Johnson, guard
T. F. Wilson, end

1923
A. J. Evans, end
W. D. Johnson, guard

1924
W. W. Wilson, back
Neeley Allison, end

1925
Joel Hunt, halfback
L. G. Dietrich, tackle
W. M. Dansby, guard
Barlow Irvin, tackle
W. W. Wilson, back

1926
Joel Hunt, halfback
L. G. Dietrich, tackle
J. A. Tektorik, guard
J. B. Sikes, end
C. D. Watts, center

1927
Joel Hunt, quarterback
J. B. Sikes, end
J. G. Holmes, guard
A. C. Sprott, tackle
E. E. Fegari, guard
W. S. Lister, tackle

1928
Z. W. Bartlett, center
H. E. Burgess, fullback
S. J. Petty, end

1929
Tommy Mills, quarterback
Charlie Richter, guard

1930
Adrain Tracey, end

1931
Carl Moulden, guard
Cliff Dominque, quarterback
Charlie Malone, end

1932
Willis Nolan, center
Charley Cummings, tackle

1933
Ted Spencer, fullback
Ray Murray, end
W. T. Jordan, tackle

1934
John Crow, guard

1936
Joe Routt, guard
Charles DeWare, center
Roy Young, tackle

1937
Joe Routt, guard
Roy Young, tackle
Dick Todd, halfback
Virgil Jones, guard

1938
Dick Todd, halfback
Joe Boyd, tackle

1939
Joe Boyd, tackle
John Kimbrough, fullback
Marshall Robnett, guard
Herb Smith, end
Jim Thomason, halfback

1940
James Sterling, end
John Kimbrough, fullback
Marshall Robnett, guard
Jim Thomason, halfback
Ernie Pannell, tackle

1941
Derace Moser, running back
James Sterling, end
Bill Sibley, center
Martin Ruby, tackle

1942
Bill Henderson, end
Felix Bucek, guard
Cullen Rogers, back
Leo Daniels, back

1943
Marian Flanagan, back
M. E. Settegast, end
Goble Bryant, tackle
Jim Hallmark, back

1944
Monty Moncrief, tackle
Clarence Howell, end
Paul Yates, fullback

1945
Monty Moncrief, guard
Grant Darnell, guard
Preston Smith, halfback
Bob Goode, halfback

1946
Monty Moncrief, tackle

1947
Jim Winkler, tackle

1948
Jim Winkler, tackle
Bob Goode, halfback
Odell Stautzenberger, guard
Andy Hillhouse, end

1949
Bob Smith, fullback

1950
Bob Smith, fullback
Max Greiner, tackle
Andy Hillhouse, end
Carl Molberg, guard

1951
Jack Little, tackle
Glenn Lippmann, back
Hugh Meyer, center
Yale Lary, back
Billy Tidwell, back

1952
Jack Little, tackle
Ray Graves, quarterback
Joe Boring, safety

1953
Don Ellis, quarterback

1954
Elwood Kettler, quarterback
Bennie Sinclair, end

1955
Gene Stallings, end
Dennis Goehring, guard

1956
Jack Pardee, fullback
Lloyd Hale, center
Dennis Goehring, guard
John David Crow, halfback
John Tracey, end
Charlie Krueger, tackle
Roddy Osborne, quarterback

1957
John David Crow, halfback
Charles Krueger, tackle
Bobby Marks, end

1958
Charles Milstead, quarterback
John Tracey, end

1960
Sam Byer, fullback

1961
Jerry Hopkins, center

1962
Jerry Hopkins, center

1963
Ronney Moore, guard

1964
Ray Gene Hinze, offensive tackle
Mike Pittman, defensive halfback

1965
Ken (Dude) McLean, offensive end
Joe Wellborn, linebacker

1966
Maurice Moorman, offensive tackle
Gary Kovar, offensive guard
Wendell Houseley, offensive halfback

1967
Edd Hargett, quarterback
Bob Long, offensive end
Tommy Maxwell, safety
Rolf Krueger, defensive tackle
Bill Hobbs, linebacker
Grady Allen, defensive end
Larry Stegent, offensive halfback
Steve O'Neal, punter
Dan Schneider, offensive tackle

1968
Edd Hargett, quarterback
Steve O'Neal, punter
Rolf Krueger, defensive tackle
Bill Hobbs, linebacker
Mike DeNiro, defensive end

1969
Larry Stegent, tailback
Lynn Odom, defensive guard
Dave Elmendorf, safety
Mike DeNiro, defensive end
Ross Brupbacher, end

1970
Homer May, end
Dave Elmendorf, safety

1971
Leonard Forey, guard
David Hoot, safety
Boice Best, defensive tackle
Grady Hoermann, linebacker
Buster Callaway, tackle
Mark Green, halfback

1972
Grady Hoermann, linebacker
Boice Best, defensive tackle
Robert Murski, cornerback
Ed Simonini, linebacker

1973
Ed Simonini, linebacker
Don Long, defensive end
Skip Walker, halfback

1974
Pat Thomas, cornerback
Ed Simonini, linebacker
Tim Gray, cornerback
Warren Trahan, defensive tackle
Bubba Bean, offensive halfback
Randy Haddox, place kicker
Glenn Bujnoch, offensive tackle
Garth TenNapel, linebacker
Mark Stanley, punter

1975
Ed Simonini, linebacker
Pat Thomas, cornerback
Garth TenNapel, linebacker
Bubba Bean, halfback
Edgar Fields, defensive tackle
Blake Schwarz, defensive end
Jimmy Dean, defensive tackle
Jackie Williams, safety
Lester Hayes, safety
Richard Osborne, tight end
Glenn Bujnoch, offensive tackle
Tank Marshall, defensive end
Bruce Welch, offensive guard
Robert Jackson, linebacker

1976
Jimmy Dean, defensive tackle
Edgar Fields, defensive tackle
Tony Franklin, kicker
Gary Haack, tight end
Lester Hayes, safety
Robert Jackson, linebacker
Tank Marshall, defensive end
Frank Myers, tackle
Dennis Swilley, guard
George Woodard, fullback

1977
Mark Dennard, center
Frank Myers, offensive tackle
Cody Risien, offensive tackle
Carl Grulich, safety

1978
Curtis Dickey, tailback
Tony Franklin, kicker
Jacob Green, defensive end
Russell Mikeska, tight end
Cody Risien, offensive tackle

1979
Jacob Green, defensive end
Gerald Carter, split end
Ed Pustejovsky, offensive guard

1980
No selections from A&M

1981
No selections from A&M

1982
Domingo Bryant, defensive back
David Hardy, kicker

1983
Rich Siler, tight end
Ray Childress, defensive end/tackle

1984
Ray Childress, defensive end/tackle

1985
Johnny Holland, linebacker
Doug Williams, offensive tackle
Kevin Murray, quarterback
Domingo Bryant, defensive back
Anthony Toney, fullback
Jeff Nelson, flanker
Rod Saddler, defensive end
Randy Dausin, offensive guard

1986
Kevin Murray, quarterback
Rod Bernstine, tight end
Johnny Holland, linebacker
Roger Vick, fullback
Keith Woodside, halfback
Scott Slater, kicker
Jay Muller, defensive end
Kip Corrington, defensive back
Louis Cheek, offensive tackle
Terrance Brooks, defensive back

1987
Rod Harris, split end
Louis Cheek, offensive tackle
Matt Wilson, center
Scott Slater, kicker
Sammy O'Brient, defensive guard
John Roper, linebacker
Kip Corrington, free safety

1988
Darren Lewis, running back
Jerry Fontenot, guard
Matt McCall, tackle
John Roper, linebacker
Aaron Wallace, linebacker
Mickey Washington, cornerback

1989
Mike Jones, tight end
Kevin Smith, defensive back
William Thomas, linebacker
Aaron Wallace, linebacker
Richmond Webb, offensive tackle

1990
Darren Lewis, runing back
Mike Arthur, center
Matt McCall, offensive tackle
William Thomas, linebacker
Kevin Smith, cornerback

1991
Kevin Smith, cornerback
Bucky Richardson, quarterback
Quentin Coryatt, linebacker
Greg Hill, running back
Keith Alex, offensive tackle
Marcus Buckley, linebacker
John Ellisor, offensive tackle
Patrick Bates, free safety

1992
Marcus Buckley, linebacker
John Ellisor, guard
David Davis, punter
Patrick Bates, free safety
Greg Schorp, tight end
Aaron Glenn, cornerback
Chris Dausin, center
Terry Venetoulias, placekicker
Greg Hill, running back
Sam Adams, defensive end

1993
Sam Adams, defensive end
Antonio Armstrong, linebacker
Jason Atkinson, linebacker
Calvin Collins, offensive guard
Chris Dausin, center
Eric England, defensive end
Aaron Glenn, cornerback
Tyler Harrison, offensive guard
Michael Hendricks, safety
Greg Hill, running back
Jason Matthews, offensive tackle
Greg Schorp, cornerback
Steve Solari, linebacker
Lance Teichelman, noseguard
Rodney Thomas, running back
Dexter Wesley, offensive tackle
Junior White, safety

AGGIE FOOTBALL LETTERMEN SINCE 1894

A
Abbey, Dan R. '29, '30
Abbott, John A. '39
Abraham, Arthur A. '44, '45
Adair, Chad '86, '87
Adamek, Jody '90
Adami, Buster '67, '68, '69
Adams, Brent (Manager) '87, '88
Adams, Darrell '79, '80, '81, '82
Adams, Jimmy '67, '68, '69
Adams, Kent '80, '81
Adams, Sam '91, '92, '93
Aday, Temple '78, '79, '80, '81
Alex, Keith '88, '89, '90, '91
Alexander, Al (Manager) '74
Alexander, Scott '17, '18, '19
Allen, Corey '86
Allen, Dennis '92, '93
Allen, Grady L. '65, '66, '67
Allison, Bill '84
Allison, J. Neely '23, '24
Alsabrook, O. D. '27, '28, '29
Altegelt, George A. '10, '11
Anderson, Gary Lee '50
Anderson, George D. '17
Anderson, Gerald R. (Manager) '53
Anderson, Percy J. '47
Andricks, Dennis B. '41
Andrus, Jason '92
Angermiller, Roy L. '59
Anglin, M. H. '20
Anthony, Shane '93
Appleby, David '76, '77, '78, '79
Armbrister, Gary '69
Armstrong, Adger '75, '76, '77, '78
Armstrong, Coy (Manager) '90, '91
Arndt, Charles '73, '74, '75
Arnold, D. C. '26
Arnold, W. J. '13
Arthur, Mike '87, '88, '89, '90
Arthur, Tom '83, '84
Asberry, Wayne '82, '83, '84, '85
Aschenbeck, Harvey '66, '67, '68
Ashley, Mike '81, '82, ;'83
Askey, N. '19
Astin, Erwin H. 1896, '97, '98, '99
Aston, James W. '30, '31, '32
Atkinson, Jason '90, '91, '92, '93
Audish, William '37, '38, '39
Austin, Darrell '82, '83, '84, '85

B
Bairrington, David '75
Baker, Keith '75, '76
Baker, Paul (Manager) '74
Balcar, Danny '85, '86, '87
Baldwin, Keith '79, '80, '81
Balenti, Michael R. '09
Ballard, William R. '51
Ballentine, John R. '45, '46, '47
Bandy, David '79, '80, '81
Barfield, R. E. '31
Barhorst, Warren '87
Barker, John (Manager) '89
Barker, William O. '65
Barnes, George W. '09, '10, '11
Barnett, Billy Bob '69
Barnett, Robert W. '65, '66
Barnett, Ray R. '52, '53, '54
Barnett, Van '79, '80, '81, '82
Barrett, James '83, '84
Barrett, Ralph '77
Barry, Mark '90
Bartlett, Z. W. Jr. '26, '27, '28
Bartley, Arthur N. '02
Bartley, Tony '86, '87
Barton, Dorbandt J. '49, '50
Bateman, A. R. '10, '11
Bates, Gus '39
Bates, Larry E. '64
Bates, Patrick '91, '92
Bates, Robert G. '48, '49, '50
Batiste, Dana '85, '86, '87, '88
Batts, Marcus '92, '93
Baty, Robert B. '46, '47, '48
Baum, Spencer '86
Baumgarten, Charles 1897, '98
Bayless, Frederick '32
Beal, David '77, '78, '79, '80
Beam, Winston '67, '70
Bean, Earnest (Bubba) '72, '73, '74, '75
Beard, Glenn G. '45
Beasley, Wyatte G. '10, '11, '12, '13
Beavers, Robby '80
Beck, Kenneth '56, '57, '58
Beeman, Del S. '04
Beesley, Ben B. '21
Beesley, E. G. '43
Beilharz, William '01, '02
Beirne, Kevin '93
Belcher, Raymond '78
Bell, Charles '75, '76
Bell, Jim (Trainer) '79, '80
Bell, Luther E. '31
Bell, Tyree L. '10, '11, '12, '14
Bellar, Mike '69, '70, '71
Belville, Vernon R. '42
Benjamin, Joseph W. '02, '03
Bennett, Gary L. '62
Bennett, James '93
Bennett, Phil '76, '77
Bernay, Camp L. '03
Bernstine, Rod '83, '84, '85, '86
Berry, Dean '85, '86, '87
Berry, Greg '80, '81, '82, '83
Berry, Murry P. '58, '59, '60
Berry, R. H. '24, '25
Best, Boice Watts '70, '71, '72
Best, Bruce Allen '70
Beutel, H. W. '24, '25
Bevans, Tom '83, '84
Bible, Hollis U. '28
Biggens, Wilbert '91, '92, '93
Billingsley, Charles '71
Bird, Max Dwayne '70, '71, '72
Birdwell, Russ '87
Bitters, Bob (Trainer) '81, '82
Black, Jayson '87, '88, '89, '90
Black, Marc '69, '70, '71
Blackburn, George S. (Manager) '39
Blair, W. G. '52
Blake, Robert E. '05
Blake, Thomas M. '01, '02, '03
Blalock, Travis '90
Blankenship, Tony '74, '75
Blavier, Steve (Manager) '84, '85
Blessing, William '39
Bob, Adam '85, '86, '87, '88
Boettcher, Reinhardt B. 1896, '03, '04
Bolcerek, Tommy '88
Bonner, H. L. '13
Booker, Herbert '79
Booth, Ellison S. '03
Boring, Joseph '52, '53
Boswell, James R. '48
Bouldin, Steve (Manager/Trainer) '93
Bounds, James Y. '62, '63, '64
Boutwell, Jeff '86
Bowers, Alvin '72, '73
Bowler, Sam E. '12
Box, Steve '80, '82, '83
Boyce, C. William Jr. '05
Boyd, Hugh F. Jr. '39
Boyd, Joe M. '37, '38, '39
Boyd, Wm. O. Jr. '35, '36
Brack, Vance '67
Bradberry, Ramsey '89, '90, '91
Bradford, J. B. '23
Bransom, George E. Jr. '37, '38
Braselton, J. W. '24
Braumiller, N. M. '14, '15
Brawley, Lance (Trainer) '89
Breding, Edward V. '64, '65, '66
Breedlove, H. M. '32, '33
Breihan, Stacy '75, '77, '78
Brice, Roland G. '60, '61, '62
Britt, A. Rankin '36, '37, '38
Broaddus, Larry G. '59, '60
Brooks, Hugh '14
Brooks, Terrance '84, '85, '86, '87
Broom, Guy '84, '85, '86, '87
Brothers, David '76, '77, '78, '79
Brotherton, John R. '62, '63, '64
Broussard, Fred E. '53
Browder, Harris M. '39
Brown, Billy '82, '83
Brown, Charles W. '14
Brown, Chris '81
Brown, Darrell W. '54, '55, '57
Brown, J. E. '28, '29
Brown, J. S. '09
Brown, Leandrew '77, '78, '79, '80
Brown, Reaville M. 1900, '01, '04
Brown, Reggie '92, '93
Brupbacher, Ross '67, '68, '69
Bruton, Alfred L. (Manager) '54
Bruton, Mike '73
Bryant, Domingo '82, '83, '84, '85
Bryant, Goble W. '43
Bucek, Felix A. '41, '42
Bucek, Roy E. '39, '40, '41
Buchanan, A. B. '39, '40
Buckley, Marcus, '90, '91, '92
Buckman, Tom '66, '67, '68
Buckner, F. K. '21
Bujnoch, Glenn '73, '74, '75
Bull, A. C. '15
Bullard, Steve '90
Bullitt, Jerry '80, '81, '82, '83
Bullitt, Steve '83, '84, '85, '86
Bulovas, John '89
Bumgardner, Tom '83
Bunger, Mike '69, '70, '71
Buntin, R. F. (Manager) '42, '47
Burditt, Jesse N. '43, '44, '45, '46
Burger, George '74
Burgess, Edwin B. 1894
Burgess, Herschel E. '26, '27, '28
Burks, Steve '69, '70, '71
Burleson, Russell W. 1894
Burney, John W. 1894
Burnett, John '87
Burns, Darrace B. '14, '15, '16
Burns, Dennis '83
Burrell, Charles '91
Burton, Alan M. (Manager) '51
Burchofsky, R. L. '43, '44, '45
Butler, Marvin M. '14
Byer, Sam A. '60, '61, '62

C
Caffey, Kenneth D. '64, '65, '66
Caffey, Lee Roy '60, '61, '62
Callahan, A. Paul '34
Callaway, David Earl '70, '71, '72
Calcott, George V. (Trainer) '62
Callcott, Wm. H. (Trainer) '64, '65
Callender, Richard '48, '49
Caldwell, Fred '80, '81, '82
Campbell, Henry '88
Campbell, Jerry '66, '67, '68
Cangelose, Marty (Manager) '79, '80
Cannon, Billy '80, '81, '82, '83
Capt, Louis E. '52, '53
Cardwell, John E. '13
Carlin, William J. '09
Carlton, Lawton '77
Carmody, T. J. '80, '81
Carpenter, Brian '89
Carpenter, Miles 1899, 1900, '01
Carpenter, Ronnie D. '61, '62, '63
Carr, Chuck '77, '78, '79
Carr, Doug '77, '78, '79, '80
Carroll, Mike (Trainer) '88
Carruth, Dennis Paschall '70, '71, '72
Carruthers, B. V. '05
Carruthers, R. L. '19, '20, '21
Carson, C. 1894
Carter, Doug '89, '90, '91, '92
Carter, Gerald '78, '79
Casas, René '88, '89
Case, Frank '84, '86
Case, Stormy '93
Cashion, James T. '44, '45, '46, '47
Caskey, Robert D. '60, '61
Caswell, Mike '67, '68, '69
Cauble, Richard C. III (Trainer) '71
Cauthorn, Sidney W. '58
Cavanaugh, Bill '86, '87, '88
Cawthon, Frank W. '14
Chaffee, Tom '67
Chaney, David (Trainer) '84, '85
Chapin, R. Tuck '48, '49, '50
Chatham, Kefa '90, '91, '92, '93
Cheek, Louis '84, '85, '86, '87
Childress, Jay 1894
Childress, Ray '81, '82, '83, '84
Childress, Trent '88, '89
Chiles, H. T. 1894
Choyce, Ken '81
Christensen, John L. '49
Christian, J. P. '29, '30, '31
Christner, Tom '83
Christopher, Todd Dennis '70, '71, '72
Church, Warren E. '37
Clare, Gary (Trainer) '83, '84
Clark, Gregory '77
Clark, Henry F. '55
Clark, Michael V. '60, '61, '62
Clark, Stuart '81
Clark, Willard W. '39
Clay, Hayward '92, '93
Clendennan, Robert J. '55, '56
Cole, Leon '87, '88
Coleman, Wiley L. '14
Colgin, P. C. '26
Collins, Calvin '93
Collins, H. W. '16, '17
Collins, Bubba J. '64, '65
Collins, Ray (Manager) '78
Collins, Melvin '86, '87
Collins, William A. '14, '15
Colon, Chris '92, '93
Conatser, William E. '38, '39, '40
Connelley, R. E. '32
Conoley, Odell M. '33, '34
Conover, Brooks W. '28, '29
Conrad, Bobby J. '55, '56, '57
Cook, Greg '91, '92
Cooley, Arthur '67, '68
Coolidge, David '86
Cooper, Brad '92
Cooper, Jeff (Trainer) '72
Cooper, John '88, '89

Copeland, Cedric D. K. '48, '59
Cornell, Albert L. '05, '06, '07
Corona, Craig (Manager) '86, '87
Corrington, Kip '84, '85, '86, '87
Cortez, Roberto '65, '66, '67
Coryatt, Quentin '90, '91
Costar, Gary '87, '88
Coston, F. M. '36, '37, '38
Coulter, Hiram T. 1894
Couser, W. L. '33, '34
Cousins, R. W. 1898
Cover, Robert J. '03
Cowley, Harold E. '39, '40, '41
Cox, Jessie '90, '92
Cox, Truman D. '42
Cox, William E. 1896
Craig, George W. '60, '61
Craig, James W. Jr. '62, '63
Cretcher, J. C. '08, '09, '10
Crooms, Chris '88, '89, '90, '91
Crossman, Jerry M. '50 '51, '52
Crouch, Robert '84
Crow, Floyd A. '14
Crow, J. W. '32
Crow, John David '55, '56, '57
Crow, M. O. '34, '35
Crutsinger, Larry L. '61
Cummings, Charley M. '31, '32, '33
Cummings, Leslie L. '34, '35, '36
Cunningham, Pat '88, '89
Curbello, Jimmy (Trainer) '79
Cure, Wayne O. '42
Curington, Lloyd D. '64, '65, '66
Cushman, Cecil A. '12
Cuthrell, J. H. '28

D

Dale, Ivan '06, '07
Dale, Jay '77, '79
Dale, Jesse D. '05, '06, '07
Daniel, Edwin R. '46, '47, '48
Daniel, Thomas C. '44, '45
Daniels, James '73, '74
Daniels, Leo H. '41, '42, '46
Dansby, M. W. '24
Dansby, N. J. '23, '24, '25
Darbyshire, Russell O. '08
Darnell, Grant S. '43, '44, '45
Darwin, Matt '81, '82, '83, '84
Darwin, William B. '57, '58, '59
Dausin, Bryan '79, '81, '82
Dausin, Chris '91, '92, '93
Dausin, Randy '83, '84, '85
Davis, Alan (Trainer) '91
Davis, Dan '78, '79, '80, '81
Davis, David '91, '92
Davis, James M. '02
Davis, Jeff (Trainer) '81
Davis, Jewel '19
Davis, Robin '69
Davis, W. E. '27, '38
Davis, W. E. '30, '31
Dawkins, Marvin H. '63, '64
Dawson, John '78, '79, '81
Dawson, Oran '31
Dawson, William H. '38, '39, '40
Dean, Don '72
Dean, James S. (Manager) '05
Dean, Jeff (Manager/Trainer) '93
Dean, Jimmy '73, '74, '75, '76
Deaton, Thomas Weldon '70
Debenport, Dan '89
DeBusk, Kelly S. '64
Decker, Jack (Trainer) '68
Deere, Donal R. '43
Deffebach, J. A. '26, '27
Delery, H. B. '28, '29
DeLong, Raleigh '14
Dendy, Billy G. '55
Dennard, Mark '75, '76, '77
Denton, Dean M. '45
Descant, Dennis '89
DeSilva, Jim '81
Devine, Michael D. '64
Dew, Bobby W. '47
DeNiro, Mike '68, '69
DeWare, Charles A. Sr. '05, '06, '07, '08
DeWare, Charles A. Jr. '34, '35, '36
DeWare, Robert R. 1899, 1900, '01
DeWitt, Bernard John III '70
DeWitt, Mike (Manager) '73
Dickey, Curtis '76, '77, '78, '79
Dickey, Leonard M. '41, '45, '46
Dickie, Byron H. '14
Dickson, Preston '77, '78, '79
Dieterich, A. F. '20, '21
Dietrich, L. G. '24, '25, '26
Dillon, Greg '84, '87
Dillon, Paul G. '62
Dittman, Henry '37, '38
Dixon, Robert H. '51, '52
Dockery, Seth '88, '89, '90, '91
Dollar, Roy I. '52
Dominque, G. C. '31, '32, '33
Donahue, Johnnie '76, '77, '78
Dorsey, R. R. '27, '28, '29
Doucet, Raymond L. '57, '58
Dowell, David '82, '83, '84, '85
Dowell, George S. 1897
Drake, C. R. '18, '19, '20
Dreiss, Ed Jr. '10, '11
Drennan, James L. '62, '63, '64
Dubcak, James Louis '70, '71
DuBois, H. V. '21, '22, '23
Dudley, Edward R. '55, '58
Duncan, William M. '38, '39
Dunn, Ralph B. '03
Dupree, Calvin R. '47, '48
Dusek, Ed D/ '42, '46, '47
Dusek, John Bradley '70, '71, '72
Dwoskin, Blake '87
Dwyer, W. F. 1897, '98
Dwyer, Tom J. '08, '09, '10

E

Easley, Robert A. Jr. '53, '54
Eberle, A. A. '43, '44
Ebrom, Edwin '69, '70, '71
Eddington, Ashley '84, '85
Edmondson, Larry '81
Edwards, Brian '87, '88
Edwards, Bryan '88
Eenigenburg, Todd '90
Eillers, Joseph A. '60, '61
Eitt, Henry W. '22
Elam, John '87
Elam, K. C. '17, '18
Elder, Jim M. '02
Elkins, John '81, '82, '84
Elledge, Jerry R. (Trainer) '61
Elliott, Jay '91, '92
Ellis, Cedric '81
Ellis, Donald E. '52, '53
Ellis, Herbert W. '44, '45, '47, '48
Ellis, J. P. (Manager) '66
Ellis, Kevin '89, '90
Ellis, Larry '71, '72, '73
Ellis, Oscar L. '07
Ellisor, John '88, '90, '91, '92
Elmendorf, Dave '68, '69, '70
Emerson, Steve '92, '93
Endsley, Lindon C. '64
England, Eric '90, '91, '92, '93
Engle, William F. '45
Erhard, Earl 1900
Erickson, Jalmer L. '61, '62
Ermis, Harvey J. '64
Eschenberg, Arthur C. '14, '15
Esquivel, Carlos '56, '57
Estes, Teddy J. '58, '59, '60
Evans, A. J. '21, '22, '23
Evans, David (Trainer) '77
Evans, Greg (Manager) '89, '90
Evans, Rick (Trainer) '73
Evans, Robert D. '61, '64
Evans, Scott (Manager) '90, '93
Everett, G. Dudley '12, '13, '14
Ewell, W. L. '28

F

Faber, Benny H. '14
Farr, Reso 1896, '97
Farrar, Jeff '80, '81, '82
Farrar, Troy (Trainer) '88
Few, Jon W. '58, '60
Figari, E. E. '27
Fields, Edgar '74, '75, '76
Fields, Mike '69, '70
Finley, Bruce Kent '70, '71, '72
Fischler, Chris '90
Fisher, Donnie '80, '82
Fisher, Franklin C. '60, '61
Fister, Lynn '67, '68
Flanagan, Marion D. '43, '46
Fletcher, Pierce H. '63, '65, '66
Flinchem, James M. '07, '10
Flinn, Pat '79, '80
Flournoy, James '90
Flowers, James '83, '84, '85, '86
Flowers James L. '48, '49, '50
Floyd, Mike '74, '75
Floyd, J. G. '28, '29, '30
Foldberg, Henry C. '42
Foldberg, John D. '45
Fontenot, Jerry '85, '86, '87, '88
Foote, J. M. '11, '12
Force, Henry H. '39
Ford, Chris '85, '86
Ford, Ken '83, '84
Ford, M. H. '17
Ford, William J. '62, '63, '64
Forey, Leonard '69, '70, '71
Forgason, J. Y. '22, '23, '24
Forgsard, Charles H. '09
Foster, Edmund J. '02, '03, '04, '05
Foster, H. 1899, 1900
Foster, John (Trainer) '79, '80
Foster, Kermit '80, '81, '84
Fowler, E. Odell '32, '34
Fowler, James B. '49, '50, '51
Franklin, Carter L. '58, '59, '60
Franklin, Eric '84, '85
Franklin, Tony '75, '76, '77, '78
Francis, Keith '90
Frazee, Dick '77
Frazelle, Billy J. (Trainer) '51
Frazier, Derrick '89, '90, '91, '92
Freeman, Matt '74, '75, '76
Freiling, Wayne E. '59, '60, '61
Frey, Richard H. '50, '51, '52
Fronk, Dave '88
Fry, David '87
Frymire, Tom (Manager) '87
Fuller, Jeff '80, '81, '82, '83

G

Galloway, Gerald '78
Gantt, Greg (Manager) '80, '81
Gardemal, Richard D. '49, '50, '51
Gardner, John '69, '70, '71
Garner, Robert A. '58
Garrett, Shane '88, '89, '90
Garrett, T. H. 1897, '98, '99, 1900
Garrison, Chris '85, '86
Garrity, John '13, '14, '15
Garth, J. W. '18
Gary, R. J. '43, '44, '46, '47
Gay, Richard C. '56, '57, '58
Gebhart, P. C. 1899, 1900
Geer, Carl E. '39
Geer, W. E. '43, '44, '45
Gerasimowicz, Robert W. '70, '71
Gerrity, Johnny '13, '14
Gibson, Charles B. '43
Gilbert, John R. '55, '56, '57
Gilbert, O'Neill '85, '86, '87, '88
Gilbert, Warren A. (Manager) '07
Gilbert, Warren A. Jr. '46, '47
Gilby, John '90
Gilfillan, Max D. '14, '15, '16
Gill, E. King '22, '23
Gillar, George E. '55, '56
Gillmore, L. M. '17
Gillis, Alton '91
Gillum, Lee (Trainer) '87, '88
Gilman, Greg (Trainer) '82, '83
Glenn, Aaron '92, '93
Glendenning, Craig '73, '74, '75, '76
Glenn, Ronnie '85, '86, '87
Godwin, W. G. '33
Godwin, Willis H. Jr. '57, '58, '59
Goehring, Allen G. '57, '58, '59
Goehring, Dennis H. '54, '55, '56
Goff, Robert E. '44, '48, '49
Golansinski, Joe A. '32
Golson, Kyle '77, '78, '79
Goode, Robert L. '45, '46, '47, '48
Goodwin, Tommy '70, '71
Gosney, Robert R. '53
Gouger, G. Bryan '17, '19, '20
Gough, Carl '67, '68
Graham, M. C. '16
Graham, Mark '83
Graham, Reggie '91, '92, '93
Graham, Thomas '81, '82
Granger, Jeff '91, '92
Grant, Donald G. '55
Graves, Henry L. '31, '32
Graves, Ray D. '51, '52
Gray, Frank M. 1900, '02
Gray, George W. '44, '45
Gray, George William '58
Gray, Tim '73, '74
Green, Jacob '77, '78, '79
Green, Mark '71, '72
Greene, Taylor H. (Manager) '54
Greeno, David '73, '74, '75
Greer, Donavan '93
Gregory, Thomas '76, '78, '79
Gregory, J. C. '33
Greiner, Max G. '47, '48, '49, '50
Griesenbeck, C. T. '17
Griffin, Mike (Trainer) '74
Grimmer, Gib (Manager) '79, '80
Grissom, Roy J. '10
Groce, Clif '91, '92, '93
Gruben, Gary '68
Grudt, Darren '88, '89
Grulich, Carl '76, '77, '78, '79
Gunnels, Roy '67
Gurley, Matt '86, '87, '88
Guseman, Oliver J. '31
Guthrie, Keith '80, '81, '82, '83
Guthrie, Zach '76, '78, '79, '80
Gwin, Clinton D. '50

H

Haack, Gary '74, '75, '76
Haas, Raymond A. Jr. '52
Haddox, Bennie R. '72, '73, '74
Hagerty, Paul '78
Hail, George (Trainer) '59
Gale, Gordon '83
Hale, Lloyd R. '54, '55, '56
Hall, Charles L. '52, '54
Hall, Luther H. '58
Hall, Robert L. '38
Hallman, Curley '66, '67, '68
Hallman, Leroy '83
Hallmark, James L. '43, '46
Hallmark, Kenzy D. '50
Haltom, Bart U. '48
Haltom, Guy V. '04, '05
Hamilton, Jimmy '76, '77, '78, '79

Hamiilton, Louis A. '06, '07, '08, '09
Hamner, Stayton W. '02, '03
Hampton, Gary Wayne (Manager) '77
Hampton, Keith (Manager) '83
Hampton, Neil (Manager) '79
Hand, Floyd '42
Hanick, C. F. '05
Hanna, Howard E. '03, '05
Hanna, T. W. '22, '23
Hanson, Allan '68, '69
Hardin, Eddie '75, '76, '77
Hardman, J. J. '22
Hardy, David '79, '80, '81, '82
Hargett, Edd '66, '67, '68
Hargett, George W. '61, '62, '63
Harper, James L. '60, '61, '62
Harris, Barney '67, '68, '69
Harris, David B. (Manager) '05, '09
Harris, Joey '83
Harris, Rod '85, '86, '87, '88
Harris, Jay (Trainer) '81
Harrison, R. H. Jr. '18, 19
Harrison, Tony '90, '91, '92, '93
Harrison, Tyler '91, '92, '93
Hart, Lilliard D. '45
Hart, William T. '45
Hartley, Wally '86, '87, '88, '89
Hartman, Jim '73, '74, '75
Harvey, Karl '83
Harvey, Randy '77, '78, '79
Hauerland, Leroy '67, '68
Hauser, Henry '38, '39, '40
Haverda, Lance '83, '84, '85, '86
Hawkins, Jimmie '82, '83, '84, '85
Hayes, Lester '73, '74, '75, '76
Haynes, Marlin '90, '91
Hays, Scott '79, '80
Heath, Eddie '76, '77, '78
Heaton, Robert (Trainer) '85, '86, '87
Heck, David (Trainer) '89, '90, '91
Hector, Johnny '79, '80, '81, '82
Heidelberg, Frank T. '07, '08
Heimann, Chester E. '39
Henderson, Daniel E. '55
Henderson, Mike (Manager) '91
Henderson, Robert W. '40, '41, '42
Hendricks, Michael '91, '92, '93
Hendrickson, Glenn '83, '85
Henke, Charles E. '38, '39, '40
Henry, Patrick '89, '91
Henry, Peter C. '39
Herman, Odell C. '38, '39, '40
Hernandez, Frank P. (Manager) '58
Herold, Brian (Manager) '90
Herr, Joey '69, '70, '71
Herring, Julian C. '50
Herrold, Brian (Manager) '89
Hewitt, W. W. '30, '31, '32
Higginbotham, G. H. '12
Higginbotham, Roswell G. '17, '19, '20
Higgins, Norton '44, '45, '46, '47
Hill, Carl R. '49
Hill, David '79, '80, '81
Hill, Greg '91, '92, '93
Hill, Russell E. '59, '60, '61
Hill, Walter R. '50, '51, '52
Hillhouse, Andy L '48, '50
Hillje, Bubba '88, '89
Hinnant, Barb '69, '70
Hinze, Ray G. '62, '63, '64
Hitt, Lee Ellison '70, '71
Hobbs, Bill '66, '67, '68
Hodge, Charles H. '50, '51
Hodges, Gene (Trainer) '71
Hoermann, Grady '70, '71, '72
Hogan, George A. '60, '61
Hohn, Caesar '09, '10, '11, '12
Hohn, Charles M. '43
Holder, Leonard D. '41
Holditch, Murry W. '49, '50
Holland, Johnny '83, '84, '85, '86
Holley, Jeff '83, '84, '85, '86
Holliday, T. C. '11
Hollmig, Stanley E '46, '47
Holmes, Doug '77, '78, '79
Holmes, J. G. '27
Holmes, R. C. (Manager) '47, '48
Honeycutt, Lynn '78, '79
Honore, Jerry '73, '74
Hood, Billy (Trainer) '83, '84
Hooker, Roger M. '07, '08, '09
Hooper, Clarence D. '50, '51, '52
Hoot, David '69, '70, '71
Hope, George N. '02
Hopkins, Jerry W. '60, '61, '62
Hornsby, H. R. '30, '31
Horton, Larry '87, '88, '89, '90
Housley, Wendell '66, '67, '68
Howard, Albert L. '64, '65, '66
Howard, Thomas V. Jr. '56, '57, '58
Howard, Todd '83, '84, '85, '86
Howell, John C. '44, '46, '47
Howse, James '85, '86
Hoyl, Basil L. (Manager) '42
Hubby, Ronnie G. '72, '73, '74, '75
Huddleston, Billy P. '53, '54, '55
Hudeck, Russell R. '49, '50, '51
Hudgins, Charles M. '50
Huff, Jeff '87, '88
Huff, Leslie N. (Manager) '07
Huggins, Alan K. '60, '61
Huggins, Harold '87
Hullin, Paul '72, '73, '74
Hull, Burt E. (Manager) '04
Hundl, Philip '90
Hunnicutt, Jesse '74, '75, '76
Hunt, O. Joel '25, '26, '27
Huntington, Bobby N. '60, '61, '62
Hyde, Walter 1900, '01

I

Irvin, Barlow '23, '24, '25
Irvwin, B. M. '32
Ivy, Kyle '90

J

Jackson, Basil '85, '86, '87, '88
Jackson, Earnest '79, '80, '81, '82
Jackson, Lance '83, '84, '85
Jackson, Larry '91, '92, '93
Jackson, Robert '75, '76
James, Arlis '78, '79, '80
James, Lex Forrest '70, '71, '72
James, Ronnie '79
Janner, Calvin F. '61
Jay, Mike '73, '74, '75
Jay, Monte '85, '86
Jeffrey, William M. '38, '39, '40
Jeffries, Craig '92
Jenkins, Jerry S. '60, '61
Jenkins, Joseph S. (Manager) '64
Jennings, Curtis '77, '78
Joeris, Leonard '39, '42
Johnson, A. L. '16
Johnson, B. L. '46
Johnson, Chris '69, '70, '71
Johnson, F. S. (Manager) '03
Johnson, George R. '55
Johnson, Harry '85
Johnson, Joe '87, '88
Johnson, Joe B. '60
Johnson, Larry '76, '79
Johnson, Larry '83, '84
Johnson, Scott (Trainer) '79
Johnson, William D. '22, '23
Johnson, Wilbur G. '45
Joiner, David '86
Jones, Albert '87, '88, '89, '90
Jones, Don '80, '81, '82, '83
Jones, Donald (Manager) '89, '90
Jones, Donald H. (Manager) '60
Jones, Gary '86, '87, '88, '89
Jones, Ivan '66, '67, '68
Jones, Jeff '91, '92, '93
Jones, Michael '88, '89
Jones, Tony '86, '87, '88
Jones, Troy '86
Jones, Virgil B. '36, '37
Jordan, Jim '82, '83
Jordan, W. T. '32, '33, '34

K

Kachtick, Jerry V. '63, '64, '65
Kachtik, Edward D. '52, '53, '54
Kahler, Mike (Manager) '78
Kamp, Charles H. '70
Kapchinski, Karl (Trainer) '78
Kauffman, James H. '65
Kazmierski, Jim '68
Keeling, Thomas D. '60, '61
Keen, L. S. '21, '22
Keese, Mike '73, '74
Keith, Robert D. '54, '55, '56
Kellen, John '82, '83
Keller, James L '61, '62, '63
Kelley, Victor M. '05, '06, '07, '09
Kelm, Larry '83, '84, '85, '86
Kemph, Gary S. '65
Kenderdine, J. M. '33
Kendrick, J. M. '15
Kendrick, Robert T. '04, '05
Kennedy, Kevin '80
Kenney, Steve '91, '93
Kennon, Paul A. '54
Kern, R. A. '10, '12
Kern, Ryan '91, '93
Kesey, David A. (Statistician) '69
Kettler, Elwood N. '53, '54
Kidwell, Richard (Manager) '85, '86
Kildow, P. C. 1899
Killion, Reed '82
Kimbrough, Jack C. '39, '40
Kimbrough, John A. '38, '39, '40
Kimbrough, William R. '33, '34
King, Joe Mac '69, '70, '71
Kipp, Kenneth W. '60, '61, '62
Kirby, Selmer M. '34, '35
Kirchmer, John T. '64
Kirk, Kenny '76, '77
Kirkpatrick, Roy '69
Kishi, Taro '24, '25
Kitchens, Gary '67
Klein, Terry (Manager) '77
Knickerbocker, A. G. '19
Knickerbocker, H. W. '22, '23
Knight, Charles J. '64
Kocurek, Jimmy '76, '77
Koehn, Donald W. '64, '65, '66
Kohlman, Joe M. '62, '64
Kotch, Jim (Trainer) '74
Kovar, Gary W. '64, '65, '66
Kovar, Jack '67, '68, '69
Krahl, Shane '88, '89, '90
Kramm, Raymond E. '62
Krenek, Benedict J. '60, '61, '62
Krueger, Charles A. '55, '56, '57
Krueger, Rolf '66, '67, '68
Krug, William 1894
Kubala, Raymond G. '61, '62, '63
Kubecka, Bill '67
Kubiak, Gary '80, '81, '82
Kubesch, Raymond A. '62
Kuehn, Russell '71, '72

L

Labar, Harry W '58, '59, '60
LaBauve, Dwight '71, '72
LaGrange, Charles R. '63, '64, '65
LaGrone, Walter A. '60, '61
Lakin, Greg '88, '89, '90, '91
Lambert, H. G. '10, '11, '12
Lamkin, Kenneth A. '64, '65, '66
Lammers, Chris '83
Lamp, Ted '73, '74
Land, Marshall '86
Land, Mike (Trainer) '81, '82
Landrum, Tim '85, '86, '87
Langford, Alvin L. '50, '51, '52
Langston, James E. '56
Lark, Scott '85, '86, '87, '88
Lary, Robert Y. '49, '50, '51
Latham, Joel P. '60, '61, '62
Lawson, Bruce '82, '83
Lawson, Clarence O. '49
Lazarine, Marshall M. '50
League, Thomas '44
LeBouef, Gordon E. '57, '58, '59
Ledbetter, Harry L. '65, '66
Ledbetter, Ronald P. '60, '61, '62
Lee, Larry L. '65, '66
Lee, Robert G. '63
Leggett, Charles W. '09
Lehrer, Robert (Trainer) '86, '87
Leiper, Sam E. '22
Leisner, Lane (Manager) '82, '83
Lemmons, Bernard '50
Lemons, Billy '73, '74, '75, '76
Lemons, Frank '76, '77
Lewis, Darren '87, '88, '89, '90
Lewis, Mark '80, '81, '82, '84
Lewis, Steve '79
Lewis, Trent '89, '90, '91
Leyendecker, Dan '88
Liles, Ike '83, '84
Lillard, Steve T. '09
Lindsey, Ernedst M. '35
Lindsey, Glynn '64, '65, '66
Lindsey, Ronald L. '64, '65, '66
Linnstaedter, James A. '61, '62, '63
Linscombe, Corry '84, '85
Lippman, Glenn E. '49, '50, '51
Lister, W. S. '26, '27
Littig, Michael '83
Little, Jack H. '50, '51, '52
Little, Mike '78, '79, '80, '81
Litterst, Frank C. '16
Lockett, Bobby J. '56
Lofton, Steve '89
Long, Bob '66, '67, '68
Long, Don '72, '73, '74
Long, Eldon W. '43
Lopez, Ricky '81
Lord, George P. '30, '31
Lord, Mike '69, '70, '71
Love, Andrew C. 1894, '98
Love, J. N. '33
Love, Richard L. '59
Loving, James W. '04
Lowery, Gene '93
Luebbehusen, Steve '69, '70, '71
Luethy, Don R. '42
Luna, Otie C. '57, '58
Lutrick, J. A. '11
Lyles, John V. '12

M

Maddox, Randy '69
Magourik, Conrad W. '51, '52, '53
Magrill, O. B. '29, '30, '31
Maham, Scott '87, '88
Mahan, Jack '17, '19, '20
Malone, C. C. '30, '31
Malone, Grant (Manager) '89, '90, '91
Malone, Tyronne '90
Maltz, Hershel (Manager) '47
Manning, Waylon E. '35, '36
Maples, Weldon L. '41, '42
Marcus, James '87, '89

Marks, Jared '84, '85, '86
Marks, Robert E. '55, '56, '57
Marquette, Leo J. '52
Marshall, Mike '82
Marshall, Tank '73, '74, '75, '76
Martin, G. W. '18, '19, '20
Martin, Gary Wayne '70
Martin, Harry 1894
Martin, John '88
Martin, Sidney T. '34
Masey, Chris (Trainer) '78
Masterson, L. '02
Matthews, Mason L. '44, '45
Mathews, Jason '91, '92, '93
Mathews, Ryan '91, '92, '93
Mathison, Todd '91, '92, '93
Maughmer, Lynn '78
Mauk, Albert '03, '05
Maxfield, Kyle '91, '92, '93
Maxwell, Stapp N. '32
Maxwell, Tommy '66, '67, '68
May, Homer H. '70, '71, '72
Mayeaux, Hayden E. '51, '52
Mayfield, J. D. Jr. (Manager) '49, '50
Mazur, John '83, '84
McAfee, Keith '88, '89, '90, '91
McAllister, G. T. '43, '44
McAnelly, Phil '68
McArthur, O. A. '12
McCaffrey, Gary '70
McCall, Mark (Trainer) '89, '90, '91
McCall, Matt '87, '88, '89, '90
McCarley, Robert E. '52
McClatchy, Scott (Trainer) '89, '90, '91
McClelland, Don A. '57, '60
McClelland, H. W. '22
McClintock, J. R. '17
McCoy, Joe (Manager) '89, '90, '91
McCoy, Torin '89, '90
McCray, Danny '93
McCrumbly, John '73, '74
McDermott, Pat '70, '71, '72
McDonald, Andy '88, '89
McDonald, Charles N. '49, '50, '51
McDonald, Hugh F. 1894
McDonald, Pace '18
McDonald, William A. '09
McDowell, Charles H. '10
McElroy, Hugh '70, '71
McElroy, Leeland '93
McFadden, P. M. '30, '31
McFarland, Arthur '03, '04
McFarland, H. F. 1893, '94
McFarland, James L. '11
McGinnis, Francis K. 1900
McGonagill, J. D. 1894
McGonagle, Brad '90
McGowan, Billy Joe '52, '54
McGregor, Flint '02
McGuire, Eddy (Trainer) '89, '90
McGuire, Joseph D. '24, '25
McGuire, Trace '85, '86, '87
McIlhany, Joe D. '62, '63, '64
McKaughan, Edward W. '64, '65
McKeehan, James '91, '92, '93
McKnight, J. B. '16, '17
McLean, Ken J. '62, '63, '65
McMahan, Billy M. '53
McMahan, James T. '50
McMillan, M. Blaisdale 1894
McMillan, W. G. '21, '22
McMullen, Typail '93
McMurrey, J. D. '17
McNeill, J. C. 1894
McQueen, Mark '81, '82
Meeks, Thomas E. '62, '63, '64
Meitzen, J. B. '24
Mercer, Arthur J. '41, '42
Merka, Jeremiah H. '33
Meyer, D. '02
Meyer, William H. '49, '50, '51
Mickens, Ray '92, '93
Middleton, Bobby '84, '85, '86
Middleton, Doug '85
Mikeska, Russell '76, '77
Miles, Wadine '77
Miller, A. R. '12
Miller, Eric E. '51, '52, '53
Miller, John '89, '90
Miller, L. '02
Miller, Steve (Manager/Trainer) '93
Miller, T. L. '21, '22
Miller, Thomas B. '39
Miller, Vance W. '12, '13
Milligan, Garry '76, '77, '78
Milligan, Wayne '03, '07
Mills, J. Kenneth '37
Mills, Thomas W. '27, '28, '29
Millsap, Lenard '70
Milstead, Charles F. '57, '58, '59
Minnock, W. A. '37, '38
Mitchell, Billy '90, '92, '93
Mitchell, Brandon '93
Mitchell, Brian '91, '92, '93
Mitchell, Keith '93
Mitchell, Merlin '15, '16
Mohn, Walter '67
Molberg, Carl '48, '49, '50
Moncrief, Monte P. '43, '44, '45, '46
Monk, Kevin '74, '75, '76, '77
Montgomery, J. B. '42
Montgomery, Roark '12
Moon, L. B. '87, '88
Moore, A. A. '30, '31
Moore, Doyle H. '49
Moore, Eric '89, '90
Moore, George F. '07, '08
Moore, Kirk (Manager/Trainer) '93
Moore, Mack '79, '80
Moore, William R. '62, '63, '64
Moore, W. Scott '07, '08, '09, '10
Moorman, Maurice '66
Morgan, Sylvester '84, '85, '86, '87
Morris, A. B. '20, '21, '22
Morris, Alex '85, '86, '87, '88
Morrison, D. E. '12
Morrison, P. M. 1896
Morrow, Johnnie '35, '36
Mortensen, James E. '45
Moseley, Hal 1897, '98, '99, 1900
Mosley, Mike '77, '78, '79, '80
Moser, R. Derace '39, '40, '41
Moses, Sam F. '49, '50, '51
Mossenburg, W. G. 1894
Motley, Larry '86
Motley, Zolus C. '39, '41
Moulden, Carl D. '29, '30, '31
Mudd, Dennis '85
Mulhollan, Ray W. '40, '41, '42
Mullen, Steve '68
Muller, Jay '84, '85, '86
Munson, George (Manager) '72
Munson, Joe U. Jr. '57, '58
Murchison, Phil (Manager/ Trainer) '93
Murname, T. (Manager) '44, '45, '46
Murphy A. L. (Manager) '52, '53
Murphy, James L. '59, '60, '61
Murphy, Mike (Manager) '80, '81
Murrah, Thomas F. '63, '64, '65
Murrah, W. E. '18, '19, '20, '21
Murray, Kevin '83, '84, '85, '86
Murray, Paul '79
Murray, R. L. '32, '33
Murski, Robert '70, '71, '72
Myers, Frank '74, '75, '76, '77
Myers, O. W. 1897, '98, '99

N

Naiser, Derek '88
Nakos, Alex (Manager) '88, '89
Nakos, Spiro (Manager) '90, '93
Nasser, Al '78
Nealy, Otis '89, '90, '91, '92
Neece, Clarence M. '08, '09
Neely, Roy G. '22, '23
Neff, Asa J. '02
Nehib, Greg '88
Nelms, Milton R. '12
Nelson, Freddie A. '65
Nelson, Jeff '82, '83, '84, '85
Neill, Doug '69, '70, '71
Nesrsta, J. O. '35, '36, '37
Netardus, Jaro G. Jr. '49, '51
Nettles, Rusty '81, '82
Neville, Henry A. '43
Newton, Keith '83, '84
Nicholas, Don R. '49
Nichols, Jerry D. '64, '65
Niland, Thomas K. '51, '52
Nilson, John H. '63, '64, '65
Noble, Elton 1899, 1900
Nohavitza, Elo E. '49, '50, '51
Nolan, Willis '30, '31, '32
Nolen, Lockhart (Manager) '48
Northup, Roy F. '58, '59, '60

O

O'Brient, Sammy '84, '85, '86, '87
Ochterbeck, W. J. '24, '25
Odom, Lynn '647, '68, '69
Odom, Van '69, '70, '71
Ogdee, Edward '42
Ohlendorf, Norbert K. '52, '53, '54
Olbrich, Alvin P. '38
Oliver, Gale G. '57, '58, '59
Oliver, Gary '87, '88, '89, '90
O'Neal, Hardy E. '02
O'Neal, Steve '66, '67, '68
Osborn, John '79, '80
Osborne, Carl R. '55, '56, '57
Osborne, Richard '72, '73, '74, '75
Osgood, Chris '88, '89
Overly, Charles R. '43, '46, '47
Overly, James A. (Trainer) '48, '49
Overshiner, E. M. 1896
Overton, Andrew J. '63, '64
Owens, Bob (Manager) '73
Ozee, Kevin (Manager/Trainer) '93

P

Page, Sean '87
Paine, Jeff '80, '81, '82, '83
Palasota, Vince '88
Pannell, E. W. '38, '39, '40
Pappas, Mike '87, '89, '90
Pardee, John P. '54, '55, '56
Parish, Joseph M. '39
Park, Mike '70, '71, '72
Parker, James H. (Manager) '39, '40
Parker, Jim '68, '69, '70
Parker, William E. '08, '09, '10, '12
Parmer, James R. '44
Patterson, Cornelius '88, '89, '90
Pavlas, Lance '87, '88, '89, '90
Payne, Brian '89, '90, '91
Payne, H. B. (Buddy) '57, '58, '59
Payne, Lawrence J. '45
Payne, Rick (Manager) '76
Payne, W. O. '42
Pearson, Henry A. '57
Pender, Paul '79, '80, '81, '82
Peoples, Dan '71
Perkins, Frank D. 1894, '96, '97
Persons, David H. '13
Peter, Philip '61
Petty, Kent '89, '90, '91, '92
Petty, S. J. '26, '27
Peveto, Cal '78, '79
Philley, Andy '69, '70, '71
Phillips, David '84
Phillips, H. D. '30
Phillips, James D. '60, '61, '62
Phillips, Michael L. '64
Phillips, Robert H. '59, '60
Phythian, Walter R. '35, '36
Pickard, Billy (Trainer) '78
Pickett, Tom B '41, '46
Pierce, J. A. '18, '19, '20
Pierce, Kirk '88
Pinson, C. T. '23
Pinson, Harry T. '21
Piper, Jim '67, '68, '69
Piper, Paul K. '59, '60
Pirie, James E. '01, '02, '03
Pirtle, David (Trainer) '76
Pitman, Mike J. '62, '63, '64
Pitner, H. M. '34, '35, '36
Pittman, Lee (Manager) '81, '82
Pizzitola, Michael J. '61, '62
Polasek, Billy Joe '69, '71
Polk, Scott '80, '81, '82, '83, '84
Pollacia, Tony '85
Pollard, Dan '86
Pollock, Oscar L. '47
Polocheck, Layne '85
Pool, Rusty '71
Porter, Greg '81, '82, '83
Poss, John M. '65, '66
Powell, Jack E. '53, '55
Powell, Louis H. '14
Powell, William D. '54, '55, '56
Power, Robert (Manager) '67
Power, Richard S. (Manager) '69
Price, C. Walemon '37, '38, '39
Price, Harold L. '56
Price, P. M. '25
Price, Terry '86, '87, '88, '89
Prokop, Merl A. '47
Puckett, Felix S. '05, '06
Puckett, John W. '02, '03
Pugh, Marion C. '38, '39, '40
Pullig, Corey '92, '93
Pustejovsky, Ed '76, '77, '78, '79
Pyburn, Jack H. '64, '65, '66

R

Ragsdale, Robert 1897, '98
Rahn, Leon F. '39, '40
Raiford, Aubrey '81
Randle, Floyd '77, '78
Ransby, Felton '88, '90
Ransom, Dennis '87, '88, '89, '90
Rau, Tim (Manager) '88, '89
Rawlins, Harry E. 1897
Ray, Tom '85
Reagan, Travis H. '61, '62, '63
Red, Darrell '91, '92, '93
Redus, James '79
Reed, Roderick '76, '77
Reed, Roman '83
Rees, W. Nelson '31
Reeves, John R. '39, '40
Reeves, Ken '81, '82, '83, '84
Reid, Steve (Manager) '83, '84
Reinarz, Brandon '92
Reinarz, Cole '93
Rektorek, J. A. '26
Resley, George '68
Reynolds, James '68
Reynolds, John W. '65
Reynolds, Ron '84
Richard, John '92
Richardson, Bucky '87, '88, '90, '91
Richardson, Lester S. '39, '41
Richardson, Rod '82

Richenstein, Charles A. '05
Richey, Derrick '87, '88, '89
Richter, Charles E. '27, '28, '29
Ricke, Mike (Trainer) '80, '81
Rickman, Ricky (Manager) '68
Ridenhower, Ray '01, '02
Riggs, Charlie '66, '67, 68
Rion, Dennis '83
Risien, Cody '76, '77, '78
Risien, Flint '80, '81, '82
Roach, James B. '33
Roaches, Carl '72, '73, '74, '75
Robbins, Cooper P. Jr. '52, '53
Robbins, Donald '55
Robbins, Doug '70
Robbins, Mike '79, '81, '82
Roberts, F. A. (Manager) '13
Roberts, William C. '08
Robertson, Art Mitchell '70, '71
Robertson, John E. '31, '33
Robinson, Jeroy '86, '87, '88, '89
Robison, Tommy '80, '81, '82, '83
Robnett, Edward '39
Robnett, Marshall R. '38, '39, '40
Rockhold, Jason '89, '90
Roepke, Robert E. (Manager) '61
Rogers, Cullen J. '39, '41, '42
Rogers, Gary '82
Rogers, Gerald G. '61, '62, '63
Rogers, Joe C. '15, '16
Rogers, Owens A. '36, '37, '38
Rollins, Gerald D. (Manager) '56
Rollins, John W. '14, '15, 16
Roper, James S. '58
Roper, John '85, '86, '87, '88
Roquemore, Michael A. '62
Ross, Brian '86, '87, '88, '89
Ross, James B. '06, '07
Rothe, Joe H. '39, '40
Rother, Randy '82
Routt, Joe E. '35, '36, '37
Routt, William A. '38, '39, '40
Royalty, Charlie A. '48, '49
Ruby, Martin O. '39, '40, '41
Rudder, James Earl '31
Rugel, Dan F. '07, '08, '09
Rush, Marshall N. '51, '52
Rush, William T. '49, '50, '51
Rushing, Eli '37, '38
Rylander, W. E. '15

S

Sacra, Joseph R. '44, '46, '47
Sacra, Joseph R. '70, '71, '72
Saddler, Rod '83, '84, '85, '86
Sagraves, Steven '90, '91
Sallee, Bill D. '65, '66, '67
Salyer, Johnny A. '51, '52, '53
Sammons, Thomas B. '04
Sams, Bucky '73, '74, '75
Sanders, Chris '91, '92
Sanders, Eugene '76, '77, '78
Sanders, Robert W. '57, '58, '59
Sanders, S. H. '21
Sanders, Scot '91
Sanders, Thomas '80, '81, '82, '84
Sarkissian, Steve '89
Sawyer, Buzzy '81
Sawyer, Randy '82
Saxe, Augie W. '50, '51
Saxe, Charles S. '51, '52
Scarborough, J. S. '08
Schaedel, Charles T. '10, '11
Schero, Joe E. '52, '53, '54
Schmid, Joe H. (Manager) '57
Schmidt, Hubert '06, '07
Schneider, Daniel W. '65, '66, '67
Schorp, Greg '90, '91, '92, '93
Schroeder, Bruno E. '35, '37, '38
Schroeder, William H. '53, '54
Schultz, Earl 1900, '01, '02, '03
Schwarz, Blake '72, '73, '74, '75
Scoggins, Phillips C. '64, '65
Scott, David '79, '80
Scott, Herbert B. '52
Scott, Johnny D. '52, '53
Scott, Joseph O. '44, '46
Scott, Richard E. '49
Scott, Verne A. '14
Scovell, J. Field '28
Scudder, Carl F. '18, '19, '20
Seago, H. W. '36
Seeker, Ricky '72, '73, '74
Seely, Bill '68, '69
Self, Rocky '69
Settegast, Marion E. Sr. '14, '15, '16
Settegast, Marion E. Jr. '43
Shaeffer, Robert J. '49, '50, '51
Shanks, Jeff '88, '89
Shaw, Joe '69
Sheffield, Corky '69, '72
Sheffield, Jimmy '68, '69, '70
Shefts, Morton '44, '46
Shelton, J. Howard '39, '40
Shiller, Steve '83
Shipman, David '74, '75, '76
Shippix '09
Shira, Charles N. '43, '44
Shockey, Jacob C. '35, '36, '37
Shorter, Antonio '91, '92, '93
Sibley, William R. '41, '42
Sikes, Delmar D. '50
Sikes, Jules V. '25, '26, '27
Siler, Rich '83, '84, '85
Simmons, A. L. '56, '57
Simmons, Elvis A. '40, '41, '42
Simmons, J. A. '26
Simmons, Melvin D. '62, '63, '64
Simmons, Randy '88, '89, '90, '91
Simmons, Wayland A. '59, '60, '61
Simon, Burnis '80, '81, '82, '83
Simonini, Edward '72, '73, '74, '75
Simpson, J. V. '02, '03, '04
Simpson, O. M. 1897, '98, '99
Simpson, Phillip '77, '78, '79
Sims, Arthur R. '58, '59, '60
Sims, J. P. (Trainer) '88, '89
Sims, M. W. 1894
Sinclair, Bennie C. '53, '54
Singleton, James M. '65, '66
Singleton, Percy '92
Sipe, Brent (Trainer) '89
Skinner, Ben S. (Manager) '52
Slater, Scott '85, '86, '87, '88
Slaton, Tony '82, '83, '84
Slaughter, Marion P. '42
Slocum, Shawn '84
Amelser, Dennis '73, '74, '75
Smith, Alan '80, '81, '83, '84
Smith, Bland '70, '71
Smith, Brent '85, '86, '87, '88
Smith, Darrell '76, '77, '78
Smith, Darrell '82, '83, '84
Smith, Detron '92, '93
Smith, Don G. '56, '57, '58
Smith, Earl L. '39, '40
Smith, George '82, '83
Smith, Gilbert '66
Smith, H. E. '37, '38, '39
Smith, Kevin '88, '89, '90, '91
Smith, Langston M. '14, '15
Smith, M. V. '20, '21
Smith, Preston W. '45, '46, '47, '48
Smith, Ralph W. '58, '59, '60
Smith, Randy (Trainer) '82, '83
Smith, Robert L. '49, '50, '51
Smith, Ted '69, '70, '71
Smitham, Verner R. (Manager) '14
Snow, Dion '88, '89
Solari, Steve '91, '92, '93
Sooy, Tom '647, '68, '69
Sorrell, Gary '87, '88, '89
Spadora, Joseph (Manager) '65
Spake, W. E. '12
Speed, Carleton D. '25
Spencer, Michael F. '49, '50
Spencer, Oliver E. '14
Spencer, Rick '71
Spencer, Ted L. '31, '32, '33
Spires, Truman E. '45
Spitzenberger, Steve '75, '76, '77
Spivey, Marshall '39, '40, '41
Sprott, Alton C. '26, '27
Stabler, James M. '64, '65
Stach, Stanfield A. '33, '35
Stages, William E. '36
Stahr, Richard (Trainer) '89
Stallings, Eugene C. '54, '55, '56
Stallings, Rusty '68, '69
Stanley, James L. '55, '56, '57
Stanley, Mark '73, '74, '75
Stansberry, Robert '69
Stautzenberger, Weldon O. '46, '47, '48
Steadman, Nate '82, '83, '84
Steen, Elroy '77, '78, '79
Steffens, Karl K. '38
Stegent, Larry '67, '68, '69
Stephenson, Phillip (Manager) '80, '81
Sterling, James R. '39, '40, '41
Sterns, James B. 1896, '97, '98
Steymann, Walter R. '42
Stinson, Mike '68, '69
Stiteler, Robert H. '30
Stoss, Robert '79, '80, '81, '82
Stratton, Carl K. '72, '73, '74
Street, Gus C. 1899, '01, '02, '03, '04
Street, Robert L. (Manager) '48, '49
Stringfellow, Jack C. '33
Strogen, Bobby '79, '80, '81, '82
Stuard, Kyle '80, '81, '82, '83
Stump, Craig '84, '85, '86, '87
Sturcken, Edward B. '42
Sugg, Tommy '82
Sullivan, Mike '89
Surovik, John H. (Manager) '52, '53
Svatek, Johnnie '77, '78, '79
Swan, Michael K. '63
Swedeen, John '70
Swilley, Dennis '73, '74, '75, '76
Symes, Clarence '06, '07

T

Talbot, Layne '87, '88, '89, '90
Taliaferro, Darrell '73
Tankersley, Rick '85, '86
Tassos, Damon G. '43, '44
Tate, Marvin P. '52, '53, '54
Taylor, Anthony '86, '87
Taylor, Arthur W. '08, '09
Taylor, Kenneth '77, '78
Taylor, Loyd F. '55, '56, '57
Teague, Doug '76, '77, '78, '79
Teague, Foster S. '53
Teague, Sammie R. (Manager) '59
Teal, Jimmy '82, '83, '84
Teate, Randall '76
Teichelman, Lance '90, '91, '92, '93
TenNapel, Garth '73, '74, '75
Tewell, Dennis (Trainer) '67
Thelen, David '89, '90
Theriot, Sidney J. '52, '53, '54
Thomas, Clifford '69
Thomas, Clifton '70
Thomas, Edwin W. '13, '14
Thomas, Patrick S. '72, '73, '74, '75
Thomas, Rodney '91, '92, '93
Thomas, William '88, '89, '90
Thomason, James N. '38, '39, '40
Thompson, George E. '80
Thompson, Nash O. '34
Thompson, Thomas E. '09
Thompson, Tony '85, '86, '87
Thompson, William '73, '74, '75, '76
Thornton, Penn B. '16
Thrower, John D. 1899, 1900
Thurmond, Albert N. '72, '73, '74
Tidwell, Billy R. '49, '50, '51
Todd, Dick S. '36, '37, '38
Tolleson, Mike '86
Toney, Anthony '84, '85
Torno, Frank V. '46
Tracey, John '56, '57, '58
Tracy, Carroll A. '28, '29, '30
Tracy, Henry C. '72, '73, '74, '75
Tracy, H. H. 1897
Trahan, Warren '73, '74
Trammell, Bud '73
Trimble, Murry H. '55, '56
Trimmier, Tim '73
Trew, Robert L. '13
Trott, Bobby (Trainer) '66
Tschantz, Todd '84, '85, '86
Tucker, Kevin '89, '90
Tucker, Lanning (Trainer) '85, '86
Tucker, M. Dwayne, '48, '49, '50
Tulis, Robert F. '41, '46, '47
Turley, Herbert E. '43, '46, '47, '48
Turner, J. G. '37
Turner, Lafayette '86, '87, '88
Turner, Stanley S. '43
Turney, John '68

U

Ullrich, Charles E. '33
Underwood, James '90
Uriegas, Alberto (Trainer) '84
Utay, Joe '05, '06, '07
Uzzell, William J. '63, '64

V

Vaden, Frank S. (Manager) '55
Valentine, Ira '82, '84, '85, '86
Vandervoort, A. S. '18, '19
Van Dyke, Lewis E. '60, '62
Van Pelt, Thomas E. (Trainer) '60
Van Sant, Jon '80, '81, '82
Van Zandt, Roscoe L. '28, '30
Vassar, William C. (Manager) '63
Vaughn, John (Manager) '81, '82
Vaughn, Tommie '38, '39, '40
Veckert, Harman H. 1896, '97
Vela, Javier '67, '68
Velasquez, Joe '81, '82, '83, '84
Venetoulias, Terry '90, '91, '92, '93
Vesmirovsky, E. '10, '11, '12, '13
Vick, Richard P. '54
Vick, Roger '83, '84, '85, '86
Vincent, Kary '90, '91
Vitek, Richard D. '35, '36, '37
Vordenbaumen, Tim '93
Voss, Kenneth R. '48

W

Waddle, Percy '87, '88, '89
Walker, Alvin (Skip) '72, '73, '74, '75
Walker, Bill '86
Walker, David '73, '74, '76, '77
Walker, Elvis '82
Walker, George '66
Walker, L. E. '18
Walker, Larry '93
Walker, Shawn '83, '84
Walker, Shea '83, '84, '85, '86
Walker, Weldon F. '35
Walker, William E. '44

Walker, William T. '02, '03, '04, '05
Wallace, Aaron '86, '87, '88, '89
Wallace, Larry '91, '93
Ward, Arland L. '09
Ward, C. E. '09, '10
Ward, Tim '79, '80, '82
Ward, Waylon O. '63, '64
Ward, William R. '63
Ware, Derek '90
Warnke, Carl '73, '74, '75
Washington, Mickey '87, '88, '89
Washington, William H. '12
Watkins, Ronald '81
Watson, Donald A. '54, '55, '56
Watson, Steve '83
Watts, Arthur P. 1894
Watts, Claude D. '25, '26
Watts, Dale '68, '69
Waugh, C. A. '23, '24
Weaver, Mark '66, '67
Webb, Duncan '83, '84, '85
Webb, James '88, '89, '91
Webb, Richmond '86, '87, '88, 89
Webster, J. D. '40, '41, '42
Weghorst, Allan (Manager) '85
Weinert, Arthur 1900, '08
Weir, David (Trainer) '87, '88
Weir, H. B. '17
Weir, W. C. '19, '20, '21
Weiss, Joe H. '64, '65, '66
Welch, Bruce '73, '74, '75
Welch, F. Barney '42, '46, '47
Wellborn, Joseph H. '63, '64, '66
Wells, Gaddy '67
Wendt, F. T. '21
Wesley, Dexter '90, '91, '92, '93
Wesson, T. Euel '39, '40, '41
West, Donald E. '64
Westbrook, Wm. A. (Manager) '62
Westerberg, Tom (Manager) '84
Westerfield, Ira Dan '64, '65, '66
Whatley, Richard E. '63, '64, '65
Wheat, Shannon (Trainer) '84, '85
Wheat, Wayne '69
Wheeler, Lee (Manager) '82, '83
Wheeler, Mark '90, '91
White, Finis L. '39
White, Joe R. '37, '38, '39
White, Junior '91, '92, '93
White, Oscar M. '45
Whitehead, Gary '71, '72
Whitfield, Calvin '84, '85, '86
Whitfield, John T. '35, '36
Whitmore, Jack '67, '68, '69
Whittaker, Wray W. '46, '47, '48, '49
Whitwell, Mike '78, '79, '80, '81
Whyte, James A. '10
Wickerhan, James B. '64
Wiebold, Bill '71, '72
Wiley, J. E. '43
Wilkerson, Grady '73, '74, '75, '76
Wilkins, W. Taylor '34, '35
Willenborg, James C. '62, '63, '64
Williams, Andre '93
Williams, Anthony '89, '90
Williams, Cedric '93
Williams, Doug '84, '85
Williams, George '39
Williams, Greg '80, '81, '82
Williams, Jackie '73, '74, '75
Williams, Jimmie '80, '81, '82, '83
Williams, J. Maurice '39
Williams, Michael '75, '76, '77
Williams, Reggie '73, '74
Williams, Robert H. '41, '42
Williams, Sammy '68
Williams, T. J. '05
Williams, W. B. '31, '32
Willis, Nicholas W. '34, '35
Willoughby, Jack (Manager) '71
Wilson, E. S. '16, '17, '18, '19
Wilson, Fay '23, '24, '25
Wilson, Matt '84, '85, '86, '87
Wilson, Richard O. '22, '23
Wilson, Robert '88, '89, '90
Wilson, Roy D. (Trainer) '63
Wilson, Sean '87, '88, '89, '90
Wilson, T. F. '20, '21, '22, '23
Wilson, W. W. '24
Winkler, Andrew 1897, '98
Winkler, James C. '45, '46, '47, '48
Winkler, Lawrence E. '52, '53, '54
Winn, W. E. '21
Withers, John '82
Wolf, Herbert J. '54, '55
Wolf, William M. '30
Wood, Frank M. '39
Wood, Joe '66
Woddard, George '75, '76, '77, '79
Woodard, Mike (Trainer) '76
Woodfin, Jim (Manager) '86, '87, '88
Woodland, Sully '32, '33
Woodman, Cony N. '04, '06
Woodman, James O. '30
Woodman, V. W. '25, '26
Woodside, Keith '83, '85, '86, '87
Work, Chris '88
Worthing, Evan E. '01, '02
Wright, Charlie E. '43, '46, '47, '48
Wright, Don '77, '78
Wright, Fred G. '35
Wright, James '55, '56, '57
Wright, Larry '73
Wright, R. C. '43, '46
Wright, Richard H. '32
Wright, Will '79, '80, '81, '82
Wurzback, Mark '84, '85, '86
Wylie, H. P. '26
Wylie, Randy '83, '84, '85

Y

Yates, Paul T. '44
Yeargain, C. W. '44, '45
Yeoman, William F. '45
Yocum, Gill '71
Young, Gary '76
Young, Roy O. '35, '36, '37

Z

Zachery, James '77, '78, '79
Zachry, Ben '84, '85
Zapalac, Willie F. '41, '42, '46
Zarafonetis, George H. '28, '29
Zedler, Otto F. (Manager) '16
Zuch, Howard W. '51, '52